A STREET SCENE—EARLY XIXTH CENTURY.

THE DAWN OF THE XIXTH CENTURY IN ENGLAND

A SOCIAL SKETCH OF THE TIMES

BY

JOHN ASHTON

AUTHOR OF "SOCIAL LIFE IN THE REIGN OF QUEEN ANNE," "ENGLISH
CARICATURE AND SATIRE ON NAPOLEON I.," "OLD TIMES," ETC.

WITH 114 ILLUSTRATIONS DRAWN BY THE AUTHOR
FROM CONTEMPORARY ENGRAVINGS

With an Introduction
by
LESLIE SHEPARD

LONDON

T. FISHER UNWIN

Now Reissued by
Singing Tree Press
1249 Washington Blvd., Detroit, Michigan 1968

Library of Congress Card Number: 67-23941

9 - 12 - 72

INTRODUCTION

John Ashton compiled some thirty works, mainly in the
fields of social history and folklore, but never received
proper biographical notice. There are stray bibliograph-
ical notes in Allibone's *Critical Dictionary of English
Literature* and Cousin's *Short Biographical Dictionary of
English Literature* (Appendix to 1910 edition) but there
are no details of his life, and even his death was not
recorded in any standard reference work. The present
reissue of a group of his books is a good opportunity to
list the few facts it has been possible to discover about
this interesting author.

John Ashton was born in London, September 22,
1834, son of Thomas and Isabella Ashton. Thomas
Ashton was a shipbroker in the city of London and his
wife followed the specialized trade of gun maker in the
Goodman's Fields area. In addition to John Ashton
there were two sisters and one brother. Thomas Ashton
died in 1851 at his residence in Lewisham, Kent, and
Isabella Ashton in 1875. We have no details of the early
education and employment of John Ashton, but by the
age of 40 he had settled down to regular research at the
British Museum, London. In 1882 he published three
books: *The Earliest Known Printed Ballad. A ballade of
the Scottysshe King* (a facsimile of the first printing of
Skelton's ballad, with introductory notes), *Chap-books
of the Eighteenth Century*, and *Social Life in the Reign of
Queen Anne*—the latter book was the first of a series of
valuable compilations on social history. Ashton read
steadily at the British Museum for more than thirty
years, producing a new book about once a year.

In 1895 he lived at 4 Middleton Road (now Grove),
Islington, in north west London, a rather dreary area
near Camden Road. It was in this district that novelist

George Gissing lodged his character Alfred Yule in *New Grub Street*, and John Ashton must have been one of many struggling authors contemporary with Gissing, living frugally in a furnished room and making his way each day to the British Museum by omnibus, studying under the great glass dome of the Reading Room. It is doubtful whether Ashton made much money out of his books. Although they sold well, the rewards of authors in those days were modest, especially for non-fiction books. But clearly Ashton studied the kind of subjects that interested him—curiosities of history, and manners, modes and customs of past times. Living in an uninspiring district of endless rows of houses, he plodded away at his books, living in a romantic past. He had some skill in sketching, and embellished his books with many copies of old prints. Two of his books—*The Old Bailey and Newgate* [1902] and *Old-Time Aldwych, Kingsway and Neighbourhood* [1903] were published under the pseudonym "Charles Gordon", possibly to avoid complications on a publishing contract.

Ashton wrote little in his last few years and his death on July 29, 1911 seems to have passed unnoticed. Between 1906 and 1913 *Who's Who* had noted his works and it continued to list him until 1913 (though he does not appear in *Who Was Who*).

Ashton did not claim to be more than a compiler, but his compilations were thorough and entertaining, avoiding the extremes of heavy scholarship or over popularisation. He was a typical dedicated researcher with a keen delight in the everyday customs and traditions of ordinary people of former times. His books are not dated, and more than half a century after his death they remain as interesting and instructive as when they were first published.

London, England   Leslie Shepard
1967

BIBLIOGRAPHY OF WORKS WRITTEN OR EDITED
BY JOHN ASHTON

(Publication dates are for British editions; American editions sometimes vary.)

Chap-books of the Eighteenth Century; with facsimiles, notes, and introductions. 1882.

[SKELTON, John] *The Earliest known printed English Ballad. A ballade of the Scottysshe King* (facsimile reprint without introduction). 1882.

Social Life in the Reign of Queen Anne, taken from original sources. 1882.

The Adventures and Discourses of Captain John Smith, sometime President of Virginia. 1883.

Humour, Wit, and Satire of the Seventeenth Century. 1883.

Lord Mayor's Show in the Olden Times [Drawings by F. C. Price] [1883].

English Caricature and Satire on Napoleon I 2 vols. 1884; new edition 1888.

Old Times: a picture of social life at the end of the Eighteenth Century. 1885.

The Dawn of the XIXth Century in England. A social sketch of the times. 1886 [1885]; Popular edition 1886.

The Legendary History of the Cross. A series of sixty-four woodcuts from a Dutch book published by Veldener, A.D. 1483. Introduction by J. Ashton; Preface by S. Baring-Gould. 1887 [1886].

Romances of Chivalry told and illustrated in facsimile. 1887. [1886].

A Century of Ballads . . . Edited, and illustrated in facsimile of the originals. 1887.

[MANDEVILLE, Sir John] *The Voiage and Travayle of Sir John Maundeville* (Edited, annotated and illustrated by J. Ashton). 1887.

The Fleet: its River, Prison, and Marriages. 1888. [1887].

Eighteenth Century Waifs [essays]. 1887.

Modern Street Ballads. 1888.

Men, Maidens and Manners a Hundred Years Ago. 1888.

Curious Creatures in Zoology. 1890. [1889].

Social England under the Regency, 1890; New edition 1899.

[HOOD, Thomas] *The Poetical Works of T. Hood* [with memoir and notes by J. Ashton] [1891].

Real Sailor-Songs. Collected and edited. 1891.

[with MEW, James] *Drinks of the World.* 1892.

A History of English Lotteries. 1893.

Charles Letts's Date Book and Chronological Diary, or record of important events in English history [1893].

A Righte Merrie Christmasse!!! The story of Christmastide [1894].

Varia [essays]. 1894.

Hyde Park from Domesday-Book to date. 1896 [1895].

When William IV was King. 1896.

The Devil in Britain and America. 1896.

The History of Gambling in England. 1898

Florizel's Folly. George IV and Brighton. 1899.

[under pseudonym of GORDON, Charles] *The Old Bailey and Newgate.* 1902.

[under pseudonym of GORDON, Charles] *Old-Time Aldwych, Kingsway and Neighbourhood.* 1903.

Gossip in the First Decade of Victoria's Reign. 1903.

The History of Bread from prehistoric to modern times. 1904.

PREFACE.

THAT Sir Walter Scott, when he called his novel "Waverley; or, 'Tis Sixty Years Since," thought that the time had come, when the generation, then living, should be presented with a page of history, which would bring to their remembrance the manners and customs of their grandfathers, must be my excuse for this book.

For, never, in the world's history, has there been such a change in things social, as since the commencement of the Nineteenth Century ; it has been a quiet revolution—a good exemplar of which may be found in the Frontispiece, which is a type of things past, never to be recalled. The Watchman has long since given place to the Police ; the climbing boy, to chimney-sweeping on a more scientific plan ; and no more is "Saloop" vended at street corners ; even the drummer-boys are things of the past, only fit for a Museum—and it is of these things that this book treats.

The times, compared with our own, were so very different ; Arts, Manufactures, Science, Social Manners, Police, and all that goes to make up the sum of life, were

PREFACE.

then so widely divergent, as almost to make one disbelieve, whilst reading of them, that such a state of things could exist in this Nineteenth Century of ours. In the first decade, of which I write, Steam was in its very babyhood ; locomotives, and steamships, were only just beginning to be heard of ; Gas was a novelty, and regarded more as an experiment, than the useful agent we have since found it ; whilst Electricity was but a scientific toy, whose principal use was to give galvanic shocks, and cause the limbs of a corpse to move, when applied to its muscles.

Commerce was but just developing, being hampered by a long and cruel war, which, however, was borne with exemplary patience and fortitude by the nation—England, although mistress of the seas, having to hold her own against all Europe in arms. The Manners, Dress, and Food, were all so different to those of our day, that to read of them, especially when the description is taken from undoubtedly contemporary sources, is not only amusing, but instructive.

The Newspapers of the day are veritable mines of information ; and, although the work of minutely perusing them is somewhat laborious and irksome, the information exhumed well repays the search. Rich sources, too, to furnish illustrations, are open, and I have availed myself largely of the privilege ; and I have endeavoured, as far as in my power lay, to give a faithful record of the Dawn of the Nineteenth Century in England, taken absolutely from original, and authentic, sources.

JOHN ASHTON.

CONTENTS.

CONTENTS.

CHAPTER V.

CHAPTER VI.

CHAPTER VII.

CHAPTER VIII.

CHAPTER IX.

CHAPTER X.

CONTENTS.

CONTENTS.

CHAPTER XVII.

CHAPTER XVIII.

CHAPTER XIX.

CHAPTER XX.

CHAPTER XXI.

CHAPTER XXII.

CHAPTER XXIII.

CONTENTS.

CONTENTS.

CHAPTER XXXI.

CHAPTER XXXII.

CHAPTER XXXIII.

CHAPTER XXXIV.

CHAPTER XXXV.

CHAPTER XXXVI.

CHAPTER XXXVII.

CONTENTS.

CHAPTER XXXVIII.

CHAPTER XXXIX.

CHAPTER XL.

CHAPTER XLI.

CHAPTER XLII.

CHAPTER XLIII.

CONTENTS.

CHAPTER XLIV.

CHAPTER XLV.

CHAPTER XLVI.

CHAPTER XLVII.

CHAPTER XLVIII.

CHAPTER XLIX.

CONTENTS.

ILLUSTRATIONS.

ILLUSTRATIONS.

ILLUSTRATIONS.

ILLUSTRATIONS.

THE DAWN OF THE XIXᵀᴴ CENTURY
IN ENGLAND.

A SOCIAL SKETCH OF THE TIMES.

CHAPTER I.

1799–1800.

Retrospect of Eighteenth Century—Napoleon's letter to George III.—Lord Gren-
ville's reply—French prisoners of war in England—Scarcity of provisions—
Gloomy financial outlook—Loan from the Bank of England—Settlement of the
Union with Ireland.

HE old Eighteenth Century lay
a-dying, after a comparatively
calm and prosperous life.

In its infancy, William of Orange
brought peace to the land, besides
delivering it from popery, brass
money, and wooden shoes ; and,
under the Georges, civil war was
annihilated, and the prosperity,
which we have afterwards enjoyed,
was laid down on a broad, and solid basis.

2

But in its last years, it fell upon comparatively evil days, and, although it was saved from the flood of revolution which swept over France, yet, out of that revolution came a war which embittered its closing days, and was left as a legacy to the young Nineteenth Century, which, as we know, has grappled with and overcome all difficulties, and has shone pre-eminent over all its predecessors.

The poor old century had lost us America, whose chief son, General George Washington, died in 1799. In 1799 we were at war with France truly, but England itself had not been menaced—the war was being fought in Egypt. Napoleon had suddenly deserted his army there, and had returned to France post-haste, for affairs were happening in Paris which needed his presence, if his ambitious schemes were ever to ripen and bear fruit. He arrived, dissolved the Council of Five Hundred, and the Triumvirate consisting of himself, Cambacérès, and Le Brun was formed. Then, whether in sober earnest, or as a bit of political by-play, he wrote on Christmas day, 1799, the following message of goodwill and peace :

"*Bonaparte, First Consul of the Republic, to His Majesty the King of Great Britain and Ireland.*

"Paris, 5 Nivôse, year VIII. of the Republic.

" Called by the wishes of the French nation to occupy the first magistracy of the French Republic, I deem it desirable, in entering on its functions, to make a direct communication to your Majesty.

" Must the war, which for four years has ravaged every part of the world, be eternal? Are there no means of coming to an understanding?

" How can the two most enlightened nations of Europe, more powerful and stronger than is necessary for their safety and independence, sacrifice to the idea of a vain grandeur, the benefits of commerce, of internal prosperity, and domestic happiness? How is it they do not feel that peace is as glorious as necessary?

"These sentiments cannot be strangers to the heart of your Majesty, who rules over a free nation, with no other view than to render them happy.

"Your Majesty will only see in this overture, my sincere desire to effectually contribute to a general pacification, by a prompt step, free and untrammelled by those forms which, necessary perhaps to disguise the apprehensions of feeble states, only prove, in the case of strong ones, the mutual desire to deceive.

"France and England, by abusing their strength, may, for a long time yet, to the misery of all other nations, defer the moment of their absolute exhaustion; but I will venture to say, that the fate of all civilized nations depends on the end of a war which envelopes the whole world.   "(*Signed*) BONAPARTE."

Fair as this looks to the eye, British statesmen could not even then, in those early days, implicitly trust Napoleon, without some material guarantee. True, all was not *couleur de rose* with the French army and navy. The battle of the Nile, and Acre, still were in sore remembrance. Italy had emancipated itself, and Suwarrow had materially crippled the French army. There were 140,000 Austrians hovering on the Rhine border, and the national purse was somewhat flaccid. No doubt it would have been convenient to Napoleon to have patched up a temporary peace in order to recruit—but that would not suit England.

On Jan. 4, 1800, Lord Grenville replied to Talleyrand, then Minister for Foreign Affairs, in a long letter, in which he pointed out that England had not been the aggressor, and would always be glad of peace if it could be secured on a sure and solid basis. He showed how France had behaved on the Continent, cited the United Provinces, the

Swiss Cantons, and the Netherlands; how Germany had been ravaged, and how Italy, though then free, "had been made the scene of unbounded anarchy and rapine;" and he wound up thus :

"His Majesty looks only to the security of his own dominions and those of his Allies, and to the general safety of Europe. Whenever he shall judge that such security can in any manner be attained, as resulting either from the internal situation of that country from whose internal situation the danger has arisen, or from such other circumstances of whatever nature as may produce the same end, His Majesty will eagerly embrace the opportunity to concert with his Allies the means of immediate and general pacification.

"Unhappily no such security hitherto exists: no sufficient evidence of the principle by which the new Government will be directed; no reasonable ground by which to judge of its stability. In this situation it can for the present only remain for His Majesty to pursue, in conjunction with other Powers, those exertions of just and defensive war, which his regard to the happiness of his subjects will never permit him either to continue beyond the necessity in which they originated, or to terminate on any other grounds than such as may best contribute to the secure enjoyment of their tranquillity, their constitution, and their independence."[1]

So the war was to go on, that ever memorable struggle which cost both nations so much in treasure, and in men. France has never recovered the loss of those hecatombs driven to slaughter. Nor were they always killed. We kept a few of them in durance. On Dec. 21, 1799, the French Government refused to provide any longer for their compatriots, prisoners in our hands, and, from a report then taken, we had in keeping, in different places, as follows, some 25,000 men.[2]

[1] *Morning Post*, Jan. 7, 1800.   [2] *Annual Register*, Jan. 25, 1800.

Plymouth	...	...	...	...	7,477
Portsmouth	...	...	...	10,128
Liverpool	...	...	...	...	2,298
Stapleton	...	...	...	...	693
Chatham	...	...	...	...	1,754
Yarmouth	...	...	...	...	50
Edinburgh	...	...	...	...	208
Norman Cross	...	...	...	3,038

$$25,646$$

There is no doubt but these poor fellows fared hard, yet their ingenuity enabled them to supplement their short commons, and I have seen some very pretty baskets made in coloured straw, and little implements carved out of the bones of the meat which was served out to them as rations.

Their captors, however, were in somewhat evil case for food, and gaunt famine began to stare them in the face. There never was a famine, but there was a decided scarcity of provisions, which got worse as time went on. The Government recognized it, and faced the difficulty. In February, 1800, a Bill passed into law which enacted "That it shall not be lawful for any baker, or other person or persons, residing within the cities of London and Westminster, and the Bills of Mortality, and within ten miles of the Royal Exchange, after the 26th day of February, 1800, or residing in any part of Great Britain, after the 4th day of March, 1800, to sell, or offer to expose for sale, any bread, until the same shall have been baked twenty-four hours at the least; and every baker, or other person or persons, who shall act contrary hereto, or offend herein, shall, for every offence, forfeit and pay the sum of £5 for every loaf of bread so sold, offered, or exposed to sale." By a previous Bill, however, new bread might be lawfully sold to soldiers on the march. Hunger, however, although staring the people in the face, had not yet absolutely touched them, as it did later in the year.

The year, too, at its opening, was gloomy financially. The Civil List was five quarters in arrear ; and the King's servants were in such straits for money, that the grooms and helpers in the mews were obliged to present a petition to the King, praying the payment of their wages. Some portion, undoubtedly, was paid them, but, for several years afterwards, the Civil List was always three or six months in arrears.

The Bank of England came forward, and on the 9th of January agreed to lend the Government three millions without interest, but liable to be called in if the Three per Cent. Consols should get up to eighty, on condition that the Bank Charter be renewed for a further term of twenty-one years, to be computed from the 1st of August, 1812.

The question of the Union between Great Britain and Ireland had been discussed for some time, and on the 11th of February it was carried by a great majority in the Irish House of Lords. On the 2nd of April the King sent the following message to Parliament :

"GEORGE R.—It is with most sincere satisfaction that his Majesty finds himself enabled to communicate to this House the joint Address of his Lords and Commons of Ireland, laying before his Majesty certain resolutions, which contain the terms proposed by them for an entire union between the two kingdoms. His Majesty is persuaded that this House will participate in the pleasure with which his Majesty observes the conformity of sentiment manifested in the proceedings of his two parliaments, after long and careful deliberation on this most important subject; and he earnestly recommends to this House, to take all such further steps as may best tend to the speedy and complete execution of a work so happily begun, and so interesting to the security and happiness of his Majesty's subjects, and to the general strength and prosperity of the British Empire.

"G. R." [1]

[1] " Parliamentary History," vol. xxxv. pp. 25, 26

Lord Grenville presented this message in the Lords, and Mr. Pitt in the Commons. The resolutions mentioned are " Resolutions of the two Houses of Parliament of Ireland, respecting a Union of the Kingdoms of Great Britain and Ireland ; and their Address thereon to His Majesty. *Die Mercurii, 26 Martii,* 1800." They are somewhat voluminous, and settled the basis on which the Union was to take place.

On the 21st of April, both Lords and Commons began to debate on the Union. The Commons continued it on the 22nd, 25th, 28th, 29th, and 30th of April, and May 1st and 2nd—on which date, the question being put "That the said Resolutions be now read a second time," the House divided. Yeas, 208 ; Noes, 26. An address was afterwards drawn up, and communicated to the Lords at a Conference.

The Lords began their deliberations also on the 21st of April, and continued them on the 25th, 28th, and 30th, May 7th and 8th, when the House divided. Contents, 55 ; Proxies, 20 ; Not Contents, 7. The dissentients were the Earls of Hillsborough, Fitzwilliam, Carnarvon, and Buckinghamshire, and Lords Dundas, Holland, and King— the two latter entering a formal written protest.

The Lords and Commons agreed to an address which they presented to the King on the 12th of May, and, on the 2nd of July, the King went in state to the House of Lords, and gave his Royal Assent to the Bill, which thus became law, and was to take effect on the 1st of January, 1801. The Royal Assent was a very commonplace affair— there were but about thirty Peers present, and it was shuffled in with two other Bills—the Pigott Diamond Bill and the Duke of Richmond Bill. There was no enthusiasm in England, at all events, over the Union, no rejoicings, no illuminations, hardly even a caricature. How it has worked, we of these later days of the century know full well.

CHAPTER II.

ON the 15th of May, the King, who, while his health was good, was always most active in fulfilling the onerous duties which devolved upon him, attended the field exercises of the Grenadier battalion of the Guards, in Hyde Park, when a gentleman named Ongley, a clerk in the Navy Office, was shot by a musket ball, during the volley firing, whilst standing but twenty-three feet from the King. The wound was not dangerous —through the fleshy part of the thigh—and it was immediately dressed ; and it might have passed off as an accident, but for an event which occurred later in the day. The cartouch-boxes of the soldiers were examined, but none but blank cartridges were found. So little indeed was thought of it, that the King, who said it was an accident, stopped on the ground for half an hour afterwards, and four more volleys were fired by the same company before he left.

The King was a great patron of the Drama, and on that evening he visited Drury Lane Theatre, where, "by command of their Majesties," were to be performed " She would, and

she would not,"[1] and "The Humourist;"[2] but scarcely had
he entered the box, before he had taken his seat, and whilst
he was bowing to the audience, than a man, who had previously taken up a position in the pit close to the royal box,
took a good and steady aim with a horse-pistol, with which
he was armed, at His Majesty, and fired : luckily missing the
King, who with the utmost calmness, and without betraying
any emotion, turned round to one of his attendants, and
after saying a few words to him, took his seat in apparent
tranquillity, and sat out the whole entertainment. He had,
however, a narrow escape, for one of the two slugs with which
the pistol was loaded, was found but a foot to the left of
the royal chair.

Needless to say, the would-be assassin was seized at once—
as is so graphically depicted in the illustration—and, by the
combined exertions of both pit and orchestra, was pulled
over the spikes and hurried across the stage, where he was
at once secured and carried before Sir William Addington,
who examined him in an adjoining apartment. The audience was furious, and with difficulty could be calmed by
the assurance that the villain was in safe custody. Then, to
avert attention, the curtain drew up, and the stage was
crowded by the whole strength of the house—scene-shifters,
carpenters, and all; and "God save the King" was given
with all the heartiness the occasion warranted.

Then, when that was done, and the royal party was seated,
came the reaction. The Princesses Augusta, Sophia, and
Mary fainted away, the latter twice. The Princess Elizabeth
alone was brave, and administered smelling salts and cold
water to her less courageous sisters. The Queen bore it well
—she was very pale, but collected—and during the performance kept nodding to the princesses, as if to tell them
to keep up their spirits.

The name of the man who fired the shot was James
Hadfield. He was originally a working silversmith ; after-

---

[1] By Colley Cibber.   [2] By James Cobb.

wards he enlisted in the 15th Light Dragoons, and his
commanding officer gave him the highest character as a
soldier. He deposed that Hadfield, "while in the regiment,
was distinguished for his loyalty, courage, and irreproachable
conduct. On all occasions of danger he was first to volunteer. On the memorable affair at Villers en Couche, on the
24th of April, 1794, which procured the 15th Regiment so
much honour, and the officers the Order of Merit from his
Imperial Majesty, Hadfield behaved with the most heroic
bravery. On the 18th of May following, when the Duke
of York retreated in consequence of the attack of Pichegru
on his rear, Hadfield, in the action at Roubaix, fought with
desperation. He volunteered on a skirmishing party, withstood the shock of numbers alone, was often surrounded by
the enemy, and called off by his officers, but would not
come. At last he fell, having his skull fractured, his cheek
separated from his face, his arm broken, and he was otherwise so shockingly mangled, that the British troops, after
seeing him, concluded he was dead : and he was returned
among the killed in the *Gazette*. The French having
obtained possession of the field, Hadfield fell into their
hands, and recovered. He remained upwards of a year a
prisoner, his regiment all the time supposing him dead ;
but in August, 1795, he joined it at Croydon, to the great
astonishment and joy of his comrades, who esteemed him
much. It soon became manifest, however, that his wounds
had deranged his intellect. Whenever he drank strong
liquors he became insane ; and this illness increased so much
that it was found necessary to confine him in a straight-
waistcoat. In April, 1796, he was discharged for being a
lunatic." His officers gave him the highest character, particularly for his loyalty ; adding that they would have
expected him to lose his life in defending, rather than
attacking, his King, for whom he had always expressed
great attachment.

After his discharge he worked at his old trade ; but even

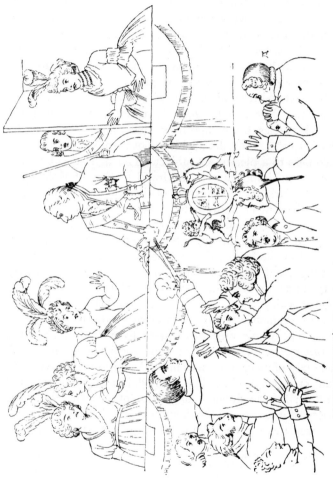

JAMES HADFIELD'S ATTEMPT TO KILL GEORGE III., MAY 15, 1800.

his shopmates gave testimony before the Privy Council as to his insanity. He was tried on June 26th by Lord Kenyon, in the Court of King's Bench, and the evidences of his insanity were so overwhelming, that the Judge stopped the case, and the verdict of acquittal, on the ground that he was mad, was recorded. He was then removed to Newgate. He seems to have escaped from confinement more than once —for the *Annual Register* of August 1, 1802, mentions his having escaped from his keepers, and been retaken at Deal ; whilst the *Morning Herald* of August 31st of the same year chronicles his escape from Bedlam, and also on the 4th of October, 1802, details his removal to Newgate again.[1]

To pass to a pleasanter subject. The next event in the year of social importance is the Grand Review of Volunteers in Hyde Park, on the occasion of the King's 63rd birthday.

The Volunteer movement was not a novelty.   The Yeomanry were enrolled in 1761, and volunteers had mustered strongly in 1778, on account of the American War.   But the fear of France caused the patriotic breast to beat high, and the volunteer rising of 1793 and 1794 may be taken as the first grand gathering of a civic army.

On this day the largest number ever brigaded together, some 12,000 men, were to be reviewed by the King in Hyde Park. The whole city was roused to enthusiasm, and the *Morning Post* of the 5th of June speaks of it thus : " A finer body of men, or of more martial appearance, no country could produce. While they rivalled, in discipline, troops of the line ; by the fineness of their clothing, and the great variety of uniform and the richness of appointments, they far exceeded them in splendour. The great number of beauti-

---

[1] Silver medals in commemoration of the King's escape were struck by order of Sheridan.   The Obverse represents Providence protecting the King from the attempt upon his life, figuratively displayed by a shield and shivered arrows, portraying the Sovereign's safety ; and encircled are the words "GOD SAVE THE KING." On the Reverse is the British Crown in the centre of a wreath of laurel, the radiant beams of glory spreading their influence over it, with the words, " *Preserved from Assassination, May* 15, 1800 ; " and on the knot of the wreath, " *Give God Praise.*"   Hadfield died in Bedlam.

ful standards and colours—the patriotic gifts of the most
exalted and distinguished females—and the numerous music,
also contributed much to the brilliancy and diversity of the
scene.   It was with mixed emotions of pride and gratitude
that every mind contemplated the martial scene.   Viewing
such a body of citizen soldiers, forsaking their business
and their pleasures, ready and capable to meet all danger
in defence of their country—considering, too, that the same
spirit pervades it from end to end, the most timid heart is
filled with confidence.   We look back with contempt on
the denunciations of the enemy, ' which, sown in serpents'
teeth, have arisen for us in armed men,' and we look with
gratitude to our new-created host, which retorted the insult,
and changed the invader into the invaded."

But, alack and well-a-day! to think that all this beautiful
writing should be turned in bathos by the context ; and
that this review should be for ever memorable to those who
witnessed it, not on account of the martial ardour which
prompted it, but for the pouring rain which accompanied
it !   No language but that of an eye-witness could properly
portray the scene and give us a graphic social picture of
the event.

" So early as four o'clock the drums beat to arms in every
quarter, and various other music summoned the reviewers
and the reviewed to the field.   Even then the clouds were
surcharged with rain, which soon began to fall ; but no
unfavourableness of weather could damp the ardour of
even the most delicate of the fair.   So early as six o'clock,
all the avenues were crowded with elegantly dressed women
escorted by their beaux ; and the assemblage was so great,
that when the King entered the Park, it was thought advisable to shut several of the gates to avoid too much pressure.
The circumstance of the weather, which, from the personal
inconvenience it produced, might be considered the most
inauspicious of the day, proved in fact the most favourable
for a display of beauty, for a variety of scene, and number of

incidents. From the constant rain and the constant motion, the whole Park could be compared only to a newly ploughed field. The gates being locked, there was no possibility of retreating, and there was no shelter but an old tree or an umbrella. In this situation you might behold an elegant

THE LOYAL DUCKING; OR, RETURNING FROM THE REVIEW ON THE FOURTH OF JUNE, 1800.

woman with a neat yellow slipper, delicate ankle, and white silk stocking, stepping up to her garter in the mire with as little dissatisfaction as she would into her coach—there another making the first *faux pas* perhaps she ever did, and seated reluctantly on the moistened clay.

" Here is a whole group assembled under the hospitable roof of an umbrella, whilst the exterior circle, for the advantage of having one shoulder dry, is content to receive its dripping contents on the other. The antiquated virgin laments the hour in which, more fearful of a speckle than a wetting, she preferred the dwarfish parasol to the capacious umbrella. The lover regrets there is no shady bower to which he might lead his mistress, ' nothing loath.' Happy she who, following fast, finds in the crowd a pretence for closer pressure. Alas ! were there but a few grottos, a few caverns, how many Didos—how many Æneas' ? Such was the state of the spectators. That of the troops was still worse—to lay exposed to a pelting rain ; their arms had changed their mirror-like brilliancy [1] to a dirty brown ; their new clothes lost all their gloss, the smoke of a whole campaign could not have more discoloured them. Where the ground was hard they slipped ; where soft, they sunk up to the knee. The water ran out at their cuffs as from a spout, and, filling their half-boots, a squash at every step proclaimed that the Austrian buckets could contain no more."

[1] The barrels and locks of the muskets of that date were bright and burnished. Browning the gun-barrels for the army was not introduced till 1808.

CHAPTER III.

High price of gold—Scarcity of food—Difference in cost of living 1773-1800—
Forestalling and Regrating—Food riots in the country—Riot in London at
the Corn Market—Forestalling in meat.

THE people were uneasy. Gold was scarce—so
scarce, indeed, that instead of being the normal
£3 17s. 6d. per oz., it had risen to £4 5s., at which
price it was a temptation, almost overpowering, to melt
guineas. Food, too, was scarce and dear ; and, as very few
people starve in silence, riots were the natural consequence.
The Acts against "Forestalling and Regrating"—or, in
other words, anticipating the market, or purchasing before
others, in order to raise the price—were put in force. Acts
were also passed giving bounties on the importation of
oats and rye, and also permitting beer to be made from
sugar. The House of Commons had a Committee on the
subject of bread, corn, &c., and they reported on the
scarcity of corn, but of course could not point out any
practical method of remedying the grievance. The cost of
living, too, had much increased, as will appear from the
following table of expenses of house-keeping between 1773
and 1800, by an inhabitant of Bury St. Edmunds : [1]

[1] *Annual Register*, vol. xlii. p. 94.

	1773.			1793.			1799.			1800.		
	£	s.	d.	£	s.	d.	£	s.	d.	£	s.	d.
Comb of Malt¹	0	12	0	1	3	0	1	3	0	2	0	0
Chaldron of Coals	1	11	6	2	0	6	2	6	0	2	11	0
Comb of Oats	0	5	0	0	13	0	0	16	0	1	1	0
Load of Hay	2	2	0	4	10	0	5	5	0	7	0	0
Meat	0	0	4	0	0	5	0	0	7	0	0	9
Butter	0	0	6	0	0	11	0	0	11	0	1	4
Sugar (loaf)	0	0	8	0	1	0	0	1	3	0	1	4
Soap	0	0	6	0	0	8	0	0	9½	0	0	10
Window lights, 30 windows	3	10	0	7	10	0	12	12	0	12	12	0
Candles	0	0	6	0	0	8	0	0	9½	0	0	10½
Poor's Rates, per quarter	0	1	0	0	2	6	0	3	0	0	5	0
Income Tax on £200		...			...		20	0	0	20	0	0
	8	4	0	16	2	8	42	9	4	45	14	1½

With everything advancing at this amazing rate of progression, it is not to be wondered at that the price of the staff of life was watched very narrowly, and that if there were any law by which any one who enhanced it, artificially, could be punished, he would get full benefit of it, both from judge and jury. Of this there is an instance given in the *Annual Register*, July 4, 1800 :

"This day one Mr. Rusby was tried, in the Court of King's Bench, on an indictment against him, as an eminent cornfactor, for having purchased, by sample, on the 8th of November last, in the Corn Market, Mark Lane, ninety quarters of oats at 41s. per quarter, and sold thirty of them again in the same market, on the same day, at 44s. The most material testimony on the part of the Crown was given by Thomas Smith, a partner of the defendant's. After the evidence had been gone through, Lord Kenyon made an address to the jury, who, almost instantly, found the defendant guilty. Lord Kenyon—'You have conferred, by your verdict, almost the greatest benefit on your country that was ever conferred by any jury.' Another indictment against the defendant, for engrossing, stands over.

¹ A comb is four bushels, or half a quarter.

3

"Several other indictments for the same alleged crimes were tried during this year, which we fear tended to aggravate the evils of scarcity they were meant to obviate, and no doubt contributed to excite popular tumults, by rendering a very useful body of men odious in the eyes of the mob."

As will be seen by the accompanying illustration by Isaac Cruikshank, the mob did occasionally take the

HINTS TO FORESTALLERS; OR, A SURE WAY TO REDUCE THE PRICE OF GRAIN.

punishment of forestallers into their own hands. (A case at Bishop's Clyst, Devon, August, 1800.)

A forestaller is being dragged along by the willing arms of a crowd of country people; the surrounding mob cheer, and an old woman follows, kicking him, and beating him with the tongs. Some sacks of corn are marked 25s. The mob inquire, "How much now, farmer?" "How much now, you rogue in grain?" The poor wretch, half-strangled, calls out piteously, "Oh, pray let me go, and I'll let you have it at a guinea. Oh, eighteen shillings! Oh, I'll let you have it at fourteen shillings!"

In August and September several riots, on account of the scarcity of corn, and the high price of provisions, took place in Birmingham, Oxford, Nottingham, Coventry, Norwich, Stamford, Portsmouth, Sheffield, Worcester, and many other places. The markets were interrupted, and the populace compelled the farmers, &c., to sell their provisions, &c., at a low price.

At last these riots extended to London, beginning in a small way. Late at night on Saturday, September 13th, or early on Sunday, September 14th, two large written placards were pasted on the Monument, the text of which was:

"Bread will be sixpence the Quartern if the People will assemble at the Corn Market on Monday.

FELLOW COUNTRYMEN,

How long will ye quietly and cowardly suffer yourselves to be imposed upon, and half starved by a set of mercenary slaves and Government hirelings? Can you still suffer them to proceed in their extensive monopolies, while your children are crying for bread? No! let them exist not a day longer. We are the sovereignty; rise then from your lethargy. Be at the Corn Market on Monday."

Small printed handbills to the same effect were stuck about poor neighbourhoods, and the chance of a cheap loaf, or the love of mischief, caused a mob of over a thousand to assemble in Mark Lane by nine in the morning. An hour later, and their number was doubled, and then they began hissing the mealmen, and cornfactors, who were going into the market. This, however, was too tame, and so they fell to hustling, and pelting them with mud. Whenever a Quaker appeared, he was specially selected for outrage, and rolled in the mud; and, filling up the time with window

breaking, the riot became somewhat serious—so much so,
that the Lord Mayor went to Mark Lane about 11 a.m.
with some of his suite.   In vain he assured the maddened
crowd that their behaviour could in no way affect the
market.   They only yelled at him, " Cheap bread !   Birmingham and Nottingham for ever ! Three loaves for
eighteenpence," &c.   They even hissed the Lord Mayor,
and smashed the windows close by him.   This proved
more than his lordship could bear, so he ordered the Riot
Act to be read.   The constables charged the mob, who of
course fled, and the Lord Mayor returned to the Mansion
House.

No sooner had he gone, than the riots began again, and
he had to return ; but, during the daytime, the mob was
fairly quiet.   It was when the evening fell, that these
unruly spirits again broke out ; they routed the constables,
broke the windows of several bakers' shops, and, from one
of them, procured a quantity of faggots.   Here the civic
authorities considered that the riot ought to stop, for, if
once the fire fiend was awoke, there was no telling where
the mischief might end.

So the Lord Mayor invoked the aid of the Tower Ward
Volunteers—who had been in readiness all day long, lying
perdu in Fishmongers' Hall—the East India House Volunteers, and part of the London Militia.   The volunteers
then blocked both ends of Mark Lane, Fenchurch Street,
and Billiter Lane (as it was then called).   In vain did
the mob hoot and yell at them ; they stood firm until
orders were given them, and then the mob were charged
and dispersed—part down Lombard Street, part down
Fish Street Hill, over London Bridge, into the Borough.
Then peace was once more restored, and the volunteers
went unto their own homes.

True, the City was quiet ; but the mob, driven into the
Borough, had not yet slaked their thirst for mischief.
They broke the windows, not only of a cheesemonger's

in the Borough, but of a warehouse near the church. They then went to the house of Mr. Rusby (6, Temple Place, Blackfriars Road)—a gentleman of whom we have heard before, as having been tried, and convicted, for forestalling and regrating—clamouring for him, but he had prudently escaped by the back way into a neighbour's house. However, they burst into his house and entered the room where Mrs. Rusby was. She begged they would spare her children, and do as they pleased with the house and furniture. They assured her they would not hurt the children, but they searched the house from cellar to garret in hopes of getting the speculative Mr. Rusby, with the kindly intention of hanging him in case he was found. They then broke open some drawers, took out, and tore some papers, and took away some money, but did not injure the furniture much. In vain they tried to find out the address of Mrs. Rusby's partner, and then, having no *raison d'être* for more mischief, they dispersed; after which a party of Light Horse, and some of the London Militia, came up, only to find a profound quiet. The next day the riotous population were in a ferment, but were kept in check by the militia and volunteers.

Whether by reason of fear of the rioters, or from the fact that the grain markets were really easier, wheat did fall on that eventful Monday ten and fifteen shillings a quarter; and, if the following resolutions of the Court of Aldermen are worth anything, it ought to have fallen still lower:

" Combe, Mayor.

" A Court of Lord Mayor and Aldermen held at the Guildhall of the City of London, on Tuesday, the 16th of September, 1800.

" Resolved unanimously—That it is the opinion of this Court, from the best information it has been able to procure, that, had not the access to the Corn Market been, yesterday, impeded, and the transactions therein interrupted, a fall in the price of Wheat and Flour, much more considerable than that which actually took place, would have ensued ; and this Court is further of opinion, that no means can so effectually lead to reduce the present excessive prices of the principal articles of food, as the holding out full security and indemnification to such lawful Dealers as shall bring their Corn or other commodities to market. And this Court does therefore express a determination to suppress, at once, and by force, if it shall unhappily be necessary, every attempt to impede, by acts of violence, the regular business of the markets of the Metropolis.

" RIX."

A butcher was tried and convicted at the Clerkenwell Sessions, September 16th, for " forestalling the market of Smithfield on the 6th of March last, by purchasing of Mr. Eldsworth, a salesman, two cows and an ox, on their way to the market." His brother was also similarly convicted. The chairman postponed passing sentence, and stated that " he believed there were many persons who did not consider, that, by such a practice, they were offending against the law ; but, on the contrary, imagined that, when an alteration in the law was made, by the repeal of the old statutes against forestalling, there was an end of the offence altogether. It had required the authority of a very high legal character, to declare to the public that the law was not repealed, though the statutes were." He also intimated that whenever sentence was passed, it would be the lightest possible. Still the populace would insist on pressing these antiquated prosecutions, and an association was formed to supply funds for that purpose.

CHAPTER IV.

Continuation of food riots in London—Inefficiency of Police—Riots still continue—Attempts to negotiate a Peace—A political meeting on Kennington Common—Scarcity of corn—Proclamation to restrict its consumption—Census of the people.

THE Lord Mayor in vain promulgated a pacific Proclamation ; the Riots still went on.

"COMBE, MAYOR.

"*Mansion House, Sept.* 17, 1800.

"Whereas the peace of this City has been, within these few days, very much disturbed by numerous and tumultuous assemblies of riotous and disorderly people, the magistrates, determined to preserve the King's peace, and the persons and property of their fellow-citizens, by every means which the law has intrusted to their hands, particularly request the peaceable and well-disposed inhabitants of this City, upon the appearance of the military, to keep themselves away from the windows ; to keep all the individuals of their families, and servants, within doors ; and, where such opportunities can be taken, to remain in the back rooms of their houses.

"By order of his Lordship.

"W. J. NEWMAN, *Clerk.*"

In reading of these Riots we must not forget that the

civil authorities for keeping the peace were, and had
been, for more than a century previous, utterly inefficient
for their purpose, and the laughing-stock of every one ;
added to which, there was a spirit of lawlessness abroad,
among the populace, which could hardly exist now-a-
days. The male portion of the Royal Family were fearlessly
lampooned and caricatured, and good-natured jokes were
made even on such august personages as the King and
Queen—the plain, homely manner of the one, and the
avaricious, and somewhat shrewish temper of the other,
were good-humouredly made fun of. The people gave of
their lives, and their substance, to save their country from
the foot of the invader ; but they also showed a sturdy
independence of character, undeniably good in itself, but
which was sometimes apt to overpass the bounds of
discretion, and degenerate into license.

So was it with these food riots. The mob had got an
idea in their heads that there was a class who bought food
cheap, and held it until they could sell it dear ; and nothing
could disabuse their minds of this, as the following will
show.

On the morning of the 18th of September, not having
the fear of the Lord Mayor before their eyes, the mob
assembled in Chiswell Street, opposite the house of a Mr.
Jones, whose windows they had demolished the previous
night, and directed their attentions to a house opposite, at
the corner of Grub Street, which was occupied by a Mr.
Pizey, a shoemaker, a friend of the said Jones, to accommo-
date whom, he had allowed his cellars to be filled with
barrels of salt pork. These casks were seen by the mob,
and they were immediately magnified into an immense
magazine of butter and cheese, forestalled from the market,
locked up from use, and putrefying in the hands of unfeeling
avarice. Groaning and cursing, the mob began to mutter
that " it would be a d—d good thing to throw some stuff
in and blow up the place." Poor Pizey, alarmed, sent

messengers to the Mansion House, and Worship Street office : a force of constables was sent, and the mob retired.

At night, however, the same riot began afresh. Meeting in Bishopsgate Street, they went on their victorious career up Sun Street, through Finsbury Square, overthrowing the constables opposed to them, down Barbican into Smithfield, Saffron Hill, Holborn, and Snow Hills, at the latter of which they broke two cheesemongers' windows. Then they visited Fleet Market, breaking and tossing about everything moveable, smashed the windows of another cheesemonger, and then turned up Ludgate Hill, when they began breaking every lamp ; thence into Cheapside, back into Newgate Street, St. Martin's-le-Grand, and Barbican to Old Street, where they dispersed for the night. From Ludgate Hill to Barbican, only one lamp was left burning, and of that the glass was broken. Somehow, in this night's escapade the military were ever on their track, but never near them.

On the 18th of September the King arose in his Majesty, and issued a proclamation, with a very long preamble, "strictly commanding and requiring all the Lieutenants of our Counties, and all our Justices of the Peace, Sheriffs, and Under-Sheriffs, and all civil officers whatsoever, that they do take the most effectual means for suppressing all riots and tumults, and to that end do effectually put in execution an Act of Parliament made in the first year of the reign of our late royal ancestor, of glorious memory, King George the First, entituled 'An Act for preventing tumults and riotous assemblies, and for the more speedy and effectual punishing the rioters,'" &c.

Still, in spite of this terrible fulmination, the rioters again "made night hideous" on the 19th of September ; but they were not so formidable, nor did they do as much mischief, as on former occasions. On the 20th they made Clare Market their *rendezvous*, marched about somewhat, had one or two brushes with the St. Clement Danes

Association, and, finally, retired on the advent of the Horse Guards. Another mob met in Monmouth Street, the famous old-clothes repository in St. Giles's, but the Westminster Volunteers, and cavalry, dispersed them ; and, the shops shutting very early—much to the discomfiture of the respectable poor, as regarded their Saturday night's marketings—peace once more reigned. London was once more quiet, and only the rioters who had been captured, were left to be dealt with by the law. But the people in the country were not so quickly satisfied ; their wages were smaller than those of their London brethren, and they proportionately felt the pinch more acutely. In some instances they were put down by force, in others the price of bread was lowered ; but it is impossible at this time to take up a newspaper, and not find some notice of, or allusion to, a food riot.

The century would die at peace with all men if it could, and there was a means of communication open with France, in the person of a M. Otto, resident in this country as a kind of unofficial agent. The first glimpse we get of these negotiations, from the papers which were published on the subject, is in August, 1800 ; and between that time, and when the *pourparlers* came to an end, on the 9th of November, many were the letters which passed between Lord Grenville and M. Otto. Peace, however, was not to be as yet. Napoleon was personally distrusted, and the French Revolution had been so recent, that the stability of the French Government was more than doubted.

A demonstration (it never attained the dimensions of a riot)—this time political and not born of an empty stomach —took place at Kennington on Sunday, the 9th of November. So-called "inflammatory" handbills had been very generally distributed about town a day or two beforehand, calling a meeting of mechanics, on Kennington Common, to petition His Majesty on a redress of grievances.

This actually caused a meeting of the Privy Council, and

orders were sent to all the police offices, and the different volunteer corps, to hold themselves in readiness in case of emergency. The precautions taken, show that the Government evidently over-estimated the magnitude of the demonstration. First of all the Bow Street patrol were sent, early in the morning, to take up a position at "The Horns," Kennington, there to wait until the mob began to assemble, when they were directed to give immediate notice to the military in the environs of London, who were under arms at nine o'clock. Parties of Bow Street officers were stationed at different public-houses, all within easy call.

By and by, about 9 a.m., the conspirators began to make their appearance on the Common, in scattered groups of six or seven each, until their number reached *a hundred*. Then the police sent round their fiery-cross to summon aid; and before that could reach them, they actually tried the venturesome expedient of dispersing the meeting themselves—with success. But later—or lazier—politicians continued to arrive, and the valiant Bow Street officers, thinking discretion the better part of valour, retired. When, however, they were reinforced by the Surrey Yeomanry, they plucked up heart of grace, and again set out upon their mission of dispersing the meeting —and again were they successful. In another hour, by 10 a.m., these gallant fellows could breathe again, for there arrived to their aid the Southwark Volunteers, and the whole police force from seven offices, together with the river police.

Then appeared on the scene, ministerial authority in the shape of one Mr. Ford, from the Treasury, who came modestly in a hackney coach; and when he arrived, the constables felt the time was come for them to distinguish themselves, and two persons, "one much intoxicated," were taken into custody, and duly lodged in gaol—and this glorious intelligence was at once forwarded to the Duke of

Portland, who then filled the post of Secretary to the Home Department.

The greatest number of people present at any time was about five hundred ; and the troops, after having a good dinner at "The Horns," left for their homes—except a party of horse which paraded the streets of Lambeth. A terrible storm of rain terminated this political campaign, in a manner satisfactory to all ; and for this *ridiculus mus* the Guards, the Horse Guards, and all the military, regulars or volunteers, were under arms or in readiness all the forenoon !

I have here given what, perhaps, some may consider undue prominence to a trifling episode ; but it is in these things that the contrast lies as to the feeling of the people, and government, in the dawn of the nineteenth century, and in these latter days of ours. The meeting of a few, to discuss grievances, and to petition for redress, in the one case is met with stern, vigorous repression : in our times a blatant mob is allowed, nay encouraged, to perambulate the streets, yelling, they know not what, against the House of Lords, and the railings of the park are removed, by authority, to faciliate the progress of these Her Majesty's lieges, and firm supporters of constitutional liberty.

The scarcity of corn still continued down to the end of the year. It had been a bad harvest generally throughout the Continent, and, in spite of the bounty held out for its importation, but little arrived. The markets of the world had not then been opened—and among the marvels of our times, is the large quantity of wheat we import from India, and Australia. So great was this scarcity, that the King, in his paternal wisdom, issued a proclamation (December 3rd) exhorting all persons who had the means of procuring other food than corn, to use the strictest economy in the use of every kind of grain, abstaining from pastry, reducing the consumption of bread in their respective families at least one-third, and upon no account to allow it "to exceed one quartern loaf for each person in each week ; " and also all persons keeping horses, especially those for pleasure, to restrict their consumption of grain, as far as circumstances would admit.

If this proclamation had been honestly acted up to, doubtless it would have effected some relief ; which was sorely needed, when we see that the average prices of corn and bread throughout the country were—

Wheat per qr.	Barley per qr.	Oats per qr.	Quartern loaf.
113s.	60s.	41s.	1s. 9d.

And, looking at the difference in value of money then, and now, we must add at least 50 per cent., which would make the average price of the quartern loaf 2s. 7½d.!—and, really, at the end of the year, wheat was 133s. per quarter, bread 1s. 10½d. per quartern.

Three per Cent. Consols were quoted, on January 1, 1800, at 60 ; on January 1, 1801, they stood at 54.

A fitting close to the century was found in a Census of the people. On the 19th of November Mr. Abbot brought a Bill into Parliament "to ascertain the population of Great Britain." He pointed out the extreme ignorance which prevailed on this subject, and stated "that the best opinions of modern times, and each of them highly respectable, estimate our present numbers, according to one statement, at 8,000,000; and according to other statements—formed on more extensive investigation and, as it appears to me, a more correct train of reasoning, showing an increase of one-third in the last forty years—the total number cannot be less than 11,000,000."

This, the first real census ever taken of the United Kingdom, was not, of course, as exhaustive and trustworthy, as those decennial visitations we now experience. Mr. Abbot's plan was crude, and the results must of necessity have been merely approximate. He said, " All that will be necessary will be to pass a short Act, requiring the resident clergy and parish officers, in every parish and township, to answer some few plain questions, perhaps four or five, easy to be understood, and easy to be executed, which should be specified in a schedule to the Act, and to return their answers to the clerk of the Parliament, for the inspection of both Houses of Parliament.   From such materials it will be easy (following the precedent of 1787) to form an abstract exhibiting the result of the whole."

When the numbers, crudely gathered as they were, were published, they showed how fallacious was the prediction as to figures.

England and Wales		8,892,536
Scotland		1,608,420
Ireland		5,216,331
Total ...		15,717,287[1]

One thing more was necessary before the dying giant expired, and that was to rectify the chronology of the century.[2] "From the 1st day of March last there has been a difference of twelve days between the old and new style, instead of eleven as formerly, in consequence of the regulations of the Act passed in 1752, according to which

---

[1] G. Fr. Kolb, "The Condition of Nations," &c.

[2] W. Toone, "The Chronological Historian."—[When the Julian Calendar was introduced, the Vernal Equinox fell on the 25th of March. At the time of the Council of Nice, A.D. 325, it had retrograded to the 21st of March; and when the reformation was made in 1582, to the 11th of March. Pope Gregory XIII., to restore it to its place, directed ten days to be suppressed in the calendar; and as the use of the Julian intercalation was found to be three days in 400 years, he ordered the intercalation to be omitted in all the centenary years except those which were multiples of 400. According to Gregorian rule, therefore, every year of which the number is divisible by four, without a remainder, is a leap year, excepting the centenary years, which are only leap years when divisible by four, on suppressing the units and tens. Thus—

16(00) is a leap year.
17(00), 18(00), 19(00), are not leap years.
20(00) is a leap year.

The shifting of days caused great disturbance in festivals dependent on Easter. Pope Gregory, in 1582, ordered the 5th of October to be called 15th of October; the Low Countries made 15th of December 25th of December. Spain, Portugal, and part of Italy, accepted the Gregorian change, but the

the year 1800 was only to be accounted a common year, and not a leap year ; therefore old Lady-day was the 6th of April, old May-day 13th May, old Midsummer-day 6th July, old Lammas 13th August, old Michaelmas-day 11th October, &c., and so to continue for one hundred years."

Protestant countries and communities resisted up to 1700. In England the ten days' difference had increased to eleven days, and the Act of 24 Geo. II. was passed to equalize the style in Great Britain and Ireland to the method now in use in all Christian countries, except Russia. In England, Wednesday, September 2, 1752, was followed by Thursday the 14th of September, and the New Style date of Easter-day came into use in 1753.—*Note by John Westby Gibson, Esq., LL.D.*]

DRAW THE CURTAINS—THE OLD CENTURY
IS DEAD.

CHAPTER V.

1801.

"LE Roi est mort. Vive le Roi." Ring the bells
to welcome the baby Nineteenth Century, who
is destined to utterly eclipse in renown all his
ancestors.

Was it for good, or was it for evil, that its first act should
be that of the Union with Ireland ? It was compulsory,
for it was a legacy bequeathed it. There were no national
rejoicings. The new Standard was hoisted at the Tower,
and at St. James's, the new "Union" being flown from
St. Martin's steeple, and the Horse Guards; and, after
the King and Privy Council had concluded the official
recognition of the fact, both the Park and Tower guns
fired a salute. The ceremonial had the merit, at least, of
simplicity.

A long Royal Proclamation was issued, the principal
points of which were: " We appoint and declare that our

Royal Stile and Titles shall henceforth be accepted, taken, and used, as the same are set forth in manner and form following ; that is to say, the same shall be expressed in the Latin tongue by these words, ' *GEORGIUS TER-TIUS, Dei Gratiâ, Britanniarum Rex, Fidei Defensor.*' And in the English tongue by these words, 'GEORGE the THIRD, by the Grace of God, of the United Kingdom of Great Britain and Ireland, King, Defender of the Faith.' And that the Arms or ensigns armorial of the said United Kingdom shall be quarterly—first and fourth, England ; second, Scotland ; third, Ireland ; and it is our will and pleasure, that there shall be borne therewith, on an escocheon of pretence, the Arms of our dominions in Germany, ensigned with the Electoral bonnet. And it is our will and pleasure that the Standard of the said United Kingdom shall be the same quartering as are herein before declared to be the arms or ensigns armorial of the said United Kingdom, with the escocheon of pretence thereon, herein before described : and that the Union flag shall be azure, the Crosses-saltires of St. Andrew and St. Patrick quarterly per saltire countercharged argent and gules ; the latter fimbriated of the second ; surmounted by the Cross of St. George of the third, fimbriated as the saltire." There is a curious memorial of these arms to be seen in a stained-glass window in the church of St. Edmund, King and Martyr, Lombard Street, which window was put up as a memento of the Union. In the above arms it is to be noticed that the *fleur de lys*, so long used as being typical of our former rule in France, is omitted. A new Great Seal was also made—the old one being defaced.[1] On

---

[1] The Great Seal in use in 1800, was the fifth made during the reign of George III. Its Obverse was the King, in Roman costume, with flying mantle, on horseback, facing left hand. In his right hand he holds a marshal's baton. Legend—both Obv. and Rev. "Georgius III. D.G. BRIT. FR. REX. F.D. BRVNS. ET. LVN. DVX. S.R.I.A.T. ET. PR. ELECT. ETC." The Reverse has the King royally robed and crowned, seated on a throne, on the back of which is emblazoned the Royal arms. He holds the sceptre in his right, the orb in his left hand. He is surrounded by allegorical

January 1, 1801, the King issued a proclamation for holding the first Parliament under the Union, declaring that it should " on the said twenty-second day of January, one thousand, eight hundred and one, be holden, and sit for the dispatch of divers weighty and important affairs."

On the 1st of January, also, was a proclamation issued, altering the Prayer-book to suit the change, and, as some readers would like to know these alterations, I give them.

" In the Book of Common Prayer, Title Page, instead of ' The Church of England,' put ' of the United Church of England and Ireland.'

" Prayer for the High Court of Parliament, instead of Our Sovereign, and his Kingdoms,' read 'and his Dominions.'

" The first Prayer to be used at sea, instead of ' His Kingdoms,' read ' His Dominions.'

" In the form and manner of making, ordaining, and consecrating of Bishops, Priests, and Deacons, instead of the order ' of the Church of England,' read ' of the United Church of England and Ireland.'

" In the preface of the said form, in two places, instead of ' Church of England,' read ' in the United Church of England and Ireland.'

" In the first question in the Ordination of Priests, instead of ' Church of England,' read ' of this United Church of England and Ireland.'

" In the Occasional Offices, 25th of October, the King's accession, instead of ' these realms,' read ' this realm.'

" In the Collect, before the Epistle, instead of ' these Kingdoms,' read ' this United Kingdom.'

figures. On his right (heraldically) stand Hercules, typical of Power, Minerva, of Wisdom, and Justice with sword and scales ; on his left are Britannia with spear, shield, and palm branch, and a female, figurative of piety, carrying the model of a church. The Seal of 1801 is identical, except that BRITANNIANUM is substituted for BRIT., and FR. is left out. Also in the Royal arms on the throne, the French *fleur de lys* is omitted, and the harp of Ireland is introduced. It is worthy of note, that the medallist has omitted the Cross of St. Patrick in Britannia's shield, although proclaimed.

" For the Preachers, instead of ' King of Great Britain, France, and Ireland,' say, ' King of the United Kingdom of Great Britain and Ireland.' "

The Union gave seats in the Imperial Parliament to one hundred commoners, twenty-eight temporal peers, who were elected for life, and four bishops representing the clergy, taking their places in rotation.[1]

The heavens marked the advent of the New Century by the discovery, by the Italian astronomer Piazzi, of the Planet Ceres on the 1st of January ; and, to begin the year in a proper and pious manner, a proclamation was issued that a general fast was to be observed in England and Ireland, on the 13th, and in Scotland, on the 12th of February.

The cry of scarcity of food still continued ; wheat was mounting higher and higher in price. In January it was 137s. a quarter, and it rose still higher. The farmers must have had a good time of it, as the Earl of Warwick declared in Parliament (November 14, 1800), they were making 200 per cent. profit. " Those who demanded upwards of 20s. a bushel for their corn, candidly owned that they would be contented with 10s. provided other farmers would bring down their prices to that standard." And again (17th of November) he said : " He should still contend that the gains of the farmer were enormous, and must repeat his wish, that some measure might be adopted to compel him to bring his corn to market, and to be contented with a moderate profit. He wondered not at the extravagant style of living of some of the farmers, who could afford to play guinea whist, and were not contented

---

[1] There is verily " nothing new under the sun." On January 22nd, the first Parliament of the United Kingdom met. Addington was chosen Speaker, and members were sworn in. On the 2nd of February the King opened the Session with a speech, and on the very next day, 3rd of February, *an Irish member was twice called to order by the Speaker.* He was a Mr. Martin of Galway, a gentleman who afterwards complained of his speech being reported in italics, and plaintively asked, " Mr. Speaker, did I speak in italics ? "

with drinking wine only, but even mixed brandy with it ; on farms from which they derived so much profit, they could afford to leave one-third of the lands they rented wholly uncultivated, the other two-thirds yielding them sufficient gain to support all their lavish expenditure."

Still the prosperity of the farmer must have been poor consolation to those who were paying at the rate of our half-crown for a quartern loaf, so that it is no wonder that the authorities were obliged to step in, and decree that from January 31, 1801, the sale of fine wheaten bread should be forbidden, and none used but that which contained the bran, or, as we should term it, brown, or whole meal, bread.

The poor French prisoners, of course, suffered, and were in a most deplorable condition, more especially because the French Government refused to supply them with clothes. They had not even the excuse that they clothed their English prisoners, for our Government looked well after them in that matter, however much they may have suffered in other ways.

On the 18th of February Pitt opened his budget, and as an increase was needed of over a million and three quarters, owing to the war, and interest of loan, new taxes were proposed as follows :

		£
Ten per cent. on all Teas over 2s. 6d. per lb., which would probably produce		30,000
Doubling the tax on Paper except Paper-hangings and glazed Paper	,,	130,000
Drawback on the export of Calicoes to be taken off, and an extra duty of one penny imposed	,,	155,000
Increase of one-third on the tax on Timber, Staves, and Deals	,,	95,000
Sixpence per lb. export duty, and threepence per lb. on home consumption to be levied on Pepper	,,	119,000
Twenty pence per cwt. extra on Sugar	,,	166,000
A duty on Raisins	,,	10,000
do. on Lead	,,	120,000
Ten shillings per pleasure Horse if only one were kept, and an additional ten for each horse so kept	,,	170,000
Horses used in agriculture 4s. each	,,	136,000
Increase of stamp duty on Bills and Notes	,,	112,000

Double stamp on Marine Insurance Policies	probably produce	145,000
An additional duty on deeds of Conveyance	,,	93,000
Modified Postal arrangements	,,	80,000
The Penny Post to be Twopence	,,	17,000
Other modifications of the Post-office	,,	53,000

There had been political dissatisfactions for some time past, which was dignified with the name of sedition, but the malcontents were lightly dealt with. On the 2nd of March those who had been confined in the Tower and Tothill Fields were liberated on their own recognizances except four—Colonel Despard, Le Maitre, Galloway, and Hodgson, who, being refused an unconditional discharge, preferred to pose as martyrs, and were committed to Tothill Fields. Of Colonel Despard we shall have more to say further on. Vinegar Hill had not been forgotten in Ireland, and sedition, although smothered, was still alight, so that an Act had to be introduced, prolonging the suspension of the Habeas Corpus Act in that kingdom.

In this year, too, was brought in a Bill which became law, preventing clergymen in holy orders from sitting in the House of Commons. This was brought about by the election (this sessions) of the Rev. John Horne Tooke for Old Sarum, a rotten borough, which in 1832 was disfranchised, as it returned two members, and did not have very many more voters. Tooke had been a partizan of Wilkes, and belonged, as we should now term it, to the Radical party, a fact which may probably have had something to do with the introduction of the Bill, as there undoubtedly existed an undercurrent of dissatisfaction, which was called sedition. Doubtless societies of the disaffected existed, and a secret commission, which sat for the purpose of exposing them, reported, on the 27th of April, that an association for seditious purposes had been formed under the title of United Britons, the members whereof were to be admitted by a test.

The question of feeding the French prisoners of war again turned up, and as it was not well understood, the *Morning Post*, 1st of September, 1801, thus explains matters: " Much abuse is thrown out against the French Government for not providing for the French prisoners in this country. We do not mean to justify its conduct ; but the public should be informed how the question really stands. It is the practice of all civilized nations to feed the prisoners they take. Of course the French prisoners were kept at the expense of the English Government till, a few years ago, reports were circulated of their being starved and ill-treated. The French Government, in hopes of stigmatizing the English Ministry as guilty of such an enormous offence, offered to feed the French prisoners here at its own expense; a proposal, which was readily accepted, as it saved much money to this country ; but the French Government has since discontinued its supplies, and thus paid a compliment to our humanity at the expense of our purse. In doing this, however, France has only reverted to the established practice of war, and all the abuse of the Treasury journals for withholding the supplies to the French prisoners, only betrays a gross ignorance of the subject."

Of their number, the *Morning Post*, 16th of October, 1801, says, " The French prisoners in this country at present amount to upwards of 20,000, and they are all effective men, the sick having been sent home from time to time as they fell ill. Of these 20,000 men, nine out of ten are able-bodied seamen ; they are the best sailors of France, the most daring and enterprising, who have been mostly employed in privateers and small cruisers." Some of them had been confined at Portsmouth for eight years !

M. Otto, in spite of the rebuff he had experienced, the former negotiations for peace having been broken off, was still in London, where he acted as Commissary for exchange of prisoners. Napoleon was making treaties of peace all round, and, if it were to be gained in an honourable manner, it would be good also for England. So Lord Hawkesbury, who was then Secretary of State for Foreign Affairs, entered into communication with M. Otto, on the 21st of March, signifying the King's desire to enter into negotiations for peace, and they went on all the summer. Of course all did not go smoothly, especially with regard to the liberty of the English press, which Napoleon cordially hated, and wished to see repressed and fettered; but this, Lord Hawkesbury either would not, or dared not, agree to. The public pulse was kept in a flutter by the exchange of couriers between England and France, and many were the false rumours which caused the Stocks to fluctuate. Even a few days before the Preliminaries were signed, a most authentic report was afloat that all negotiations were broken off; so we may imagine the universal joy when it was proclaimed as an authentic fact.

It fairly took the Ministry by surprise when, on Wednesday, the 30th of September, an answer was received from Napoleon, accepting the English proposals. Previously, the situation had been very graphically, if not very politely, described in a caricature by Roberts, called "Negotiation See-saw," where Napoleon and John Bull were represented as playing at that game, seated on a plank labelled, "Peace or War." Napoleon expatiates on the fortunes of the game: "There, Johnny, now I'm down, and you are up; then I go up, and you go down, Johnny; so we go on." John Bull's appreciation of the humour of the sport is not so keen; he growls, "I wish you would settle it one way or other, for if you keep bumping me up and down in this manner, I shall be ruined in Diachilem Plaster."

But when the notification of acceptance did arrive, very little time was lost in clinching the agreement. A Cabinet Council was held, and an express sent off to the King, whose sanction returned next afternoon. The silver box, which had never been used since the signature of peace with America, was sent to the Lord Chancellor at 5 p.m. for the Great Seal, and his signature; and, the consent of the

other Cabinet Ministers being obtained, at 7 p.m. Lord
Hawkesbury and M. Otto signed the Preliminaries of Peace
in Downing Street, and his lordship at once despatched
the following letter, which must have gladdened the hearts
of the citizens, to the Lord Mayor.

"TO THE RIGHT HONOURABLE THE LORD MAYOR.
"*Downing Street, Oct.* 1, 1801, *at night.*

"MY LORD,

"I have great satisfaction in informing your Lordship that Preliminaries of Peace between Great Britain and
France have been signed this evening by myself, on the
part of His Majesty, and by M. Otto, on the part of the
French Government. I request your Lordship will have
the goodness to make this intelligence immediately public
in the City.

"I have the honour to be, &c.,
"(*Signed*) HAWKESBURY."

The Lord Mayor was not at the Mansion House, and
the messenger had to proceed to his private house at
Clapham. His lordship returned to town, and by nine
o'clock the good news was known all over London. The
Lord Mayor read the letter at the Stock Exchange, and
also at Lloyd's Coffee House, at the bar of which it was
afterwards posted ; for Lloyd's was then a great power in
the City, from which all public acts, subscriptions, &c.,
emanated, as was indeed but right, as it was the assembly
which embraced all the rich and influential merchants.

Among this class all was joy, and smiles, and shaking of
hands. The Three per Cents., which only the previous day
were at 59½, rose to 66, and Omnium, which had been at
8, rose to 18.

The news came so suddenly, that the illuminations on
the night of the 2nd of October were but very partial.
We, who are accustomed to brilliant devices in gas, with

coruscating crystal stars, and transparencies, would smile
at the illuminations of those days. They generally took
the shape of a wooden triangle in each window-pane, on
which were stuck tallow candles, perpetually requiring
snuffing, and guttering with every draught ; or, otherwise, a
black-painted board with a few coloured oil-lamps arranged
in the form of a crown, with G. R. on either side.

As is observed in the *Morning Post* of the 3rd
October, 1884: "The sensation produced yesterday among
the populace was nothing equal to what might have been
expected. The capture of half a dozen men-of-war, or
the conquest of a colony, would have been marked with a
stronger demonstration of joy. The illumination, so far
from being general, was principally confined to a few
streets—the Strand, the Haymarket, Pall Mall, and Fleet
Street. In the last the Globe Tavern was lighted up at
an early hour, with the word *Peace* in coloured lamps.
This attracted a considerable mob, which filled the street
before the door. It was apprehended that they would
immediately set out on their tour through the whole town,
and enforce an universal illumination. This induced a few
of the bye-streets to follow the example, but nothing
more. There were several groups of people, but no crowd,
in the neighbourhood of Temple Bar. The other streets,
even those that were illuminated, were not more frequented
than usual. St. James's Street, Bond Street, and the west
part of the town ; east of St. Paul's, together with Holborn,
and the north part, did not illuminate. Several flags were
hoisted in the course of the day, and the bells of all the
churches were set a-ringing."

To us, who are accustomed to have our news reeled out
on paper tapes hot and hot from the telegraph, or to converse with each other, by means of the telephone, many miles
apart, the method used to disseminate the news of the
peace throughout the country, seems to be very primitive, and
yet no better, nor quicker mode, could have been devised

in those days. The mail coaches were placarded PEACE
WITH FRANCE in large capitals, and the drivers all wore
a sprig of laurel, as an emblem of peace, in their hats.

   The Preliminaries of Peace were ratified in Paris on the
5th of October, but General Lauriston, who was to be the
bearer of this important document, did not set out from
Paris until the evening of the 7th, having been kept waiting
until a magnificent gold box, as a fitting shrine for so
precious a relic, was finished; and he did not land at Dover
until Friday evening, the 9th of October, about 9 p.m.
He stayed a brief time at the City of London Inn, Dover,
to rest and refresh himself, sending forward a courier,
magnificently attired in scarlet and gold, to order horses
on the road, and to apprise M. Otto of his arrival. He
soon followed in a carriage, with the horses and driver
bedecked with blue ribands, on which was the word PEACE.
Of course the mob surrounded him, and cheered and yelled
as if mad—indeed they must have been, for they actually
shouted " Long live Bonaparte ! " At M. Otto's house, the
general was joined by that gentleman, who was to accompany him to Reddish's Hotel, in Bond Street.   In Oxford
Street, however, the mob took the horses out of his carriage,
and drew him to the hotel, rending the air with shouts of
joy ; some amongst them even mounting a tricoloured
cockade.   From the hotel window General Lauriston
scattered a handful of guineas among his friends, the mob,
who afterwards, when he went to Lord Hawkesbury's
office, once more took out the horses, and dragged him
from St. James's Square to Downing Street.

   At half-past two the Park guns boomed forth the welcome
news, and at three the Tower guns proclaimed the fact to
the dwellers in the City, and the East end of London.

   It was in vain that the general's carriage was taken
round to a back entrance ; the populace were not to be
baulked of their amusement, and, on his coming out, the
horses were once more detached, men took their places,

and he was dragged as far as the Admiralty. Here he remained some time, and was escorted to his carriage by Earl St. Vincent. Said he to the mob, "Gentlemen! gentlemen!" (three huzzas for Earl St. Vincent) "I request of you to be careful, and not overturn the carriage." The populace assured his lordship they would be careful of, and respectful to, the strangers; and away they dragged the carriage, with shouts, through St. James's Park, round the Palace, by the Stable-yard, making the old place ring with their yells, finally landing the general uninjured at his hotel.

At night the illuminations were very fine, and there were many transparencies, one or two of which were, to say the least, peculiar. One in Pall Mall had a flying Cupid holding a miniature of Napoleon, with a scroll underneath, "Peace and Happiness to Great Britain." Another opposite M. Otto's house, in Hereford Street, Oxford Street, had a transparency of Bonaparte, with the legend, "Saviour of the Universe." Guildhall displayed in front, a crown and G. R., with a small transparency representing a dove, surrounded with olive. The Post Office had over 6,000 lamps. The India House was brilliant with some 1,700 lamps, besides G. R. and a large PEACE. The Mansion House looked very gloomy. G. R. was in the centre, but one half of the R was broken. The pillars were wreathed with lamps. The Bank only had a double row of candles in front.

Squibs, rockets, and pistols were let off in the streets, and the noise would probably have continued all night, had not a terrible thunder-storm cleared the streets about 11 p.m.

On the 12th, the illuminations were repeated with even more brilliancy, and all went off well. One effect of the peace, which could not fail to be gratifying to all, was the fact, that wheat fell, next market day, some 10s. to 14s. per quarter.

The popular demonstrations of joy occasionally took odd forms, for it is recorded that at Falmouth, not only the horses, but the cows, calves, and asses were decorated with ribands, in celebration of the peace; and a publican at Lambeth, who had made a vow that whenever peace was made, he would give away all the beer in his cellar, actually did so on the 13th of October.

As was but natural, the Lord Mayor's installation, on the 9th of November, had a peculiar significance. The Show was not out of the way, at least nothing singular about it is recorded, except the appearance of a knight in armour with his page at the corner of Bride Lane, Bridge Street, had anything to do with it; probably he was only an amateur, as he does not seem to have joined the procession. In the Guildhall was a transparency of Peace surrounded by four figures, typical of the four quarters of the globe returning their acknowledgments for the blessings showered upon them. There were other emblematic transparencies, but the contemporary art critic does not speak very favourably of them. M. Otto and his wife, an American born at Philadelphia, were *the* guests of the evening, even more than the Lord Chancellor, and the usual ministerial following.

Bread varied in this year from 1s. 9¼d. on the 1st of January to 1s. 10½d. on the 5th of March, 10¼d. on the 12th of November, and 1s. 0¼d. on the 31st of December. Anent the scarcity of wheat at the commencement of the year, there is a singular item to be found in the "Account of Moneys advanced for Public Services from the Civil List (not being part of the ordinary expenditure of the Civil List)," of a "grant of £500 to Thomas Toden, Esq., towards enabling him to prosecute a discovery made by him, of a paste as a substitute for wheat flour."

Wheat was on January 1st, 137s. per quarter; it reached 153s. in March; and left off on the 31st of December at 68s.

The Three per Cents. varied from 54 on the 1st of January, to 68 on the 31st of December.

CHAPTER VI

1802.

THE year 1802 opened somewhat dully, or, rather, with a want of sensational news. Disarmament, and retrenchment, were being carried out with a swiftness that seemed somewhat incautious, and premature. But the people had been sorely taxed, and it was but fitting that the burden should be removed at the earliest opportunity.

Provisions fell to something like a normal price, directly the Preliminaries of Peace were signed, and a large trade in all sorts of eatables was soon organized with France, where prices ruled much lower than at home. All kinds of poultry and pigs, although neither were in prime condition, could be imported at a much lower rate than they could be obtained from the country.

Woodward gives an amusing sketch of John Bull

enjoying the good things of this life, on a scale, and at a
cost, to which he had long been a stranger.

On the 10th of February the Right Hon. Charles Abbot,
afterwards Lord Colchester, was elected Speaker to the
House of Commons, in the room of the Right Hon. John
Nutford, who had accepted the position of Chancellor of

JOHN BULL AND HIS FRIENDS COMMEMORATING THE PEACE.

Ireland; and, on the 15th of February, Mr. Chancellor
Addington presented the following message from the
King:

"GEORGE R.

"His Majesty feels great concern in acquainting the
House of Commons that the provision made by Parlia-

ment for defraying the expenses of his household, and civil government, has been found inadequate to their support. A considerable debt has, in consequence, been unavoidably incurred, an account of which he has ordered to be laid before this House. His Majesty relies with confidence on the zeal and affection of his faithful Commons, that they will take the same into their early consideration, and adopt such measures as the circumstances may appear to them to require.

"G. R."

This message was referred to a Committee of Supply, and, at the same time, the Prince of Wales, not to be behind his father, made a claim for the amount of the revenues of the Duchy of Cornwall received during his minority, and applied to the use of the Civil List. The King had "overrun the constable" at an alarming rate. He only wanted about a million sterling, and this state of indebtedness was attributed to many causes. The dearness of provisions, &c., during the last three years; the extra expenses caused by the younger princes and princesses growing up, which ran the Queen into debt; the marriage of the Prince of Wales, the support of the Princess Charlotte, pensions to late ministers to foreign courts, &c. In the long run John Bull put his hands in his pockets, and paid the bill, £990,053—all which had been contracted since the passing of Burke's Bill on the subject, and exclusive of the sums paid in 1784 and 1786. The Prince of Wales was not so lucky with his application at this time. The Chancellor of the Exchequer could not stand two heavy pulls upon his purse.

Well, as a sop, John got rid of the Income Tax. Like the "Old Man of the Sea," which we have to carry on our shoulders, it was originally proposed as a war tax; but, unlike ours, faith was kept with the people, and, with the cessation of the war, the tax died. A very amusing satirical print, given here, is by Woodward, and shows the departure of the Income Tax, who is flying away, saying, "Farewell, Johnny—remember me!" John Bull, relieved of his presence, growls out: "Yes, d—n thee; I have reason to remember thee; but good-bye. So thou'rt off; I don't care; go where thou wilt, thou'lt be a plague in the land thou lightest on."

JOHN BULL AND HIS FAMILY TAKING LEAVE OF THE INCOME TAX.

The negotiations for peace hung fire for a long time. Preliminaries were ratified, as we have seen, in October, but the old year died, and the new year was born, and still no sign to the public that the peace was a real fact; they could only see that a large French armament had been sent to the West Indies; nor was it until the 29th of March, that the citizens of London heard the joyful news, from the following letter to the Lord Mayor:

"*Downing Street, March* 29, 1802.

"MY LORD,

"Mr. Moore, assistant secretary to Marquis Cornwallis, has just arrived with the definite treaty of peace, which was signed at Amiens, on the 27th of this month, by His Majesty's plenipotentiary, and the plenipotentiaries of France, Spain, and the Batavian Republic.[1]

"I have the honour, &c.,

"HAWKESBURY."

It must have been a great relief to the public mind, as the armistice was a somewhat expensive arrangement, costing, it is said, a million sterling per week! One of the causes, said to be the principal, of the delay in coming to an understanding, was the question respecting the payment of the expenses, incurred by our Government, for the maintenance of the French prisoners of war. They amounted to upwards of two millions sterling, and a proposal was made by England, but rejected on the part of the French, to accept the island of Tobago as an equivalent. It was afterwards left to be paid as quickly as convenient. There were no regular illuminations on the arrival of this news, but of course many patriotic individuals vented their feelings in oil lamps, candles, and transparencies.

But what were the conditions of this Peace? The English restored "to the French Republic and its Allies, viz., His Catholic Majesty, and the Batavian Republic, all the possessions, and colonies, which respectively belonged to them, and which have been either occupied, or conquered, by the British forces during the course of the present war, with the exception of the island of Trinidad, and of the Dutch possessions in the island of Ceylon."

"The Port of the Cape of Good Hope remains to the Batavian Republic in full sovereignty, in the same manner as it did previous to the war. The ships of every kind belonging to the other contracting parties, shall be allowed to enter the said port, and there to purchase what provisions they may stand in need of, as heretofore, without

---

[1] Signed by the Marquis Cornwallis for England, Joseph Bonaparte for France, Azara for Spain, and Schimmelpenninck for Holland.

being liable to pay any other imports than such as the Batavian Republic compels the ships of its own nation to pay."

A portion of Portuguese Guiana was ceded to the French in order to rectify the boundaries ; the territories, possessions, and rights of the Sublime Porte were to be maintained as formerly.

The islands of Malta, Goza, and Comino were to be restored to the Order of St. John of Jerusalem, and the forces of His Britannic Majesty were to evacuate Malta, and its dependencies, within three months of the exchange of the ratifications, or sooner, if possible. Half the garrison should be Maltese, and the other half (2,000 men) should be furnished, for a time, by the King of Naples ; and France, Great Britain, Austria, Spain, Russia, and Prussia were the guarantors of its independence.

The French troops were to evacuate the kingdom of Naples, and the Roman States, and the English troops were to evacuate Porto Ferrajo, and all the ports, and islands they occupied in the Mediterranean, and the Adriatic.

The Prince of Orange was to have adequate compensation for the losses suffered by him in Holland, in consequence of the revolution ; and persons accused of murder, forgery, or fraudulent bankruptcy, were to be given up to their respective Powers, on demand, accompanied by proof.

This, then, was the Treaty of Amiens, in which France certainly came best off ; and so the popular voice seemed to think, although thankful for any cessation of the constant drain of men and treasure, combined with privations at home, and loss of trade.

A satirical print by Ansell, clearly shows this feeling.

Peace greets John Bull with—" Here I am, Johnny, arrived at last ! Like to have been lost at sea ; poles of the chaise broke at Dover, springs of the next chaise gave way at Canterbury, and one of the horses fell, and overturned the other chaise at Dartford. Ah, Johnny! I wonder we have ever arrived at all." John Bull replies, "Odds niggins!!! Why, is that you? have I been waiting all this time to be blessed with such a poor ugly crippled *piece?* and all you have with you is a quid of tobacco and some allspice." Mrs. Bull asks her husband, "Why, John, be this she you have been talking so much about?"

There was a wild rush of English over to France, and the French returned the compliment, but not in the same

LONG-EXPECTED COME AT LAST; OR, JOHN BULL DISAPPOINTED AT HIS
CRIPPLED VISITOR.

ratio; the Continental stomach having then, the same antipathy to the passage of the Channel, as now. Still there was an attempt at an *entente cordiale*, which was well exemplified by a contemporary artist (unknown), in a picture called "A Peaceable Pipe, or a Consular Visit to John Bull." Napoleon is having a pleasant chat with his old foe, smoking, and drinking beer with him. John Bull toasts his guest. "Here's to you, Master Boney Party. Come, take another whiff, my hearty." Napoleon accepts the invita-

tion with, " Je vous remercie, John Bull ; I think I'll take
another pull." Whilst the gentlemen are thus pleasantly
engaged, Mrs. Bull works hard mending John's too well-
worn breeches ; and as she works, she says, " Now we are
at peace, if my husband does take a drop extraordinary, I
don't much mind ; but when he was at war, he was always
grumbling. Bless me, how tiresome these old breeches are
to mend ; no wonder he wore them out, for he had always
his hands in his pockets for something or other."

Among the other Englishmen who took advantage of
the peace to go over to France, was Charles James Fox,
who, immediately after his election for Westminster, on
July 15, 1802, started off for Paris, professedly to search
the archives there, for material for his introductory chapter
to " A History of the Early Part of the Reign of James
the Second." A history of this trip was afterwards written
by his private secretary, Mr. Trotter.[1]   He and Mrs. Fox,
who was now first publicly acknowledged as his wife, were
introduced to Napoleon ; a subject most humorously
treated by Gillray, in his " Introduction of Citizen Volpone
and his Suite at Paris." Napoleon, in full Court costume,
and wearing an enormous cocked hat and feathers, is seated
on a chair, which is emblematical of his sovereignty of the
world, and is surrounded by a Mameluke guard. Fox and
his wife, both enormously fat, yet bowing and curtseying
respectively, with infinite grace, are being introduced by
O'Connor, who had, aforetime, been in treaty with the
French Government for the invasion of Ireland. Erskine,
in full forensic costume, bows, with his hand on his heart ;
and Lord and Lady Holland help to fill the picture. But
the real account of his reception was very different (*teste*
Mr. Trotter). " We reached the interior apartment, where
Bonaparte, First Consul, surrounded by his generals,
ministers, senators, and officers, stood between the second

---

[1] " Memoirs of the Later Years of the Right Hon. Charles James Fox."
By John Bernard Trotter, Esq., late private secretary to Mr. Fox. London, 1811.

and third Consuls, Le Brun and Cambacérès, in the centre
of a semicircle, at the head of the room! The numerous
assemblage from the *Salle des Ambassadeurs*, formed into
another semicircle, joined themselves to that, at the head
of which stood the First Consul. . . . The moment the
circle was formed, Bonaparte began with the Spanish
Ambassador, then went to the American, with whom he
spoke some time, and so on, performing his part with
ease, and very agreeably, until he came to the English
Ambassador, who, after the presentation of some English
noblemen, announced to him Mr. Fox. He was a great
deal flurried, and, after indicating considerable emotion,
very rapidly said, 'Ah, Mr. Fox! I have heard with
pleasure of your arrival, I have desired much to see you;
I have long admired in you the orator and friend of his
country, who, in constantly raising his voice for peace,
consulted that country's best interests, those of Europe,
and of the human race. The two great nations of Europe
require peace; they have nothing to fear; they ought to
understand and value one another. In you, Mr. Fox, I see,
with much satisfaction, that great statesman who recommended peace, because there was no just object of war;
who saw Europe desolated to no purpose, and who struggled
for its relief.' Mr. Fox said little, or rather nothing, in
reply—to a complimentary address to himself, he always
found invincible repugnance to answer—nor did he bestow
one word of admiration or applause upon the extraordinary and elevated character who addressed him. A
few questions and answers relative to Mr. Fox's tour,
terminated the interview."

According to Article II. of the Treaty of Amiens, "All
the prisoners made on one side and the other, as well by
land as by sea, and the hostages carried off, or delivered up,
during the war, and up to the present day, shall be restored,
without ransom, in six weeks at the latest, to be reckoned
from the day on which the ratifications of the present

treaty are exchanged, and on paying the debts which they shall have contracted during their captivity."

The invaluable M. Otto wrote the *detenus* a letter, in which, whilst congratulating them, he exhorted them to subdue all spirit of party, if, indeed, it had not already been effected by their years of suffering, and captivity, and cautioned them as to their behaviour on their return, telling them of the change for the better which they would not fail to observe. Glad, indeed, must these poor captives have been at the prospect of once more setting foot on *La belle France ;* and that the English Government made no unnecessary delay in helping them to the consummation of their wishes, is evident, for, on the 10th of April, upwards of 1,000 of them were liberated from the depôt at Norman Cross, preparatory to their being conveyed to Dunkirk. The others—at least, all those who were willing and able to go—soon left England.

"Several of the French prisoners who embarked at Plymouth on Thursday, on board the coasters and trawl boats, having liberty to come on shore until morning, thought the indulgence so sweet, that they stayed up the whole night. This morning, at three o'clock, they sung in very good style through the different streets, the 'Marseillais Hymn,' the 'Austrian Retreat,' with several other popular French songs, and concluded with the popular British song of 'God save the King,' in very good English."—*Morning Herald*, April 19, 1802.

CHAPTER VII.

ON the 21st of April, a proclamation was issued, ordering a public thanksgiving for Peace, to be solemnized on 1st of June. On the 26th of April, the King proclaimed Peace, in the following terms:

"By the KING. A Proclamation.

"G. R.,

"Whereas a definitive treaty of peace, and friendship, between us, the French Republic, His Catholic Majesty, and the Batavian Republic, hath been concluded at Amiens on the 27th day of March last, and the ratifications thereof have been duly exchanged; in conformity thereunto, We have thought fit, hereby, to command that the same be published throughout all our dominions; and we do declare to all our loving subjects our will and pleasure, that the said treaty of peace, and friendship, be observed inviolably, as well by sea as by land, and in all places whatsoever; strictly charging, and commanding, all our loving subjects to take notice hereof, and to conform themselves thereunto, accordingly.

"Given at our Court at Windsor, the 26th day of April, 1802, in the forty-second year of our reign.

"God save the King."

On the 29th of April, a public proclamation of the same was made, and it must have been a far more imposing spectacle than the very shabby scene displayed in 1856. All mustered in the Stable-yard, St. James's. The Heralds and Pursuivants were in their proper habits, and, preceded by the Sergeant Trumpeter with his trumpets, the Drum Major with his drums, and escorted on either side by Horse Guards, they sallied forth, and read aloud the Proclamation in front of the Palace. We can picture the roar of shouting, and the waving of hats, after the Deputy Garter's sonorous " God save the King ! " A procession was then formed, and moved solemnly towards Charing Cross, where another halt was made, and the Proclamation was read, the Herald looking towards Whitehall. The following is the order of the procession :

Two Dragoons.
Two Pioneers, with axes in their hands.
Two Trumpeters.
Horse Guards, six abreast.
Beadles of Westminster, two and two, with staves.
Constables of Westminster.
High Constable, with his staff, on horseback.
Officers of the High Bailiff of Westminster, with white wands, on horseback.
Clerk of the High Bailiff.
High Bailiff and Deputy Steward.
Horse Guards.
Knight Marshal's men, two and two.
Knight Marshal.
Drums.
Drum Major.
Trumpets.
Sergeant Trumpeters.
Pursuivants.

Sergeants-at-Arms. { Heralds. } Sergeants at-Arms.
King-at-Arms.
Horse Guards.

Horse Guards flanked the Procession. (left margin)

Horse Guards flanked the Procession. (right margin)

Thence to Temple Bar, which, according to precedent, was shut—with the Lord Mayor, Sheriffs, and civic officials on the other side. The minor Officer of Arms stepped out of the procession between two trumpeters, and, preceded by two Horse Guards, rode up to the gates, and after the trumpeters had sounded thrice, he knocked thereat with a cane. From the other side the City Marshal asked, "Who comes there?" and the Herald replied: "The Officers of Arms, who demand entrance into the City, to publish His Majesty's Proclamation of Peace." The gates being opened, he was admitted alone, and the gates were shut behind him. The City Marshal, preceded by his officers, conducted him to the Lord Mayor, to whom he showed His Majesty's Warrant, which his lordship having read, returned, and gave directions to the City Marshal to open the gates, who duly performed his mission, and notified the same to the Herald in the words—"Sir, the gates are opened." The Herald returned to his place, the procession entered the Bar, and, having halted, the Proclamation was again read.

The Lord Mayor, Sheriffs, &c., then joined the procession in the following order :

The Volunteer Corps of the City.
The King's Procession, as before stated.
Four Constables together.
Six Marshal's men, three and three, on foot.
Six Trumpeters, three and three.
Band of Music.

| Sheriff's Officers on foot. | { | Two Marshals on horseback.
Two Sheriffs on horseback.
Sword and Mace on horseback. | } | Sheriff's Officers on foot. |
| Porter in a black gown and staff. | { | LORD MAYOR, mounted on a beautiful bay horse. | } | Beadle. |

Household on foot.
Six Footmen in rich liveries, three and three.
State Coach with six horses, with ribands, &c.
Aldermen in seniority, in their coaches.
Carriages of the two Sheriffs.
Officers of the City, in carriages, in seniority.
Horse Guards.

The line of procession was kept by different Volunteer Corps.

The Proclamation having been read a fourth time, at Wood Street, they went on to the Exchange, read it there, and yet once again, at Aldgate pump, after which they returned, and, halting at the Mansion House, broke up, the Heralds going to their College, at Doctor's Commons, the various troops to their proper destinations ; and so ended a very beautiful sight, which was witnessed by crowds of people, both in the streets, and in the houses, along the route.

The illuminations, at night, eclipsed all previous occasions, Smirk, the Royal Academician, painting a transparency for the Bank of England, very large, and very allegorical. M. Otto's house, in Portman Square, was particularly beautiful, and kept the square full of gazers all the night through.   There were several accidents during the day, one of which was somewhat singular.   One of the outside ornaments of St. Mary le Strand, then called the New Church, fell down, killing one man on the spot, and seriously damaging three others.

The day of General Thanksgiving was very sober, comparatively.   Both Houses of Parliament attended Divine service, as did the Lord Mayor and Sheriffs, who went in state to St. Paul's.   Most of the churches were well filled, and flags flew, and bells rung, all day.

In July came a General Election, which evoked a lawless saturnalia throughout the length and breadth of the land. An election in our own times—before the ballot brought peace—was bad enough, but then the duration of the polling was nothing like it was in the days of which I write.   The County polling lasted fourteen days ; Boroughs, seven days.

The *Morning Herald*, July 14, 1802, thus speaks of the Middlesex election : " During the business of polling, the populace amused themselves in varieties of whimsicalities, one of which was the exhibition of a man on the shoulders of another, handcuffed and heavily ironed, while a third was employed in flogging him with a tremendous cat-o'-nine-tails, and the man who received the punishment, by his contortions of countenance, seemed to experience all the misery which such a mode of punishment inflicts. The shops were all shut in Brentford, and the road leading to London was lined on each side with crowds of idle spectators. It is impossible for any but those who have witnessed a Middlesex election to conceive the picture it exhibits; it is one continual scene of riot, disorder, and tumult."

And, whilst on the subject of Politics, although they have no proper place in this history, as it deals more especially with the social aspect of this portion of the Century, yet it is interesting to be acquainted with the living aspect of some of the politicians of the time, and, thanks to Gillray, they are forthcoming in two of his pictures I have here given.

This is founded on a serio-comic incident which occurred in a debate on Supply, on March 4, 1802.[1] " The report of the Committee of Supply, to whom the Army estimates were referred, being brought up, Mr. Robson proceeded to point out various heads of expenditure, which, he said, were highly improper, such as the barracks, the expenses of corn and hay for the horses of the cavalry, the coals and candles for the men, the expenses of which he contended to be enormous. The sum charged for beer to the troops at the Isle of Wight, he said, was also beyond his comprehension. He maintained that this mode of voting expenditure, by months, was dangerous ; the sum, coming thus by driblets, did not strike the imagination in the same manner as they would do, if the whole service of the year came before the public at once, and that the more particularly, as money was raised by Exchequer bills, to be hereafter provided for, instead of bringing out at once the budget of taxes for the year. He alleged that those things

[1] " Parliamentary History," vol. xxxvi. p. 346, &c.

were most alarming, and the country was beginning to feel the effects of them. Gentlemen might fence themselves round with majorities; but the time would come when there must be an account given of the public money. The finances of the country were in so desperate a situation,

Nichol.   *Tierney.*   *Addington.*
Lord Hawkesbury.   *Dickenson.*

SKETCH OF THE INTERIOR OF ST. STEPHEN'S AS IT NOW STANDS.

that Government was unable to discharge its bills; for a fact had come within his knowledge, of a bill, accepted by Government, having been dishonoured. (A general exclamation of hear! hear!)

"Mr. Robson, however, stuck to it as a fact, saying that

'it was true that a banker, a member of that House, did take an acceptance to a public office—the sum was small. The answer at that public office was "that they had not money to pay it."' On being pressed to name the office, he said it was the Sick and Hurt Office.

"Later on in the evening Addington said, 'I find that the amount of the bill accepted by Government, and non-payment of which was to denote the insolvency of Government, is —

£19 7s. Whether or not the bill was paid, remains to be proved ; but my information comes from the same source as the hon. member derives his accusation. At all events, the instance of the hon. member of the insolvency of the Government is a bill of £19 7s.'

" Mr. Robson said that was so much the worse, as the bill was in the

R. B. *Robson.* Horne *Tooke.* Sir F. *Burdett·*
T. T. *Jones.*

" DESPAIR."

hands of a poor man who wanted the money."

In August some riots occurred in Wiltshire, caused by the introduction of machinery into cloth-working. What Hargreaves, Arkwright, and Crompton, had done for the cotton trade, was bound, sooner or later, to be followed by other textile industries. In this case a shearing machine had been introduced into a large factory, some three years back, and, like the silversmiths at Ephesus, the cloth-workers thought that "thus our craft is in danger of being set at nought ; " and they did what most poor ignorant men have done under like circumstances, they thought they could retard the march of intellect, by breaking the objectionable machines. Not only so, but, in their senseless folly, they cut, and destroyed, much valuable property in the cloth-racks—altogether the damage done was computed at over £100,000. For this, one man was tried at Gloucester Assizes, and hanged—a fate which seems to have acted as a warning to his brother craftsmen, for there was no repetition of the outrage. In this case, the machinery, being very expensive, could only be introduced into large mills, the owners of which did not discharge a man on its account, and the smaller masters were left to plod on in the old way, in which their soul delighted, and to go quietly to decay, whilst their more go-ahead neighbours were laying the foundation of a business which, in time, supplied the markets of the world. But there was the same opposition to the *Spinning Jenny,* and we have seen, in our time, the stolid resistance offered by agricultural labourers to every kind of novel machine used in farming, so that we can more pity, than blame, these deluded, and ignorant, cloth-workers, because they were not so far-seeing as the manufacturers.

It was mysteriously whispered about on the evening of the 18th of November, that a plot had been discovered, having for its object the assassination of the King ; and next day the news was confirmed—Colonel Despard, of whom I have before spoken (see p. 37), was at the head of this plot. He was an Irishman, and had seen military service in the West Indies, on the Spanish Main, and in the Bay of Honduras, where he acted as Superintendent of the English Colony ; but, owing to their complaints, he was recalled, and an inquiry into his conduct was refused. This, no doubt, soured him, and made him disaffected, causing him to espouse the doctrines of the French Revolution. On account of his seditious behaviour, he was arrested under the " Suspension of the Habeas Corpus " Act (1794), and passed some years in prison ; and, as we have seen, preferred continuing there, to having a conditional pardon. On his liberation, this misguided man could not keep quiet, but must needs plot, in a most insane manner, not for any good to be done to his country, to redress no grievances, but simply to assassinate the King, forgetting that another was ready to take the place of the slaughtered monarch.

Of course, among a concourse of petty rogues, one was traitor, a discharged sergeant of the Guards ; and, in consequence of his revelations to Sir Richard Ford, the chief magistrate at Bow Street, a raid, at night, was made upon the Oakley Arms, Oakley Street, Lambeth (still in existence at No. 72), and there they found Colonel Despard and thirty-two labouring men and soldiers—English, Irish, and Scotch—all of whom they took into custody, and, after being examined for eight hours, the Colonel was committed to the County Gaol, twelve of his companions (six being soldiers) to Tothill Fields Bridewell, and twenty others to the New Prison, Clerkenwell.

Next day he was brought up, heavily ironed, before the Privy Council, and committed to Newgate for trial, the charge against him being, that he administered a secret oath to divers persons, binding them to an active co-operation in the performance of certain treasonable, and murderous, practices. As a matter of history, his fate belongs to the next year, but 1803 was so full of incident that it is better to finish off this pitiful rogue (for he was no patriot) at once.

On the 20th of January, 1803, the Grand Jury brought in a true bill against him and twelve others, on the charge of high treason ; and on the 5th of February their trial, by Special Commission, commenced, at the Sessions House, Clerkenwell, before four judges. They were tried on eight counts, the fifth and sixth of which charged them with

" intending to lie in wait, and attack the King, and treating
of the time, means, and place, for effecting the same;" also
" with a conspiracy to attack and seize upon the Bank,
Tower, &c., to possess themselves of arms, in order to kill
and destroy the soldiers and others, His Majesty's liege
subjects," &c.   The trial lasted until 8 a.m. on the 10th
of February, when Despard, who was found guilty on the
8th, and nine others, were sentenced to be hanged, disem-
bowelled, beheaded, and quartered.   But the day before
they were executed, it was " thought fit to remit part of the
sentence, viz., taking out and burning their bowels before
their faces, and dividing the bodies into four parts."   They
were to be hanged, and afterwards beheaded ; and this
sentence was fully carried out on Despard, and six of his
accomplices, on the 21st of February, 1803.

And so the year came to an end, but not quietly ; clouds
were distinctly visible in the horizon to those who watched
the political weather.   England hesitated to fulfil her portion of the treaty, with regard to the evacuation of Malta ;
and the relations of Lord Whitworth, our Ambassador, and
the French Court, became somewhat strained.

Still the Three per Cents. kept up—in January 68, July 70,
December 69 ; and bread stuffs were decidedly cheaper
than in the preceding year—wheat averaging 68s. per.
quarter, barley 33s., oats 20s., whilst the average quartern
loaf was 1s.

CHAPTER VIII.

1803.

Strained relations with France—Prosecution and trial of Jean Peltier for libel against Napoleon—Rumours of war—King's proclamation—Napoleon's rudeness to Lord Whitworth—Hoax on the Lord Mayor—Rupture with France—Return of Lord Whitworth, and departure of the French Ambassador.

POLITICAL Caricatures, or, as they should rather be called, Satirical Prints, form very good indications as to the feeling of the country; and, on the commencement of 1803, they evidently pointed to a rupture with France, owing to the ambition of Napoleon. Lord Whitworth found him anything but pleasant to deal with. He was always harping on the license of the British press, and showed his ignorance of our laws and constitution by demanding its suppression. Hence sprung the prosecution, in our Law Courts, of one Jean Peltier, who conducted a journal in the French language—called *L'Ambigu.*

Napoleon's grumbling at the license of our press, was somewhat amusing, for the French press was constantly publishing libels against England, and, as Lord Hawkesbury remarked, the whole period, since the signing of the treaty, had been " one continued series of aggression, violence, and insult, on the part of the French Government." Still, to show every desire to act most impartially towards Napoleon,

6

although the relations with his government were most strained, Jean Peltier was indicted ; and his trial was commenced in the Court of King's Bench, on the 21st of February, 1803, before Lord Ellenborough and a special jury.

The information was filed by the Attorney General, and set forth : " That peace existed between Napoleon Bonaparte and our Lord the King ; but that M. Peltier, intending to destroy the friendship so existing, and to despoil said Napoleon of his consular dignity, did devise, print, and publish, in the French language, to the tenor following "—— what was undoubtedly calculated to stir up the French against their ruler. The Attorney General, in his speech, details the libels, and gives the following description of the paper. " The publication is called *The Ambigu, or atrocious and amusing Varieties.* It has on its frontispiece a sphinx, with a great variety of Egyptian emblematical figures, the meaning of which may not be very easy to discover, or material to inquire after. But there is a circumstance which marks this publication, namely, the head of the sphinx, with a crown on it. It is a head, which I cannot pretend to say, never having seen Bonaparte himself, but only from the different pictures of him, one cannot fail, at the first blush, to suppose it was intended as the portrait of the First Consul," &c.

It is very questionable, nowadays, whether such a press prosecution would have been inaugurated, or, if so, whether it would have been successful, yet there was some pretty hard hitting. " And now this tiger, who dares to call himself the founder, or the regenerator, of France, enjoys the fruit of your labours, as spoil taken from the enemy. This man, sole master in the midst of those who surround him, has ordained lists of proscription, and put in execution, banishment without sentence, by means of which there are punishments for the French who have not yet seen the light. Proscribed families give birth to children, oppressed before they are born ; their misery has commenced before their life. His wickedness increases every day." The Attorney General gave many similar passages, which it would be too tedious to reproduce, winding up with the following quotation : "'Kings are at his feet, begging his favour. He is desired to secure the supreme authority in his hands. The French, nay, Kings themselves, hasten to congratulate him, and would take the oath to him like subjects. He is proclaimed Chief Consul for life. As for me, far from envying his lot, let him name, I consent to it, his worthy successor. Carried on the shield, let him be elected Emperor ! Finally (and Romulus recalls the thing to mind), I wish, on the morrow, he may have his apotheosis. Amen.' Now, gentlemen, he says, Romulus suggests that idea. The fate that is ascribed to him is well known to all of us—according to ancient history, he was assassinated."

Peltier's counsel, a Mr. Mackintosh, defended him very ably, asking pertinently : "When Robespierre presided over the Committee of Public Safety, was not an Englishman to canvass his measures ? Supposing we had then been at peace with France, would the Attorney General have filed an information against any one who had expressed due abhorrence of the furies of that sanguinary monster ? When Marat demanded 250,000 heads in the Convention, must we have contemplated that request without speaking of it in the terms it provoked ? When Carrier placed five hundred children in a square at Lyons, to fall by the musketry of the soldiery, and from their size the balls passed over them, the little innocents flew to the knees of the soldiery for protection, when they were butchered by the bayonet ! In relating this event, must man restrain his just indignation, and stifle the expression of indignant horror such a dreadful massacre must excite ? Would the Attorney General in his information state, that when Maximilian Robespierre was first magistrate of France, as President of the Committee of Public Safety, that those

who spoke of him as his crimes deserved, did it with a
wicked and malignant intention to defame and vilify
him. . . .

"In the days of Cromwell, he twice sent a satirist upon
his government to be tried by a jury, who sat where this
jury now sit. The scaffold on which the blood of the
monarch was shed was still in their view. The clashing of
the bayonets which turned out the Parliament was still
within their hearing; yet they maintained their integrity,
and twice did they send his Attorney General out of court,
with disgrace and defeat."

However, all the eloquence, and ingenuity, of his counsel
failed to prevent a conviction. Peltier was found guilty
and, time being taken to consider judgment, he was bound
over to appear, and receive judgment when called upon.
That time never came, for war broke out between France
and England, and Peltier was either forgotten, or his offence
was looked upon in a totally different light.

The English Government looked with great distrust upon
Napoleon, and the increasing armament on the Continent,
and temporized as to the evacuation of Malta, to the First
Consul's intense disgust. But the Ministry of that day were
watchful, and jealous of England's honour, and as early as
the 8th of March, the King sent the following message to
Parliament:

"GEORGE R.

"His Majesty thinks it necessary to acquaint the House
of Commons, that, as very considerable military preparations are carrying on in the ports of France and Holland,
he has judged it expedient to adopt additional measures of
precaution for the security of his dominions; though the
preparations to which His Majesty refers are avowedly
directed to Colonial service, yet, as discussions of great
importance are now subsisting between His Majesty and
the French Government, the result of which must, at pre-

sent, be uncertain, His Majesty is induced to make this communication to his faithful Commons, in the full persuasion that, whilst they partake of His Majesty's earnest and unvarying solicitude for the continuance of peace, he may rely with perfect confidence on their public spirit, and liberality, to enable His Majesty to adopt such measures as circumstances may appear to require, for supporting the honour of his Crown, and the essential interests of his people.   " G. R."

An address in accordance with the message was agreed to by both Houses, and, on the 10th, the King sent Parliament another message, to the effect he intended to draw out, and embody, the Militia. On the 11th of March the Commons voted the following resolution, " That an additional number of 10,000 men be employed for the sea service, for eleven lunar months, to commence from the 26th of February, 1803, including 3400 Marines."

Events were marching quickly. On the 13th of March Napoleon behaved very rudely to Lord Whitworth ; in fact it was almost a parallel case with the King of Prussia's rudeness to M. Benedetti on the 13th of July, 1870. But let our Ambassador tell his own story :

" *Despatch from Lord Whitworth to Lord Hawkesbury dated Paris the 14th of March,* 1803.

" MY LORD,
        " The messenger, Mason, went on Saturday with my despatches of that date, and, until yesterday, Sunday, I saw no one likely to give me any further information, such as I could depend upon, as to the effect which His Majesty's Message had produced upon the First Consul.

" At the Court which was held at the Tuileries upon that day, he accosted me, evidently under very considerable agitation. He began by asking me if I had any news from England. I told him that I had received letters from your lordship two days ago. He immediately said, ' And so you are determined to go to war.' 'No!' I replied, 'we are too sensible of the advantages of peace.' 'Nous avons,' said he, 'déjà fait la guerre pendant quinze ans.' As he seemed to wait for an answer, I observed only, 'C'en est déjà trop.' 'Mais,' said he, 'vous voulez la faire encore quinze années, et vous m'y forcez.' I told him that was very far from His Majesty's intentions. He then proceeded to Count Marcow, and the Chevalier Azara, who were standing together, at a little distance from me, and said to them, 'Les Anglais veulent la guerre, mais s'ils sont les premiers à tirer l'epée, je serai le dernier à la remettre. Ils ne respectent pas les traités. Il faut dorénavant les couvrir de crêpe noir.' He then went his round. In a few minutes he came back to me, and resumed the conversation, if such it can be called, by saying something civil to me. He began again : 'Pourquoi des armémens? Contre qui des mesures de précaution? Je n'ai pas un seul vaisseau de ligne dans les ports de France ; mais, si vous voulez armer, j'armerai aussi ; si vous voulez vous battre, je me battrai aussi. Vous pourrez peut—être tuer la France, mais jamais l'intimider.' 'On ne voudrait,' said I 'ni l'un, ni l'autre. On voudrait vivre en bonne intelligence avec elle.' 'Il faut donc respecter les traités,' replied he ; 'malheur a ceux qui ne respectent pas les traités ; ils en serait responsible à toute l'Europe.' He was too much agitated to make it advisable for me to prolong the conversation ; I therefore made no answer, and he retired to his apartment, repeating the last phrase.

"It is to be remarked, that all this passed loud enough to be overheard by two hundred people who were present, and I am persuaded that there was not a single person, who did not feel the extreme impropriety of his conduct, and the total want of dignity as well as of decency, on the occasion.

"I propose taking the first opportunity of speaking to M. Talleyrand on this subject.

"I have the honour to be, &c.

"(*Signed*) WHITWORTH."

He did call on Talleyrand, who assured him that it was very far from the First Consul's intention to distress him, but that he had felt himself personally insulted by the charges which were brought against him by the English Government ; *and that it was incumbent upon him to take the first opportunity of exculpating himself, in the presence of the ministers of the different Powers of Europe :* and Talleyrand assured Lord Whitworth that nothing similar would again occur.

And so things went on, the French wishing to gain time, the English temporizing also, well knowing that the peace would soon be broken.

We are not so virtuous ourselves, in the matter of false news, as to be able to speak of the following Stock Exchange *ruse* in terms of proper indignation. It was boldly conceived, and well carried out.

On the 5th of May, 1803, at half-past eight in the morning, a man, booted and spurred, and having all the appearance of just having come off a long journey, rushed up to the Mansion House, and inquired for the Lord Mayor, saying he was a messenger from the Foreign Office, and had a letter for his lordship. When informed that he was not within, he said he should leave the letter, and told the servant particularly to place it where the Lord Mayor should get it the moment of his return. Of course the thing was well carried out ; the letter bore Lord Hawkesbury's official seal, and purported to be from him. It ran thus :

"*Downing Street*, 8 a.m.

"To the Right Hon. the Lord Mayor.

"Lord Hawkesbury presents his compliments to the Lord Mayor, and is happy to inform him that the negotiations between this country, and the French Republic, have been amicably adjusted."

His lordship made inquiries as to the messenger, and,

as the whole thing seemed to be genuine, he wrote one copy, which was straightway stuck up outside the Mansion House, and sent another to Lloyd's, going himself to the Stock Exchange with the original, and, about 10 a.m., wrote to Lord Hawkesbury expressing his satisfaction.   Before a reply could be obtained, and the whole fraud exposed, Mr. Goldsmid called at the Mansion House, saw the letter, and pronounced it a forgery.   Meanwhile, the excitement on the Stock Exchange had been terrible.   Consols opened at 69, and rose, before noon, to over 70, only to sink, when the truth came out, to 63.   If the bargains had been upheld, it would have been hopeless ruin to many ; so a committee of the Stock Exchange decided that all transactions on that day, whether for money or time, were null and void.   The perpetrators of this fraud, consequently, did not reap any benefit ; nor were they ever found out, although the Lord Mayor offered a reward of £500.

The Caricaturists were, at this time, very busy with their satirical pictures, some of which are very good, especially one by Gillray (May 18, 1803) called "Armed Heroes." Addington, in military costume, with huge cocked hat and sword, bestrides a fine sirloin of the "Roast Beef of Old England," and is vapouring at little Bonaparte, who, on the other side of the Channel, is drawing his sword, and hungrily eyeing the beef.   Says he :

> "Ah, ha ! sacrè dieu ! vat do I see yonder?
> Dat look so invitingly Red and de Vite ?
> Oh, by Gar ! I see 'tis de Roast Beef of Londres,
> Vich I vill chop up, at von letel bite !"

Addington alternately blusters and cringes, "Who's afraid? damme !   *O Lord, O Lord, what a Fiery Fellow he is!* Who's afraid ? damme !   *O dear ! what will become of ye Roast Beef ?*   Damme! who's afraid ?   *O dear ! O dear !* " Other figures are introduced, but they are immaterial.

But the crisis was rapidly approaching.   On the 12th of

May Lord Whitworth wrote Lord Hawkesbury : " The remainder of this day passed without receiving any communication from M. de Talleyrand. Upon this, I determined to demand my passports, by an official note, which I sent this morning by Mr. Mandeville, in order that I might leave Paris in the evening. At two I renewed my demand of passports, and was told I should have them immediately. They arrived at five o'clock, and I propose setting out as soon as the carriages are ready." He did not, however, land at Dover until a quarter to twelve on the night of the 17th of May, where he found the French Ambassador, General Andreossi, almost ready to embark. This he did early in the morning of the 19th of May, being accompanied to the water side by Lord Whitworth.

CHAPTER IX.

Declaration of War against France—Napoleon makes all the English in France prisoners of war—Patriotic Fund—Squibs on the threatened invasion—"The New Moses"—Handbill signed "A Shopkeeper"—"Britain's War-song"—"Who is Bonaparte?"—"Shall Frenchmen rule over us?"—"An Invasion Sketch."

ON the 16th of May the King sent a message to Parliament announcing his rupture with the French Government, and the recall of his ambassador, and laying before them the papers relating to the previous negotiations ; and on the 18th of May, His Majesty's Declaration of War against France (a somewhat lengthy document) was laid before Parliament. No time was lost, for, on the 20th of May, Lord Nelson sailed from Portsmouth in the *Victory*, accompanied by the *Amphion*, to take the command in the Mediterranean ; and prizes were being brought in daily.

Whether it was in reprisal for this, or not, there are no means of telling, but Napoleon, on the 22nd of May, took the most unjustifiable step of making prisoners of war of all the English in France, and Holland, where, also, an embargo was laid on all English vessels. This detention of harmless visitors was unprecedented, and aroused universal reprobation. They were not well treated, and, besides, were harassed by being moved from place to place.

In the *Annual Register*, vol. xlv. p. 399, we read :

" In consequence of orders from the Government, the English, confined at Rouen, have been conducted to Dourlens, six miles from Amiens. The English that were at Calais when Bonaparte visited that place, have all been sent to Lisle. The English prisoners at Brussels have been ordered to repair to Valenciennes. The great Consul, like a politic shepherd, continually removes the pen of his bleating English flock from spot to spot, well knowing that the soil will everywhere be enriched by their temporary residence. How their wool will look when they return from their summer pasture is of little consequence !"

It is not my province to write on the progress of the war, except incidentally, and as it affected England socially. The old Volunteer Corps, which had been so hastily disbanded, again came to the fore, in augmented strength, and better organization ; but of them I shall treat in another place. As both men, and money, constitute the sinews of war, the volunteers found one, the merchants helped with the other. On the 20th of July the merchants, underwriters, and subscribers of Lloyd's, held a meeting for the purpose of " setting on foot a general subscription, on an extended scale, for the encouragement and relief of those who may be engaged in the defence of their country, and who may suffer in the common cause ; and of those who may signalize themselves during this present most important contest." The Society of Lloyd's gave £20,000 Stock in the Three per Cent. Consols, and over £12,000 was subscribed at once, five subscriptions each of £1000 coming from such well-known City names as Sir F. Baring, John J. Angerstein, B. and A. Goldsmid, John Thomson, and Thomson Bonar. Other loyal meetings took place, and everything was done that could be done, to arouse the enthusiasm of the people, and the spirit of patriotism.

One method was by distributing heart-stirring handbills, serious or humorous, but all having the strongest patriotic basis. Of these very many hundreds are preserved in the

British Museum,[1] and very curious they are. That they answered their purpose no one could doubt, for, although the threatened invasion of England was a patent fact, to which no one could shut their eyes, nor doubt its gravity, these handbills kept alive an enthusiasm that was worth anything at the time, and it was an enthusiasm, that although in its style somewhat bombastic, and with some insular prejudice, was deep-seated and real; and, had the invasion ever taken place, there can be little doubt but that, humanly speaking, it would have resulted in a disastrous defeat for Napoleon, or, had it been otherwise, it would not have been the fault of the defenders, for, like Cromwell's Ironsides, "Every man had a heart in him."

In these handbills, Bonaparte was accused of many things—that he became Mohammedan, poisoned his sick at Jaffa, with many other things which do not come within the scope of this work, and have been fully treated in my " English Caricature and Satire on Napoleon I.," and which I do not wish to reproduce; only, naturally, Napoleon's name can hardly be kept out, and, as I took the best for that book, this must not suffer therefrom. They are of all dates, as can be seen from internal evidence, but very few are dated, so that they may be taken nearly haphazard. The following, from its mention of Lord Whitworth, and his recall, is evidently an early one:

" THE NEW MOSES

or

"BONAPARTE'S TEN COMMANDMENTS.

" Translated from a French Manuscript

by

SOLIMAN the TRAVELLER.

"And when the great man came from Egypt, he used

---

[1] Notably the following, $\frac{806.\ \text{k.}\ \text{I.}}{\text{I—154}}$ Squibs on Bonaparte's threatened Invasion ; 1890 e. Miss Banks' Collection, Threatened Invasion ; and 554 f. 25 Squibs on the Threatened French Invasion.

cunning and force to subject the people. The good as well as the wicked of the land trembled before him, because he had won the hearts of all the fighting men ; and after he had succeeded in many of his schemes, his heart swelled with pride, and he sought how to ensnare the people more and more, to be the greatest man under the sun.

"The multitude of the people were of four kinds : some resembled blind men, that cannot see ; some were fearful, who trembled before him ; others courageous, and for the good of the people, but too weak in number ; and others yet, who were as wicked as the great man himself. And when he was at the head of the deluded nation, he gave strict laws and the following commandments, which were read before a multitude of people, and in a full congregation of all his priests—

" 1. Ye Frenchmen, ye shall have no other commander above me ; for I, Bonaparte, am the supreme head of the nation, and will make all nations about you bow to you, and obey me as your Lord and Commander.

"2. Ye shall not have any graven images upon your Coin, in marble, wood, or metal, which might represent any person above me ; nor shall ye acknowledge any person to excel me, whether he be among the living, or the dead, whether he be in the happy land of the enlightened French, or in the cursed island of the dull English ; for I, the Chief Consul of France, am a jealous hero, and visit disobedience of an individual upon a whole nation, and of a father upon the children, and upon the third and fourth generation of them that hate me ; and show mercy unto them that love me, and humble themselves.

" 3. Ye shall not trifle with my name, nor take it in vain ; nor shall you suffer that any other nation, treat it disrespectfully ; for I will be the sole commander of the earth, and make you triumph over your enemies.

"4. Remember that ye keep the days of prayers, and pray for me as the head of the nation, and the future conqueror of the base English. Ye shall pray fervently with your faces cast upon the ground, and not look at the priest when he pronounces my name ; for I am a jealous hero, and delight in my priests because they are humble, and I have regarded the lowliness of their hearts, and forgiven them all their past iniquities. And, ye priests, remember the power of him who made you his creatures, and do your duty.

" 5. Respect and honour all French heroes, that ye may find mercy in mine eyes for all your iniquities, and that ye may live in the land in which I, the Lord your Commander, lives.

" 6. Ye shall not murder each other, save it be by my own commands, for purposes that may be known to me alone ; but of your enemies, and all those nations that will not acknowledge your, and my greatness, ye may kill an infinite number ; for that is a pleasing sight in the eyes of your supreme Commander.

" 7. Ye shall not commit adultery at home, whatever ye may do in the land of the infidels, and the stiff-necked people ; for they are an abomination to the Lord your Commander.

" 8. Ye shall not steal at home, but suppress your covetousness and insatiable desire for plunder until ye may arrive in the land of your enemies. Ye shall neither steal from them with indiscretion, but seem to give with the left hand, when the right taketh.

"9. Ye shall not bear false witness against your neighbour, if he should distinguish himself in the land of the enemies.

" 10. Ye shall not covet anything of your neighbour, but everything of your enemies—his jewels, his gold, his silver, his horse or ass, his maid, his daughter, his wife, or anything in which your hearts find delight ; and ye may take it, but still with cunning ; for the Lord your Commander loveth mildness more than strength, to please the people when he plunders. Use the sword in battle, cunning after it ; look for plunder, but subject the people to me. Herein lie all my Commandments, and those who keep them shall be protected by my power, and prosper in all their undertakings.

" When the reading of these Commandments were over, the multitude gazed with amazement. There were present the gentiles, and ambassadors of various nations, and many looked at each other as if they were looking for the sense of what they had heard. The Chief Priest, however, more cunning than all the rest, thus broke silence :

" *Bishop.* Our mouths shall glorify thee for ever ; for thou hast regarded the lowliness of our hearts, and hast raised thy servants from the dust.

" *Pope.* And I will support your holy endeavours ; for without him I would not sit upon the holy seat of Peter.

" *All* (Priests and many of the Multitude). Praise be to him, for he has mercy on those that are humble, and fear him—throughout all the world, and all nations but the English, who are an abomination in his sight.

" *Bishop of Amiens.* Bow to him, for he commands ye.

" *An Italian to a Swiss.* I bow to him, for I fear and dread him.

" *A Dutchman* (to the two former). Ay, ay ! I must bow, at present, with you ; but I would rather make him bow before me and my nation.

" *French Gentleman.* Dat be very right to you ! Vy vere ye sush fools, and bigger fools yet, as we French, to submit to him, and even to court his tyranny ?

" *Bonaparte* (in one corner of the hall, and not hearing part of the preceding discourse, to one of his slaves). Do you observe that proud Englishman ?

" *1st Slave.* He neither bows, nor does he seem to approve of the homage paid to thee by the worshippers.

" *2nd Slave.* Ay, he is one of the stiff-necked Englishmen.

" *Bonaparte.* And so are all of his breed, except some of the meanest rabble.

"*Lord Whitworth* (to himself). I shall bow to thee with all my heart and soul, as soon as I may have the pleasure of being recalled.

"*Bonaparte.* This is an insult which shall be revenged on the whole nation."

There is not much "go" in the above, but it is mild, as being one of the first; they soon developed.

"Fellow Citizens,

"Bonaparte threatens to invade us; he promises to enrich his soldiers with our property, to glut their lust with our Wives and Daughters. To incite his Hell Hounds to execute his vengeance, he has *sworn* to permit everything. Shall we Merit by our Cowardice the titles of sordid Shopkeepers, Cowardly Scum, and Dastardly Wretches, which in every proclamation he gives us? No! we will loudly give him *the lie:* Let us make ourselves ready to shut our Shops, and march to give him the reception his malicious calumnies deserve. Let every brave young fellow instantly join the *Army* or *Navy;* and those among us who, from being married, or so occupied in business, cannot, let us join some Volunteer Corps, where we may learn the use of arms, and yet attend our business. Let us encourage recruiting in our neighbourhood, and loudly silence the tongues of those whom Ignorance or Defection (if any such there be) lead them to doubt of the attempt to invade or inveigh against the measures taken to resist it. By doing this, and feeling confidence in ourselves, we shall probably prevent the attempt; or, if favoured by a dark night, the enemy should reach our shores, our Unanimity and Strength will paralyze his efforts, and render him an easy prey to our brave *Army.* Let *us*, in families and neighbourhood, thus contribute to so desirable an event, and the *bloodstained banners of the Vaunted Conquerors of Europe will soon be hung up in our Churches, the honourable Trophies of our brave Army*—an Army ever Victorious when not doubled in numbers, and the only Army who can stand the charge of Bayonets. What *Army* ever withstood THEIRS !!! Let the welfare of our Country animate all, and 'come the World in Arms against us, and we'll shock 'em !'

" A SHOPKEEPER."

" Prave 'orts," but they answered their purpose. It was an article of faith that an Englishman was certainly a match for two ordinary foes, perhaps three, and this, no doubt, was to a certain extent true. The history of that time shows victories, both by land and sea, gained against fearful odds. What then might not have been done under such stimulant as

"BRITAIN'S WAR-SONG.

" BRITONS rouse ; with Speed advance ;
Seize the Musket, grasp the Lance ;
See the Hell-born Sons of France !

Now Murder, Lust, and Rapine reign
Hark ! the Shriek o'er Infants slain !
See the desolated Plain !

Now's the Day, and now's the Hour,
See the Front of Battle lower !
See curs'd Buonaparte's Power !

Who will be a Traitor Knave ?
Who can fill a Coward's Grave ?
Who so base as live a Slave ?

Rush indignant on the Foe !
Lay the Fiend Invaders low !
Vengeance is on every Blow !

Forward ! lo, the Dastards flee ;
Drive them headlong to the Sea ;
Britons ever will be free !
Huzza, Huzza, Huzza !"

7

"Who is BONAPARTE?

"WHO IS HE? Why an obscure Corsican, that began his Murderous Career with turning his Artillery upon the Citizens of Paris—who boasted in his Public Letters from Pavia, of *having shot the whole Municipality*—who put the *helpless, innocent,* and *unoffending* Inhabitants of Alexandria, *Man, Woman,* and *Child,* to the SWORD, till *Slaughter* was tired of its work—who, against all the Laws of War, put near 4000 Turks to death, in cold blood, after their Surrender—who destroyed his own Comrades by *Poison,* when lying sick and wounded in Hospitals, because they were unable to further the plan of Pillage which carried him to St. Jean d'Acre—who, having thus stained the profession of Arms, and solemnly and publicly renounced the religious Faith of Christendom, and embraced Mohametanism, again pretended to embrace the Christian Religion—who, on his return to France, destroyed the Representative System—who, after seducing the Polish Legion into the Service of his pretended Republic, treacherously transferred it to St. Domingo, where it has perished to a Man, either by Disease or the Sword—and who, finally, as it were to fill the Measure of his Arrogance, has *Dared* to attack what is most dear and useful to civilized Society, the FREEDOM of the PRESS and the FREEDOM of SPEECH, by proposing to restrict the *British Press* and the Deliberations of the *British Senate.* Such is the *Tyrant* we are called upon to oppose; and such is the Fate which awaits ENGLAND should WE suffer him and his degraded Slaves to pollute OUR Soil."

"SHALL FRENCHMEN RULE O'ER US? King Edward said, No!
And No! said King Harry, and Queen Bess she said, No!
And No! said Old England, and No! she says still;
They never shall rule Us; let them try if they will.
   Hearts of Oak we are all, both our Ships and our Men;
    Then steady, Boys, steady,
    Let's always be ready;
  We have trimmed them before, let us trim them again.

Shall Frenchmen rule o'er us? King George he says No!
And No! say our Lords, and our Commons they say No!
And No! say All Britons of every degree;
They shall never rule Britons, United and Free.

> Hearts of Oak, &c.

Shall Frenchmen rule us, the Free Sons of the Waves?
Shall England be ruled by a Nation of Slaves?
Shall the Corsican Tyrant, who bound on their Chains,
Govern Us, in the room of Our Good King who reigns?

> Hearts of Oak, &c.

Though He'd fain stop our Press, yet we'll publish his shame;
We'll proclaim to the World his detestable Fame;
How the Traitor Renounced his Redeemer, and then
How he murder'd his Pris'ners and Poison'd his Men.

> Hearts of Oak, &c.

Then Down with the Tyrant, and Down with his Rod!
Let us stand by our Freedom, our King, and our God!
Let us stand by our Children, our Wives, and our Homes!
Then Woe to the Tyrant Whenever he Comes!

> Hearts of Oak, &c."

The following is particularly good, as it gives a very vivid description of what might have occurred, had Napoleon's threatened invasion been successful, and it will favourably contrast with its congener of modern times, "The Battle of Dorking."

"Our Invasion Sketch.

"If there be one Person so lost to all Love for his Country, and the British Constitution, as to suppose that his Person or his Property, his Rights and his Freedom, would be respected under a Foreign Yoke, let him contemplate the following Picture—not Overcharged, but drawn from Scenes afforded by every Country: Italy, Holland, Switzerland, Germany, Spain, Hanover, which has been exposed to the Miseries of a French Invasion.

" LONDON, 10 *Thermidor Year* ——.

"General BONAPARTE made his public entrance into the Capital, over London Bridge, upon a charger from his BRITANNIC MAJESTY'S Stables at Hanover, preceded by a detachment of Mamelukes. He stopped upon the bridge for a few seconds, to survey the number of ships in the river ; and, beckoning to one of his Aide-de-camps, ordered the French flags to be hoisted above the English—the English sailors on board, who attempted to resist the execution of this order, were bayonetted, and thrown overboard.

"When he came to the Bank, he smiled with Complaisance upon a detachment of French Grenadiers, who had been sent to load all the bullion in waggons, which had previously been put in requisition by the Prefect of London, Citizen MENGAUD, for the purpose of being conveyed to France. The Directors of the Bank were placed under a strong guard of French soldiers, in the Bank parlour.

"From the Bank, the FIRST CONSUL proceeded, in grand procession, along Cheapside, St. Paul's, Ludgate Hill, Fleet Street, and the Strand, to St. James's Palace. He there held a grand Circle, which was attended by all his officers, whose congratulations he received upon his entrance into the Capital of these once proud Islanders. BONAPARTE, previous to his arrival, appointed two Prefects, one for London, and one for Westminster. Citizen MENGAUD, late Commissary at Calais, is the Prefect of London, and Citizen RAPP, of Westminster. He also nominated Citizen FOUCHÉ to the office of Minister of Police. The Mansion-house has been selected for the residence of the Prefect of London, and Northumberland House,[1] for the residence of the Prefect of Westminster. As it has been deemed necessary to have the Minister of Police always near the person of the FIRST CONSUL, Marlborough House has been given to Citizen Fouché. Lodgings have been prepared elsewhere, for the late owners of that splendid palace.

[1] On the site of which The Grand Hotel, Charing Cross, now stands.

" London was ordered to be illuminated, and detachments of French Dragoons paraded the principal streets, and squares, all night.

" 11 Thermidor.

" BONAPARTE, at five o'clock in the morning, reviewed the French troops on the Esplanade at the Horse Guards. A Council was afterwards held, at which the following Proclamations were drawn up, and ordered to be posted in every part of the City :

"' BY ORDER OF THE FIRST CONSUL.
" ' PROCLAMATION.

"' St. James's Palace.

"' Inhabitants of London, be tranquil. The Hero, the Pacificator, is come among you. His moderation, and his mercy, are too well known to you. He delights in restoring peace and liberty to all mankind. Banish all alarms. Pursue your usual occupations. Put on the habit of joy and gladness.

"' The FIRST CONSUL orders,

"' That all the Inhabitants of London and Westminster remain in their own houses for three days.

"' That no molestation shall be offered to the measures which the French Soldiers will be required to execute.

"' All persons disobeying these Orders, will be immediately carried before the Minister of Police.

"' (Signed) BONAPARTE.
"' The Minister of Police, FOUCHÉ.'

"' Proclamation.
" ' To the French Soldiers.

"' Soldiers ! BONAPARTE has led you to the Shores, and the Capital of this proud island. He promised to reward his brave companions in arms. He promised to give up the Capital of the British Empire to pillage. Brave

Comrades, take your reward. London, the second Carthage, is given up to pillage for three days.

" '(*Signed*) BONAPARTE.

" 'The Minister of War, par interim, ANGEREAU.'

"The acclamations of the French Soldiery—*Vive Bonaparte—le Héros—le Pacificateur—le Magnanime*—resound through every street.

" 12th, 13th, 14th Thermidor.

" LONDON PILLAGED! The doors of private houses forced. Bands of drunken soldiers dragging wives, and daughters, from the hands of husbands and fathers. Many husbands, who had the *temerity* to resist, butchered in the presence of their Children. Flames seen in a hundred different places, bursting from houses which had been set fire to, by the *vivacity* of the troops. Churches broken open, and the Church plate plundered—the pews and altars converted into Stabling. Four Bishops murdered, who had taken refuge in Westminster Abbey—the screams of women and of children mix with the cries of the Soldiers—*Vive la Republique ! Vive Bonaparte !*

" St. Martin's Church converted into a *depôt* for the property acquired by the pillage of the Soldiery.

" 15 Thermidor.

" A proclamation published by the FIRST CONSUL, promising *protection* to the inhabitants.

"The houses of the principal Nobility and Gentry appropriated to the use of the French Generals. Every house is required to furnish so many rations of bread and meat for the troops.

" At a Council of State, presided over by BONAPARTE, the two Houses of Parliament are solemnly abolished, and ordered to be replaced by a Senate, and a Council of State. General MASSENA appointed Provisional President of the former, and General DESSOLLES of the latter. The

Courts of Law are directed to discontinue their sittings, and are replaced by Military Tribunals.

"16 *Thermidor.*

"A contribution of twenty millions ordered to be levied upon London. A deputation was sent to BONAPARTE to represent the impossibility of complying with the demand, the Bank and the Capital having been pillaged. After waiting in the ante-chamber of the Consul for four hours, the deputation are informed by a Mameluke guard, that BONAPARTE will not see them. Two hundred of the principal Citizens ordered to be imprisoned till the Contribution is paid.

"17 *Thermidor.*

" A plot discovered by FOUCHÉ against the FIRST CONSUL, and three hundred, supposed to be implicated in it, sent to the Tower.

"Insurrections in different parts of the Capital, on account of the excesses of the Soldiers, and the contribution of twenty millions. Cannon planted at all the principal avenues, and a heavy fire of grape shot kept up against the insurgents.

" Lords NELSON, ST. VINCENT, and DUNCAN, Messrs. ADDINGTON, PITT, SHERIDAN, GREY, twenty Peers and Commons, among the latter is Sir SIDNEY SMITH, tried by the Military Tribunals for having been concerned in the *insurrection* against France, and sentenced to be shot. Sentence was immediately carried into execution in Hyde Park.

"18 *Thermidor.*

"The Dock-yards ordered to send all the timber, hemp, anchors, masts, &c., to France. The relations of the British sailors at sea, sent to prison till the ships are brought into port, and placed at the disposal of the French. Detachments dispatched to the different Counties to disarm the people.

"The Island ordered to be divided into departments, and military divisions—the name of London to be changed for *Bonapart-opolis*—and the appellation of the Country to be altered from Great Britain, to that of *La France insulaire.*—Edinburgh to take the name of *Lucien-ville*—Dublin, that of *Massen-opolis.*

"BRITONS! can this be endured? shall we suffer ourselves thus to be parcelled off? I hear you one and all say, NO! NO! NO! To your Tents, O Israel!—for BRITONS NEVER WILL BE SLAVES."

CHAPTER X.

SEE yet another :
" The Consequences of Buonaparte's succeeding in
his designs against this Country :—Universal Pillage,
Men of all parties slaughtered, Women of all Ranks
violated, Children Murdered, Trade Ruined, the Labouring
Classes thrown out of Employment, Famine with all its
Horrors, Despotism Triumphant. The remaining Inhabi-
tants Carried away by Ship Loads to Foreign Lands.
Britons look before you."

There were sham playbills such as—" THEATRE ROYAL,
ENGLAND. In Rehearsal, and meant to be speedily at-
tempted, A FARCE in one Act, called THE INVASION OF
ENGLAND. Principal Buffo, Mr. BUONAPARTE ; being his
FIRST (and most likely his last) Appearance on the Stage,"
&c. " In Rehearsal, THEATRE ROYAL OF THE UNITED
KINGDOMS. Some dark, foggy night, about November next,
will be ATTEMPTED, by a Strolling Company of French
Vagrants, an Old Pantomimic Farce, called HARLEQUIN'S

INVASION, or the DISAPPOINTED BANDITTI," &c. " THEA-
TRE ROYAL, THE OCEAN. In preparation, A *magnificent*
NAVAL *and* MILITARY SPECTACLE, superior to anything
of the kind ever witnessed ; consisting of an immense
display of Flat-bottomed Boats Burning, Sinking, &c., to

THE FREEMAN'S OATH.

be called BUONAPARTE ; or The FREE-BOOTER running
away ; the Triumph of the British Flag," &c.

"THE FREEMAN'S OATH.

" OUR bosoms we'll bare for the glorious strife,
  And our oath is recorded on high ;
  To prevail in the cause that is dearer than life,
  Or, crush'd in its ruins, to die.
  Then rise, fellow freemen, and stretch the right hand,
  And swear to prevail in your dear native land.

'Tis the home we hold sacred is laid to our trust,
God bless the green isle of the brave,
Should a conqueror tread on our forefathers' dust,
It would rouse the old dead from their grave.
Then rise, fellow freemen, and stretch the right hand,
And swear to prevail in your dear native land.

In a Briton's sweet home shall the spoiler abide,
Prophaning its loves and its charms?
Shall a Frenchman insult the lov'd fair at our side?
To arms! Oh, my country, to arms!
Then rise, fellow freemen, and stretch the right hand,
And swear to prevail in your dear native land.

Shall Tyrants enslave us, my Countrymen? No!
Their heads to the sword shall be given:
Let a deathbed repentance be taught the proud foe,
And his blood be an offering to Heaven.
Then rise, fellow freemen, and stretch the right hand,
And swear to prevail in your dear native land."

Turning from the sublimity of this patriotic effusion, we shall find a change in "JOHN BULL and BONAPARTE ! ! to the tune of the BLUE BELLS OF SCOTLAND :"

"WHEN and O when does this little Boney come?
Perhaps he'll come in August! perhaps he'll stay at home;
But it's O in my heart, how I'll hide him should he come.

Where and O where does this little Boney dwell?
His birth place is in Corsica—but France he likes so well,
That it's O the poor French, how they crouch beneath his spell.

What cloathes and what cloathes does this little Boney wear?
He wears a large cock'd hat for to make the people stare;
But it's O my oak stick! I'd advise him to take care!

What shall be done, should this little Boney die?
Nine cats shall squall his dirge, in sweet melodious cry,
And it's O in my heart, if a tear shall dim my eye!

Yet still he boldly brags, with consequence full cramm'd
On England's happy island, his legions he will land;
But it's O in my heart, if he does may I be d——d."

I will give but one more example, not that the stock is exhausted by some hundreds, but that I fear to be wearisome, and this one shows that if occasionally the matter of invasion was treated with a light heart, there were many, nay, the large majority, who looked upon its possibility *au grand serieux.*

"THE EVE OF INVASION.

" THE hour of battle now draws nigh,
We swear to conquer, or to die ;
Haste quick away, thou slow pac'd Night,
To-morrow's dawn begins the fight.

CHORUS.
Brothers, draw th' avenging sword,
Death or Freedom be the word.

A SOLDIER.
Did ye not leave, when forc'd to part,
Some treasure precious to the heart ?
And feel ye not your bosoms swell,
Whene'er ye think of that farewell ?
Chorus.

ANOTHER SOLDIER.
My Lucy said, no longer stay,
Thy country calls thee hence away,
Adieu ! may angels round thee hover,
But no slave shall be my lover.
Chorus.

ANOTHER.
My Grandsire cried, I cannot go,
But thou, my Son, shall meet the foe ;
I need not say, dear Boy, be brave,
No Briton sure would live a slave.
Chorus.

ANOTHER.
My Wife, whose glowing looks exprest,
What patriot ardour warm'd her breast,
Said, ' In the Battle think of me ;
These helpless Babes, they shall be free.'
Chorus.

ALL.

Shades of Heroes gone, inspire us,
Children, Wives, and Country fire us.
Freedom loves this hallow'd ground—
Hark ! Freedom bids the trumpet sound.

CHORUS.

Brothers, draw th' avenging sword,
Death or Freedom be the word."

If the foregoing examples of the Patriotic Handbills of
1803 are not choice specimens of refined literature, they
are at least fairly representative. I have omitted all the
vilification of Napoleon, which permeates all the series in
a greater or less degree, because I have already given it in
another work. It was gravely stated that his great grandfather was the keeper of a wine-shop, who, being convicted
of robbery and murder, was condemned to the galleys,
where he died in 1724. His wife, Napoleon's great grandmother, was said to have died in the House of Correction
at Genoa. " His grandfather was a butcher of Ajaccio,
and his grandmother daughter of a journeyman tanner at
Bastia. His father was a low pettyfogging lawyer, who
served and betrayed his country by turns, during the Civil
Wars. After France conquered Corsica, he was a spy
to the French Government, and his mother their trull."
General Marbœuf was said to have been Napoleon's father.
He was accused of seducing his sisters, and his brothers
were supposed to be a very bad lot. He massacred the
people at Alexandria and Jaffa, besides poisoning his own
sick soldiers there. There was nothing bad enough for
the *Corsican Ogre ;* they even found that he was the real,
original, and veritable Apocalyptic BEAST, whose number
is 666. It is but fair to say that the majority of these
accusations came originally from French sources, but they
were eagerly adopted here; and, although they might be,
and probably were, taken at their proper valuation by the

educated classes, there is no doubt but the lower classes
regarded him as a ruffianly murderer. " Boney will come
to you," was quite enough to quiet and overawe any re-
fractory youngster, who, however, must have had some
consolation, and satisfaction, in crunching, in sweetstuff,
Bonaparte's Ribs.   It was all very well to sing—

> " Come, BONAPARTE, if you dare ;
> John Bull invites you ; bring your Host,
> Your slaves with Free men to compare ;
> Your Frogs shall croak along the Coast.
>
> When slain, thou vilest of thy Tribe,
> Wrapped in a sack your Bones shall be,
> That the Elements may ne'er imbibe
> The venom of a Toad like thee "—

but there was the flat-bottomed Flotilla, on the opposite
shore, which we were unable to destroy, or even to appreci-
ably damage, and the " Army of England," inactive certainly, was still there, and a standing menace.   The
Volunteers were fêted, and praised to the top of their bent.
An old air of Henry Purcell's (1695), which accompanied
some words interpolated in Beaumont and Fletcher's play
of "Bonduca" or "Boadicæa," became extremely popular ; and
the chorus, " Britons, strike home," was married to several
sets of words, and duly shouted by loyal Volunteers.   The
Pictorial Satirist delineates the Volunteer as performing
fabulous deeds of daring.   Gillray gives us his idea of the
fate of " Buonaparte forty-eight hours after Landing !"
where a burly rustic Volunteer holds the bleeding head of
Napoleon upon a pitchfork, to the delight of his comrades,
and he thus apostrophises the head : " Ha, my little Boney!
what do'st think of Johnny Bull, now?   Plunder Old
England ! hay ? make French slaves of us all ! hay ? ravish
all our Wives and Daughters ! hay ?   O Lord, help that
silly Head !   To think that Johnny Bull would ever suffer
those lanthorn Jaws to become King of Old England Roast
Beef and Plum Pudding !"

Ansell, too, treats Bonaparte's probable fate, should he
land, in a somewhat similar manner. His etching is called
"After the Invasion. The Levée en Masse, or, Britons, strike
home." The French have landed, but have been thoroughly
routed, of course, by a mere handful of English, who drive
them into the sea. Our women plunder the French dead,
but are disgusted with their meagre booty—garlic, onions,
and pill-boxes. A rural Volunteer is, of course, the hero of
the day, and raises Napoleon's head aloft on a pitchfork,
whilst he thus addresses two of his comrades. "Here he
is exalted, my Lads, 24 Hours after Landing." One of his
comrades says, "Why, Harkee, d'ye zee, I never liked
soldiering afore, but, somehow or other, when I thought of
our Sal, the bearns, the poor Cows, and the Geese, why I
could have killed the whole Army, my own self." The other
rustic remarks, "Dang my Buttons if that beant the head
of that Rogue Boncy. I told our Squire this morning,
'What! do you think,' says I, 'the lads of our Village can't
cut up a Regiment of them French Mounseers? and as soon
as the lasses had given us a kiss for good luck, I could
have sworn we should do it, and so we have."

Well! it is hard to look at these things in cold blood, at
a great distance of time, and without a shadow of a shade
of the fear of invasion before our eyes, so we ought to be
mercifully critical of the bombast of our forefathers. It
certainly has done us no harm, and if it kept up and nour-
ished the flame of patriotism within their breasts, we are
the gainers thereby, as there is no doubt but that the bold
front shown by the English people, and the unwearying
vigilance of our fleet, saved England from an attempted, if
not successful, invasion. Upwards of 400,000 men voluntarily rising up in arms to defend their country, must have
astonished not only Bonaparte, but all Europe; and by being
spontaneous, it prevented any forced measures, such as a
levée en masse. The Prince of Wales, in vain, applied for
active service; but, it is needless to say, it was refused, not

to the colonel of the regiment, but to the heir to the throne.
The refusal was tempered by the intimation that, should
the enemy effect a landing, the Prince should have an
opportunity of showing his courage, a quality which has
always been conspicuous in our Royal Family.

But before we leave the subject of the threatened Invasion, it would be as well to read some jottings respecting
it, which have no regular sequence, and yet should on no
account be missed, as they give us, most vividly, the state
of the public mind thereon.

Napoleon was at Boulogne, at the latter end of June,
making a tour of the ports likely to be attacked by the
British, and, as an example of how well his movements
were known, see the following cutting from the *Times* of 4th
of July : " The Chief Consul reached Calais at five o'clock
on Friday afternoon (the 1st of July). His entry, as might
be expected, was in a grand style of parade : he rode on a
small iron grey horse of great beauty. He was preceded
by about three hundred Infantry, and about thirty Mamelukes formed a kind of semicircle about him. . . . In a
short time after his arrival he dined at *Quillac & Co's.* (late
Dessin's) hotel. The time he allowed himself at dinner
was shorter than usual ; he did not exceed ten minutes or
a quarter of an hour. Immediately after dinner he went,
attended by M. Francy, Commissary of Marine, Mengaud,
Commissary of Police, and other municipal officers, through
the Calais gates, to visit the different batteries erected there.
As soon as he and his attendants had passed through the
gates, he ordered them to be shut, to prevent their being
incommoded by the populace. The execution of this
order very much damped the ardour of the Corsican's
admirers, who remained entirely silent, although the moment
before, the whole place resounded with *Vive Buonaparte!*
The same evening the General went on board the *Josephine*
packet, Captain Lambert, and, after examining everything
there minutely, he took a short trip upon the water in a

boat as far as the pier-head to the Battery at the entrance
of the harbour, where he himself fired one of the guns ;
afterwards, he visited all the different Forts, and at night
slept at Quillac's Hotel."

They had a rough-and-ready method, in those days, of
recruiting for the services, apprehending all vagrants, and
men who could not give a satisfactory account of themselves, and giving them the option of serving His Majesty
or going to prison.   There is a curious instance of this in
the following police report, containing as it does an amusing anecdote of "diamond cut diamond." *Times*, the
7th July, 1803 : "PUBLIC OFFICE, BOW STREET.   Yesterday upwards of forty persons were taken into custody,
under authority of privy search warrants, at two houses
of ill fame ; the one in Tottenham Court Road, and
the other near Leicester Square.   They were brought
before N. Bond, Esq., and Sir W. Parsons, for examination ; when several of them, not being able to give a
satisfactory account of themselves, and being able-bodied
men, were sent on board a tender lying off the Tower.
Two very notorious fellows among them were arrested
in the office for pretended debts, as it appeared, for
the purpose of preventing their being sent to sea, the
writs having been just taken out, at the suit of persons
as notorious as themselves.   The magistrates, however,
could not prevent the execution of the civil process, as
there was no criminal charge against them, which would
justify their commitment."   Take also a short paragraph
in the next day's *Times :* "Several young men, brought
before the Lord Mayor yesterday, charged with petty
offences, were sent on board the tender."

But, perhaps, this was the best use to put them to, as idle
hands were not wanted at such a juncture.   Men came
forward in crowds as volunteers.   Lloyd's, and the City
generally, subscribed most liberally to the Patriotic Fund, and
even in minor things, such as transport, the large carriers

came forward well—as, for instance, the well-known firm of Pickford and Co. offered for the service of the Government, four hundred horses, fifty waggons, and twenty-eight boats.[1] County meetings were held all over England to organize defence, and to find means of transport for cannon, men, and ammunition in case of invasion. The people came forward nobly ; as the *Times* remarked in a leader (6th of August, 1803): " ELEVEN WEEKS are barely passed since the Declaration of War, and we defy any man living, to mention a period when *half so much* was ever effected, in the same space of time, for the defence of the country. 1st. A naval force such as Great Britain never had before, has been completely equipped, manned, and in readiness to meet the enemy. 2nd. The regular military force of the kingdom has been put on the most respectable footing. 3rd. The militia has been called forth, and *encamped* with the regular forces. 4th. The supplementary militia has also been embodied, and even encamped. 5th. An army of reserve of 50,000 men has been already added to this force, and is now in great forwardness. 6th. A measure has been adopted for calling out and arming the whole mass of the people, in case of emergency ; and we are confident that our information is correct, when we say, that at *this moment* there are nearly 300,000 men enrolled in different Volunteer, Yeomanry, and Cavalry Corps, of whom at least a *third* may be considered as already disciplined, and accoutred."

But, naturally, and sensibly, the feeling obtained of what might occur in case the French did actually land, and, among other matters, the safety of the King and the Royal Family was not forgotten. It was settled that the King should not go far, at least at first, from London, and both Chelmsford, and Dartford, as emergency might direct, were settled on as places of refuge for His Majesty: the

---

[1] In two advertisements only of voluntary offers of horses and carriages, in August, we find they amount to 2,370 horses and 510 carriages.

Queen, the Royal Family, and the treasure were to go to Worcester the faithful, *Civitas in bello, et in pace fidelis.* The artillery and stores at Woolwich were to be sent into the Midland districts by means of the Grand Junction Canal. Beacons were to be affixed to some of the seaside churches, such as Lowestoft and Woodbridge, and these were of very simple construction—only a tar barrel!

But, by and by, a better, and more organized, system of communication by beacon was adopted, and the beacons themselves were more calculated to effect their object. They were to be made of a large stack, or pile, of furze, or faggots, with some cord-wood—in all, at least, eight waggon loads, with three or four tar barrels, sufficient to yield a light unmistakable at a distance of two or three miles. These were to be used by night; by day, a large quantity of straw was to be wetted, in order to produce a smoke.

When the orders for these first came out, invasion was only expected on the Kent and Sussex coasts, and the beacon stations were proportionately few ; afterwards, they became general throughout the country. The first lot (17th of November) were

1. Shorncliffe.	5. Egerton.
1. Canterbury.	5. Tenderden.
2. Barham.	6. Coxheath.
2. Shollenden.	6. Highgate near Hawkehurst.
2. Lynne Heights.	7. Boxley Hill.
3. Isle of Thanet.	7. Goodhurst.
3. Postling Down.	8. Chatham Lines.
4. Charlmagna.	8. Wrotham Hill.

N.B. Stations marked with the same figures, communicate directly with each other.

Of course, naturally, there was the Spy craze, and it sometimes led to mistakes, as the following will show: *Times*, the 29th of August, " A respectable person in town a short time ago, went on a party of pleasure to the Isle of Wight, and, being anxious to see all the beauties of the place, he rose early one day to indulge himself with a long morning's walk. In his way he took a great pleasure in viewing with his glass, the vessels at sea. In the midst of his observations he was interrupted by an officer, who, after a few questions, took him into custody upon suspicion of being a spy. After a proper investigation of his character, he was liberated."

In more than one case, however, the charge of *espionage* seems to have rested on a far more solid basis; but, of course, the "Intelligence Department" of every nation will have its agents, in the enemy's camp, if possible. Two persons, one named Nield, the other Garrick (nephew to the famous actor), were actually arrested as being Bonaparte! I do not know how Mr. Nield fared, but Mr. Garrick was enabled to prosecute his journey under the protection of the following certificate from the Mayor of Haverfordwest :

"This is to certify whom it may concern, that the bearer, Mr. George Garrick, is known to me ; who is on a tour through the country, and intends returning to England, by the way of Tenby.

"RICHARD LLOYD, *Mayor.*"

We cannot wonder at the rumour of spies being in their midst, when we think of the number of French prisoners of war there were in our keeping, one prison alone (Mill Prison, Plymouth) having 2,500.

Many were out on parole, which I regret to say all did not respect, many broke prison and got away; in fact, they did not know where to put them, nor what to do with them, so that it was once seriously proposed that, in an hour of danger, should such ever arrive, they should be shut up in the numerous spent mines throughout England. When on parole, the following were the regulations—they were allowed to walk on the turnpike road within the distance of one mile from the extremity of the town in which they resided, but they must not go into any field or cross road, nor be absent from their lodgings after five o'clock in the afternoon, during the months of November, December, and January ; after seven o'clock in the months of February, March, April, August, September, and October ; or, after eight o'clock in the months of May, June, and July ; nor quit their lodgings in the morning until the bell rang at six o'clock.

If they did not keep to these regulations, they were liable to be taken up and sent to prison, a reward of one guinea being offered for their recapture. Should they not behave peaceably, they would also have to return to durance.

There were also very many refugees here who were not prisoners of war, and, in order to keep them under super-vision, a Royal Proclamation was issued on the 12th of October, citing an Act passed the last session of Parliament, respecting the Registration of Aliens, and proclaiming that all aliens must, within eighteen days from date, register themselves and their place of abode—if in London, before the Lord Mayor, or some magistrate at one of the police offices ; if in any other part of Great Britain, before some neighbouring magistrate.

However, enemies nearer home were plaguing John Bull. " Mannikin Traitors " verily, but still annoying. Then, as now, England's difficulty was Ireland's opportunity ; and o course, the chance was too tempting to be resisted. The Union (curious phrase!) was but in the third year of its ex-istence, and Ireland was once more in open rebellion. Chief of the spurious patriots was one Robert Emmett, whose picture in green and gold uniform coat, white tights and Hessian boots, waving an immense sword, appears periodi-cally, in some shop windows, whenever Irish sedition is peculiarly rampant, only to disappear when the inevitable petty rogue, the approver, has done his work, and the wind-bag plot is pricked.

Emmett was the son of one of the State physicians in Dublin, and brother to that Thomas Eddis Emmett, who was prominent in the rebellion of 1798. Robert had so compromised himself, by his speech and behaviour, that he deemed it wise to live abroad during the suspension of the Habeas Corpus Act, but he returned when his father died, having become possessed of about £2,000, which he must needs spend, in " regenerating " Ireland.

Silly boy ! (he was only twenty-four) with such a sum, and about one hundred followers, he thought it could be done. His crazy brain imagined his down-trodden compatriots hastening to his side, to fight for the deliverance of their beloved country from the yoke of the hated Saxon despot. There were meetings *sub rosâ*—assemblages on the quiet—as there always will be in Ireland when the pot is seething ; and at last the curtain was to be drawn up, for the playing of this farce, on the 23rd of July, when towards evening, large bodies of men began to assemble in some of the streets of Dublin—but vaguely, and without leaders.

At last a small cannon was fired, and a single rocket went upwards to the sky ; and the deliverer, Emmett, sallied out, waving that big sword. A shot from a blunder-buss killed Colonel Browne ; and the Lord Chief Justice of Ireland, Lord Kilwarden, and his nephew, Rev. Richard Wolfe, were dragged from their carriage, and brutally murdered.

A little more bluster, and then, some three hours after its rising, this scum was put down by about one hundred and twenty soldiers. The ringleaders were caught and executed. Emmett, tried on the 19th of September, was hanged next day.

To show how slowly news travelled in those days, the *Times* has no notice of this riot on the 23rd till the 28th of July, and then not a full account. The Government, however, seems to have estimated the situation quite at its full gravity, for there was a message from the King to his faithful Parliament on the subject ; the Habeas Corpus

Act was once more suspended, and martial law proclaimed.

On the 19th of October the religious panacea of a general fast was tried, and "was observed with the utmost decorum" in the Metropolis. The Volunteers, especially, won the encomia of the *Times* for their goodness in going to church, and the *Annual Register* also warms up into unusual fervour on the occasion : " Such a number of corps attended this day, that it is impossible to enumerate them. Every principal church was crowded with the ardent patriots who fill the voluntary associations ; and there can be no doubt that, in the present temper of the people of this country, not only every other great city and town, but even the smallest village or hamlet throughout the island, evinced a proportionate degree of fervour and animation in the holy cause. The corps who had not before taken the oath of allegiance, did so this day, either on their drill grounds, or in their respective churches."

Of the latter part of the year, other than the Invasion Scare, there is little to say. Among the Acts passed this year, however, was one of hopeful import, as showing a glimmer of a better time to come in the era of religious toleration. It was to relieve the Roman Catholics of some pains and disabilities to which they were subject, on subscribing the declaration and oath contained in the Act 31 George III.

Three per Cent. Consols opened this year at 69 ; dropped in July to 50, and left off the 31st of December at 55.

Bread stuffs were cheaper, the average price of wheat being 77s. per quarter, and the quartern loaf, 9d.

CHAPTER XI.

1804.

THE year 1804 opens with Britain still in arms, watching that flotilla which dare not put out, and cannot be destroyed ; but somehow, whether familiarity had bred contempt, or whether it had come to be looked upon as a " bugaboo "—terrible to the sight, but not so very bad when you knew it—the patriotic handbills first cooled down, and then disappeared, and the satirical artist imparted a lighter tone to his pictures. Take one of Gillray's (February 10, 1804) : " The KING of BROBDING-NAG and GULLIVER " (Plate 2). Scene — " Gulliver manœuvring with his little boat in the cistern," *vide Swift's Gulliver:* " I often used to row for my own diversion, as well as that of the Queen and her ladies, who thought themselves well entertained with my skill and agility. Sometimes I would put up my sail and show my art by steering starboard and larboard. However, my attempts produced nothing else besides a loud laughter, which all the respect due to His Majesty from those about him, could not make them contain. This made me reflect how vain an attempt it is for a man to endeavour to do himself honour among those who are out of all degree of equality or comparison with him!!!" The King and Queen look on with amusement at the pigmy's vessel, for the better sailing of which, the young princes are blowing; and creating quite a gale.

Take another by West (March, 1804), which shows equally, that terror is turning to derision. It is called "A French Alarmist, or, John Bull looking out for the Grand Flotilla!" John Bull is guarding his coast, sword on thigh, and attended by his faithful dog. Through his telescope he scans the horizon, and is thus addressed by a Frenchman who is behind him. "Ah, ah! Monsieur Bull, dere you see our Grande Flotilla, de grande gon boats, ma foi—dere you see 'em sailing for de grand attack on your nation—dere you see de Bombs and de Cannons—dere you see de Grande Consul himself at de head of his Legions? Dere you see—" But John Bull, mindful of the old saying, anent the Spanish Armada, replies, "Monsieur, all this I cannot see, because 'tis not in sight."

Money was scarce in this year; and in spite of the all-but million given the King not so long since to pay his debts, we find (*Morning Herald*, April 26, 1804), "The Civil List is now paying up to the Lady-day quarter, 1803."

So scarce was money—*i.e.*, bullion—that a means had to be found to supplement the currency; and it so happened that a large quantity of Spanish dollars were opportunely taken in prizes. In 1803 the idea of utilizing these as current English coins was first mooted, and some were stamped with the King's head, the size of the ordinary goldsmith's mark; but in 1804 a much larger issue of them was made, and they were stamped with a profile likeness of the King, in an octagon of about a quarter of an inch square. They were made to pass for five shillings each, which was about threepence-halfpenny over their value as bullion; and this extra, and fictitious, value was imposed upon them in order that they should not be melted down. They were also to be taken back for a time at that price, and on the 12th of January, 1804, every banking house received £1,000 worth of them from the Bank of England, against the Bank's paper. But, as currency, they did not last long, the Bank refusing, as early as April the same year, to receive them back again, on "various frivolous and ill-founded pretensions." For some reason, probably forgery, they were recalled, and on the 22nd of May there was a notice in the *Gazette* to the effect that a new issue of them would be made, which would be stamped by the famous firm of Boulton, Soho Mint, at Birmingham, whose series of tradesmen's tokens of George the Third's reign is familiar to every numismatist. They varied from those stamped at the Tower, by having on the obverse, "Georgius III., Dei Gratiâ Rex," and on the reverse, the figure of Britannia, with the words—" Five shillings dollar, Bank of England, 1804," but even these were soon forged.

On the 14th of February the King was taken ill so seriously that bulletins had to be issued. His malady was stated to be "an *Hydrops Pectoris*, or a water in the chest of the body ;" to counteract which they scarified his legs.[1] The probability is, that this treatment was not the proper one, for I observe that the next day's bulletin is signed by four, instead of two doctors, who, however, on the succeeding day, certify that their patient *could walk*. On the 26th, which was Sunday, prayers were offered up in all churches and chapels of the Metropolis, and a week later throughout England, for His Majesty's recovery. On the 27th of February, there was a long debate in Parliament on the subject of His Majesty's health ; some members holding that, looking at the gravity of our relations with France, the people were not kept sufficiently informed as to the King's illness. Addington, then Prime Minister, contended that more information than was made public would be

[1] *Morning Herald*, February 18, 1804.

injudicious, and prejudicial to the public good ; and after a long discussion, in which Pitt, Fox, Windham, and Grenville took part, the subject dropped.   Towards the end of March, the King became quite convalescent, a fact which is thus quaintly announced in the *Morning Herald* of the 28th of March : " We have the sincerest pleasure in stating that a certain personage is now perfectly restored to all his domestic comforts.   He saw the Queen for the first time on Saturday (March 24th) afternoon.   The interview, as may well be conceived, was peculiarly affecting."

Yet another Fast Day; this time on the 25th of May, and its cause—" for humbling ourselves before Almighty God, in order to obtain pardon of our sins, and in the most solemn manner to send up our prayers and supplications to the Divine Majesty, for averting those heavy judgments which our manifold provocations have most justly deserved; and for imploring His blessing and assistance on our arms, for the restoration of peace and prosperity to these dominions."   A contemporary account tells how it was kept : " Yesterday, being the day appointed for the observance of a solemn Fast, was duly observed in the Metropolis, at least as far as outward show and decorum can go.   Every shop was shut ; for those who on similar occasions, kept their windows open, have probably learnt that, to offend against public example and decency, is not the way to ensure either favour or credit.   Most of the Volunteer Corps attended at their several churches, where sermons suitable to the day were preached."

The Addington Ministry was on its last legs, and died on or about the 11th of May ; and a very strong government was formed by Pitt, which included the Duke of Portland, Lord Eldon, Lord Melville, the Earl of Chatham, Dundas, Canning, Huskisson, and Spencer Perceval.

They were not very long in power before they stretched forth their long arm after the notorious William Cobbett for the publication of certain libels with intent to traduce His Majesty's Government in Ireland, and the persons employed in the administration thereof, particularly Lord Hardwicke, Lord Redesdale, Mr. Marsden, and the Hon. Charles Osborne, contained in certain letters signed Juverna. He was tried on the 24th of May, and found guilty. On the 26th he had another action brought against him for slandering Mr. Plunket, in his official capacity as Solicitor-General for Ireland, and was cast in a verdict for £500.

On the 27th of June the Abolition of the Slave Trade was read a third time in the Commons, and some curious facts came out in debate. One member called attention to the fact that there were 7,000 French prisoners on the Island of Barbadoes, besides a great number in prison-ships, and feared they would foment discontent among the negroes, who did not distinguish between the abolition of the slave trade and immediate emancipation. He also pointed out that the Moravian missionaries on the island were teaching, most forcibly, the fact that all men were alike God's creatures, and that the last should be first and the first last.

An honourable member immediately replied in vindication of the missionaries, and said that no fewer than 10,000 negroes had been converted in the Island of Antigua, *and that their tempers and dispositions had been, thereby, rendered so much better, that they were entitled to an increased value of £10.*

Next day the Bill was taken up to the Lords and read for the first time, during which debate the Duke of Clarence said : " Since a very early period of his life, when he was in another line of profession—which he knew not why he had no longer employment in—he had ocular demonstration of the state of slavery, as it was called, in the West Indies, and all that he had seen convinced him that it not only was not deserving of the imputations that

had been cast upon it, but that the abolition of it would
be productive of extreme danger and mischief."

Before the second reading he also presented two petitions
against it, and when the second reading did come on, on
the 3rd of July, Lord Hawkesbury moved that such reading
should be on that day three months, and this motion was
carried without a division, so that the Bill was lost for that
year.

The Invasion Scare, although dying out, in this year was
far from dead ; but, though people did not talk so much
about it, the Government was vigilant and watchful, as was
shown by many little matters—notably the signals.   In the
eastern district of England were 32,000 troops ready to
move at a moment's notice ; whilst the hoisting of a red
flag at any of the following stations would ensure the
lighting of all the beacons, wherever established :

Colchester.	Mum's Hedge
Brightlingsea.	White Notley.
Earls Colne.	Ongar Park.
Gosfield.	Messing.
Sewers End.	Rettenden.
Littlebury.	Danbury.
Thaxted.	Langdon Hill.
Hatfield Broad Oak.	Corne Green.

Transport seems to have been the weakest spot in the
military organizations, and a Committee sat both at the
Mansion House, and Thatched House Tavern, to stimulate
the patriotic ardour of owners of horses and carriages, in
order that they might offer them for the use of the Government.   A large number of job-masters, too, offered to lend
their horses, provided their customers would send their
coachmen and two days' forage with them.

There was in this year a very close election for Middlesex,
between Sir Francis Burdett and Mr. Mainwaring.   The
election lasted, as usual, a fortnight, and Sir Francis claimed
a majority of one.   This so elated his supporters that they

formed a triumphal procession from Brentford, the county
town, to Piccadilly, composed as under :

A Banner, on orange ground, inscribed
VICTORY.
Horsemen, two and two.
Flags borne by Horsemen.
Persons on foot in files of six, singing " Rule, Britannia."
Handbell Ringers.
Body of foot, as before.
Car with Band of Music.
Large Body of Horsemen.
SIR FRANCIS BURDETT
In his Chariot, accompanied by his Brother, and another
Gentleman covered with Laurels and drawn by
the Populace, with an allegorical painting of
Liberty *and* Independence,
and surrounded with lighted flambeaux.
A second Car, with a Musical Band.
A Body of Horsemen.
Gentlemen's and other Carriages in a long Cavalcade,
which closed the Procession.

Was it not a pity, after all this excitement, that on a
scrutiny, the famous majority of one was found to be
fallacious, and that Mr. Mainwaring had *a majority of
five ?* a fact of which he duly availed himself, sitting for
Middlesex at the next meeting of Parliament.

The close of the year is not particularly remarkable for
any events other than the arrival in England, on the 1st
of November, of the brother of Louis XVIII. (afterwards
Charles X.), and the reconciliation which took place between
the Prince of Wales, and his royal father, on the 12th of
November, which was made the subject of a scathing
satirical print by Gillray (November 20th). It is called
" THE RECONCILIATION." " And he arose and came to
his Father, and his Father saw him, and had compassion,
and ran, and fell on his Neck and kissed him." The old
King is in full Court costume, with brocaded Coat and
Ribbon of the Garter, and presents a striking contrast to

the tattered prodigal, whose rags show him to be in pitiable case, and who is faintly murmuring, "*Against Heaven and before thee.*" The Queen, with open arms, stands on the doorstep to welcome the lost one, whilst Pitt and Lord Moira, as confidential advisers, respectively of the King and the Prince, look on with a curious and puzzled air.

Consols were, January 56⅞; December 58⅝; having fallen as low as 54½ in February. The quartern loaf began the year at 9¼d. and left off at 1s. 4¼d. Average price of wheat 74s.

CHAPTER XII.

1805.

Doings of Napoleon—His letter to George III.—Lord Mulgrave's reply—War declared against Spain—General Fast—Men voted for Army and Navy—The Salt Duty—Withdrawal of " The Army of England "—Battle of Trafalgar and death of Nelson—General Thanksgiving.

THE year 1805 was uneventful for many reasons, the chief of which was that Bonaparte was principally engaged in consolidating his power after his Coronation. He was elected Emperor on the 20th of May, 1804, but was not crowned until December of the same year. In March, 1805, he was invited by the Italian Republic to be their monarch, and, in April, he and Josephine left Paris for Milan, and in May he crowned himself King of Italy.

He was determined, if only nominally, to hold out the olive branch of peace to England, and on the 2nd of January, 1805, he addressed the following letter to George the Third.

" SIR AND BROTHER,—Called to the throne of France by Providence, and by the suffrages of the senate, the people, and the army, my first sentiment is a wish for peace. France and England abuse their prosperity. They may contend for

ages ; but do their governments well fulfil the most sacred
of their duties, and will not so much blood, shed uselessly,
and without a view to any end, condemn them in their own
consciences ?   I consider it as no disgrace to make the
first step.   I have, I hope, sufficiently proved to the world
that I fear none of the chances of war ; it, besides, presents
nothing that I need to fear : peace is the wish of my heart,
but war has never been inconsistent with my glory.   I
conjure your Majesty not to deny yourself the happiness
of giving peace to the world, nor to leave that sweet satisfaction to your children ; for certainly there never was a
more fortunate opportunity, nor a moment more favourable,
to silence all the passions and listen only to the sentiments
of humanity and reason.   This moment once lost, what end
can be assigned to a war which all my efforts will not be
able to terminate ?   Your Majesty has gained more within
the last ten years both in territory and riches than the
whole extent of Europe.   Your nation is at the highest
point of prosperity : to what can it hope from war ?   To
form a coalition with some Powers of the Continent !   The
Continent will remain tranquil—a coalition can only increase the preponderance and continental greatness of
France.   To renew intestine troubles ?   The times are no
longer the same.   To destroy our finances ?   Finances
founded on flourishing agriculture can never be destroyed.
To take from France her colonies ?   The Colonies are to
France only a secondary object ; and does not your
Majesty already possess more than you know how to
preserve ?   If your Majesty would but reflect, you must
perceive that the war is without an object, without any
presumable result to yourself.   Alas ! what a melancholy
prospect to cause two nations to fight merely for the sake
of fighting.   The world is sufficiently large for our two
nations to live in it, and reason is sufficiently powerful to
discover means of reconciling everything, when the wish
for reconciliation exists on both sides.   I have, however,

fulfilled a sacred duty, and one which is precious to my heart. I trust your Majesty will believe in the sincerity of my sentiments, and my wish to give you every proof of it.   " NAPOLEON."

When the King opened Parliament on the 15th of January, 1805, he referred to this letter thus : " I have recently received a communication from the French Government, containing professions of a pacific disposition. I have, in consequence, expressed my earnest desire to embrace the first opportunity of restoring the blessings of peace on such grounds as may be consistent with the permanent safety and interests of my dominions ; but I am confident you will agree with me that those objects are closely connected with the general security of Europe."

The reply of Lord Mulgrave (who had succeeded Lord Harrowby as Secretary of State for Foreign Affairs) was both courteous and politic. It was dated the 14th of January, and was addressed to M. Talleyrand.

" His Britannic Majesty has received the letter which has been addressed to him by the head of the French Government, dated the 2nd of the present month. There is no object which His Majesty has more at heart, than to avail himself of the first opportunity to procure again for his subjects the advantages of a peace, founded on bases which may not be incompatible with the permanent security and essential interests of his dominions. His Majesty is persuaded that this end can only be attained by arrangements which may, at the same time, provide for the future safety and tranquillity of Europe, and prevent the recurrence of the dangers and calamities in which it is involved. Conformably to this sentiment, His Majesty feels it is impossible for him to answer more particularly to the overture that has been made him, till he has had time to communicate with the Powers on the Continent, with whom he is engaged with confidential connexions and relations, and particularly the Emperor of Russia, who has given the strongest proofs of the wisdom and elevation of the sentiments with which he is animated, and the lively interest which he takes in the safety and independence of the Continent.   " MULGRAVE."

Very shortly after this, England declared war against Spain, and the Declaration was laid before Parliament on January 24th. A long discussion ensued thereon ; but the Government had a majority on their side of 313 against 106.

Probably, His Majesty's Government had some inkling of what was coming, for on the 2nd of January was issued a proclamation for another general Fast, which was to take place on the 20th of February, "for the success of His Majesty's arms." History records that the Volunteers went dutifully to church ; and also that "a very elegant and fashionable display of equestrians and charioteers graced the public ride about three o'clock. The Countesses of Cholmondeley and Harcourt were noticed for the first time this season, each of whom sported a very elegant landau. Mr. Buxton sported his four bays in his new phaeton, in a great style, and Mr. Chartres his fine set of blacks." Thus showing that different people have different views of National Fasting and Chastening.

That the arm of the flesh was also relied on, is shown by the fact that Parliament in January voted His Majesty 120,000 men, including marines, for his Navy ; and in February 312,048 men for his Army, with suitable sums for their maintenance and efficiency.

Of course this could not be done without extra taxation, and the Budget of the 18th of February proposed—an extra tax of 1d., 2d., and 3d. respectively on single, double, and treble letters (as they were called) passing through the post ; extra tax of 6d. per bushel on salt, extra taxes on horses, and on legacies. All these were taken without much demur, with one exception, and that was the Salt Duty

Bill. Fierce were the squabbles over this tax, and much good eloquence was expended, both in its behalf and against it, and it had to be materially altered before it was passed; one of the chief arguments against it being that it would injuriously affect the fisheries, as large quantities were used in curing. But a heavy tax on salt would also hamper bacon and ham curing, &c., and Mrs. Bull had an objection to see Pitt as

BILLY IN THE SALT-BOX.[1]

The Flotilla could not sail, and "the Army of England" was inactive, when circumstances arose that rendered the withdrawal of the latter imperative: consequently the Flotilla was practically useless, for it had no troops to transport. Austria had gone to war with France without

[1] Pitt says, as he looks from the Salt-box, "How do you do, cookey?" She exclaims, "Curse the fellow, how he has frightened me. I think in my heart he is getting in everywhere! Who the deuce would have thought of finding him in the Salt-box !!!"

the formality of a Declaration, and the forces of the Allies were computed at 250,000. The French troops were reckoned at 275,000 men, but "the Army of England" comprised 180,000 of these, and they must needs be diverted to the point of danger.

We can imagine the great wave of relief that spread over the length and breadth of this land at this good news. The papers were, of course, most jubilant, and the whole nation must have felt relieved of a great strain. Even the Volunteers must have got somewhat sick of airing and parading their patriotism, with the foe within tangible proximity, and must have greatly preferred its absence.

The *Times* is especially bitter on the subject :

" 1. The *scene* that now opens upon the soldiers of France, by being obliged to leave the coast, and march eastwards, is sadly different from that *Land of Promise* which, for two years, has been held out to them, in all sorts of gay delusions. After all the efforts of the *Imperial Boat Builder*, instead of sailing over the Channel, they have to cross the *Rhine*. The bleak *forests* of Suabia will make but a sorry exchange for the promised spoils of our *Docks* and *Warehouses*. They will not find any equivalent for the *plunder of the Bank*, in another bloody passage through 'the *Valley of Hell ;*' but they seem to have forgotten the magnificent promise of the *Milliard*." [1]

The *Times* (September 13th) quoting from a French paper, shows that they endeavoured to put a totally different construction on the withdrawal of their troops, or rather to make light of it. "Whilst the German papers, with much noise, make more troops march than all the Powers together possess, France, which needs not to augment her forces, in order to display them in an imposing manner, detaches a few thousand troops from the Army of England, to cover her frontiers, which are menaced by the imprudent conduct of Austria. England is preparing fresh

[1] September 11, 1805.

victories for us, and for herself fresh motives for decrying her ambition. After all, those movements are not yet a certain sign of war," &c.

The greatest loss the English Nation sustained this year, was the death of Admiral Lord Nelson at the Battle of Trafalgar, which was fought on the 21st of October, 1805.

On the 6th of November the glorious news of the Victory was published, and there was but one opinion—that it was

DEATH OF NELSON.

purchased too dearly. That evening London was but partially illuminated. On the 7th these symptoms of rejoicing were general, but throughout them there was a sombre air—a mingling of the cypress with the laurel, and men went about gloomily, thinking of the dead hero : at least most did—some did not ; even of those who might have worn a decent semblance of woe—old sailors—some of whom, according to the *Times*, behaved in a somewhat unseemly manner. " A squadron of shattered *tars* were drawn up in *line of battle*, opposite the Treasury, at anchor, with their lights *aloft*, all *well stowed with grog*, flourishing their mutilated stumps, cheering all hands, and making the best of their position, in collecting *prize money.*"

A General Thanksgiving for the Victory was proclaimed to take place on the 5th of December. The good Volunteers were duly marched to church, and one member of the Royal Family—the Duke of Cambridge—actually attended Divine Worship on the occasion. At Drury Lane Theatre, " the Interlude of *The Victory and Death of Lord Nelson* seemed to affect the audience exceedingly ; but the tear of sensibility was wiped away by the merry eccentricities of *The Weathercock*"—the moral to be learned from which seems to be, that the good folks of the early century seemed to think that God should not be thanked, nor heroes mourned, too much. This must close this year, for Nelson's funeral belongs to the next.

After the Battle of Trafalgar, the Patriotic Fund was again revived, and over £50,000 subscribed by the end of the year.

Consols were remarkably even during this year, varying very little even at the news of Trafalgar: January, 61⅞ ; December, 65.

The quartern loaf varied from January 1s. 4¼d., to December 1s. 0¼d.

Wheat varied from 95s. to 90s. per quarter.

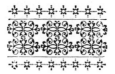

CHAPTER XIII.

1806.

Nelson's funeral—Epigrams—Death of Pitt—His funeral--General Fast—Large
coinage of copper—Impeachment of Lord Melville—The Abolition of the
Slave Trade passes the House of Commons—Death and funeral of Fox—His
warning Napoleon of a plot against him—Negotiations for peace—Napoleon
declares England blockaded.

THE year opens with the Funeral of Nelson, whose
Victory at Trafalgar had made England Mistress of
the Ocean.   He was laid to his rest in St Paul's on
January 9th, much to the profit of the four vergers of that
Cathedral, who are said to have made more than £1000, by
the daily admission of the throngs desirous of witnessing
the preparations for the funeral.   The *Annual Register*
says, " The door money is taken as at a puppet show, and
amounted for several days to more than forty pounds a
day."   Seats to view the procession, from the windows
of the houses on the route, commanded any price,
from One Guinea each ; and as much as Five Hundred
Guineas is said to have been paid for a house on Ludgate
Hill. [1]

Enthusiasm was at its height, as it was in later times,

[1] *Morning Post*, January 8, 1806.

within the memory of many of us, when the Duke of
Wellington came to rest under the same roof as the Gallant
Nelson. His famous signal—which, even now, thrills the
heart of every Englishman—was prostituted to serve trade
Advertisments, *vide* the following : " ENGLAND EXPECTS
EVERY MAN TO DO HIS DUTY. NELSON'S VICTORY, or
TWELFTH DAY. To commemorate that great National
Event, which is the pride of every Englishman to hand
down to the latest posterity, as well as to contribute towards
alleviating the sufferings of our brave wounded Tars, &c.,
H. WEBB, Confectioner, Little Newport Street, will, on
that day, Cut for SALE, the LARGEST RICH TWELFTH
CAKE ever made, weighing near 600 lbs., part of the
profits of which H. W. intends applying to the Patriotic
Fund at Lloyd's." [1]

His body lay in State at Greenwich in the " Painted
Hall" (then called the "Painted Chamber") from Sunday the
5th of January until the 8th. Owing to Divine Service not
being finished, a written notice was posted up, that the
public could not be admitted until 11. a.m.; by which time
many thousands of people were assembled. Punctually at
that hour, the doors were thrown open, and, though express
orders had been given that only a limited number should
be admitted at once, yet the mob was so great as to bear
down everything in its way. Nothing could be heard but
shrieks and groans, as several persons were trodden under
foot and greatly hurt. One man had his right eye literally
torn out, by coming into contact with one of the gate-posts.
Vast numbers of ladies and gentlemen lost their shoes,
hats, shawls, &c., and the ladies fainted in every direction.   .

The Hall was hung with black cloth, and lit up with
twenty-eight Silver Sconces, with two wax candles in each
—a light which, in that large Hall, must have only served
to make darkness visible. High above the Coffin hung

[1] *Morning Post*, January 3, 1806.

a canopy of black velvet festooned with gold, and by the coffin was the Hero's Coronet. Shields of Arms were around, and, at back, was a trophy, which was surmounted by a gold shield, encircled by a wreath having upon it "Trafalgar" in black letters.

The bringing of the body from Greenwich to Whitehall by water, must have been a most impressive sight—and one not likely to be seen again, owing to the absence of rowing barges. That which headed the procession bore the Royal Standard, and carried a Captain and two Lieutenants in full uniform, with black waistcoats, breeches, and stockings, and crape round their hats and arms.

In the second barge were the Officers of Arms, bearing the Shield, Sword, Helm, and Crest, of the deceased, and the great banner was borne by Captain Moorsom, supported by two lieutenants.

The third barge bore the body, and was rowed by forty-six men from Nelson's flag-ship the *Victory*. This barge was covered with black velvet, and black plumes, and Clarencieux King-at-Arms sat at the head of the coffin, bearing a Viscount's Coronet, upon a black velvet cushion.

In the fourth barge came the Chief Mourner, Admiral Sir Peter Parker, with many assistant Mourners and Naval grandees.

Then followed His Majesty's barge, that of the Lords Commissioners of the Admiralty, the Lord Mayor's barge, and many others ; and they all passed slowly up the silent highway, to the accompaniment of minute guns, the shores being lined with thousands of spectators, every man with uncovered head. All traffic on the river was suspended, and the deck, yards, masts, and rigging of every vessel were crowded with men.

The big guns of the Tower boomed forth, and similar salutes accompanied the mournful train to Whitehall, from whence the body was taken, with much solemnity, to the Admiralty, there to lie till the morrow.

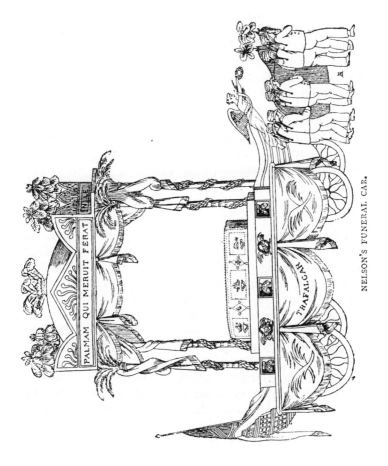

NELSON'S FUNERAL CAR.

His resting-place was not fated to be that of his choice.
" Victory, or Westminster Abbey," he cried, forgetful that
the Nation had apportioned the Abbey to be the Pantheon
of Genius, and St. Paul's to be the Valhalla of Heroes—and
to the latter he was duly borne.

I refrain from giving the programme of the procession,
because of its length, which may be judged by the fact,
that the first part left the Admiralty at 11 a.m., and the
last of the mourning coaches a little before three.   The
Procession may be divided into three parts : the Military,
the funeral Pageant proper, and the Mourners.   There
were nearly 10,000 regular soldiers, chiefly composed of
those who had fought in Egypt, and knew of Nelson ; and
this was a large body to get together, when the means of
transport were very defective—a great number of troops
in Ireland, and a big European War in progress, causing
a heavy drain upon the Army.   The Pageant was as brave
as could be made, with pursuivants and heralds, standards
and trumpets, together with every sort of official procurable,
and all the nobility, from the younger sons of barons, to
George Prince of Wales, who was accompanied by the
Dukes of Clarence and Kent.   The Dukes of York and
Cambridge headed the Procession, and the Duke of Sussex
made himself generally useful by first commanding his
regiment of Loyal North Britons, and then riding to St.
Paul's on his chestnut Arabian.   The Mourners, besides
the relatives of the deceased, consisted of Naval Officers,
according to their rank—the Seniors nearest the body ;
and, to give some idea of the number of those who followed
Nelson to the grave, there were one hundred and eighty-
four Mourning Coaches, which came after the Body, which
was carried on a triumphal car, fashioned somewhat after
his flag-ship the *Victory*—the accompanying illustration
of which I have taken from the best contemporary engraving I could find.

The whole of the Volunteer Corps of the Metropolis, and

its vicinity, were on duty all day, to keep the line of procession.

At twenty-three and a half minutes past five the coffin containing Nelson's mortal remains was lowered into its vault. Garter King-at-Arms had pronounced his style and duly broken his staff, and then the huge procession, which had taken so much trouble and length of time to prepare, melted, and each man went his way; the car being taken to the King's Mews, where it remained for a day or two, until it was removed to the grand hall at Greenwich—and the Hero, or rather his grave, was converted into a sight for which money was taken.

"EPIGRAM,

ON THE SHAMEFUL EXHIBITION AT ST. PAUL'S.

Brave NELSON was doubtless a lion in war,
　With terror his enemies filling;
But now he is dead, they are safe from his paw,
　And the LION is *shewn* for a *shilling*." [1]

"THE INVITATION.

Lo ! where the relics of brave NELSON lie !
　And, lo ! each heart with saddest sorrow weeping !
Come then, ye throng, and gaze with anxious eye—
　But, ah ! remember, you must—*pay* for *peeping*." [2]

The cost of this funeral figures, in the expenses of the year, at £14,698 11s. 6d.

Yet another death : the great Statesman, WILLIAM PITT, who had been sinking for some time, paid the debt of Nature on the 23rd of January. Parliament voted him, by a majority of 258 to 89, a public funeral, and sepulture in Westminster Abbey ; and also a sum not exceeding £40,000 was voted, without opposition, to pay his debts.

He lay in state, in the Painted Chamber of the Palace of Westminster, on the 20th and 21st of February, and people flocked to the sight—19,800 persons passing through in the

---

[1] *Morning Post,* January 20, 1806.　　　[2] Ibid., January 21, 1806.

six hours the doors were kept open ; or, in other words, they entered and went out at the rate of fifty-five a minute. This average was exceeded next day, when the number of visitors rose to 27,000, or seventy-five a minute.

Of course the accessories of this funeral, which took place on the 22nd of February, were nothing like so gorgeous as at that of Nelson ; but there was a vast amount of State, and the Dukes of York, Cumberland, and Cambridge, were among the long line of the Nobility who paid their last respects to William Pitt. The cost of the funeral was £6,045 2s. 6d.

It would be without precedent to allow the year to pass without a Fast, so one was ordered for the 26th of February. The Houses of Lords and Commons attended Church, so did the Volunteers. Also " The Lord Mayor, Sheriffs, &c., attended Divine Service at St. Paul's, from whence they returned to the Mansion House—*where they dined.*"

The Copper Coinage having, during the King's long reign, become somewhat deteriorated, a proclamation of His Majesty's appeared in the *Gazette* of the 10th of May, for a New Coinage of 150 tons of penny pieces, 427½ tons of halfpenny pieces, and twenty-two and a half tons of farthings. The penny pieces were to be in the proportion of twenty-four to the pound, avoirdupois, of copper, and so on with the others. It was provided that no one should be obliged to take more of such penny pieces, in one payment, than shall be of the value of one shilling, or more of such halfpence and farthings than shall be of the value of sixpence.

This year witnessed the singular sight of a Parliamentary Impeachment. Lord Melville was accused on ten different counts, and his trial commenced on the 29th of April ; Westminster Hall being fitted up for the occasion. The three principal charges against him were—"First, that before January 10, 1786, he had applied to his private use and profit, various sums of public money entrusted to him, as

Treasurer of the Navy. Secondly, that in violation of the Act of Parliament, for better regulating that office, he had permitted Trotter, his paymaster, illegally to take from the Bank of England, large sums of the money issued on account of the Treasurer of the Navy, and to place those sums in the hands of his private banker, in his own name, and subject to his sole control and disposition. Thirdly, that he had fraudulently and corruptly permitted Trotter to apply the said money to purposes of private use and emolument, and had, himself, fraudulently and corruptly derived profit therefrom."

Of course Lord Melville pleaded "not guilty," and this was the verdict of his peers.

On the 10th of June, the Abolition of the Slave Trade again passed the House of Commons, by a majority of ninety-nine. On the 24th of June the Lords debated on the same subject, and they carried, without a division, an address to His Majesty, "praying that he would be graciously pleased to consult with other Powers towards the accomplishment of the same end," which would afford another opportunity to those who were anxious again to divide upon this question.

On the 13th of September of this year died Pitt's great rival, Charles James Fox, a man who, had he lived in these times, would have been a giant Statesman. For him, however, no public funeral, no payment by the nation of his debts—this latter probably because in the accounts for the year figure two items of expenditure: " For secret services for 1806, £175,000," and " For the seamen who served in the Battle of Trafalgar, £300,000." He was buried on the 10th of October in Westminster Abbey, and the funeral, under the direction of his friend, Sheridan, was a very pompous affair—though, of course, it lacked the glitter of a State ceremonial. Still there were the King's Trumpeters and Soldiers, whilst the Horse and Foot Guards and Volunteers lined the way. So he was carried to his grave in the Abbey—which, curiously, was dug within eighteen inches of his old opponent, Pitt. The relation between the two is well summed up by a contemporary writer. "We may pronounce of them, that, as rivals for power and for fame, their equals have not been known in this country, and perhaps in none were there two such Statesman, in so regular and equal a contention for pre-eminence. In the advantages of birth and fortune they were equal ; in eloquence, dissimilar in their manner, but superior to all their contemporaries ; in influence upon the minds of their hearers equal ; in talents and reputation, dividing the nation into two parties of nearly equal strength ; in probity, above all suspicion ; in patriotism rivals, as in all things else." [1]

It must not be thought that the year passed by without attempts being made to stop the war. They were begun by a charming act of international courtesy and friendship on the part of Fox, which cannot be better told than in his own words, contained in a letter to Talleyrand.

> "*Downing Street, February* 20, 1806.
>
> "SIR,—I think it my duty, as an honest man, to com-municate to you, as soon as possible, a very extraordinary circumstance which is come to my knowledge. The shortest way will be to relate to you the fact simply as it happened.
>
> "A few days ago a person informed me that he was just arrived at Gravesend without a passport, requesting me at the same time to send him one, as he had lately left Paris, and had something to communicate to me which would give me satisfaction. I sent for him ; he came to my house the following day. I received him alone in my closet ; when, after some unimportant conversation, this villain had the audacity to tell me, that it was necessary for the tranquillity of all crowned heads, to put to death the Ruler of France ; and that, for this purpose, a house had

---

[1] *Annual Register*, vol. xlviii. p. 916.

been hired at Passy, from which this detestable project could be carried into effect with certainty, and without risk. I did not perfectly understand if it was to be done by a common musket, or by fire-arms upon a new principle.

"I am not ashamed to tell you, Sir, *who know me*, that my confusion was extreme, in thus finding myself *led into* a conversation with an avowed assassin. I instantly ordered him to leave me, giving, at the same time, orders to the police officer who accompanied him, to send him out of the kingdom as soon as possible.

" It is probable that all this is unfounded, and that the wretch had nothing more in view than to make himself of consequence, by promising what, according to his ideas, would afford me satisfaction.

" At all events, I thought it right to acquaint you with what had happened, before I sent him away. Our laws do not permit us to detain him long ; but he shall not be sent away till after you shall have had full time to take pre-cautions against his attempts, supposing him still to enter-tain bad designs ; and, when he goes, I shall take care to have him landed at a seaport as remote as possible from France.

" He calls himself here, Guillet de la Gevrilliere, but I think it is a false name which he has assumed.

" At his first entrance I did him the honour to believe him to be a spy.

" I have the honour to be, with the most perfect attach-ment,

   " Sir,

     " Your most obedient servant,

       " C. J. Fox."

I have given this letter *in extenso*, to show how a *Gentle-man* of the grand Old School could act towards an enemy —feeling himself dishonoured by even conversing with a murderous traitor. It was chivalrous and manly, and well

merited Napoleon's remarks, contained in Tallyrand's reply :
" I recognize here the principles of honour and of virtue,
by which Mr. Fox has ever been actuated.   Thank him on
my part."

This episode is the most agreeable one in the whole of
the papers in connection with the negotiations for peace at
that time.   The King fully entered into the reasons why
these proposals did not come to a successful issue, in a
Declaration, dated October 21st, which, with many other
papers, was laid before Parliament on December 22nd.

If " Rien n'est sacré pour un Sapeur," it is the same with
the Caricaturist.   Here were men presumably doing their
honest best to promote peace, and do away with a war that
was exhausting all Europe ; yet the satirist takes it jauntily.
Take only one, the Caricature by Ansell (August, 1806).
" The Pleasing and Instructive Game of *Messengers ;* or,
Summer Amusement for John Bull."   Balls, in the shape
of Messengers, are being sent and returned, in lively succession, across the Channel ; their errands are of a most
extraordinary character.   " Peace—Hope—Despair.   No
Peace—Passports—Peace to a certainty—No Peace—Cre-
dentials—Despatches, &c."   Napoleon and Talleyrand like
the game.   " Begar, Talley, dis be ver amusant.   Keep it
up as long as you can, so that we may have time for our
project."   John Bull merely looks on, leaving Fox, Sheridan,
and the Ministry, to play the game on his behalf ; and, in
reply to a query by Fox, " Is it not a pretty game, Johnny ? "
the old man replies, with a somewhat puzzled air, " Pretty
enough as to that—they do fly about monstrous quick, to
be sure ; but you don't get any more money out of my
pocket for all that ! "

The failure of these pacific negotiations with France,
brought a rejoinder from the French Emperor, which, to
use a familiar expression made John Bull " set his back up."
It was no less than a proclamation of Napoleon's, dated
Berlin, November 21, 1806, in which, he attempted, on paper,

to blockade England. The principal articles in this famous proclamation are as follow :—

1. The British Isles are declared to be in a state of blockade.

2. All trade and communication with Great Britain is strictly prohibited.

3. All letters going to, or coming from England, are not to be forwarded, and all those written in English are to be suppressed.

4. Every individual, who is a subject of Great Britain, is to be made a prisoner of war, wherever he may be found.

5. All goods belonging to Englishmen are to be confiscated, and the amount paid to those who have suffered through the detention of ships by the English.

6. No ships coming from Great Britain, or having been in a port of that country, are to be admitted.

7. All trade in English Goods is rigorously prohibited.

Besides these startling facts, the time allowed for the delivery of all English property was limited to the space of twenty-four hours after the issue of the Proclamation ; and if, after that time, any persons were discovered to have secreted, or withheld, British goods, or articles, of any description, they were to be subjected to military execution. The British subjects who were arrested in Hamburgh, and had not escaped, were ordered to Verdun, or the interior of France, as Prisoners of War.

This was enough to close all hopes of reconciliation, and, although the English Newspapers took a courageous view of the blockade, and attempted to laugh at its ever being practicable to carry out, yet it undoubtedly created great uneasiness, and intensified the bitter feeling between the belligerents.

This, then, was the position of affairs at the end of 1806. Consols, during the year, varied from 61 in January to 59 in December, having in July reached 66½.

The quartern loaf was fairly firm all the year, beginning at 11¾d. and ending at 1s. 1d. Average price of wheat 52s.

CHAPTER XIV.

1807.

Passing of the Slave Trade Bill—Downfall of the " Ministry of all the Talents "—
General Fast—Election for Westminster—Death of Cardinal York—Arrival in
England of Louis XVIII.—Copenhagen bombarded, and the Danish Fleet
captured—Napoleon again proclaimed England as blockaded.

THE year 1807 began, socially, with the Abolition of
the Slave Trade, the debate on which was opened,
in the Lords, on January 2nd, and many were the
nights spent in its discussion. On Feburary 10th, it was
read a third time in the Upper House, and sent down to
the Commons, who, on March 15th, read it a third time,
and passed it without a division. On the 18th, it was sent
again to the Lords, with some amendments. It was printed,
and these amendments were taken into consideration on
the 23rd, and the alterations agreed to on the same date ;
and exactly at noon on March 25th, the bill received the
Royal Assent by Commission, and became LAW. This
Act, be it remembered, did not abolish Slavery, but only
prohibited the Traffic in Slaves ; so that no ship should
clear out from any port within the British dominions after
May 1, 1807, with slaves on board, and that no slave should
be landed in the Colonies after March 1, 1808.

This Act was somewhat hurried through, owing to the
downfall of the Coalition Ministry, which will ever be known

in the political history of England as the "Ministry of all the talents," or the "Broad-bottomed" Cabinet. While this Ministry was in existence, it afforded the Caricaturists plenty of food for their pencils. One of the last of them is by Gillray (April 18, 1807), and it is called "The Pigs Possessed, or, The Broad-bottomed Litter rushing headlong in the Sea of Perdition." Though the subject is hackneyed, the treatment is excellent. "Farmer George," as the King was familiarly termed, has knocked down a portion of his fence, which stands on the edge of a cliff, and, with brandished dung-fork, and ready heel, he speeds the swine to their destruction, thus apostrophizing them: "O, you cursed ungrateful Grunters! what! after devouring more in a twelve month, than the good old Litters did in twelve years, you turn round to kick and bite your old Master? but, if the Devil or the Pope has got possession of you all—pray get out of my Farm Yard! out with you all; no hanger-behind! you're all of a cursed bad breed; so out with you all together!!!"

Of course there was the Annual Fast, which was fixed, for February 25th. This time "the shops were all shut, and the utmost solemnity prevailed throughout the day." Their repetition, evidently, was educating the people as to their implied meaning.

Sir Francis Burdett wished to retrieve his former defeat, and we consequently find him, at the General Election in this year, putting up for Westminster. Paull, who had contested the seat with Sheridan, was one candidate, Lord Cochrane, and Elliott the brewer, at Pimlico, were the others. This election is chiefly remarkable in illustrating the manners of the times, by a duel which took place between two of the candidates, Paull and Burdett, the latter of whom had squabbled over his name having been advertised as intending to appear at a meeting, without his consent having been first obtained. They met at Combe Wood near Wimbledon, and both were wounded. Sir

Francis was successful, and a short account of his
" chairing "—a custom long since consigned to *limbo*—may
not be uninteresting.   Originally, as the name implies, the
successful candidate was seated in a chair, and carried
about on the shoulders of his enthusiastic supporters, as the
winner of the Queen's prize at Wimbledon is now honoured.
But Sir Francis's admirers had improved upon this.   The
procession and triumphal car started from Covent Garden,
and worked its way to the baronet's house in Piccadilly,
where he mounted the car.   How he did so, the contemporary account does not state, but it does say that " the
car was as high as the one pair of stairs windows," and " the
seat upon which the Baronet was placed, stood upon a lofty
Corinthian pillar."   On this uncomfortable elevation, he
rode from Piccadilly, down the Haymarket, up St. Martin's
Lane, and so into Covent Garden, where a dinner was
provided.

On the 31st of August died, at Rome, Henry Benedict
Maria Clement Stuart, Cardinal York—the last of the
Stuarts.   The feeble little attempt he made to assert his
right to the throne of England, would be amusing if it
had been serious; the coining of one medal, in which he
styled himself Henry IX., was his sole affectation of
royalty.   With him died all hope, if any such existed, of
disturbing the Hanoverian Succession.   Curiously enough,
events made him a pensioner on George the Third's bounty,
and the annuity was granted by the one, and received by
the other, not as an act of charity, but as of brotherly
friendship ; and this annuity of £4,000 he duly received for
seven years before he died.

In this year, too, England gave shelter to another un-
fortunate scion of royalty—Louis XVIII.—who came from
Sweden in the Swedish Frigate the *Freya*.   He travelled
under the name of the Comte de Lille, and landed at
Yarmouth.   He rather ungraciously declined the Palace of
Holyrood, which was placed at his disposal, on the ground

that he had not come to England as an asylum, or for safety, but on political business as King of France. Wisely, he was allowed to have his own way, and he settled down at Hartwell, in Buckinghamshire, a seat of the Marquis of Buckingham, and here he abode until the fall of Napoleon, when, of course, he went to Paris.

The year ends stormily. After having bombarded Copenhagen and captured all the Danish fleet, war was proclaimed against Denmark on the 4th of November. On the 8th of the month, Portugal was compelled by Napoleon to confiscate British property, and shut her ports against England.

Nor was he content with this. Probably he thought the effect of his former proclamation of blockading England, was wearing out, so he fulminated a fresh one on the 11th of November from Hamburgh, and another from Milan on the 27th of December; in both of which he reiterated his intention of prohibiting intercourse between all subjects under his control, and contumacious England, and that this should be properly carried out he appointed commercial residents, at different ports, to attend strictly to the matter.

This, of course, was met promptly by an Order in Council, allowing neutral Powers to trade with the enemies of Great Britain, provided they touched at British ports, and paid custom dues to the British Government.

Consols this year began at 61⅜, and left off 62⅞.

Wheat varied during the year, from 84s. to 73s., the highest price being 90s.; and the quartern loaf varied in proportion from 1s. 1¼d. to 10¾d.

CHAPTER XV.

1808.

Gloomy prospects of 1808—King's Speech—Droits of the Admiralty—Regulation of Cotton Spinners' wages—Riots in the Cotton districts—Battle of Vimiera—Convention of Cintra—Its unpopularity—Articles of the Convention.

THE year 1808 opened very gloomily. Parliament met on the 21st of January, and was opened by Commission. The " King's Speech," on this occasion sketches the political situation better than any pen of a modern historian can do. I therefore take some portions of it, not sufficient to weary the reader, but to give him the clearest idea of the state of Europe at this period.

The King informed Parliament,[1] " that, no sooner had the result of the Negotiations at Tilsit,[2] confirmed the influence, and control, of France over the Powers of the Continent, than His Majesty was apprized of the intention of the enemy to combine those Powers in one general confederacy, to be directed either to the entire subjugation of this kingdom, or to the imposing upon His Majesty, an insecure

---

[1] " Parliamentary Debates," vol. x.

[2] Napoleon met the Emperor of Russia and the King of Prussia at Tilsit. His historical meeting with the former took place on the 25th of June, 1807, on a barge, or raft, sumptuously appointed, moored in the middle of the river Niemen.

and ignominious peace. That for this purpose, it was determined to force into hostility against His Majesty, States which had hitherto been allowed by France to maintain, or to purchase, their neutrality, and to bring to bear against different points of His Majesty's dominions, the whole of the Naval Force of Europe, and specifically the Fleets of Portugal and Denmark. To place these fleets out of the power of such a confederacy became, therefore, the indispensable duty of His Majesty.

"In the execution of this duty, so far as related to the Danish Fleet, his Majesty has commanded us to assure you, that it was with the deepest reluctance that His Majesty found himself compelled, after his earnest endeavours to open a Negotiation with the Danish Government had failed, to authorize his commanders to resort to the extremity of force ; but that he has the greatest satisfaction in congratulating you upon the successful execution of this painful but necessary service.

"We are commanded further to acquaint you, that the course which His Majesty had to pursue with respect to Portugal, was, happily, of a nature more congenial to His Majesty's feelings : That the timely and unreserved communication, by the Court of Lisbon, of the demands, and designs of France, while it confirmed to His Majesty the authenticity of the advices which he had received from other quarters, entitled that Court to His Majesty's confidence in the sincerity of the assurances by which that communication was accompanied. The fleet of Portugal was destined by France to be employed as an instrument of vengeance against Great Britain ; that fleet has been secured from the grasp of France, and is now employed in conveying to its American dominions [1] the hopes, and fortunes, of the Portuguese monarchy. His Majesty implores the protection of Divine Providence upon that enterprize,

[1] The King of Portugal, and his family, fled to the Brazils, protected by a British squadron, November 29, 1807.

rejoicing in the preservation of a Power so long the friend, and ally, of Great Britain, and, in the prospect of its establishment in the New World, with augmented strength and splendour.

"We have it in command from His Majesty to inform you, that the determination of the enemy to excite hostilities between His Majesty, and his late Allies, the Emperors of Russia and Austria, and the King of Prussia, has been but too successful, and that the ministers from those Powers have demanded, and received, their passports. This measure, on the part of Russia, has been attempted to be justified by a statement of wrongs, and grievances, which have no real foundation. The Emperor of Russia had, indeed, proffered his mediation between His Majesty and France : His Majesty did not refuse that mediation ; but he is confident you will feel the propriety of its not having been accepted, until His Majesty should have been able to ascertain that Russia was in a condition to mediate impartially, and, until the principles, and the basis, on which France was ready to negotiate, were made known to His Majesty. No pretence of justification has been alleged for the hostile conduct of the Emperor of Austria, or for that of his Prussian Majesty. His Majesty has not given the slightest ground of complaint to either of those sovereigns, nor even at the moment when they have respectively withdrawn their ministers, have they assigned to His Majesty any distinct cause for that proceeding."

On the other hand, the King congratulates his people on still retaining the friendship of the Porte, and the King of Sweden ; and that he had concluded a " Treaty of Amity, Commerce, and Navigation" with the United States of America : but these were hardly fair offsets against the powerful European Confederation. Virtually, England was single-handed to fight the world ; but there was no flinching —and history records our success.

War takes money, and taxation makes every one feel

the burden, directly, or indirectly, so that it must have been with a sigh of relief that the nation read that portion of the King's Speech which related to finance. "Gentlemen of the House of Commons, His Majesty has directed the Estimates for the year to be laid before you. . . . His Majesty has great satisfaction in informing you, that, notwithstanding the difficulties which the enemy has endeavoured to impose upon the commerce of his subjects, and upon their intercourse with other nations, the resources of the country have continued, in the last year, to be so abundant, as to have produced both from the permanent, and temporary, revenue, a receipt considerably larger than that of the preceding year. The satisfaction which His Majesty feels assured you will derive, in common with His Majesty, from this proof of the solidity of these resources, cannot be greatly increased, if, as His Majesty confidently hopes, it shall be found possible to raise the necessary supplies for the present year without material additions to the public burdens."

This, the Chancellor of the Exchequer was enabled to do, by taking half a million of money from unclaimed Dividends, and by other means, shown by the following resolutions of the Court of Directors of the Bank of England :

" January 14, 1808. Resolved, That the proposal of Chancellor of the Exchequer, to take £500,000, from the unclaimed Dividends, in addition to the former sum of £376,397, be acceded to by this Court. . . .

" Resolved, That the Court of Directors do accede to the proposal of the Chancellor of the Exchequer to lend, for the use of government, £3,000,000, on Exchequer bills, without interest, during the war, provided it is stipulated to be returned within six months after the ratification of a treaty of peace, and under the complete understanding, that all transactions between the public, and the Bank, shall be continued in the accustomed manner, even though the amount of public balances should exceed the sum of ten millions."

On the 9th of February, Sir Francis Burdett asked a very pertinent question in the House, anent the presentation of £20,000 by His Majesty to the Duke of York, out of *Droits of Admiralty.* He said that " it had been stated in the public prints that His Majesty had granted large sums out of the proceeds of property belonging to nations not at war with this country, to several branches of the Royal Family, and particularly to the Duke of York. What he wished to know was, whether this statement was correct; and, if so, upon what ground it was that His Majesty could seize the property of nations not at war with this country ? "

The Chancellor of the Exchequer (Right Hon. Spencer Perceval) was willing to give the hon. baronet every information he required on the subject. But first, he must apprize the hon. baronet of a misapprehension which he seemed to labour under, with respect to the principle upon which His Majesty's right to the property in question was founded. It was true that the property had been seized previous to His Majesty's formal declaration of war, but war had since been declared, and the question respecting the property had been referred to the competent tribunal, and condemned. The right of His Majesty, therefore, grounded upon such a decision, was incontrovertible. It was true that His Majesty had granted a certain sum out of the proceeds of such property to each of the junior male branches of the Royal Family, and to the Duke of York amongst the rest.

These *Droits of the Admiralty* formed a very convenient fund upon which the King drew, as occasion required, when it was impolitic to ask Parliament for an increase of the Civil List; but Sir Francis did good service in calling attention to it, and, after its being mentioned on more than one occasion, it was settled that an account should be laid before the House, of the net proceeds paid into the Registry of the Court of Admiralty, or to the Receiver-

General of Droits, of all property condemned to His
Majesty as Droits, either in right of his Crown, or in right
of the office of Lord High Admiral, since the 1st of
January, 1793, and of the balance in hand.

The Cotton trade at Manchester was very dull, owing to
the limited trade with the Continent, and some distress
prevailed among the operatives.   On the 19th of May,
Mr. Rose asked leave of the House of Commons to bring
in a bill to fix a minimum of wages, which the workpeople
should receive.   He said they were now suffering peculiar
hardships, and, at the same time, supporting them with a
patience and resolution, which did them credit.   A short
debate took place on this proposition, which, afterwards,
was withdrawn.   One member opined that the distress
arose, not from the wages being too low, but through their
having been, at one time, too high, which had caused a
great influx of labour, thus overstocking the market.   Sir
Robert Peel said that the great cause of the distress was,
not the oppression of the masters, but the shutting-up of
the foreign markets ; and the fact was, that masters were
now suffering from this cause still more than the men.
And then, as far as Parliament went, the matter dropped.

But not so at Manchester.   The demands of the men
were absurd, and preposterous ; they wanted an advance
of 6s. 8d. in the pound, or 33⅓ per cent.   Of course, with
failing trade, and a bad market, the masters could not grant
this extraordinary rise ; but, after a meeting among themselves they offered an immediate advance of 10 per cent. on
all kinds of cotton goods weaving, to take effect that day
(June 1st), and a further rise of 10 per cent. on the 1st of
August.   The men refused to take this offer, and would be
satisfied with nothing less than their original demand, and
some 60,000 looms lay idle, whilst the operatives peram-
bulated the streets or rushed into house, cellar, or garret,
where any shuttle was going, and deprived that man of his
means of living.

On the 30th of May there had been some disturbance among the weavers at Rochdale, and some were apprehended, and put in prison ; but the mob forced the gaol, released the prisoners, and set fire to the New Prison. Thus it will be seen that it was necessary for the law to step in, and vindicate its majesty, and, consequently, cavalry was freely employed in and about Manchester, Bolton, Rochdale, and Bury ; and, on the 6th of June, a raid was made upon a house in Manchester, which resulted in the lodging of about twenty men in the New Bayley.

Still they went on with disorderly meetings, and destruction of industrious men's looms, and work, compelling the troops to be always on the alert. Of course they burnt the manufacturers in effigy, the women amongst them, relying on their sex, being the most turbulent and mischievous, acting not quite as *petroleuses*, but getting as near that type as opportunity afforded, for vitriol, or aquafortis, was squirted on to the looms, through broken panes in the windows, or dropped upon the bags containing pieces which the industrious, and well-disposed, weaver had worked hard at, for himself, and employer. It is satisfactory to know that they did not obtain their demands, and, after much simmering, and frothing, the scum subsided, and honest, and hardworking, men were once more enabled to pursue their avocation in peace.

On the 22nd of August was fought the famous battle of Vimiera, which thoroughly crippled Napoleon's power in Portugal, completely defeated Junot's fine army, and led to the Convention of Cintra, which so disgusted the English people, and called down on the head of Sir Hugh Dalrymple a formal declaration of His Majesty's displeasure. A commission sat at Chelsea, to report upon his conduct, and they exonerated him. Still, the general public were indignant. The Park and Tower guns were fired at night on the 15th of September, and, next day, came out an *Extraordinary Gazette*, with the text of the Convention.

The accompanying illustration, by Ansell, brings to our mind far more vividly than is possible to do by any verbal description, the astonishment, and disgust, with which the news was received in the City.   The scene is outside Lloyd's Coffee House, in Lombard Street, and it shows us this commercial institution as it was in its youth, with its modest premises, and two bow windows with red moreen dwarf blinds.

The print, itself, is in two parts, one called " The Tower

EXTRAORDINARY NEWS.

Guns.   Surprize the First."   Here, John Bull and his wife are in their happy home ; J. B. smoking his pipe, and enjoying his tankard.   A servant enters with " Law, sir, if there isn't the big guns at the Tower going off ! "   John kicks up his heels, waves his nightcap, and pipe, crying out, " The Tower Guns at this time of Night ! *Extraordinary* News arrived !   By Jupiter, we've sent Juno to the Devil, and taken the Russian Fleet !   Illuminate the House ! Call up the Children, and tap the Gooseberry Wine, Mrs. Bull ; we'll drink to our noble Commanders in Portugal."

The companion to this is the illustration given, and it is called "The Gazette. Surprize the Second." Here, opposite Lloyd's, an old merchant is reading to his *confrères* an *Extraordinary Gazette.* "Art. IV. The French Army shall carry with it all its artillery of French calibre, with the horses belonging to it, and the tumbrils supplied with sixty rounds per gun. All oth . . ." Universal indignation prevails, and one calls out, "What! carry away Sixty Pounds a man, that ought to have been in the pockets of our brave fellows. D—n me if I ever believe the Tower Guns again."

The Articles in this Convention which excited popular indignation were—

"II. The French Troops shall evacuate Portugal with their arms and baggage ; they shall not be considered as prisoners of war, and, on their arrival in France, they shall be at liberty to serve.

"III. The English Government shall furnish the means of conveyance for the French Army, which shall be disembarked in any of the ports of France between Rochfort, and l'Orient, inclusively.

"IV. The French Army shall carry with it, all its artillery of French calibre, with the horses belonging to it, and the tumbrils supplied with sixty rounds per gun. All other artillery, arms, and ammunition, as also the Military and Naval Arsenals, shall be given up to the British army and navy, in the state in which they may be, at the period of the ratification of the Convention.

"V. The French Army shall carry with it all its equipments, and all that is comprehended under the name of property of the army ; that is to say, its military chest, and carriages attached to the Field Commissariat, and Field Hospitals, or shall be allowed to dispose of such part of the same, on its account, as the Commander-in-chief may judge it unnecessary to embark. In like manner, all individuals of the army shall be at liberty to dispose of their private property, of every description, with full security, hereafter, for the purchasers."

On the 29th of August of this year, the Queen of France joined her husband here; where they continued, living in privacy, until their restoration.

Consols began at 64⅜, and left off at 66⅛, having reached 70⅜ in June and July.

Wheat ranged from 69s. per quarter in January, to 81s. in July, and 91s. in December. The quartern loaf varied from 11d. to 1s. 2d.

CHAPTER XVI.

1809.

EARLY in the year 1809 (on February 8th) was a day of Fasting, and prayer, for the success of His Majesty's arms.

Also, in January, began the celebrated Clarke Scandal, which ended in the Duke of York resigning his position as Commander-in-chief; but this will be fully treated of in another place, as will the celebrated O. P. Riots, which occurred in this year.

Socially, the only other important event which occurred in this year was " THE JUBILEE," or the celebration of the fiftieth anniversary of the accession of George III., he having succeeded to the throne on the 25th of October, 1760; and this Jubilee created quite a craze. A Jubilee Medal was struck by Bisset, of Birmingham, having, on the Obverse, a bust of the King, with the following legend: " KING GEORGE THE THIRD ascended the Throne of the Imperial Realms of Great Britain and Ireland, October 25, A.D. 1760. Grand National Jubilee, celebrated October 25, 1809." On the Reverse, was the Guardian

Genius of England, represented as Fame, seated in the clouds, and triumphing over Mortality; she displayed a centenary circle, one half of which showed the duration of the King's reign up to that time, whilst rays from heaven illuminate a throne.

Not content with this, it was suggested that there should be a special costume worn on the occasion, and that gentlemen should dress in the " Windsor uniform," *i.e.*, blue frock coats, with scarlet collars, and the ladies' dresses were to be of garter blue velvet, or satin, with head-dresses containing devices emblematical of the occasion.

It is no wonder that people went somewhat crazy over this Jubilee, for it was an event of very rare occurrence, only three monarchs of England having kept jubilees— Henry III., Edward III., and George III. Let us, however, hope that this generation may add yet another to the list in Queen Victoria. Edward III. celebrated the jubilee of his birth in a good and kindly manner in 1363, as we may learn from Guthrie: " Edward was now in the fiftieth year of his age, and he laid hold of that æra as the occasion of his performing many other popular acts of government. For he declared, in his parliament, by Sir Henry Green, that he was resolved to keep it as a jubilee; and that he had given orders to issue out general and special pardons, without paying any fees, for recalling all exiles, and setting at liberty all debtors to the Crown, and all prisoners for criminal matters. He further created his third son, Lionel, Duke of Clarence, and his fifth son, Edmund, Earl of Cambridge. The Parliament, on their parts, not to be wanting in gratitude, having obtained their petitions, on the day of their rising, presented the King with a duty of twenty-six shillings and eight pence upon every sack of wool, for three years, besides continuing the former duty upon wools, fells, and skins. This year being declared a year of jubilee, the reader is to expect little business, as it was spent in hunting throughout the great forests of England, and other magnificent diversions, in which the King laid out an immense sum.   But we are not to close the transactions of this year before we inform the reader that it was from the jubilee then instituted, that the famous custom took its rise of our Kings washing, feeding, and clothing, on Maunday Thursday, as many poor people, as they are years old." [1]

The whole of the country was determined to celebrate this occasion in a way worthy of it, and, of course, every one had his own theory, and aired it ; some were for a general illumination and feasting everybody, others to relieve poor debtors, and rejoice the hearts of the poor ; others mingled the two.   " Sir, benevolence is no less amiable for being attended with gaiety ; without a general illumination the day would be like a public mourning, or fast ; the shops shut, the bells tolling, the churches open, a cloudy night, a howling wind, a Jubilee ! ! !   But no such dull Jubilee for JOHN BULL."

Perhaps one of the most popular ways for people to spend their money, in order to show their gratitude for the beneficent sway of the sovereign who had ruled them for fifty years, and who was much beloved of his subjects, was the release of prisoners for small debts.   Their case was cruelly harsh, and it must have been felt as one of the hardest, and most pressing, of social evils.   Take the following advertisement from the *Morning Post*, October 23, 1809: " JUBILEE.   PRISONERS for DEBT in the Prison of the Marshalsea of His Majesty's Household.   There are now confined in the above prison in the Borough, seventy-two persons (from the age of twenty-three to seventy-four, leaving fifty-three wives, and two hundred and three children) for various debts from seven guineas, up to £140. The total amount of the whole sum is £2092, many of whom (*sic*) are in great distress, and objects of charity,

---

[1] " A General History of England from the Landing of Julius Cæsar to the Revolution of 1688," by William Guthrie, London, 1744–1751, vol. ii. p. 213.

every way worthy the notice of a generous and feeling public, who are interesting themselves in the cause of suffering humanity against the approaching Jubilee. It is, therefore in contemplation to raise a sufficient sum, for the purpose of endeavouring to effect their release, by offering compositions to their respective creditors in the following proportions, *viz.*, 10s. in the pound for every debt not exceeding £20; above that sum, and not exceeding £50, the sum of 7s. 6d.; and above £50, the sum of 5s. in the pound, in full for debt and costs. Subscriptions . . . will be received by . . . with whom are left lists containing the names of the unfortunate Persons immured within the Prison, and other particulars respecting them, for the inspection of such Persons as may be desirous of promoting so benevolent an undertaking."

And that large sums were so raised, we have evidence in many instances. Take one case :

" At a meeting of MERCHANTS and BANKERS appointed to conduct the ENTERTAINMENT to be given at Merchant Taylors' Hall on the 25th inst., held this day—

" BEESTON LONG, Esq., in the Chair.

" Resolved, That since the advertisement published by this Committee on the 5th day of September last, various communications having been made to this Committee which lead them to imagine that a general Illumination will not be so acceptable to the Public as was at first supposed, and, wishing that the day may pass with perfect unanimity of proceeding, on so happy an Occasion, this Committee no longer think it expedient to recommend a general Illumination.

"Resolved, That it appears to this Committee that, instead of such general Illumination, it will be more desirable to open a SUBSCRIPTION for the Relief of Persons confined for Small Debts, and that the sums collected be paid over to the Treasurer of the Society established for that purpose."

To show how warmly this idea of releasing the debtor was taken up, in this instance alone, considerably more than £2,000 was collected.

"JUBILEE SONG.

" For WEDNESDAY, 25th OCTOBER, 1809.

" *Tune—*'GOD SAVE THE KING.'

" BRITONS ! your Voices raise,
Join cheerful Songs of praise,
　　With grateful lay ;
May all our Island ring,
Her Sons' Orisons sing
For their Beloved King
　　On this bright day.

May he the vale of life
Close free from ev'ry strife ;
　　His subjects see.
Bless'd with a lasting Peace,
May War for ever cease,
Pris'ners each Pow'r release,
　　And all be free.

King George's Fiftieth Year
Of Sceptred greatness cheer
　　Each loyal Heart ;
May the stain'd Sword be sheath'd ;
Amity once more breath'd ;
Commerce, with Plenty wreath'd,
　　Sweet Joy impart.

Thus may our Children find
Cause which will e'er remind
　　Them to agree,
That we with Justice sing,
God bless our good old King,
For him, our Noble King,
　　This Jubilee."

This is not the sole attempt at a Jubilee literature. There was a satirical pamphlet called " The Jubilee ; or, John Bull in his Dotage. A Grand National Pantomime.

As it was to have been acted by His Majesty's subjects on the 25th of October, 1809." Another pamphlet, by Dr. Joseph Kemp, was entitled "The Patriotic Entertainment, called the Jubilee." And yet another book of 203 pages printed in Birmingham, which had for title, "An Account of the Celebration of the Jubilee of 1809 in various parts of the Kingdom." This was arranged in alphabetical order, and gave an account of the doings, on this occasion, in the various cities, towns, and villages of England. It was published by subscription, and the profits were to go to the "Society for the Relief of Prisoners for Small Debts."

There was a poem, too, which is too long to be reproduced in its entirety, but which contains some pretty lines, such as would go home to a people who really loved their king—who had suffered when God had afflicted him, and yearned for his recovery, and who were then spending both blood, and treasure, to preserve his throne and their own country.

> " *Seculo festas referente luces,*
> *Reddidi carmen.*"—HORACE.

> "OFT (ah! how oft) has the revolving Sun
> Smiled on Britannia's joy at battles won?
> How oft our bosoms felt the conscious glow
> For brilliant triumph o'er the stubborn foe?
> If, then, our patriot hearts could proudly feel
> Such zealous transports at our Country's weal,
> Shall not the Bard his cheerful efforts lend
> To praise that Country's first and truest friend?
> For such is GEORGE, the pride of England's Throne,
> True to his people's rights as to his own.

> Mild is the Prince, and glorious were the arts,
> That gave him sov'reign empire o'er our hearts.
> Our love for him is such as ever flows
> Spontaneous, warm, and strength'ning as it glows;
> Unlike the smiles, and flattery of Courts,
> Which int'rest prompts, and tyranny extorts;

A Monarch so belov'd has nought to fear
From mad ambition's turbulent career ;
For subjects ne'er from their allegiance swerve,
Who love his person they are bound to serve.

   .   .   .   .

History shall tell how deep was every groan
When 'erst black sickness struck at England's throne :
For her lov'd KING was heard the Nation's sigh,
While public horror star'd in ev'ry eye ;
But, when restor'd, to many a daily pray'r,
What heartfelt joy succeeded to despair.

   .   .   .   .

Then oh ! Thou KING of KINGS, extend thy arm
To shield thine own anointed George from harm ;
Grant, if it so comport with thy behest,
For thy decrees must ever be the best ;
Grant that he long may live, and long may stand
' A tow'r of strength ' to guard our native land."

The King, on the 18th of October, issued a proclamation
pardoning all deserters from the Navy and Marines, but not
allowing them any arrears of pay or prize-money ; and he
also pardoned all deserters from the Army, who should give
themselves up within two months from the 25th of October,
but then they must rejoin the Army. Not particularly
inviting terms when they come to be analyzed, for the
sailors would certainly be marked, and, eventually, pressed,
and the soldiers were simply asked to exchange their
present liberty, for their old slavery. But he really did a
graceful, and, at the same time, a kindly action in sending
through Mr. Perceval, to the Society for the Relief of
Persons confined for Small Debts, £2,000 from his privy
purse.

CHAPTER XVII.

IN the Court of Common Council this feeling of helping the poor debtor was prevalent, and a Mr. Jacks, at a Court held on October 5th, proposed, if the Corporation wished to appropriate a sum for the celebration of the Jubilee, that they should follow the example of the Jewish Law, and liberate the prisoner, and captive, which, he said, would be a much better method of applying their money than for eating and drinking, and the following resolution was carried :

" That it will be more acceptable to Almighty God, and more congenial to the paternal feelings of our beloved Monarch, if the Court would proceed to the liberation of the prisoners and captives, on the joyful Jubilee about to be celebrated, than in spending sums of money in feasting and illuminations. We therefore resolve, that the sum of £1,000 be applied to the relief of persons confined for small debts, and for the relief of persons confined within the gaols of the City, especially freemen of London."

It would be impossible within the limits of this work, even to *sketch* a tithe part of the ways in which the Jubilee was celebrated throughout the country ; but a notice, in some detail, is necessary, as illustrating the social habits of this portion of the Century.   Take, for instance, the ox and sheep roasting at Windsor.   Roasting beasts whole, is a relic of barbarism all but exploded in England, a type of that rude, and plentiful, hospitality which might be expected from a semi-civilized nation.   As it is not probable that the custom will survive, and as the details may be useful for some antiquarian reproduction, I give the *modus operandi* in full, premising, that from all I have heard from those who have feasted upon an animal so treated, that it is very far from being a gastronomic treat, some parts being charred to a cinder, others being quite raw.   This, then, is how it was done :

" At two yesterday morning the fire was lighted, and the ox began to turn on the spit, to the delight of the spectators, a considerable number of whom were assembled, even at that hour, to witness so extraordinary a sight.   A few of the Royal Blues attended to guard it ; a little rain fell a short time previous to the kindling of the fire, but, by the time the ox began to turn, all was fair again.

" At nine o'clock the sheep were put to the fire, on each side of the ox, in Bachelors' Acre.   The apparatus made use of on this occasion, consisted of two ranges set in brick-work, and so contrived that a fire should be made on each side of the ox, and on the outer side of each fire was the necessary machinery for roasting the sheep.   A sort of scaffolding had been erected, consisting of six poles, three of which, at each extremity, fixed in the earth, and united at the top, bore a seventh, from which descended the pulley by means of which the ox was placed between the ranges when put down, and raised again when roasted.   Over the animal a long tin dish was placed, into which large quantities of fat were thrown, which, melting, the beef was basted with it, a ladle at the end of a long pole being used for the purpose.   An immense spit was passed through the body of the animal, the extremity of which worked in a groove at each end. A bushel and a half of potatoes were placed in his belly, and roasted with him.

"At one, the ox and sheep being considered to be sufficiently done, they were taken up. The Bachelors had previously caused boards to be laid from the scene of action to a box, which had been prepared for Her Majesty, and the Royal Family, to survey it from. They graciously accepted the invitation of the Bachelors, to view it close. Their path was railed off and lined by Bachelors, acting as constables, to keep off the crowd. They appeared much gratified by the spectacle, walked round the apparatus and returned to their box. Her Majesty walked with the Duke of York. The Royal party were followed by the Mayor and Corporation. The animals were now placed on dishes to be carved, and several persons, attending for that purpose, immediately set to work. The Bachelors still remained at their posts to keep the crowd off, and a party of them offered the first slice to their illustrious visitors, which was accepted. Shortly after the carving had commenced, and the pudding had began to be distributed, the efforts of the Bachelors to keep off the crowd became useless ; some of the Royal Blues, on horseback, assisted in endeavouring to repel them, but without effect. The pudding was now thrown to those who remained at a distance, and now a hundred scrambles were seen in the same instant. The bread was next distributed in a similar way, and, lastly, the meat ; a considerable quantity of it was thrown to a butcher, who, elevated above the crowd, catching large pieces in one hand, and holding a knife in the other, cut smaller pieces off, letting them fall into the hands of those beneath who were on the alert to catch them. The pudding, [1] meat, and bread, being thus distributed, the crowd were finally regaled with what was denominated a ' *sop in the pan* ;' that is, with having the mashed potatoes, gravy, &c., thrown over them."

[1] The Bachelors had provided about twenty bushels of plum pudding.

Later in the day, Bachelors' Acre was the scene of renewed festivity, no less than a bull bait. "A fine sturdy animal, kept for the purpose, given to the Bachelors for their amusement, by the same gentleman who gave the ox, was baited ; and, in the opinion of the *amateurs* of bull baiting, furnished fine sport ; but, at length, his skin was cut by the rope so much that he bled profusely, and, as it was thought he could not recover, he was led off to be slaughtered."

At Frogmore, the King gave a fête, and a display of fireworks at night. Everything went off very well, except a portion of the water pageant, which was not a success. "Two cars, or chariots, drawn by seahorses, in one of whom (*sic*) was a figure of *Britannia*, in the other a representation of *Neptune*, appeared majestically moving on the bosom of the lake, followed by four boats filled with persons dressed to represent tritons, &c. These last were to have been composed of choristers, we understand, who were to have sung 'God save the King,' on the water, but, unfortunately, the crowd assembled was so immense, that those who were to have sung could not gain entrance. The high treat this could not but have afforded, was, in consequence, lost to the company."

The Jews celebrated the Jubilee with much enthusiasm, and, in the Spanish and Portuguese Synagogue, after hearing a sermon preached on a text from Levit. xxv. 13 : "In the year of this Jubilee ye shall return every man unto his possession," we are told "the whole of the 21st Psalm was sung in most expressive style, to the tune of '*God save the King.*"

In spite of the want of unanimity as to the expediency of a general illumination, there were plenty of transparencies, and even letters of cut-glass. I give descriptions of two of the most important.

"STUBBS'S in Piccadilly, exhibited three transparencies of various dimensions. In the centre was a portrait of His Majesty, in his robes, seated in his coronation chair ; the figure was nine feet in height, and the canvas occupied 20 square feet. On the right hand of the King was placed the crown, on a crimson velvet cushion, supported by a table, ornamented with embroidery. Over His Majesty's head appeared *Fame*, with her attributes ; in her left hand a wreath of laurel leaves ; her right pointing to a glory. At the feet of the Sovereign was a group of boys representing *Bacchanalians*, with *cornucopia*. Underneath appeared a *tablet* with the words ' Anno Regni 50. Oct. 25, 1809.' On the right and left of the above transparency, were placed representations of the two most celebrated oak-trees in England, and two landscapes—the one of Windsor, and the other of Kew."

"Messrs. RUNDELL and BRIDGE'S, Ludgate Hill. In the centre His Majesty is sitting on his throne, dressed in his coronation robes ; on his right, Wisdom, represented by Minerva, with her helmet, ægis, and spear ; Justice with her scales and sword ; on his left, Fortitude holding a pillar, and Piety with her Bible. Next to Wisdom, Victory is decorating two wreathed columns with oak garlands and gold medallions bearing the names of several successful engagements on land—as Alexandria, Talavera, Vimiera, Assaye, &c. Behind the figure of Fortitude, a female figure is placing garlands and medallions on two other wreathed columns, bearing the names of naval victories—as the First of June, St. Vincent's, Trafalgar, &c. The base of the throne is guarded by Mars sitting, and Neptune rising, holding his trident, and declaring the triumphs obtained in his dominions ; on the base between Mars and Neptune, are boys representing the liberal arts, in basso-relievo. The figures are the size of life."

The disastrous end of the campaign known as the Walcheren Expedition, brings the year to a somewhat melancholy conclusion, for on Christmas Day, Admiral Otway's squadron, with all the transports, arrived in the Downs, from Walcheren.

Consols began at 67⅛, and ended at 70, with remarkably little fluctuation.   The top price of wheat in January was 90s. 10d., and at the end of December 102s. 10d.   It did reach 109s. 6d. in the middle of October—a price we are never likely to see.   The quartern loaf, of course, varied in like proportion—January 1s. 2¾d., December 1s. 4¼d., reaching in October 1s. 5d.

CHAPTER XVIII.

1810.

ALTHOUGH the Walcheren Expedition was undertaken, and failed, in 1809, it was criticized by the country, both in and out of Parliament, in this year.

It started in all its pride, and glory, on the 28th of July, 1809, a beautiful fleet of thirty-nine sail of the line, thirty-six frigates, besides accompanying gunboats and transports. These were under the command of Sir Richard Strachan, Admiral Otway, and Lord Gardner ; whilst the land force of forty thousand men was under the chief command of the Earl of Chatham, who was somewhat notorious for his indolence and inefficiency.

At first, the destination of the fleet was kept a profound secret, but it soon leaked out that Vlissing, or Flushing, in the Island of Walcheren, which lies at the mouth of the Scheldt, was the point aimed at. Middleburgh surrendered to the English on the 2nd of August, and on the 15th

after a fearful bombardment, the town of Flushing surrendered.   General Monnet, the commander, and over five
thousand men were taken prisoners of war.

Nothing was done to take advantage of this success, and,
on the 27th of August, when Sir Richard Strachan waited
upon the Earl of Chatham to learn the steps he intended
to take, he found, to his great disgust, that the latter had
come to the conclusion not to advance.

About the middle of September, the Earl, finding that
a large army was collecting at Antwerp, thought it would
be more prudent to leave with a portion of his army for
England, and accordingly did so.   He resolved to keep
Flushing, and the Island of Walcheren, to guard the mouth
of the Scheldt, and keep it open for British commerce ;
but it was a swampy, pestilential place, and the men sick-
ened, and died of fever, until, at last, the wretched remnant
of this fine army was obliged to return, and, on the 23rd of
December, 1809, Flushing was evacuated.

Popular indignation was very fierce with regard to
the Earl of Chatham, and a scathing epigram was made
on him, of which there are scarce two versions alike.

> " Lord Chatham, with his sword undrawn,
>   Stood, waiting for Sir Richard Strachan ;
>   Sir Richard, longing to be at 'em,
>   Stood waiting for the Earl of Chatham." [1]

The Caricaturists, of course, could not leave such a
subject alone, and Rowlandson drew two (September 14,
1809).   "A design for a Monument to be erected in commemoration of the glorious and never to be forgotten
Grand Expedition, so ably planned and executed in the
year 1809."   There is nothing particularly witty about
this print.   Amongst other things it has a shield on which
is William, the great Earl of Chatham, obscured by

---

[1] This version is taken from " The Life of the Right Hon. George Canning,"
by Robert Bell, London, 1846.   The first line, however, is generally rendered,
" The Earl of Chatham, with his sword drawn."

clouds; and the supporters are on one side a "British seaman in the dumps," and on the other "John Bull, somewhat gloomy, but for what, it is difficult to guess after so glorious an achievement." The motto is—

> " Great Chatham, with one hundred thousand men,
>   To Flushing sailed, and then sailed back again."

And ten days later—on the 24th of September—he published "General Chatham's marvellous return from his Exhibition of Fireworks."

The citizens of London were highly indignant at the incapacity displayed by the Earl of Chatham, and in December, they, through the Lord Mayor, memorialized the King, begging him to cause inquiry to be made as to the cause of the failure of the expedition; but George the Third did not brook interference, and he gave them a right royal snubbing. His answer was as follows:

" I thank you for your expressions of duty and attachment to me and to my family.

" The recent Expedition to the Scheldt was directed to several objects of great importance to the interest of my Allies, and to the security of my dominions.

" I regret that, of these objects, a part, only, has been accomplished. I have not judged it necessary to direct any Military Inquiry into the conduct of my Commanders by Sea or Land, in this conjoint service.

" It will be for my Parliament, in their wisdom, to ask for such information, or to take such measures upon this subject as they shall judge most conducive to the public good."

But the citizens, who bore their share of the war right nobly, would not stand this, and they held a Common Hall on the 9th of January, 1810, and instructed their representatives to move, or support, an Address to His Majesty, praying for an inquiry into the failures of the late expeditions

to Spain, Portugal, and Holland.   They drew up a similar
address, and asserted a right to deliver such address, or
petition, to the King upon his throne.

Nothing, however, came of it, and when Parliament was
opened, by Commission, on the 23rd of January, 1810, that
part of His Majesty's speech relating to the Walcheren
Expedition was extremely brief and unsatisfactory : "These
considerations determined His Majesty to employ his forces
on an expedition to the Scheldt.   Although the principal
ends of this expedition had not been attained, His Majesty
confidently hopes that advantages, materially affecting the
security of His Majesty's dominions in the further prosecution of the war, will be found to result from the demolition
of the docks, and arsenals, at Flushing.   This important
object His Majesty was enabled to accomplish, in consequence of the reduction of the Island of Walcheren by the
valour of his fleets and armies.   His Majesty has given
directions that such documents and papers should be laid
before you, as he trusts will afford satisfactory information
upon the subject of this expedition."

And Parliament had those papers, and fought over them
many nights ; held, also, a Select Committee on the Scheldt
Expedition, and examined many officers thereon ; and,
finally, on the 30th of March, they divided on what was
virtually a vote of censure on the Government, if not carried
—a motion declaratory of the approbation of the House in
the retention of Walcheren until its evacuation ; when the
numbers were—

Ayes	255
Noes	232
Majority for the Ministry	23

John, Earl of Chatham, had, however, to bow to the
storm, and resign his post of Master General of the
Ordnance; but his Court favour soon befriended him again.
Three years afterwards, he was made full General, and on

the death of the Duke of York he was appointed Governor of Gibraltar.

The 28th of February was set apart for the Annual Day of Fasting and Humiliation, and in its routine it resembled all others. The Lords went to Westminster Abbey, the Commons to St. Margaret's Church, and the Volunteers had Church Parades.

On the 1st of February, Mr. Francis Horner, M.P. for Wendover, moved for a variety of accounts, and returns, respecting the present state of the circulating medium, and the bullion trade. The price of gold was abnormally high, and paper proportionately depreciated. His conjecture to account for this—and it seems a highly probable one—was that the high price of gold might be produced partly by a larger circulation of Bank of England paper than was necessary, and partly by the new circumstances in which the foreign trade of this country was placed, by which a continual demand for bullion was produced, not merely to discharge the balance of trade, as in the ordinary state of things, but for the purpose of carrying on some of the most important branches of our commerce ; such as the purchase of naval stores from the Baltic, and grain from countries under the control and dominion of the enemy.

Recourse was had to an issue of Dollars in order to relieve the monetary pressure ; and we read in the *Morning Post* of February 22nd, "A large boat full of dollars is now on its way by the canal, from Birmingham. The dollars have all been re-stamped at Messrs. Bolton and Watts, and will be issued on their arrival at the Bank." These must not be confounded with the old Spanish dollars which were stamped earlier in the century, and about which there was such an outcry as to the Bank refusing to retake them ; but from the same handsome die as those struck in 1804 to guard against forgery—having on the Obverse, the King's head, with the legend, "GEORGIUS III. DEI GRATIA" ; and on the Reverse, the Royal Arms,

within the garter, crowned, and the legend, "BRITAN-
NIARUM REX. FIDEI DEFENSOR," and the date.[1]

But these were snapped up, and smuggled out of the
country, as we see by a paragraph in the same paper
(March 9th) : "Thirty thousand of the re-stamped dollars
were seized on board a Dutch Schuyt in the river, a few
days since. The public are, perhaps, little aware that the
Dutch fishermen, who bring us plaice and eels, will receive
nothing in return but gold and silver." This doubtless was
so, but no cargo of fish could have been worth 30,000 dollars.

Gold was scarce, as will be seen by the following note :
(April 3rd) : " Several ships were last week paid at Plymouth
all in new gold coin ; and, on Saturday last, the artificers
belonging to the Dockyard, were paid their wages in new
half-guineas. It was pleasing to see the smiles on the
men's countenances at the sight of these strangers. The
Jews and slop merchants are busily employed in purchasing
this desirable coin, and substituting provincial and other
bank paper in its room."

That a large, and profitable, trade was done in smuggling
the gold coinage out of the country is evident. *Morning
Post*, 28th of July : "Two fresh seizures have lately been
made of guineas, which have for some time been so scarce
that it is difficult to conceive whence the supply can have
been drawn. A deposit of 9,000 guineas, was on Thursday
discovered in a *snug* recess, at the head of the mast of a
small vessel in the Thames, which had just discharged a
cargo of French wheat; another seizure of 4,500 guineas
was made at Deal on the preceding day."

Morning Post, December 10, 1810 : " The tide surveyor
at Harwich seized, a few days since, on board a vessel at

[1] The number of dollars issued by the Bank of England to February 8,
1810, inclusive, was :

Dollars stamped in	1797	and issued	2,325,099
,, ,,	1804	,,	1,419,484
,, ,,	1809 and 1810	,,	1,073,051
	Total		4,817,634

that port, twenty-two bars of gold, weighing 2,870 ounces.
He found the gold concealed between the timbers of the
vessel, under about thirty tons of shingle ballast."

In writing the social history of this year, it would be
impossible to keep silence as to the episode of Sir Francis
Burdett's behaviour, and subsequent treatment.

Curiously enough, it arose out of the Scheldt Expedition.
On the 19th of February the Right Hon. Charles Yorke,
M.P. for Cambridgeshire, rose, and complained of a breach
of privilege in a placard printed by a certain John Dean—
which was as follows : " WINDHAM AND YORKE, BRITISH
FORUM, 33, BEDFORD STREET, COVENT GARDEN,
MONDAY, FEB. 19, 1810. Question :—Which was the
greater outrage upon the public feeling, Mr. Yorke's enforce-
ment of the standing order to exclude strangers from the
House of Commons, or Mr. Windham's recent attack upon
the liberty of the press ? The great anxiety manifested by
the public at this critical period to become acquainted with
the proceedings of the House of Commons, and to ascertain
who were the authors and promoters of the late calamitous
expedition to the Scheldt, together with the violent attacks
made by Mr. Windham on the newspaper reporters (whom
he described as ' bankrupts, lottery office keepers, footmen,
and decayed tradesmen ') have stirred up the public feeling,
and excited universal attention. The present question is
therefore brought forward as a comparative inquiry, and
may be justly expected to furnish a contested and interesting debate. Printed by J. Dean, 57, Wardour Street."
It was ordered that the said John Dean do attend at the
bar of the house the next day.

He did so, and pleaded that he was employed to print
the placard by John Gale Jones—and the interview ended
with John Dean being committed to the custody of the
Serjeant-at-Arms—and John Gale Jones, was ordered to
attend the House next day.

When he appeared at the bar, he acknowledged that he

was the author of the placard, and regretted that the printer should have been inconvenienced. That he had always considered it the privilege of every Englishman to animadvert on public measures, and the conduct of public men; but that, on looking over the paper again, he found he had erred, and, begging to express his contrition, he threw himself on the mercy of the House.

John Dean, meanwhile, had presented a petition, acknowledging printing the bill, but that it was done by his workmen without his personal attention. He was ordered to be brought to the bar, reprimanded, and discharged—all which came to pass. Gale, however, was committed to Newgate, where he remained until the 21st of June, when Parliament rose, in spite of a motion of Sir Samuel Romilly (April 16th) that he be discharged from his confinement; the House divided—Ayes 112; Noes 160; majority for his further imprisonment, 48.

On a previous occasion (March 12th), Sir Francis Burdett had moved his discharge, but, on a division, fourteen only were for it, and 153 against it. In his speech he denied the legal right of the House to commit any one to prison for such an offence—and he published in *Cobbett's Weekly Political Register* of Saturday, March 24, 1810, a long address: " SIR FRANCIS BURDETT TO HIS CONSTITUENTS; DENYING THE POWER OF THE HOUSE OF COMMONS TO IMPRISON THE PEOPLE OF ENGLAND." It is too long to reproduce, but its tone may be judged of, by the following extract : " At this moment, it is true, we see but one man actually in jail for having displeased those Gentlemen ; but the fate of this one man (as is the effect of punishments) will deter others from expressing their opinions of the conduct of those who have had the power, to punish him. And, moreover, it is in the nature of all power, and especially of assumed and undefined power, to increase as it advances in age ; and, as Magna Charta and the law of the land have not been sufficient to protect Mr. Jones ; as we have seen him sent to jail for having described the conduct of one of the members, as *an outrage upon public feeling*, what security have we, unless this power of imprisonment be given up, that we shall not see other men sent to jail for stating their opinion respecting Rotten Boroughs, respecting Placemen, and Pensioners, sitting in the House ; or, in short, for making any declaration, giving any opinion, stating any fact, betraying any feeling, whether by writing, by word of mouth, or by gesture, which may displease any of the Gentlemen assembled in St. Stephen's Chapel ? " This was supplemented by a most elaborate " Argument," and on the 27th of March the attention of Parliament was called thereto by Mr. Lethbridge, M.P. for Somerset.

The alleged breach of privilege was read by a clerk, and Sir Francis was called upon to say whatever he could, in answer to the charge preferred against him. He admitted the authorship both of the Address and Argument and would stand the issue of them. Mr. Lethbridge then moved the following resolutions : " 1st. Resolved that the Letter signed Francis Burdett, and the further Argument, which was published in the paper called *Cobbett's Weekly Register*, on the 24th of this instant, is a libellous and scandalous paper, reflecting upon the just rights and privileges of this House. 2nd. Resolved, That Sir Francis Burdett, who suffered the above articles to be printed with his name, and by his authority, has been guilty of a violation of the privileges of this House."

The debate was the fiercest of the session. It was adjourned to the 28th, and the 5th of April, when Mr. Lethbridge's resolutions were agreed to without a division, and Sir Robert Salusbury, M.P. for Brecon, moved that Sir Francis Burdett be committed to the Tower. An amendment was proposed that he be reprimanded in his place ; but, on being put, it was lost by 190 to 152—38, and at seven o'clock in the morning of the 6th of April, Sir Francis's doom was decreed.

CHAPTER XIX.

UP to this time the proceedings had been grave and dignified, but Sir Francis imported a ludicrous element into his capture.

Never was any arrest attempted in so gentlemanlike, and obliging a manner.[1] At half-past seven o'clock in the morning, as soon as the division in the House of Commons was known, Mr. Jones Burdett, accompanied by Mr. O'Connor, who had remained all night at the House of Commons, set off in a post chaise to Wimbledon, and informed Sir Francis Burdett of the result. Sir Francis immediately mounted his horse, and rode to town. He found a letter on his table from Mr. Colman, the Serjeant-at-Arms, acquainting him that he had received a warrant, signed by the Speaker, to arrest and convey him to the Tower, and he begged to know when he might wait on him; that it was his wish to show him the utmost respect, and, therefore, if he preferred to take his horse, and ride to the Tower, he would meet him there.

---

[1] The account of Sir F. Burdett's arrest, &c., is mainly taken from the *Annual Register*, vol. lii.

To this very courteous and considerate letter, Sir Francis replied that he should be happy to receive him at noon next day. However, before this letter could reach the Serjeant-at-Arms, he called on Sir Francis, and verbally informed him that he had a warrant against him. Sir Francis told him he should be ready for him at twelve next day, and Mr. Colman bowed, and retired. Indeed it was so evidently the intention of the baronet to go to his place of durance quietly, that, in the evening, he sent a friend to the Tower to see if preparations had been made to receive him, and it was found that every consideration for his comfort had been taken.

But the urbane Serjeant-at-Arms, when he made his report to the Speaker, was mightily scolded by him for not executing his warrant, and at 8 p.m. he called, with a messenger, on Sir Francis, and told him that he had received a severe reprimand from the Speaker for not executing his warrant in the morning, and remaining with his prisoner.

Sir Francis replied that he should not have allowed him to have remained, and that he would not yield a voluntary assent to the warrant, but would only give in, in presence of an overwhelming force. The Serjeant-at-Arms then withdrew, having refused to be the bearer of a letter to the Speaker, which was afterwards conveyed to that dignitary by private hands. In this letter he asserted he would only submit to superior force, and insultingly said, " Your warrant, sir, I believe you know to be illegal. I know it to be so."

On the morning of the 7th of April another attempt was made by a messenger of the House to serve him with the warrant and arrest him ; but, although Sir Francis read it and put it in his pocket, he told the messenger that he might return and inform the Speaker that he would not obey it. The poor man said his orders were to remain there ; but he was commanded to retire, and had to go.

Later in the day, between twelve and one, came a troop

of Life Guards, who pranced up and down the road and pavement and dispersed the people, who heartily hissed them. A magistrate read the Riot Act; the troops cleared the road, and formed two lines across Piccadilly, where Sir Francis lived; and so strictly was this cordon kept, that they refused to allow his brother to pass to his dinner, until he was accompanied by a constable. Sir Francis wrote to the Sheriffs complaining of his house being beset by a military force.

No further attempt to execute the warrant was made that day, nor on the following day, which was Sunday.

But the majesty of Parliament would brook no further trifling, and on the Monday morning (April 9th), after breakfast, when "Sir Francis was employed in hearing his son (who had just come from Eton school) read and translate Magna Charta," a man's head was observed looking in at the window, the same man advertising his advent by smashing a pane or two of glass. Great credit was taken that no one threw this man off his ladder, but, probably, the sight of the troops in front of the house, acted as a deterrent. The civil authorities, however, had effected an entrance by the basement, and entered the drawing-room, where a pretty little farce was acted.

"The *Serjeant-at-Arms* said: 'Sir Francis, you are my prisoner.'

"*Sir Francis.* By what authority do you act, Mr. Serjeant? By what power, sir, have you broken into my house, in violation of the laws of the land?

"*Serjeant.* Sir Francis, I am authorized by the warrant of the Speaker of the House of Commons.

"*Sir Francis.* I contest the authority of such a warrant. Exhibit to me the legal warrant by which you have dared to violate my house. Where is the Sheriff? Where is the Magistrate?

"At this time there was no magistrate, but he soon afterwards appeared.

"*Serjeant.* Sir Francis, my authority is in my hand: I will read it to you: it is the warrant of the Right Honourable the Speaker of the House of Commons.

"And here Mr. Colman attempted to read the warrant, but which he did with great trepidation.

"*Sir Francis.* I repeat to you, that it is no sufficient warrant. No—not to arrest my person in the open street, much less to break open my house in violation of all law. If you have a warrant from His Majesty, or from a proper officer of the King, I will pay instant obedience to it; but I will not yield to an illegal order.

"*Serjeant.* Sir Francis, I demand you to yield in the name of the Commons House of Parliament, and I trust you will not compel me to use force. I entreat you to believe that I wish to show you every respect.

"*Sir Francis.* I tell you distinctly that I will not voluntarily submit to an unlawful order; and I demand, in the King's name, and in the name of the law, that you forthwith retire from my house.

"*Serjeant.* Then, sir, I must call in assistance, and force you to yield.

"Upon which the constables laid hold of Sir Francis. Mr. Jones Burdett and Mr. O'Connor immediately stepped up, and each took him under an arm. The constables closed in on all three, and drew them downstairs.

"*Sir Francis* then said: 'I protest in the King's name against this violation of my person and my house. It is superior force only that hurries me out of it, and you do it at your peril.'"

A coach was ready, surrounded by Cavalry, and Sir Francis and his friends entered it. The possibility of a popular demonstration, or attempt at rescue, was evidently feared, for the escort consisted of two squadrons of the 15th Light Dragoons, two troops of Life Guards, with a magistrate at their head; then came the coach, followed by two more troops of Life Guards, another troop of the 15th

Light Dragoons, two battalions of Foot Guards, the rear being formed by another party of the 15th Light Dragoons. After escorting through Piccadilly, the Foot Guards left, and marched straight through the City, to await the prisoner at the Tower.

His escort went a very circuitous route, ending in Moorfields, the result of an arrangement between the authorities and the Lord Mayor, by which, if the one did not go through Temple Bar and the heart of the City, the Lord Mayor would exert all his authority within his bounds, as indeed he did, meeting, and heading, the cavalcade.

During his ride, Sir Francis, as might have been expected, posed, sitting well forward so that he might be well seen. It could hardly be from apathy, for the lower orders considered him as their champion ; but, either from the body of accompanying troops, or the curious route taken, the journey to the Tower passed off almost without incident, except a little crying out, until the Minories was reached, when the East End—and it was a hundred times rougher than now—poured forth its lambs to welcome their shepherd. The over-awing force on Tower Hill prevented any absolute outbreak. There were shouts of " Burdett for ever ! " and a few of the mob got tumbled into the shallow water of the Tower ditch, whence they emerged, probably all the better for the unwonted wash. No attempt at rescue seems to have been made, and the Tower gates were safely reached. The coach drew up ; the Serjeant-at-Arms entered the little wicket to confer with the military authorities ; the great gates swung open ; the cannon boomed forth their welcome to the prisoner, and Sir Francis was safely caged.

Up to this time the roughs had had no fun ; it had been tame work, and, if the military got away unharmed, it would have been a day lost ; so brickbats, stones, and sticks were thrown at them without mercy. The soldiers' tempers had been sorely tried ; orders were given to fire, and some of the mob fell. The riot was kept up until the troops had left Fenchurch Street, and then the cost thereof was counted in the shape of one killed and eight wounded. A contemporary account says : " The confusion was dreadful, but the effect was the almost immediate dispersion of the mob in every direction. A great part of them seemed in a very advanced state of intoxication and otherwise infuriated to madness, for some time braving danger in every shape. In all the route of the military the streets were crowded beyond all possibility of description ; all the shops were shut up, and the most dreadful alarm for some time prevailed."

There were fears of another riot taking place when night fell, but preparations were made. The Coldstream Guards were under orders, and each man was furnished with thirty rounds of ball cartridge. Several military parties paraded the streets till a late hour, and the cannon in St. James's Park were loaded with ball. Happily, however, all was quiet, and these precautions, although not unnecessary, were un-needed.

Next day the Metropolis was quiet, showing that the sympathy with the frothy hero of the hour, however loud it might be, was not deep. Even at the Tower, which contained all that there was of the origin of this mischief, the extra Guards were withdrawn, and ingress and egress to the fortress were as ordinarily—the prisoner's friends being allowed to visit him freely. This episode may be closed with the consolatory feeling that the one man who was killed had been exceedingly active in attacking the military, and, at the moment when the shot was fired which deprived him of existence, he was in the act of throwing a brickbat at the soldiers. History does not record whether he was accompanied to his grave by weeping brother bricklayers.

We have seen that Sir Francis Burdett proffered a letter, addressed to the Speaker to the Serjeant-at-Arms, which

the latter very properly refused to deliver, and, on the 9th
of April, this letter formed the subject of a debate in the
House of Commons.   The Serjeant-at-Arms was examined
by the House as to the particulars of the recalcitrant
baronet's arrest, and the Speaker added his testimony to
the fact of his reproving the Serjeant for not obeying
orders.   The debate was adjourned until the next day, and
it ended, according to Hansard, thus :

"It appearing to be the general sentiment that the
Letter should not be inserted on the Journals, the Speaker
said he would give directions accordingly.   It being also
understood that the Amendments moved should not appear
on the Journals, the Speaker said he would give directions
accordingly, and the question was put as an original
motion, 'That it is the opinion of this House, that the said
Letter is a high and flagrant breach of the privileges of the
House; but it appearing from the report of the Serjeant-
at-Arms attending this House, that the warrant of the
Speaker for the commitment of Sir Francis Burdett to the
Tower has been executed, this House will not, at this time,
proceed further on the said letter.'   Agreed *nem con.*"

Then followed a scene that has its parallel in our days,
with another demagogue.   Sir Francis Burdett commenced
actions against the Speaker, the Serjeant-at-Arms, and the
Earl of Moira, who was then Governor of the Tower.   We
know how easily petitions are got up, and this case was
no exception ; but Sir Francis was kept in well-merited
incarceration, until the Prorogation of Parliament on the
21st of June, which set him free.   The scene on his liberation is very graphically described by a contemporary :

"The crowd for some time continued but slowly to
increase, but towards three o'clock, their numbers were
rapidly augmented ; and, shortly after three, as fitting a
rabble as ever were 'raked together' appeared on Tower
Hill.   The bands in the neighbourhood frequently struck
up a tune; and the assembled rabble as frequently huzzaed

(*they knew not why*), and thus between them, for an hour or two, they kept up a scene of continual jollity and uproar.

"The *Moorfields Cavalry*[1] had by this time arrived at the scene of action. Everything was prepared to carry Sir Francis (like the effigy of Guy Fawkes on the 5th of November) through the City. The air was rent by repeated shouts of 'Burdett for ever!' 'Magna Charta!' and 'Trial by Jury!' The blessings of the last, many of these patriots had doubtless experienced, and were, therefore, justified in expressing themselves with warmth. While these shouts burst spontaneously from the elated rabble, and every eye was turned towards the Tower, with the eagerness of hope, and the anxiety of expectation—on a sudden, intelligence was received that they had all been made fools of by Sir Francis, who, ashamed, probably, of being escorted through the City by such a band of 'ragged rumped' vagabonds, had left the Tower, crossed the water, and proceeded to Wimbledon.

"To describe the scene which followed—the vexation of the Westminster electors, the mortification of the *Moorfields Cavalry*, and the despair of '*The Hope*,' in adequate colours, is impossible. Petrified by the news, for some time they remained on the spot undetermined how to act, and affecting to disbelieve the report. Unwilling, however, to be disappointed of their fondest hope—that of showing *themselves*—they determined on going through the streets in procession, though they could not accompany Sir Francis. The pageant accordingly commenced, the *empty* vehicle intended for Sir Francis took that part in the procession which he was to have taken, and the rational part of the mob consoled themselves by reflecting that, as they had originally set out to accompany *emptiness* they were not altogether disappointed.

"It was now proposed by some of the mob, that as they

---

[1] A number of persons on horseback, who met at Moorfields.

could not have the honour of escorting Sir Francis Burdett
from the Tower, they should conclude the day by conducting
MR. GALE JONES from Newgate, and he, shortly after, fell
into the procession in a hackney coach.

"On the arrival of the procession in Piccadilly, it went off
to the northward, and the vehicles returned by a different
route from that which they went. The whole of the
streets and windows were crowded, from Tower Hill, to
Piccadilly.

"About one o'clock a party of Burdettites from Soho,
with blue cockades and colours flying, proceeded down
Catherine Street, and the Strand, for the City. They
marched two and two. At Catherine Street they were
met by the 12th Light Dragoons on their way to Hyde
Park Corner. The music of the former was playing *St.
Patrick's Day.* The Band of the Dragoons immediately
struck up *God save the King.* The 14th Light Dragoons
followed the 12th; both regiments mustering very strong.
All the Volunteers were under orders; and the Firemen
belonging to the several Insurance Offices paraded the
streets, with music, acting as constables."

CHAPTER XX.

Good harvest—Thanksgiving for same—List of poor Livings—Another Jubilee—
Illness and death of the Princess Amelia— Effect on the King—Prayers for his
restoration to health—Funeral of the Princess—Curious position of the Houses
of Parliament—Proposition for a Regency—Close of the first decade of the
XIXth Century.

IT gives great pleasure to record that the Harvest this year was plentiful, so bountiful, indeed, as to stir up feelings of gratitude in the national breast, and induce the manufacture of a "Form of prayer and thanksgiving to Almighty God, for His mercy in having vouchsafed to bestow on this Nation an abundant crop, and favourable harvest." The farmers and laics benefited thereby, but the position of the Clergy at that time was far from being very high, at least with regard to worldly remuneration — *vide* the following :

Account of Livings in England and Wales under £150 a year.

Not exceeding £10 a year		...	...	...	12
From £10 to £20 inclusive		...	...	...	72
From £20 to £30	,,	...	...	...	191
From £30 to £40	,,	...	...	...	353
From £40 to £50	,,	...	...	...	433
From £50 to £60	,,	...	...	...	407
From £60 to £70	,,	...	...	...	376
From £70 to £80	,,	...	...	...	319

From £80 to £90 inclusive	...	...	...	309
From £90 to £100 ,,		...	...	... 315
From £100 to £110 ,,		...	...	... 283
From £110 to £120 ,,		...	...	... 307
From £120 to £130 ,,		...	...	... 246
From £130 to £140 ,,		...	...	... 205
From £140 to £150 ,,		...	...	... 170
		Total ...	...	3998

"Of these very small livings three are in the diocese of Lichfield and Coventry, three in that of Norwich, two in that of St. David's, one in that of Llandaff, one in that of London, one in that of Peterborough, and one in that of Winchester."

This does not show a very flourishing state of things, although money could be spent freely in support of foreign clergy as we see by the accounts for this year : " Emigrant clergy and laity of France, £161,542 2s."

One would think that two Jubilees in one twelvemonth was almost too much of a good thing, but our great-grandfathers thought differently. There had already been one, to celebrate the fact of the King entering on the fiftieth year of his reign, they must now have one to chronicle its close. But, although there was somewhat of the " poor debtor " element introduced, it was by no means as enthusiastically received as it had been twelve months previously.

This time we hear more of festive meetings: a Jubilee Ball at the Argyle Rooms—then very decorous and proper —another at the New Rooms, Kennington, and a grand dinner at Montpelier House, whilst Camberwell, Vauxhall, Kennington, and Lambeth all furnished materials for festivity. Needless to say, there were new Jubilee medals.

But the poor old King was getting ill, and troubled about his daughter, the Princess Amelia, who lay a dying. Poor girl! she knew she had not long to live, and she wished to give the King some personal souvenir. She had a very valuable and choice stone, which she wished to have made into a ring for him. As her great thought and most earnest wish was to give this to her father before her death, a jeweller was sent for express from London, and it was soon made, and she had her desire gratified. On His Majesty going to the bedside of the Princess, as was his daily wont, she put the ring upon his finger without saying a word. The ring told its own tale: it bore as an inscription her name, and "*Remember me when I am gone.*" A lock of her hair was also worked into the ring.

The mental anguish caused by this event, and by the knowledge that death was soon to claim the Princess, was too much for the King to bear. Almost blind, and with enfeebled intellect, he had not strength to bear up against the terrible blow.

At first the papers said he had a slight cold, but the next day it was found to be of no use concealing his illness. The *Morning Post* of the 31st of October says: " It is with hearfelt sorrow we announce that His Majesty's indisposition still continues. It commenced with the effect produced upon his tender parental feelings on receiving the ring from the hand of his afflicted, beloved daughter, the affecting inscription upon which caused him, blessed and most amiable of men, to burst into tears, with the most heart-touching lamentations on the present state, and approaching dissolution, of the afflicted, and interesting Princess. His Majesty is attended by Drs. Halford, Heberden, and Baillie, who issue daily bulletins of the state of the virtuous and revered monarch, for whose speedy recovery the prayers of all good men will not fail to be offered up." And there was public prayer made " for the restoration of His Majesty's health."

The Princess Amelia died on the 2nd of November, and was buried with due state. In her coffin were "8,000 nails —6 000 small and 2,000 large; eight large plates and handles resembling the Tuscan Order; a crown at the top, of the same description as issued from the Heralds' Office; two palm branches in a cross saltier, under the crown, with P. A. (the initials of her Royal Highness). They are very massy, and have the grandest effect, being executed in the most highly-finished style, and neat manner possible. Forty-eight plates, with a crown, two palm branches in cross saltier, with the Princess Royal's coronet at top; eight bevil double corner plates, with the same ornaments inscribed, and one at each corner of the cover."

The King's illness placed Parliament in a very awkward position. It stood prorogued till the 1st of November, on which day both Houses met, but sorely puzzled how to proceed, because there was no commission, nor was the King in a fit state to sign one. The Speaker took his seat, and said, "The House is now met, this being the last day to which Parliament was prorogued; but I am informed, that notwithstanding His Majesty's proclamation upon the subject of a farther prorogation, no message is to be expected from His Majesty's commissioners upon that subject, no commission for prorogation being made out. Under such circumstances I feel it my duty to take the chair, in order that the House may be able to adjourn itself." And both Houses were left to their own devices. The head was there, but utterly incompetent to direct.

So they kept on, doing no public work, but examining the King's physicians as to his state. They held out hopes of his recovery—perhaps in five or six months, perhaps in twelve or eighteen; but, in the meantime, really energetic steps must be taken to meet the emergency. On the 20th of November the Chancellor of the Exchequer moved three resolutions embodying the facts that His Majesty was incapacitated by illness from attending to business, and that the personal exercise of the royal authority is thereby suspended, therefore Parliament must supply the defect. It was then that the Regency of the Prince of Wales was proposed, and in January, 1811, an Act was passed, entitled,

"An Act to provide for the Administration of the Royal Authority, and for the Care of the Royal Person during the Continuance of His Majesty's illness, and for the Resumption of the Exercise of the Royal Authority." The Prince of Wales was to exercise kingly powers, which, however, were much shorn in the matters of granting peerages, and granting offices and pensions ; whilst the Queen, assisted by a Council, was to have the care of His Majesty's person, and the direction of his household.

As a proof of the sympathy evinced by the people with the King in his illness, all pageantry was omitted on the 9th of November, when the Lord Mayor went to Westminster to be sworn in.

At the close of 1810 the National Debt amounted to the grand total of £811,898,083 12s. 3¾d. Three per Cent. Consols began at 70¾, touched in July 71½, and left off in December 66¼. Wheat averaged 95s. per quarter, and the quartern loaf was, in January, 1s. 4¼d. ; June, 1s. 5d. ; December, 1s. 3d.

Here ends the chronicle of the First Decade of the Nineteenth Century.

CHAPTER XXI.

PERHAPS as good a test as any, of the civilization
of a nation, is its roads. From the mere foot-tracks
of the savage, to the broader paths necessarily used
when he had brought the horse into subjugation, mark
a distinct advance. When the wheeled carriage was invented, a causeway, artificially strengthened, must be made,
or the wheels would sink into the soft earth, and make ruts,
which would need extra power in order to extricate the
vehicle ; besides the great chance there was of that vehicle
coming to utter grief. Settlers in Africa and Australia
can yet tell tales of the inconveniences of a land without
roads.

To the Romans, as for much else of our civilization, we
are indebted for our knowledge of road making—nay, even
for some of our roads still existing—but these latter were
the main arteries of the kingdom, the veins had yet to be
developed. That roads mean civilization is apparent,
because without them there could be little or no inter-
communication between communities, and no opportunity
for traffic and barter with each other. We, in our day,

have been spoilt, by, almost suddenly, having had a road
traffic thrown open to us, which renders every village in our
Isles, of comparatively easy access, so that we are apt to
look with disfavour on the old times. Seated, or lying, in
the luxurious ease of a Pullman car—going at sixty miles
an hour—it is hard to realize a tedious journey by waggon,
or even an outside journey by the swifter, yet slow, mail or
stage coach, with its many stoppages, and its not altogether
pleasant adventures. For, considering the relative numbers
of persons travelling, there were far more accidents, and of

A STAGE COACH—1804.

a serious kind, than in these days of railways. It was all
very well, on the introduction of steam to say, "If you are
upset off a coach, why there you are ! but if you are in a
railway accident, where are you ? " The coach might break
down, as it often did, a wheel come off, or an axle, or a pole
break—or the coach might be, as it ofttimes was, over-
loaded, and then in a rut—why, over all went. The horses,
too, were apt to cast shoes, slip down, get their legs over
the traces, or take to kicking, besides which the harness
would snap, either the traces, or the breeching, or the reins,

and these terrors were amplified by the probability of encountering highwaymen, who were naturally attracted to attack the stage coaches, not only on account of the money and valuables which the passengers carried with them, but because parcels of great price were entrusted to the coachman, such as gold, or notes and securities, for country banks, remittances between commercial firms, &c.

In the illustration showing a stage coach, it will be seen that there is a supplementary portion attached, made of

THE STAGE WAGGON.

wicker-work, and called "the basket." This was for the reception of parcels. The mail coaches, which took long, direct routes, will be spoken of under the heading of Post Office.

Inconvenient to a degree, as were these stage coaches, with exposure to all changes of weather, if outside—or else cooped up in a very stuffy inside, with possibly disagreeable, or invalid, companions—they were the only means of communication between those places unvisited by the mail coach, and also for those which required a more frequent service. They were very numerous, so much so that, although I began to count them, I gave up the task, as not being " worth the candle."

But it was not every one who could afford to travel by stage coach, and for them was the stage waggon, or caravan, huge and cumbrous machines, with immensely broad wheels, so as to take a good grip of the road, and make light of the ruts. These machines, and the few canals then in existence, did the inland goods carriage of the whole of England. Slow and laborious was their work, but they poked a few passengers among the goods, and carried them very cheaply. They were a remnant of the previous century, and, in the pages of Smollett, and other writers, we hear a great deal of these waggons.

To give some idea of them, their route, and the time they used to take on their journey, I must make one example suffice, taken haphazard from a quantity. (1802.)

" *Tunbridge Wells, and Tunbridge Original Waggon.* To the Queen's Head Inn, Borough.

" By J. Hunt.

" Late Chesseman and Morphew. Under an establishment of more than sixty years. Sets out from the New Inn, Tunbridge Wells, every Monday and Thursday morning, and arrives at the above Inn, every Tuesday and Friday morning, from whence it returns the same days at noon, and arrives at Tunbridge Wells every Wednesday and Saturday afternoon, and from September 1st to December 25th a Waggon sets out from Tunbridge Wells every Wednesday and Saturday morning, and arrives at the above Inn every Monday and Thursday morning, from whence it returns the same days at noon, and arrives at Tunbridge Wells every Tuesday and Friday afternoon, carrying goods and parcels to and from—

Tunbridge Wells.	Mayfield.
Tunbridge.	Wadhurst.
Groombridge.	Ticehurst.
Langton.	Mark Cross.
Spaldhurst.	Frant.
Ashurst.	Eridge.
Rotherfield.	Southboro, &c.

" No Money, Plate, Jewels, Writings, Watches, Rings, Lace, Glass, nor any Parcel above Five Pounds Value, will be accounted for, unless properly entered, and paid for as such.

" Waggons or Carts from Tunbridge Wells to Brighton, Eastbourne, &c., occasionally."

Now Tunbridge is only thirty-six miles from London, and yet it took over twenty-four hours to reach.

Of course, those who had carriages of their own, or hired them, could go " post," *i.e.*, have fresh horses at certain recognized stations, leaving the tired ones behind them. This was of course travelling luxuriously, and people had to pay for it. In the latter part of the eighteenth century, there had been, well, not a famine, but a great scarcity of corn, and oats naturally rose, so much so that the post-masters had to raise their price, generally to 1s. 2d. per horse per mile, a price which seems to have obtained until the latter part of 1801, when among the advertisements of the *Morning Post*, September 23rd, I find, " Four Swans, Waltham Cross. Dean Wostenholme begs leave most respectfully to return thanks to the Noblemen and Gentlemen who have done him the honour to use his house, and to inform them that he has lowered the price of Posting to One Shilling per mile," &c.

And there was, of course, the convenient hackney coach,

which was generally the cast-off and used up carriage of some gentleman, whose arms, even, adorned the panels, a practice (the bearing of arms) which still obtains in our cabs. The fares were not extravagant, except in view of the different values of money. Every distance not exceeding one mile 1s., not exceeding one mile and a half, 1s. 6d., not exceeding two miles 2s., and so on. There were many other clauses, as to payment, waiting, radius, &c., but they are uninteresting.

A little book[1] says: "The hackney coaches in London were formerly limited to 1,000; but, by an Act of Parliament, the number is increased. Hackney coachmen are, in general, depraved characters, and several of them have been convicted as receivers of stolen goods," and it goes on to suggest their being licensed.

The old sedan chair was not obsolete, but was extensively used to take ladies to evening parties; and, as perhaps we may never again meet with a table of the chairmen's charges, I had better take it:

RATES OF CHAIRMEN.[2]

	s.	d.
For the first hour, if paid by an hour ...	1	6
For every hour afterwards	0	6
For any distance not exceeding one mile	1	0
For one mile to one mile and a half	1	6
For every half mile afterwards	0	6

In fact, their fares were almost identical with those of the hackney coachmen, and offending chairmen were subject to the same penalties.

The roads were kept up by means of turnpikes, exemption from payment of which was very rare; royalty, the mails, military officers, &c., on duty, and a few more, were all.

The main roads were good, and well kept; the bye, and occupation roads were bad. But on the main roads there

---

[1] "A View of London; or, The Stranger's Guide, 1803-4."
[2] "The Picture of London for 1802."

was plenty of traffic to pay for repairs.   It was essentially
a horsey age—by which I do not mean to infer that our
grand and great-grandfathers, copied their grooms either in
their dress or manners, as the youth of this generation
aspire to do ; but the only means of locomotion for any
distance was necessarily on horseback, or by means of
horse-flesh.   Every man could ride, and all wore boots and
breeches when out of doors, a style of equine dress unsur-
passed to this day.

The carriages were improving in build ; no longer being
low, and suspended by leather straps, they went to the
other extreme, and were perched a-top of high C springs.
The *Times*, January 17, 1803, says : " Many alterations have
lately taken place in the building of carriages.   The roofs
are not so round, nor are the bodies hung so low, as they
have been for the last two years.   The circular springs
have given place to whip springs ; the reason is, the first
are much more expensive, and are not so light in weight
as the others.   No boots are now used, but plain coach
boxes, with open fore ends.   Barouche boxes are now the
ton.   During the last summer ladies were much oftener
seen travelling seated on the box than in the carriage.
Hammer-cloths, except on state occasions, are quite out of
date, and the dickey box is following their example.   To
show the difference between the carriages of the present
day, and those built ten years ago, it is only necessary to
add that in the year 1793 the weight of a fashionable
carriage was about 1,900 pounds ; a modern one weighs
from 1,400 to 1,500."

CHAPTER XXII.

CERTAIN of the *jeunesse dorée* took to driving,
probably arising from the fact of riding outside
the stage coaches, and being occasionally indulged
with " handling the ribbons " and " tooling " the horses for
a short distance—of course for a consideration, by means
of which " the jarvey "[1] made no mean addition to his
income, which, by the by, was not a bad one, as every
traveller gave him something, and all his refreshment at
the various inns at which the coach stopped was furnished
free. These young men started a " Whip Club," and the
following is a description of a " meet " :

"The WHIP CLUB met on Monday morning in Park
Lane, and proceeded from thence to dine at Harrow-on-
the-Hill. There were fifteen barouche landaus with four
horses to each ; the drivers were all men of known skill in
the science of charioteering. Lord Hawke, Mr. Buxton,
and the Hon. Lincoln Stanhope were among the leaders.

" The following was the style of the set out : Yellow-

---

[1] The generic name for coachman.

bodied carriages, with whip springs and dickey boxes ;
cattle of a bright bay colour, with plain silver ornaments
on the harness, and rosettes to the ears.   Costume of the
drivers : A light drab colour cloth coat made full, single
breast, with three tiers of pockets, the skirts reaching to
the ankles ; a mother of pearl button of the size of a crown
piece.   Waistcoat, blue and yellow stripe, each stripe an
inch in depth.   Small cloths corded with silk plush, made
to button over the calf of the leg, with sixteen strings and
rosettes to each knee.   The boots very short, and finished
with very broad straps, which hung over the tops and
down to the ankle.   A hat three inches and a half deep in
the crown only, and the same depth in the brim exactly.
Each wore a large bouquet at the breast, thus resembling
the coachmen of our nobility, who, on the natal day of our
beloved sovereign, appear, in that respect, so peculiarly
distinguished.   The party moved along the road at a
smart trot ; the first whip gave some specimens of superiority at the outset by ' cutting a fly off a leader's ear.' " [1]

"ON THE WHIP CLUB.

" Two varying races are in Briton born,
     One courts a nation's praises, one her scorn ;
     Those pant her sons o'er tented fields to guide,
     Or steer her thunders thro' the foaming tide ;
     Whilst these, disgraceful born in luckless hour,
     Burn but to guide with skill a coach and four.
     To guess their sires each a sure clue affords,
     These are the coachmen's sons, and those my Lord's.
     Both follow Fame, pursuing different courses ;
     Those, Britain, scourge thy foes—and these thy horses ;
     Give them their due, nor let occasion slip ;
     On those thy laurels lay—on these thy whip ! " [2]

According to the *Morning Post*, April 3, 1809, the title
of the " Whip Club " was changed then to the " Four in

[1] *Morning Post*, June 9, 1808.
[2] *Annual Register*, vol. lix. p. 883.

Hand Club," and their first meet is announced for the 28th of April. " So fine a cavalcade has not been witnessed in this country, at any period, as these gentlemen will exhibit on that day, in respect to elegantly tasteful new carriages and beautiful horses ; the latter will be all high bred cattle, and their estimated value will exceed three hundred guineas each. All superfluous ornaments will be omitted on the harness ; gilt, instead of plated furniture."

The meet took place, as advised, in Cavendish Square, the costume of the drivers being as follows : A blue (single breast) coat, with a long waist, and brass buttons, on which were engraved the words " Four in Hand Club" ; waistcoat of Kerseymere, ornamented with alternate stripes of blue and yellow ; small clothes of white corduroy, made moderately high, and very long over the knee, buttoning in front over the shin bone. Boots very short, with long tops, only one outside strap to each, and one to the back ; the latter were employed to keep the breeches in their proper longitudinal shape. Hat with a conical crown, and the *Allen* brim (whatever that was) ; box, or driving coat, of white drab cloth, with fifteen capes, two tiers of pockets, and an inside one for the Belcher handkerchief ; cravat of white muslin spotted with black. Bouquets of myrtle, pink, and yellow geraniums were worn. In May of the same year, the club button had already gone out of fashion, and "Lord Hawke sported yesterday, *as buttons*, Queene Anne's shillings ; Mr. Ashurst displayed crown pieces."

Fancy driving was not confined to one club ; besides the " Four in Hand," there were " The Barouche Club," " The Defiance Club," and " The Tandem Club."

One of the most showy of these charioteers was a gentleman, who was irreverently termed " Tommy Onslow" (afterwards Lord Cranley), whose portrait is given here. So far did he imitate the regular *Jehu* that he had his legs swathed in hay-bands. Of him was written, under the picture of which the accompanying is only a portion—

> " What can little T. O. do ?
> Why, drive a Phaeton and Two ! !
> Can little T. O. do no more ?
> Yes, drive a Phaeton and Four ! ! ! ! "

One of his driving feats may be chronicled (*Morning Herald*, June 26, 1802): "A curious bet was made last

"TOMMY ONSLOW."

week, that Lord Cranley could drive a phaeton and four into a certain specified narrow passage, turn about, and return out of it, without accident to man, horse, or carriage. Whether it was Cranbourn, or Sidney's Alley, or Russell Court, or the Ride of a Livery Stable, we cannot tell ; but, without being able to state the particulars, we understand that the phaetonic feat was performed with dexterity and success, and that his Lordship was completely triumphant."

In London, of course, the Park was the place for showing off both beautiful horses, and men's riding, and the accompanying illustration portrays Lord Dillon, an accomplished rider, showing people

IIOW TO BREAK IN MY OWN IIORSE.

The costume here is specially noteworthy, as it shows a very advanced type of dandy.

That this was not the ordinary costume for riding in "the Row," is shown in the accompanying illustration, where it is far more business-like, and fitted for the purpose.

As we see, from every contemporary print and painting, the horses were of a good serviceable type, as dissimilar as possible from our racer, but closely resembling a well-bred hunter. They had plenty of bottom, which was needful,

14

for they were often called upon to perform what now would be considered as miracles of endurance. Take the following from the *Annual Register*, March 24, 1802, and bearing in mind the sea passage, without steam, and in a little tub

ROTTEN ROW—1803.

of a boat, and it is marvellous : " Mr. Hunter performed his journey from Paris to London in twenty-two hours, the shortest space of time that journey has ever been made in "

CHAPTER XXIII.

THERE was, however, another highway, well called
"the silent." The river Thames was then really
used for traffic, and numerous boats plied for hire
from every "stair," as the steps leading down to the river
were called. The watermen were licensed by their Company,
and had not yet left off wearing the coat and badge, now alas!
obsolete—even the so-called "Doggett's coat and badge"
being now commuted for a money payment. These watermen were not overpaid, and had to work hard for their
living. By their code of honour they ought to take a fare
in strict rotation, as is done in our present cab ranks—but
they were rather a rough lot, and sometimes used to
squabble for a fare. Rowlandson gives us such a scene and
places it at Wapping Old Stairs.

In 1803 they had, for their better regulation, to wear
badges in their hats, and, according to the *Times* of July
the 7th, the Lord Mayor fined several the full penalty of
40s. for disobeying this order, "but promised, if they
brought him a certificate of wearing the badge, and other
good behaviour, for one month, he would remit the fine."

Their fares were not exorbitant, and they were generally given a little more—they could be hired, too, by the day, or half day, but this was a matter of agreement, generally from 7s. to 10s. 6d. per diem ; and, in case of misbehaviour the number of his boat could be taken, and punishment fell swiftly upon the offender.   Taking London Bridge as a centre, the longest journey *up* the river was to Windsor, and the fare was 14s. for the whole boat, or 2s. each person. *Down* the river Gravesend was the farthest, the fare for the whole boat being 6s. or 1s. each.   These were afterwards increased to 21s. and 15s. respectively.   Just to cross the water was cheap enough—1d. below, and 2d. above the bridge, for each person.   It would seem, however, as if some did not altogether abide by the legal fares, for " A Citizen " rushed into print in the *Morning Post*, September 6, 1810, with the following pitiful tale : " The other night, about nine o'clook, I took a boat (*sculls* [1]) at Westminster Bridge to Vauxhall, and offered the waterman, on landing, *two shillings (four times his fare)* in consideration of having three friends with me ; he not only refused to take my money, but, with the greatest insolence, insisted upon having three shillings, to which extortion I was obliged to yield before he would suffer us to leave the shore, and he was aided in his robbery, by his fellows, who came mobbing round us."

Gravesend was, as a rule, the " Ultima Thule " of the Cockney, although Margate was sometimes reached ; but Margate and Ramsgate, to say nothing of Brighton, were considered too aristocratic for tradespeople to frequent, although some did go to Margate.   For these long and venturesome voyages, boats called " Hoys " were used— one-masted boats, sometimes with a boom to the mainsail, and sometimes without ; rigged very much like a cutter. They are said to have taken their name from being hailed (" *Ahoy* ") to stop to take in passengers.

---

[1] Sculls, as being lighter, were always cheaper than the heavy oars.

People, evidently, thought a voyage on one of these "hoys" a desperate undertaking; for we read in a little tract, of the fearsomeness of the adventure. The gentleman who braves this voyage, is a clergyman, and is bound for Ramsgate. "Many of us who went on board, had left our dearer comforts behind us. 'Ah!' said I, 'so must it be, my soul, when the "Master comes and calleth for thee." My

"ONE OF THE MISERIES OF LONDON.

Entering upon any of the Bridges of London, or any of the passages leading to the Thames, being assailed by a group of Watermen, holding up their hands, and bawling out, " Sculls, Sculls! Oars, Oars !"

tender wife! my tender babes! my cordial friends!' . . . Our vessel, though it set sail with a fair wind, and gently fell down the river towards her destined port, yet once, or twice, was nearly striking against other vessels in the river." And he winds up with, "About ten o'clock on Friday night we were brought safely into the harbour of Margate. . . . How great are the advantages of navigation! By the skill and

care of three men and a boy, a number of persons
were in safety conveyed from one part, to another, of the
kingdom!"

Sydney Smith in an article (1808) in the *Edinburgh
Review* on "Methodism" quotes a letter in the *Evan-
gelical Magazine.* "A Religious Hoy sets off every
week for Margate. Religious passengers accommodated
To the Editor. Sir,—It afforded me considerable pleasure
to see upon the Cover of your Magazine for the present
month, an advertisement announcing the establishment of
a packet, to sail weekly between London and Margate,
during the season ; which appears to have been set on foot
for the accommodation of religious characters ; and in which
'no profane conversation is to be allowed.' . . . Totally
unconnected with the concern, and, personally, a stranger
to the worthy owner, I take the liberty of recommending
this vessel to the notice of my fellow Christians ; persuaded
that they will think themselves bound to patronize and
encourage an undertaking that has the honour of our dear
Redeemer for its professed object."

There were but three bridges over the Thames—London,
Blackfriars, and Westminster. London Bridge was doomed
to come down. It was out of repair, and shaky ; a good
many arches blocked up, and those which were open had
such a fall, as to be dangerous to shoot. Most of us can
remember Blackfriars Bridge, and a good many Old Westminster Bridge, which was described in a London guide-
book of 1802, as one of the most beautiful in the world.
The same book says, "The banks of the Thames, contiguous to the bridges, and for a considerable extent, are
lined with manufactories and warehouses ; such as iron
founders, dyers, soap and oil-makers, glass-makers, shot-
makers, boat builders, &c. &c. To explore these will
repay curiosity : in a variety of them, that powerful agent
steam performs the work, and steam engines are daily
erecting in others. They may be viewed by applying a

day or two previous to the resident proprietors, and a small fee will satisfy the man who shows the works."

The " Pool," as that portion of the river Thames below London Bridge was called, was a forest of masts. Docks were few, and most of the ships had to anchor in the stream. Loading, and unloading, was performed in a quiet, and leisurely manner, quite foreign to the rush, and hurry of steam. Consequently, the ships lay longer at anchor, and, discharging in mid stream, necessitated a fleet of lighters and barges, which materially added to the crowded state of the river. Add to this the numerous rowing boats employed, either for business, or pleasure, and the river must have presented a far more animated appearance than it does now, with its few mercantile, and pleasure, steamers, and its steam tugs, and launches. Gay, too, were the water pageants, the City Companies barges, for the Lord Mayor's Show, the Swan Upping, the Conservation of the Thames, and Civic junkettings generally ; and then there were the Government barges, both belonging to the Admiralty, and Trinity House, as brave as gold and colour could make them ; the latter making its annual pilgrimage to visit the Trinity almshouses at Deptford Strond—all the Brethren in uniform, with magnificent bouquets, and each thoughtfully provided with a huge bag of fancy cakes and biscuits, which they gave away to the rising generation. I can well remember being honoured with a cake, and a kindly pat on the head, from the great Duke of Wellington.

The pressure of the shipping was so great, extending as it did, in unbroken sequence, from London Bridge to Greenwich, that more dock accommodation was needed : the small ones, such as Hermitage and Shadwell Docks, being far too small to relieve the congested state of the river. In 1799 several plans were put forward for new Docks, and some were actually put in progress. The Bill for the West India Docks was passed in 1799. The first stone was laid on the 12th of July, 1800, and the docks were partly opened in the summer of 1802. The first stone of the London Docks was laid on the 26th of June, 1802, and the docks opened on the 30th of January, 1805 ; and, on the 4th of March of the same year, the foundation of the East India Docks was laid, and they were opened in 1806.

Early in 1801, a shaft was sunk at Gravesend, to tunnel under the Thames, which, although it ultimately came to nothing, showed the nascent power of civil engineering—then just budding—which has in later times borne such fruit as to make it the marvel of the century, in the great works undertaken and accomplished. Even in 1801, there was a steamboat on the Thames (*Annual Register*, July 1st): " An experiment took place on the river Thames, for the purpose of working a barge, or any other heavy craft, against tide, by means of a steam engine on a very simple construction. The moment the engine was set to work the barge was brought about, answering her helm quickly, and she made way against a strong current, at the rate of two miles and a half an hour."

Commerce was developing, and the roads, with the heavy and cumbrous waggons, were insufficient for the growing trade. Railways, of course, were not yet, so their precursors, and present rivals, the canals, were made, in order to afford a cheap, and expeditious, means of inter-communication. In July, 1800, the Grand Junction Canal was opened from the Thames at Brentford, to Fenny Stratford in Buckinghamshire. A year afterwards, on the 10th of July, 1801, the Paddington Canal was opened for trade, with a grand aquatic procession, and some idea may be formed of the capital employed on these undertakings, when we find that even in January, 1804, the Grand Junction Canal had a paid-up capital of £1,350,000, and this, too, with land selling at a cheaper proportional rate than now.

CHAPTER XXIV.

LONDON was considered the best paved city in the
world, and most likely it was ; but it would hardly
commend itself to our fastidious tastes. The main
thoroughfares were flagged, and had kerbs ; sewers under
them, and gratings for the water to run from the gutters
into them—but turn aside into a side street, and then you
would find a narrow *trottoir* of "kidney" stones on end,
provocative of corns, and ruinous to boots ; no sewers to
carry off the rain, which swelled the surcharged kennels
until it met in one sheet of water across the road. Cellar
flaps of wood, closed, or unclosed, and, if closed, often
rotten, made pitfalls for all except the excessively wary.
Insufficient scavenging and watering, and narrow, and
often tortuous, streets, did not improve matters, and when
once smallpox, or fever, got hold in these back streets,
death held high carnival. Wretchedly lit, too, at night,
by poor, miserable, twinkling oil lamps, flickering with
every gust, and going out altogether with anything like a

LAMPLIGHTER—1805.

wind, always wanting the wicks trimming, and fresh oil, as is shown in the following graphic illustration.

In this, we see a lamp of a most primitive description, and that, too, used at a time when gas was a recognized source of light although not publicly employed. Of course there were improved oil lamps—notably those with the burners of the celebrated M. Argand—and science had already added the reflector, by means of which the amount of light could be increased, or concentrated. In

LAMPLIGHTER—1805.

the *Times* of May 23, 1803, is a description of a new street lamp : " A satisfactory experiment was first made on Friday evening last at the upper end of New Bond Street, to dissipate the great darkness which has too long prevailed in the streets of this metropolis. It consisted in the adaptation of twelve newly invented lamps with reflectors, in place of more than double that number of common ones ; and notwithstanding the wetness of the evening, and other unfavourable circumstances, we were both pleased, and surprised to find that part of the street illuminated with at least twice the quantity of light usually seen, and that light uniformly spread, not merely on the footways, but even to the middle of the street, so that the faces of persons walking, the carriages passing, &c., could be distinctly seen ; while the lamps and reflectors themselves, presented no disagreeable glare to the eye on looking at them, a fault which has been complained of in lamps furnished with refracting lenses."

Here, then, we have a perfectly independent testimony of the inefficiency of the then method of lighting; and, when once complaint begins, the remedy soon follows.

Gas was known, and was steadily fighting its way. Murdoch, who was a metal founder at Redruth, had been experimenting upon gas made from different materials, and in 1792 he lit up with it, his house and offices. Nay, more, he nearly earned the fame, and consequent punishment, of being a wizard; for he not only had a steam carriage, but in this uncanny conveyance he would take bladders of this new inflammable air, and actually burn a light without a wick. From a scientific curiosity, he naturally wished to develop it into a commercial undertaking, by which he might reap a substantial reward for his ingenuity; and in 1795 he proposed to James Watt to take out a patent for gas, instead of oil, as an illuminating medium. In 1797 he lit up Watt's new foundry at Old Cumnock in Ayrshire; and in 1798 Boulton and Watt's premises at Soho, Birmingham, were lit with this new light; and they, on the peace of Amiens, in 1802, gave the townsfolk of Birmingham something to stare at, and talk about, for they illuminated the whole front of their house with gas. Murdoch, in 1806, received the gold (Rumford) medal of the Royal Society for a communication detailing how he had successfully applied gas to illuminate the house and factory of Messrs. Phillips and Lee at Manchester.

In London we are chiefly indebted to a German, named Frederic Albert Winzer (or, as he afterwards Anglicised his name, Winsor) for introducing gas, and we have to thank his indomitable perseverance for its ultimate adoption. In 1804, he took out a patent for the manufacture of both gas and coke, and attempted to start a society called "The National Light and Heat Company." He wrote several works not much larger than pamphlets, notably one on "The superiority of the new Patent Coke over the use of coals" (1804); and "To be sanctioned by an Act of Parliament. A National Light and Heat Company, for providing our streets and houses with light and heat, where is proved that the destruction of smoke would open unto the Empire of Great Britain new sources of inexhaustible wealth."

Of course it met with ridicule everywhere. People would be asphyxiated. The place would be blown up. Even scientific men were not agreed as to its value, and Sir Humphrey Davy openly laughed at it. But Winsor, in 1803 and 1804, demonstrated the possibility of lighting houses, &c., by means of the new light at the Lyceum Theatre, which was not then used for dramatic purposes, but more for lectures; and

THE GOOD EFFECTS OF CARBONIC GAS!

as there could be no possibility of confuting his facts, he necessarily gained proselytes, and money was forthcoming in support of his schemes. The first experiment in street lighting was in August, 1807, when Golden Lane Brewery, and a portion of Beech, and Whitecross Streets were lit. This is shown in the illustration, and, by its means, we see the shape and arrangement, of the first street gas lamps. That the gas then in use was very impure, and offensive to the smell, there can be no doubt ; but that it ever produced the effects so comically, and graphically depicted, cannot be believed.

It is generally thought that Ackerman's Fine Art Repository, in the Strand, was the first shop in London lit with gas, in 1810 ; but there is an earlier notice of its being so used (*Morning Post*, June 15, 1805) : " The shop of Lardner and Co., the corner of the Albany, Piccadilly, is illuminated every evening with the Carbonated Hydrogen Gas, obtained from the decomposition of Coals. It produces a much more brilliant light than either oil or tallow, and proves, in a striking manner, the advantages to be derived from so valuable an application." There is a story, for which I cannot find any authority, that at Ackerman's a titled lady was so pleased with the light, that she wanted to take it home with her in the carriage.

The Light and Heat Company died a natural death, but the indefatigable Winsor started the Gaslight and Coke Company, and attempted, in 1809, to obtain a Charter for the same; but it was refused by Parliament, which gave rise to the following *jeu d'esprit* : " Gaslight Company. The shareholders in this *most promising* concern are somewhat disconcerted at the decision of the House of Commons. Some think that it will prove '*a bottle of smoke*,' while others are of opinion that it will at last '*end in air.*'"

The Gaslight and Coke Company had offices in Pall Mall, and in the street, in front, lamps for public use were once more exhibited, this time for the benefit of the West-end loungers. In the engraving a gentleman explains to his fair companion thus : " The coals being steamed, produces tar or paint for the outside of houses, the smoke passing thro' water is depriv'd of substance, and burns, as you see." On hearing this peculiarly elementary scientific explanation, an Irishman exclaimed, "Arrah, honey, if this man brings fire thro' water, we shall soon have the Thames and the Liffey burnt down, and all the pretty little herrings and whales burnt to cinders."

In 1810 the Gaslight and Coke Company got their Charter, and thenceforward the use of gas sprang into life, and although it may be on its last legs, as an illuminating power, there is plenty of vitality in it yet.

Winsor was buried at Kensal Green, and on his tombstone was cut the text from the Gospel of St. John, chap. i. ver. 9: "*That* was the true Light which lighteth every man that cometh into the world."

To light this gas or, indeed, to initiate any illuminating or heating power, recourse was only to

A PEEP AT THE GAS LIGHTS IN PALL MALL.

be had to the old, original tinder-box and matches; now things utterly of the past, possibly to be found in museums, as in the Ashmolean Museum at Oxford, labelled "Method of procuring light in the Nineteenth Century." This primitive arrangement consisted of a flat round box of iron or brass, resembling closely a pocket tobacco-box, which contained tinder. This tinder was made of charred rag, *i.e.*, linen or cotton rags burnt, but smothered so as not to smoulder out in "the parson and clerk" of our childhood, and the means of obtaining light therefrom was as follows:

The lid of the tinder-box being taken off, a piece of flint or agate, and another of hard steel, were forcibly struck together, so as to produce sparks. When one of these fell upon the tinder, it had to be carefully tended, and blown, until it became a patch of incandescence, sufficient to light a thin splint of wood some six inches long, having either end pointed, and tipped with sulphur. You might be successful at first trial, or, if the tinder was not well burnt, your temper might be considerably tried. This was the ordinary mode, but there was another—made with a pistol lock, having, in lieu of the priming-pan, a reservoir of tinder. These two were combined with a small candlestick which bore a wax-taper, and are frequently to be met with in *bric-à-brac* shops. Sometimes, also, in lieu of tinder, *amadou* or German tinder, made from a fungus, was used, or else thick and bibulous paper was soaked in a strong solution of nitrate of potash, and both were ignited by a spark from the flint and steel.

The first attempt to improve upon this machine, which was nearly as primitive as an aboriginal "fire stick," came from France, where, in 1805, M. Chancel invented a very pretty apparatus for producing light. It consisted of a bottle containing asbestos, which was saturated with strong sulphuric acid, and flame was produced by bringing this into contact with matches of the ordinary type as to shape or very slightly modified, coated at the ends with sulphur, and tipped with a mixture of chlorate of potash and sugar. The phosphorous match, too, was just beginning to be known. The following advertisement probably refers to M. Chancel's invention or some cognate method of producing fire—*Morning Post*, December 27, 1808: "The success of the Instantaneous Light and Fire Machines daily increases, and the Manufactory in Frith Street, Soho, has become now the daily resort of persons of the first fashion and consequence in town, who express themselves highly gratified with the utility and ingenuity of these philosophical curiosities."

CHAPTER XXV.

THE transition from Matches to Fires is natural, and easy, and, during the time of which I have treated in this book, there were several bad ones. In 1800 on the 11th of February, three West India Warehouses, near the Custom House, were burnt down, with an estimated loss of £300,000; and on the 6th of October of the same year, thirty houses were destroyed by fire. On September 27, 1802, an immense amount of property was destroyed in Store Street, Tottenham Court Road. The great tower over the choir in Westminster Abbey perished by flames July 9, 1803. The Theatres seem absolutely to have courted cremation. Astley's, which had been burnt down on September 17, 1794, was again made a ruin on September 1, 1803, and forty houses shared its fate at the same time. Then followed the Surrey, on August 12, 1805; Covent Garden on September 20, 1808; and Drury Lane on February 24, 1809. These were only the principal conflagrations during the decade; there were, of course, as many minor ones as ever. Take one instance—the list of fires within the Bills of Mortality for 1807. In the twelve months there were 375 fires and 356 chimney alarms.

None could complain of want of Insurance Companies, for, in 1810, there existed sixteen Fire Insurance Companies, *viz.*, The Sun, Phœnix, Royal Exchange, Hand in Hand, Westminster, London, Union, British, Imperial, Globe, County, Hope, Atlas, Pelican, Albion, and Eagle. The rates at which they assured were low, looking at the duty they paid to Government—the Sun so paying, in 1806, no less a sum than £95,269 8s. 8d. Common Insurances were charged a premium of 2s. per cent., Hazardous Insurances 3s. per cent., and Doubly Hazardous 5s. per cent., or very much the present rate. And we must remember that money was dearer, many buildings were of timber, and

A FIRE ENGINE.

nearly all were faultily constructed, there being no District Surveyor in these days—added to which, the engines were but poor manuals ; steam, of course, being unknown.

Each Fire Insurance Company had its badge, or cognizance, which was stamped out in sheet lead, painted and gilt, and then nailed on to the house insured—probably as an advertisement of the Company. There was no Fire Brigade, properly so called—that did not come till 1832 ; but each Company kept a staff of firemen and engines. We have seen that these men acted as constables when Sir Francis Burdett was released from prison. Although the dress was of somewhat similar pattern, its colour, &c., was

left to the individual fancy of each Company—the illustration I have given, being the uniform of the Sun Fire
Insurance Company. The coat, waistcoat, and breeches,
were of dark blue cloth with brass buttons, whilst a brass
badge adorned both his left arm, and his helmet. This
latter was made of horse hide, strengthened by cross
bars of metal ; its inside was of leather, quilted and

A FIREMAN—1805.

stuffed with wool, to protect the head
from falling bricks or spars. The engines
were manuals, and carried with them
spare men to relieve those pumping,
when they were tired. The most powerful engine of that time could only throw
a ton of water per minute through a
$\frac{3}{4}$ inch branch, or nozzle, and, as we see,
the fire-plug was simply pulled up, and
the water very wastefully supplied.

Water, by the by, was somewhat scarce,
and certainly not good. Drinking water
was mainly supplied from pumps, both
public and private, and when we see the
arrangement of pumps, in the country,
now-a-days, how, in order to be near the
house, they are, generally, thoughtlessly
placed in close approximation to the cess-
pool—we can imagine, in some degree,
what the supply of drinking water must
have been like in crowded London, with

its defective drainage, and its festering graveyards. There
was a supply, to certain districts, of New River water.
Some yet flowed from the heights of Hampstead, and there
were also the Water Works at London Bridge, which were
inaugurated by the "Dutchman," Peter Moritz, in 1582,
and which continued to pump up the muddy, sewaged
water, until the new bridge was built. They are thus
described in a contemporary work (1802): "The *Water*

Works, on the north-west side of the Bridge, supply a considerable part of *London* with water for domestic purposes, in the same manner as is effected by the *New River.* But as *London Bridge* lies very low, the water requires to be forced up to a bason on the top of a tower, 120 feet in height. From this bason, it again descends into the main pipes, and is conveyed in all directions through the town. The water is raised by the action of four great wheels, which are turned by the stream, and every turn of the four wheels causes 114 strokes of the piston rods—by this

DRINKING WATER SUPPLY—1802.

means 40 to 50,000 hogsheads of water are raised every 24 hours."

There was yet another water supply, which was obtained from pumps and springs, and which afforded a livelihood to many hard-working, and industrious, men. Perhaps, one of the last places in the vicinity of London thus supplied, was Hampstead—a neighbourhood noted for springs, where the water used to be thus fetched from the "Conduit Meads" and other places, and retailed at 1d. or 2d. per bucket, according to distance. This only ceased when the Midland Railway ran a tunnel underneath the spring, and destroyed it.

The water supply from the Thames, and New River, it must be remembered, was only turned on three times a week.

The Streets of London in 1804 are thus contemporaneously described : " It may well excite our admiration to go from Charing Cross to the Exchange, and pass a double row of carriages, one coming, another going, with scarcely an intermission. Yet, when we recollect the numerous causes that put so many things, and persons, in motion, we may admire, but must own it was to be expected. Not only are the streets filled with carriages, but with foot passengers ; so that the great thoroughfares of London appear like a moving multitude, or a daily fair. To this deception the endless shops lend their aid ; it is, indeed, the remark of strangers in general, that London is a continual fair. The display made by the traders, the numerous wares they have to sell, and the continual crowd that is passing and re-passing, forcibly contribute to the delusion."

Yet the streets were narrow, or at least we think them so, for we have always to widen them for the perpetually increasing traffic ; and the shops could in no ways at all compare with ours. Small panes of glass, and small windows were not calculated to show off the traders' wares to advantage. Even the contemporary guide-books, can give no shops of particular excellence—except those which sold keramic ware. In this, that particular portion of the century was pre-eminent, and one longs to have had a stroll, looking in first at Wedgwood's warehouse in St. James's Square, then at the Worcester China Warehouse, Coventry Street ; from thence to the show rooms of Derby china, in Henrietta Street, Covent Garden ; and finishing up with Spode's exposition of Staffordshire ware, in Portugal Street.

The streets were not over well scavenged, and, as I have

before said, sewers did not obtain much more than in the main thoroughfares. These, too, were watered in the summer, by means of a wooden tank hung below the axle-tree of a pair of wheels, delivering the water from a perforated wooden box at its back. " The Watering Cart is usually drawn by one horse, but on some roads two horses are applied, when the leader is rode by a boy, and the driver sits on the seat upon the cart. In districts contiguous to ponds, the carts are driven into the water, and are filled very expeditiously ; but where they have not this convenience, they are obliged to supply them with water from the pump, which is hard labour for two men."

CHAPTER XXVI

LET us go to authentic sources, and, in our imaginations, people the streets as they then were, following the example which Gay has so worthily given in his "Trivia." Leaving aside the roysterers, and nightly bad characters, together with the watchmen, the first industrial perambulator, would probably be the Sweep. In the frontispiece to this volume, the "climbing boy," as he was called, is faithfully depicted, drinking his early cup of saloop, the utensils of his trade, his brush, shovel, and scraper, lying by his side ; in his cap is a brass plate containing his master's name and address. Poor little fellows! their lives were harsh ! With hard taskmasters, badly constructed chimneys, and flues to sweep, and laborious work, climbing with back and knees; with a foul atmosphere, and lungs choked with soot, their young days *must* have been joyless. Of course we cannot blame the people then living, because they had not sufficient mechanical knowledge to abolish the climbing boy's *raison d'être.* It is pleasing to register within the decade I write of, one good and kind friend of these little fellows— a Mrs. Montagu, who died in March, 1800. She was a lady of good family, and an authoress (founder of the Blue

Stocking Club), who even attempted so high a flight as an " Essay on the Writings and Genius of Shakespeare." In her practical benevolence, her heart felt for these little *pariahs*, and she annually regaled them on May-day, with roast beef and plum pudding. This conduct was so contrary to the general spirit of the age—which could see nothing more in a " climbing boy," than a boy being utilized for his own good, and for that of the community, that her conduct was scarcely understood—so much so, that a web of romance had to be woven around her, in order to account for it. It was rumoured, and credibly believed, that she had lost a son, and found him again as a " climbing boy "; and, to mark her sense of gratitude for his restoration, she feasted all the boys in London on the sweep's holiday—May-day. Of course, there is not an atom of foundation for such a story, but practical philanthropy was then so unusual, that a reason had to be found for its observance. After her death the following verses were written :

> " And is all pity for the poor sweeps fled
> Since Montagu is numbered with the dead ?
> She who did once the many sorrows weep,
> That met the wanderings of the woe-worn sweep !
> Who, once a year, bade all his griefs depart,
> On May's sweet morn would doubly cheer his heart !
> Washed was his little form, his shirt was clean,
> On that *one* day, his real face was seen.
> His shoeless feet, *now* boasted pumps, and new.
> The brush, and shovel, gaily held to view !
> The table spread, his every sense was charmed,
> And every savoury smell his bosom warmed ;
> His light heart joyed to see such goodly cheer.
> And much he longed to taste the mantling beer :
> His hunger o'er—the scene was little heaven—
> If riches thus can bless, what blessings might be given
> But she is gone ! none left to soothe their grief,
> Or, once a year, bestow their meed of beef ! "

One instance, only, of the hard life of these little ones, will I give, and then pass on to pleasanter themes.

Morning Herald, October 1, 1802: "GREAT MARLBOROUGH
STREET.   Wednesday, an interesting examination took
place at this office, relative to a male child, about eight
years old, charged to have been kidnapped by the foreman
of Mrs. Bridges, a chimney-sweeper, in Swallow Street.   It
was stated by Mrs. Wilson, of No. 5 in the same street, that,
on Saturday last, she was dreadfully alarmed by the cry
of murder, and the screams of the child at Mrs. B.'s, which
induced her to run into the house, where she found the
child stripped, and the prisoner unmercifully beating him
with two switches, or small sticks.   She remonstrated with
him, and demanded by what authority he so cruelly treated
the child, as it was well known it had been inveigled from
the street, and unlawfully detained by them.   The prisoner
threatened to strike the witness, who, nevertheless, per-
sisted in taking away the child, and did actually take
it to the workhouse, informing the committee there of
the particulars, and the prisoner, in consequence, was
indicted.

" The child, itself, told a very artless and moving tale of
its own sufferings.   The prisoner, it appears, used to strip
him naked, and flog him in the dust cellar, to make him go
up the chimney, to which, it seems, he had an utter aver-
sion.   When in the chimney, he was urged to proceed by
the prisoner having a stick, at the top of which was fastened
a pin, with which he goaded the poor infant ; at other
times he would make the poor child descend into vaults,
and used other cruelties too shocking for recital.   On
inquiry at the workhouse, the child discovered that his
father is a smith by trade, a poor man, with six children,
living near Sloane Street.   Its parents had used every
means to discover their child, and, at length found him in
the workhouse.   The prisoner was committed to Tothill
Fields Bridewell ; and we suppose that Mrs. Bridges, as
soon as she can safely leave her bed, will also be brought
up to answer this charge."

In 1803, if not before, there was in existence an "Association for Improving the Situation of Infant Chimney Sweepers," of which John Julius Angerstein, Esq. (whose collection of pictures founded the National Gallery), was the chairman.

May-day was also sacred to another class of early morning workers — the Milkmaids. Curiously enough, the carriage and delivery of milk —by no means a light task, whether looked at from the distance walked, or the load carried — was entirely in the hands of women, strapping country wenches, principally recruited from Wales. The cows were kept in hovels

"WATER CRESSES! COME BUY MY WATER CRESSES!"

in, and near, London, and a "milkmaid's" daily life began at from 4 to 6 a.m. when the cows had to be milked ; they then delivered the milk at the various houses until near ten. Then there were the dairy vessels to wash, and at noon, the cows again to be milked.

The delivery of milk again occupied them till nearly 6 p.m., when they had to wash up all cans, &c., for the morning. In 1808 it was reckoned that about 8,500 cows were kept in London and its vicinity ; one cowkeeper at Islington owning between 800 and 900 cows. It is sad

"HOT CROSS BUNS! TWO A PENNY BUNS!"

to read, however, in 1804, that "Milk is sold at fourpence per quart, or fivepence for a better sort ; yet the advance of price does not insure its purity, for it is generally mixed in a great proportion with water, by the retailers before they leave the milk houses. The adulteration of the milk, added to the wholesale cost, leaves an average profit of

cent. per cent., to the vendors of this useful article.   Few
retail trades are exercised with equal gains."

Following the milkwoman, would come the early Baker
calling out " Hot loaves ! " and ringing a bell : he would
appear on the scene between 8 and 9 a.m., selling his rolls at

" DO YOU WANT ANY BRICK-DUST ? "

one, or two, a penny—in winter he added, or substituted,
muffins and crumpets.

Then, too, for breakfast, would be heard, either from
male, or female, lips, the cry of " Water cresses ! " which
were sold in small bunches a penny each, or three for twopence.   In those days, they were to be found growing wild

in the ditches near London, and many a weary tramp of seven or eight miles, before breakfast, of a morning, did the sellers have, in order to get them fresh. There was generally a supply at Covent Garden Market—grown for sale ; but these were considered inferior in flavour to the wild ones.

From breakfast time, the cries of the miscellaneous dealers in small wares became general, and hardly any can claim pre‑emi‑ nence, unless it be on a Good Friday — when the old pagan crossed cakes were vended, and evidently as much relished by the young folks as now. "Baking, or boiling apples" were sold by women, a char‑ coal stove accom‑ panying their barrow, so that their customers might have them hot, and luscious.

"BUY A TRAP! A RAT TRAP! BUY MY TRAP!"

Then, too, might be seen a man with band-boxes, carried on either end of a pole, which rested on his shoulder. From 6d. to 3s. was their price ; whilst boxes of slight deal, with a lock and key, might be purchased from 3s. 6d. to 6s. 6d. These boxes were of home manufacture, and gave employment to many industrious families.

Brickdust was carried about on donkey back, in small sacks, and retailed at the price of one penny per quart.

A contemporary remarks, "As brickdust is scarcely used in London for any other purpose than that of knife cleaning, the criers are not numerous; but they are remarkable for their fondness, and their training, of bull dogs. This predilection they have in common with the lamplighters of the Metropolis."

The accompanying sketch of a Rat-trap Dealer is graphic and good ; and it shows one glimpse of the past, in the old cobbler (?) at his *hutch*, or low open door. This, or a cellar, always went as an accompaniment to this branch of the shoe-making trade.

To future antiquarians, it may be useful to know that, at the commencement of this century, our domestic animals had their "purveyors of food ;" that cat's, and dog's meat, consisting of horse flesh, bullock's livers, and tripe cuttings, were distributed by means of men, or preferably, women, all over London. The horse flesh, and bullock's liver, was sold by weight at 2d. per lb.; the tripe, in bundles, at 1d. each.

"Baskets" were hawked about—not as we know them (rarer and rarer, year by year) in the gipsy caravans, but slung around the sellers—of good handy size, and durable make. One article of domestic economy has all but died out —the Bellows—and *old* specimens are almost worth their weight in silver ; but the cry of "Bellows to mend!" was then heard commonly. The mender carried his tools in a bag on his back, and, like the chair-mender, plied his calling in front of his patron's house, or at any convenient street corner.

"Chairs to mend!" might be met with anywhere. Nursery and common chairs, if not having seats of wood, were of rushes, cane being a later introduction. These rushes were, and are now, cut in our rivers, preferably in the early autumn, before they begin to rot, and sold by a peculiar measure—a *bolt*—which is as much as a man can clasp of rushes, when dried, within his arms. The repairs were executed before the house, and the charge for re-seating a chair was very moderate—from 1s. 6d. to 2s. 6d.

" Door mats " were hawked about, as they are sometimes now, but Prisons and Industrial Schools had not then interfered in this trade, so that a poor man had a chance of getting rid of his handiwork, and the price for rush, and rope, mats, varied from 6d. to 4s. each.

If we can believe a contemporary account, the Dustmen of those days were the very pink of propriety. " Dust carts ply the streets through the morning in every part of the metropolis ; two men go with each cart, ringing a large bell, and calling DUST O ! These men, daily, if necessary, empty the dust bins of all the refuse that is thrown into them. They receive no gratuity from the inhabitants of the houses, the owner of the cart pays them, like other labourers, weekly wages ; and the dust is carried to yards in the outskirts of the town, where a number of women and girls are employed in sifting it, and separating the cinders and bones from the ashes, and other refuse." I much fear that this picture is as *couleur de rose* as the engraving which accompanies it, wherein the model dustman, with very clean face, is attired in a yellow jacket, green waistcoat, crimson knee-breeches, blue ribbed stockings, and brown gaiters.

The sale of " Turnery " was also a street occupation, and brooms, brushes, sieves, bowls, clothes horses and lines were thus vended. Some, the Aristos of their trade, had a cart ; but the perambulating sellers could get a good living, as their wares yielded a good profit.

The Knife-grinder, immortalized by Canning, plied his trade in the sight of the people, and his charges for grinding, and setting, scissors, were a penny or twopence each ; penknives, a penny a blade ; table knives, 1s. 6d. or 2s. per dozen, according to the polish supplied.

" Lavender " was a cry redolent of the country, yet grown near London, at Mitcham. This was generally used in linen-presses, to counteract the abominably rank smell of the soap of those days. It was a favourite scent ; as Isaac Walton says, " I'll now lead you to an honest ale house, where we shall find a cleanly room, lavender in the windows, and twenty ballads stuck against the wall."

Among the street cries, was that of "Mackerel"; and the sellers thereof might even expose them for sale, and cry them, on Sundays—a proud privilege which no other fish possessed. There never was a glut of them in the market, because they could only be brought to Billingsgate by smacks, so that they were never sold at the very cheap rates they now are, but were, as we should think, extremely dear. At first coming in they were sold for 1s. 6d. each, and they gradually dropped to 10d., 8d., 6d. each, or, if there was a great haul, three might be sold for a shilling.

" BUY MY GOOSE ! MY FAT GOOSE ! "

might probably bring to remembrance the quotation "*Caveat emptor,*" but these two purchasers seem quite able to take care of themselves.

It was but a month, or six weeks since, that I saw a sight I had not seen for some years—a man selling Rabbits slung on a pole, which he carried on his shoulder; yet this used to be the usual method of exposing them for sale, and these small dealers were called *higglers*. The price of Rabbits, thus sold, at the time of which I write, were "from ninepence to eighteenpence each, which is cheaper than they can be bought in the poulterers' shops."

"ALL A GROWING, A GROWING! HERE'S FLOWERS FOR YOUR GARDENS!"

shows the universal yearning of the dwellers in town, to make as good a *rus in urbe* of their surroundings, as possible. The atmosphere of London was then, undoubtedly purer than now, and flowers might then be grown in the open air, where, now, it would be an impossibility.

As an "Old Clothes" man the Jew was then paramount,

the Irishman not having, as yet, entered into competition with him. *Rosemary Lane* (only sweet smelling in its name) was a thoroughfare now called *Royal Mint Street*, leading from Tower Hill; and here was held a Mart, not only in shops, but all over the pavement and road, of old clothes, boots, &c., and it fully merited its name of *Rag Fair.* A market was built for the buyers and sellers, in which to transact their business; but old habits proved too strong, they would *not* use it, and "nothing less than military force constantly exercised would prevail over the obstinacy of habit." The "high" market was from twelve to three.

It was a curious custom then, of course not in good houses, but in those of poor men, such as might be on the outskirts, and in the suburbs of the Metropolis, to strew the floor, say of the kitchen, and sometimes of the parlour, with silver sand. This kept the soles of dirty boots from actual contact with the newly scrubbed boards—and saved the housewife much exercise of temper. Sand, too, was plentifully used in scouring kitchen utensils, and it was sold, the red sand, at 2½d., and the white at 1¼d., per peck.

Fruit, in its season, was cried; and at night, among other employments, by which to earn an honest penny, there were the playbill sellers, and the link boys. The former were almost invariably women, who also sold oranges; and, if a purchaser could be found to go to the extent of buying six, a "Bill of the play" was given. Awful things were those playbills—none of your dainty, lace-edged, Rimmel-scented ones—but long strips of flimsy tissue paper, yet wet from the printers, smearing the hands with ink from the large capital letters employed. No time had they to dry them; there was usually a fresh play every night, and the playbills had to be fresh also.

CHAPTER XXVII.

The Postman—His dress—The Post Office—Changes of site—Sir Robert Vyner—
Rates of postage and deliveries—Mail coaches—Places of starting and routes
—Number of houses in London—Description of them—Their furniture.

ONE particular feature of the Streets, was, and still is, one of our most trusted servants, the POSTMAN. In those days he was a *somebody*, who held

A POSTMAN.

personal relations with his clients. None of your rat-tats, and "Look in the letter box"; he generally had something to collect, for there were no postage stamps in those days, and that being the fact, people very often left the postage to be col-lected at the other end. The officials mounted a hat with a cockade, scarlet coat (the Royal livery), blue breeches, and, of course, white stockings. They used, as in my young days, to collect the letters, nay, in many country districts they do it now.

The location of the Post Office has been changed many times. We are apt to associate it with St. Martin's-le-Grand, but it was not always so. It was originally in Cloak Lane, near Dowgate, whence it was removed to the Black Swan, in Bishopsgate Street; and, at the time of which we write, it occupied the site of Sir Robert Vyner's mansion, in Lombard Street: that Sir Robert Vyner, who is historical, if only for his treatment of his king, Charles II.—a story which is well told in No. 462 of the *Spectator*: "Sir Robert was a very loyal man, and, if you will allow me the expression, very fond of his sovereign; but, what with the joy he felt at heart for the honour done him by his prince, and through the warmth he was in with the continual toasting healths to the Royal Family, his lordship grew a little fond of His Majesty, and entered into a familiarity not altogether so graceful in a public place. The King understood very well how to extricate himself in all kinds of difficulties, and, with a hint to the company to avoid ceremony, stole off and made towards his coach, which stood ready for him in Guildhall Yard. But the Mayor liked his company so well, and was grown so intimate, that he pursued him hastily, and, catching him fast by the hand, cried out with a vehement oath and accent, 'Sir, you shall stay and take t'other bottle.' The airy monarch looked kindly at him over his shoulder, and, with a smile, and graceful air, for I saw him at the time, and do now, repeated this line of the old song:

' He that's drunk is as great as a king,'

and immediately returned back, and complied with his landlord."

Then, as now, the Lombard Street Post Office was wasted. "It is a national reproach when edifices of this kind, which, from our great mercantile concerns, afford occasion for a display of public architecture, and ornament to the Metropolis, are lost to those purposes." This was the comment of a contemporary, and the site of the present Post Office in St. Martin's-le-Grand was not fixed upon or, rather, the first stone was not laid, till May, 1824. As now, the Post Office was always changing its rules and rates—to meet emergencies and keep abreast of the times —so that it would expand this notice to too great a length, were I to chronicle all its changes. Perhaps a short relation of its doings in 1804—which would be the mean of the decade — will give as good an idea as any other.

"Houses, or boxes, for receiving letters before four o'clock, at the West end of the town, and five o'clock in the City, are open in every part of the Metropolis ; after that hour bell-men collect the letters during another hour, receiving a fee of *one penny* for each letter ; but, at the General Post Office, in Lombard Street, letters are received till seven o'clock ; after that, till half an hour after seven, a fee of *sixpence* must be paid ; and from half after seven till a quarter before eight, the postage must be paid, as well as the fee of *sixpence*. Persons, till lately, were, if well known, permitted to have back any letter put in, if required ; but, by an order of June, 1802, the masters of receiving houses are not allowed to return letters on any pretence whatever.

"Letters from (? for) the East Indies must be delivered at the India House, where a letter-box is provided for their reception.

" Those for the coast of Africa, or at single settlements in particular parts of the world, may be sent either through the ship letter office, or by the bags which await the sailing of ships, and which are kept at the respective coffee houses near the Royal Exchange."

We should consider these arrangements somewhat primitive ; but then, telegrams and frequent mails have spoilt us. The twopenny post was mainly local, there being six deliveries and collections of letters in town daily, and many country places had two deliveries and collections.

The letters were distributed throughout the length and

breadth of the country by means of *Mail Coaches*, which carried passengers at an average rate of sixpence per mile. This system was inaugurated, and organized, at the latter end of the Eighteenth Century, by a Mr. John Palmer, of Bath, who not only suggested the routes, but to prevent robbery, which, previously, was rife, had every coach accompanied by a well-armed *guard*, and these coaches accomplished their journeys at a uniform rate, including stoppages, of eight miles an hour. They did not start from the Post Office, but from various inns, and the following is a list of the coaches, and places of starting:

Dover Portsmouth	Angel, St. Clements.
Bristol Bath Exeter Liverpool Manchester Norwich Taunton Yarmouth Ipswich	Swan with Two Necks, Lad Lane.
Poole	Bell and Crown, Holborn.
Chester and Holyhead Worcester	Golden Cross, Charing Cross.
Gloucester	Golden Cross, Charing Cross; and the Angel, St. Clements, Strand.
York and Edinburgh Glasgow Shrewsbury Leeds	Bull and Mouth, Bull and Mouth Street.
Harwich	Spread Eagle, Gracechurch Street.
Chichester Cambridge Rye Brighton	Unknown.

The letters were first of all sorted; then they were weighed, and their proper amount of postage marked on them; they were counted, packed in boxes for the different towns, and an account kept of their number; they were then put in bags, which were sealed, and given in charge of the mail guard. Postage was heavy in those days. Take the charges for 1810:

					d.
From any Post Office in England or Wales to any place not exceeding 15 miles from such Office					4
For any distance above 15 miles, and not exceeding 30 miles					5
„	30	„	„	50	„	6
„	50	„	„	80	„	7
„	80	„	„	120	„	8
„	120	„	„	170	„	9
„	170	„	„	230	„	10
„	230	„	„	300	„	11
„	300	„	„	400	„	12

And so on in proportion, 1*d.* for every additional 100 miles.

London, at this time, was not beautiful. Apart from the public buildings, its 160,000 houses (the number estimated in 1804) were not lovely to look upon. Utilitarian they were, to a degree—long rows of brick-built tenements, with oblong holes for windows. There was no attempt at architecture: that had gone out with the first George; and, during the first half of this century, domestic architecture in this country was at its lowest possible ebb. Just fancy! in the first decade, Baker Street was considered "perhaps the handsomest street in London." Can condemnation go further? All the houses were the same pattern, varied only by the height of the rooms, and the number of stories, which were mostly three, and very rarely exceeded four. There was the front parlour, and the back parlour, a wretched narrow passage, or hall, with a flight of stairs leading to the drawing-rooms. In the basement were the kitchen and scullery.

The inside, even, was not redeemed by beautiful furniture.

TALES OF WONDER.

The rich, of course, furnished sumptuously, after their lights — which, at that time, represented anything of classical Greek, or Roman, shape—no matter whether suitable to the purpose for which it was employed, or not. Of course, as now, those lower in the social scale, aped, as far as they could, the tastes of the upper classes ; and, as they could not afford the sumptuous gilding, and carving, of the rich, the ordinary furniture of that time was heavy, dull, and dispiriting. Take, for example, the accompanying picture, where, from the style of dress of the ladies, we can but draw one inference—that they were in a good social position.   The furniture is dull, and heavy ; stiff, high-backed chairs ; a table, which would now only be allowed in the nursery ; but one candle, and that with a cotton wick, needing snuffing ! A tall, narrow, and tasteless mantelpiece frames a poor, starved stove of semi-circular shape, with flat front ; the fire-irons stand against the mantelpiece, and a bowed fender, of perforated sheet brass, enclosed the hearth ; a small hearth-rug with a fringe, and a bell cord with a plain brass ring, complete the furniture of the room, as far as Gillray depicted it.   Not quite our idea of luxurious comfort, yet it was comfort then ; tastes were simpler, huge fortunes had not yet been made in manufactures, railway contracting, speculations on the Stock Exchange, or promoting companies—people were more localized (in fact, they could not move), and the intercourse with abroad was very little ; and, if it had existed, the hatred of anything foreign, or, especially, French, would have, at once, condemned any innovation.

CHAPTER XXVIII.

Food—Statistics as to quantity of meat consumed—Scarcity of fish and game—
Supply of latter to London—Venison—A brewer's dinner—Beer—Quantity
brewed—Wine—Its price—Supply of vegetables—Sardines and Harvey's Sauce
—Scarcity of wheat—Forestalling—Rice from India—Bounties given for its
shipment.

PEOPLE, then, were conservative with regard to food. For the ordinary Englishman was no appetizing *plat*, no refinement of cookery—anything out of the usual ruck would be promptly denounced, and fiercely spurned, as French *kickshaws*. Plain roast and boiled meats were universal, from the highest to the lowest; the quantity of animal food consumed throughout the country was enormous; and, what was more, it was all of home production. No frozen meat, no tinned provisions; the only known way of preserving then, was the time-honoured one of salting. In London alone, according to the very meagre statistics of the day, the number of bullocks slaughtered yearly was 110,000; of sheep and lambs 776,000; calves 210,000; hogs 210,000; sucking pigs, 60,000; besides an unknown quantity of animals of other kinds. This may be an approximate estimate of the number, based, probably, on the quantity sold at the various markets to the butchers, but can give us no idea of the weight, and consequent average consumption per head.

Fish was scarce, and dear; the war, naturally, prevented

the fishermen from going far from the coast, and their numbers, moreover, were thinned by impressment. No railways to bring this very perishable commodity quickly to market, no ice to preserve it on its journey; the smack must go to port to unload her cargo, and, being entirely dependent on her sails, was at the mercy of the winds.

Inland, they never knew the taste of salt-water fish, unless some kind friend sent a cod, or turbot, packed in straw, in a basket, as a present by the mail, or stage, coach. Nor could the Londoner, then, get the abundant supply of our salmon rivers, which he now, in common with the whole of England, enjoys.

Game was very scarce, and dear. A country gentleman would not have dared to brave the public opinion of his county, by selling his game, and battues were unknown. The poachers did, undoubtedly, a good trade; and about Christmas time the mail, and stage, coaches came up, loaded with hares, &c.—a fact amusingly chronicled in the *Morning Post* of the 26th of December, 1807: "The first of the Norwich and Yarmouth coaches arrived at a late hour on Thursday, when, strange to relate, every one of the passengers, inside and outside, were found *dead!* Not less than four hundred brace of *dead game* being unloaded from it, for the banqueting of the *living Londoners* at this luxurious season." If, however, a story told in the *Times* of the 20th of January, 1803, is true, it was not always safe to buy game from the coaches: "Saturday night last, an epicure from Fish Street Hill, anxiously watched for the arrival of a Kentish coach, at the King's Head, in the Borough, in order to purchase a *Hare* from the coachman, for his Sunday's dinner; an outside passenger, having learned his errand, brought him under the gateway, and sold him a very large one, as he thought, for nine shillings, which, however, upon his return home, proved to be a *badger.*"

Poultry was seldom seen except at the tables of the very well to do. The supply was deficient, and they had not the resources we have of railway carriage, and especially of the Continental markets; consequently prices were exorbitant. Venison was considered *the* dish for an epicure, and was sold—chiefly by pastry cooks—at a reasonable rate: in fact, there were coffee houses where a venison dinner could be obtained for 2s. 6d. Probably the following advertisement indicates a somewhat better style of entertainment—*Morning Herald*, July 18, 1804: "VENISON in perfection. At the Worcester Coffee House, corner of Swallow Street, Oxford Street, Gentlemen may depend on having prime Venison. A Haunch and Neck dressed every day, ready precisely at five o'clock, at the reasonable charge for dinner of 3s. 6d. Wines and Liquors of the finest flavour; best old Port 4s. 6d. per bottle. Venison ready dressed, and pasties sent out. N.B. Fifty brace of good Bucks wanted."

It was an age of eating and drinking—*i.e.*, men ate and drank in larger quantities than now; but we must not take the following as a typical feast of the time; it was simply a brewer's dinner, cooked after a brewer's fashion—yet it was also typical, for then the cult of beefsteak and porter was at its culminating point, and people bowed down, and reverenced them exceedingly. The *Morning Post*, May 30, 1806: "Alderman Combe's Annual Dinner. Yesterday, Mr. Combe gave his annual dinner at his brewery, near Long Acre. The party consisted of the Prince of Wales, Duke of Norfolk, Lord Chancellor, Earl of Lauderdale, Lord Robert Spencer, Lord Howick, Sir Gilbert Heathcote, Lord John Townshend, Mr. R. B. Sheridan, Mr. Tierney, Mr. Harvey Combe, and Mr. Alderman Combe. At half an hour past six, the company sat down to dinner. The entertainment consisted of beefsteaks and porter. It was served up in the same style as it was last year. An oaken table, of an oblong form, was set out in the long room of the brewhouse. This table was covered with a large hempen sack, and covers, consisting of wooden trenchers, were laid for each of the guests. The other paraphernalia of the table, namely, the spoons, salt-cellars, salad bowls, &c., were composed of the same material as the plates. The Steaks were cooked by *the Stoker*, a man so called from his being always employed to keep the fires. This Stoker dressed the Steaks upon a large plate of iron, which was placed in the Copper-hole. When done, the Cook took them out with a pair of tongs, conveyed them into a wooden dish, and, in that style, they were served up. At the expiration of half an hour, the Prince, and the company, retired to Mr. Combe's house, in Great Russell Street, Bloomsbury, where they partook of a second course, consisting of every delicacy of the season, together with a dessert of fruits, the most rare and abundant we have ever seen. The Madeira, Port, and Claret were the objects of every one's panegyric."

Beer was the national beverage, and it was brewed from good malt and hops ; not out of sugar, and chemical bedevilments, as at present : and the quantity drunk in London, alone, seems to be enormous. *Vide* the *Annual Register* for 1810 :

" The Quantity of strong beer brewed by the first twelve houses in the London Porter Brewery, from the 5th of July, 1809, to the 5th of July, 1810.

	BARRELS.
Barclay, Perkins and Co.	235,053
Meux, Read and Co.	211,009
Truman, Hanbury and Co.	144,990
Felix, Calvert and Co.	133,491
Whitbread and Co.	110,939
Henry Meux and Co.	93,660
Combe and Co.	85,150
Brown and Parry	84,475
Goodwin, Skinner and Co.	74,223
Elliott and Co.	57,251
Taylor	44,510
Clowes and Co.	41,594

Wines, of course, were drunk by the higher classes, but

French wines were comparatively dear, owing to the closing of the trade with France; still there was a very fair quantity captured in the prizes taken at sea, and there was a great deal more smuggled.

Frontignac in 1800 might be bought for 19s. 6d. per doz., and Muscatel at 24s. In 1804, the following are the prices from a respectable wine merchant's list.

Superior Old Port	38s.	per dozen.
Prime Old Sherry	42s.	,,
,, Madeira	63s.	,,
Bucellas	40s.	,,
Mountain, Lisbon, and Calcavella ...	38s.	,,
Superior Claret...	70s.	,,
Cognac Brandy	20s.	per gallon.
Old Jamaica Rum	15s.	,,
Holland's Geneva	10s.	,,

In 1806, Vin de Grave was 66s. per dozen.

For the supply of vegetables, and fruit, large tracts of land were utilized for the supply of London alone. It was reckoned that this city swallowed the produce of 10,000 acres of vegetables, and about 4,000 acres of fruit trees. The market gardens have been gradually disappearing, but they used to be situated principally at Camberwell, Deptford, Fulham, Battersea, Mortlake, Barnes, and Chiswick. This produce found its way to Covent Garden, where the market days were the same as now—Tuesday, Thursday, and Saturday.

During the latter part of the first decade of the century, provisions were not so dear:

Beef averaged from	6d. to 9½d.	per lb.
Mutton ,, ...	6d. to 10d.	,,
Pork ,, ...	6d. to 1s.	,,
Lamb at first coming in... ...	10d. to 1s. 2d.	,,
,, Mid Season	6½d. to 8d.	,,
Sugar was about	5d. to 5½d.	,,
Salt ,, ...	20s. per bushel.	
Store Candles about	1s. 3d. per lb.	

Whilst on the subject of food, I cannot help chronicling the first notices I have ever met with, of two articles familiar to us—Sardines, and Harvey's Sauce. The first occurs in an advertisement in the *Morning Post*, August 10, 1801 : " SARDINIAS, a Fish cured in a peculiar manner, are highly esteemed as a Sandwich, and deemed of superior flavour to the Anchovy. Sold," &c. The second is in the *Morning Herald*, February 9, 1804 : " HARVEY'S Sauce for Fish, &c. Black Dog, Bedford. Mr. Harvey respectfully informs the Nobility and Gentry, he has appointed Mrs. Elizabeth Lazenby to prepare and sell the above sauce, at her Oil Warehouse, No. 6, Edward's Street, Portman Square, and that she, alone, is in possession of the original receipt—signed Peter Harvey."

If, however, the times were somewhat gross feeding, yet, early in the century, they also knew the pinch, if not of absolute hunger, yet of that which comes nigh akin to it— scarcity. As we have seen in the History of the decade, bread stuffs were, through bad harvests, very dear; and the strictest attention to economy in their use, even when mixed with inferior substitutes, practised. The unreasoning public laid the whole of the rise in price on the shoulders of the middle-men, or factors ; and they were branded with the then opprobrious, but now obsolete, term of "Forestallers and Regraters." Take one plaintive wail, which appeared in the *Morning Post* of March 7, 1800 : "We are told that one cause of the high price of Corn is, the consequence of the practice of selling by sample, instead of the Corn being fairly brought to market. The middle-man buys the Corn, but desires the farmer to keep it for him, until he wants it ; or, in other words, until he finds the price suits his expecta- tions." This rage against "forestalling" was, of course, very senseless; but it had the advantage of being applied indiscriminately, and to every description of food. Two women at Bristol were imprisoned for "forestalling" a cart load of mackerel; whilst the trial of Waddington for "forestalling" *hops* is almost a *cause célèbre*. Now, hops could hardly be construed into food; and, after having carefully read his trial, I can but come to the conclusion that he was a very hardly-used man, and was imprisoned for nothing at all.[1] I merely mention his case as a proof of the senseless irritation which the price of food caused upon the unreasoning public.

Food had to be looked for anywhere. The Continent was no field for speculation; a bad harvest had been universal; and, besides, we were at war. Then, for the first time, was India drawn upon for our food supply, and the East India Company—that greatest marvel of all trade—offered every facility towards the export of rice. Their instructions were as follow: "That every ship, which takes on board three quarters of her registered tonnage in rice, shall have liberty to fill up with such goods as have been usually imported by country ships. That ships embarking in this adventure shall be allowed to carry out exports from this country. That they shall be excused the payment of the Company's duty of 3 per cent., on the rice so imported. That, after the ship shall have been approved by the Company's surveyors, the risk of the rice which she brings, shall be on account of Government, which will save the owners the expense of insurance. That, in case the price of rice shall, on the ships' arrival, be under from 32s. to 29s. the hundredweight, the difference between what it may sell for, and the above rates shall be made good to the owners, on the following conditions—That the ship which departs from her port of lading, within one month from the promulgation of these orders, shall be guaranteed 32s. the hundredweight; if in two months, 31s.; if in three months, 30s.; and if in four months, 29s. But, that dependence may be safely placed on the rice being of

[1] *Par parenthèse.* This Mr. Waddington, whilst in the King's Bench Prison, gave away a ton of potatoes a day, about Christmas time. They were first of all sold at one halfpenny a pound, and the produce in money was put in the poor's box, for the benefit of the poor prisoners.

superior quality, that is, equal, at least, to the best cargo of
rice, it shall be purchased by an agent appointed by
Government.   Coppered   ships   to   be   preferred,   and,
although Convoy [1] will, if possible, be obtained for them,
they must not be detained for Convoy."

[1] Owing to the war, it was found safer for many merchant vessels to sail in
company, and these fleets usually had two or three men-of-war in attendance
to act as guards, and to protect them ; they were called " the Convoy."

CHAPTER XXIX.

PARLIAMENT bestirred itself in the matter of food supply, not only in appointing "a Committee to consider the high price of provisions," who made their first report on the 24th of November, 1800; but Mr. Dudley Ryder (afterwards Earl of Harrowby) moved, on the 12th of November, in the same year, the following resolutions, which were agreed to :—

" 1. That the average price at which foreign corn shall be sold in London, should be ascertained, and published, in the *London Gazette*.

" 2. That there be given on every quarter of wheat, weighing 424 lbs., which shall be imported into the port of London, or into any of the principal ports of each district of Great Britain, before the 1st of October, 1801, a bounty equal to the sum by which the said average price in London, published in the *Gazette*, in the third week after the importation of such wheat, shall be less than 100s per quarter.

" 3. That there shall be given on every quarter of barley,

weighing 352 lbs., which shall be imported into the port of London, or any of the principal ports of each district of Great Britain before the 1st of October, 1801, a bounty equal to the sum by which the said average price in London, published in the *Gazette* in the third week after the importation of such barley, shall be less than 45s. per quarter.

"4. That there be given on every quarter of rye, weighing 408 lbs., which shall be imported into the port of London, or into any of the principal ports of each district of Great Britain, before the 1st of October, 1801, a bounty equal to the sum by which the said average price in London, published in the *Gazette* of the third week after the importation of such rye, shall be less than 65s. per quarter.

"5. That there be given on every quarter of oats, weighing 280 lbs., which shall be imported into the port of London, or into any of the principal ports of each district of Great Britain, before the 1st of October, 1801, a bounty equal to the sum by which the average price in London, published in the *Gazette* in the third week after the importation of such oats, shall be less than 30s. per quarter.

"6. That there be given on every barrel of superfine wheaten flour, of 196 lbs. weight, which shall be imported into such ports before the 1st of October, 1801, and sold by public sale by auction, within two months after importation, a bounty equal to the sum by which the actual price of each barrel of such flour so sold, shall be less than 70s.

"7. That there be given on every barrel of fine wheaten flour, of 196 lbs. weight, which shall be imported into such ports before the 1st of October, 1801, and sold by public sale, by auction, within two months after importation, a bounty equal to the sum by which the actual price of each barrel of such flour so sold shall be less than 68s.

"8. That there be given on every cwt. of rice which shall be imported into such ports in any ship which shall have cleared out from any port in the East Indies before the

1st of September, 1801, and which shall be sold by public sale, a bounty equal to the sum by which the actual price of each cwt. of rice so sold shall be less than 32s.

"9. That there be given on every cwt. of rice, from America, which shall be imported into such ports, before the 1st of October, 1801, and sold by public sale by auction, within two months after importation, a bounty equal to the sum by which the actual price of each cwt. of such rice so sold, shall be less than 35s."

Thus we see that the paternal government of that day did all they could to find food for the hungry ; and it is somewhat curious to note the commencement of a trade for food, with two countries like India and the United States of America. Still more did the Government attempt to alleviate the distress by passing an Act (41 Geo. III. c. 16), forbidding the manufacture of fine bread, and enacting that all bread should contain the whole meal—*i.e.*, all the bran, &c.—and be what we term "brown bread." Indeed the Act was called, popularly, "The Brown Bread Bill." It came into force on the 16th of January, 1801, a date which was afterwards extended to the 31st of January, but did not last long ; its repeal receiving the Royal Assent on the 26th of February of the same year.

So also the authorities did good service in prosecuting bakers for light weight ; and the law punished them heavily. I will only make one quotation—*Morning Post*, February 5, 1801. "PUBLIC OFFICE, BOW STREET. LIGHT BREAD. Several complaints having been made against a baker in the neighbourhood of Bloomsbury, for selling bread short of weight, he was, yesterday, summoned on two informations ; the one for selling a quartern loaf deficient of its proper weight eight ounces, and the other for a quartern loaf wanting four ounces. A warrant was also issued to weigh all the bread in his shop, when 29 quartern loaves were seized, which wanted, together, 58 ounces of their proper weight ; the light bread was brought to the office, and the defendant appeared to answer the charges. The parties were sworn as to the purchase of the first two loaves, which being proved, and the loaves being weighed in the presence of the Magistrates, the defendant was convicted in the full penalty of five shillings per ounce for the twelve ounces they were deficient ; and, Mr. Ford observing that as the parties complaining were entitled to one moiety of the penalty, he could not with justice remit any part of it.

" Respecting the other 29 loaves, as it was the report of the officers who executed the warrant, that there were a considerable number more found in his shop that were of full weight, it was the opinion of him, and the other Magistrates then present, that the fine should be mitigated to 2s. per ounce, amounting to £5 16s., which the defendant was, accordingly, obliged to pay, and the 29 loaves, which, of course, were forfeited, Mr. Ford ordered to be distributed to the poor.

"A search warrant was also executed at the shop of a baker near Drury Lane, against whom an information had also been laid for selling light bread ; but, it being near three o'clock in the afternoon when the officers went to the shop, very little bread remained, out of which, however, they found eight quarterns, three half quarterns, and four twopenny loaves, short of weight 28 ounces, and on which the baker was adjudged to pay 2s. per ounce, and the bread was disposed of in the same manner as the other."

As we have seen, the price of bread in London was regulated by the civic authorities, according to the price of flour—and it is gratifying to find that they fearlessly exercised their functions. September 1, 1801 : "A number of Bakers were summoned to produce their bills of parcels of flour purchased by them during the last two weeks, according to the returns. Many of them were very irregular, which they said was owing to the mealmen not giving in their bills of parcels with the price at the time of delivering

the flour. They were ordered to attend on a future day,
when the mealmen will be summoned to answer that
complaint."

Nor were the bakers, alone, subject to this vigilance, the
butchers were well looked after, and, if evil doers, were
punished in a way worthy of the times of the "Liber
Albus." *Vide* the *Morning Post*, April 16, 1800 : "Yesterday, the carcase of a calf which was condemned by the
Lord Mayor, as being unwholesome, was burnt before the
butcher's door, in Whitechapel. His Lordship commended
the Inquest of Portsoken Ward very much for their exertions in this business, and hoped it would be an example
to others, that when warm weather comes on they may
have an eye to stalls covered with meat almost putrified,
and very injurious to the health of their fellow citizens."

Just at that time meat was extraordinarily high in price
—in May, only a few weeks after the above quotation,
beef was 1s. 6d. and mutton 1s. 3d. per lb., whilst fowls
were 6s. 6d. each, and every other article of food at pro-
portionally high rates. Yet, as was only natural, every
means were taken to increase the food supply. Cattle
shows were inaugurated, and great interest was taken in
them by the neighbouring gentry. As an example we will
take one held in September, 1801, where Mr. Tatton Sykes
was judge, and there were such well-known county gentlemen present as Mr. Denison, Major Osbaldeston, Major
Topham, &c., &c. The prizes were not high ; but, then,
as now, in agricultural contests, honour went before the
money value of the prize.

				£	s.	d.
Best shearling tup from any part of England	...	.0	10	0
Best do bred in the East Riding ...	...	10	10	0
Best year old bull do	...	...	8	8	0
Second best do do	...	...	6	6	0
Third best do do	...	...	5	5	0
Fourth best do do	...	...	4	4	0
Fifth best do do	...	...	2	2	0

			£	s.	d.
Best two year old heifer bred in the East Riding			3	3	0
Second best	do	do ...	3	3	0
Third best	do	do ...	2	2	0
Best boar		do ...	3	3	0

But, with the treaty of peace with France came comparative plenty. The French were keen enough to, at once, take advantage of the resumption of friendly relations ; and, knowing that an era of cheaper food was to be inaugurated, prices fell rapidly here. For instance, no sooner did the news of peace reach Ireland, than the price of pork fell, in some markets from 63s. to 30s. per cwt. ; and beef dropped to 33s. 6d. or 30s. 6d. per cwt. Butter, and other farm produce had proportionable reductions. In London, one shopkeeper somewhat whimsically notified the change. At the time of illumination for the peace, he displayed a transparency, on one side of which was a quartern loaf, under which were the words, "*I am coming down,*" and by its side appeared a pot of porter, which rejoined, "*So am I.*"

When the pioneer boat, loaded with provisions from France, arrived at Portsmouth, the authorities were at a loss as to what to do with her ; so she was detained until an order could be received permitting her to trade and depart within 24 hours. Her cargo was sold out at once, and no wonder, for she sold pigs at 16s. each, turkeys 2s. 6d. each, and fowls 2s. a couple, whilst eggs were going at 1s. 6d. a score.

Whilst on this subject, mention may be made of the kind of provision made for the men's feeding, otherwise than at home. The Hotel proper, as we know it, was but in its infancy ; and, as far as I can gather, there were but some fifteen hotels in London. This does not, of course, include the large coaching inns, which made up beds, because they catered for a fleeting population ; nor does it take cognizance of the coffee houses, many of which made up beds, especially for visitors from various counties, where they might possibly meet with friends, or hear the last news about them, and see the county newspaper; whilst all, without exception, and most of the taverns, supplied their customers with dinners, and other food—in fact, they acted as *victuallers*, and not as the keepers of *drinkeries*, as now. There were, besides, many of the cheaper class of eating houses, called *cook shops*, scattered over every part of the town, at which a plentiful dinner might be obtained at, from a shilling, to eighteenpence. In addition, there were very many *à la mode* beef houses, and soup shops, so that every taste, and purse, was consulted.

Before closing these notes on feeding, early in the century, I must chronicle a "little dinner." *Morning Post*, July 26, 1800: "At a village in Cheshire, last year, three clergymen, after dinner, ate fourteen quarts of nuts, and, during their sitting, drank six bottles of port wine, and NO other liquor!"

CHAPTER XXX.

Men's dress—the "Jean de Bry" coat—Short coats fashionable at watering-places
—"All Bond Street trembled as he strode"—Rules for the behaviour of a
"Bond Street Lounger."

OF Dress, either of men, or women, there is little to chronicle during this ten years. The mutations during a similar period, at the close of the previous century, had been so numerous, and radical, as to be sufficient to satisfy any ordinary being; so that, with the exception of the ordinary changes of fashion, which tailors, and milliners will impose upon their victims, there is little to record.

At the commencement of the year 1800, men wore what were then called "Jean de Bry" coats, so named from a French statesman, who was somewhat prominent during the French Revolution—born 1760, died 1834. The accompanying illustration is somewhat exaggerated, not so much as regards the padding on the shoulders, as to the Hessian boots, which latter might, almost, have passed a critical examination, had it not have been that they are furnished with bells, instead of tassels. The coat was padded at the shoulders, to give breadth, and buttoned tight to show the slimness of the waist; yet, as this, under ordinary circumstances, would have hidden the waistcoat—the coat had to be made short-waisted.

Then, the same year, only towards its close, came a craze for short coats, or jackets, resembling the Spencers, but they did not last long, being only fashionable at Brighton, Cheltenham, &c. There seems to have been very little change until 1802, when a modification of the Jean de Bry coat was worn, with the collar increasing very much in height, and boots were discarded in walking.

A JEAN DE BRY.

The portrait of Colonel Duff, afterwards Lord Fyfe, on the next page, is only introduced as an exemplar of costume, and not as a " Bond Street Lounger," of whom we hear so much, and, as not only may many of my readers like to know something about him, but his character is so amusingly sketched by a contemporary, and the account gives such a vivid picture of the manners of the times, that I transcribe it. It is from the *Morning Post* of the 6th of February, 1800 ; and, after premising that the Lounger is comfortably settled at an hotel, the following instructions are given him, as being necessary to establish his character as a young man of fashion. " In short, find fault with every *single* article, without exception, d——n the *waiter* at almost regular intervals, and never let him stand *one moment still*, but 'keep him *eternally* moving ;' having it in remembrance that he is only an *unfortunate*, and *wretched* subordinate, of course, a *stranger* to feelings which are an ornament to Human Nature ; with this recollection on your part that the more illiberal the abuse he has from *you*, the greater will be his admiration of your *superior* abilities, and *Gentleman*-like qualifications.

ALL BOND STREET TREMBLED AS HE STRODE.

Confirm him in the opinion he has so justly imbibed, by *swearing* the *fish* is not *warm* through; the poultry is *old*, and 'tough as your *Grandmother*'; the pastry is made with butter, *rank Irish*; the cheese, which they call *Stilton*, is nothing but *pale Suffolk*; the malt liquor *damnable*, a mere infusion of *malt*, *tobacco*, and *cocculus Indicus*; the port *musty*; the sherry *sour*; and the whole of the dinner and dessert were 'infernally infamous,' and, of course, not fit for the entertainment of a *Gentleman*; conclude the lecture with an oblique hint, that without *better* accommodations, and more ready *attention*, you shall be under the necessity of leaving the house for a more *comfortable* situation. This *spirited* declaration at *starting* will answer a variety of purposes, but none so essential as an *anticipated* objection to the payment of *your bill* whenever it may be presented. With no small degree of personal ostentation, give the waiter your name 'because you have ordered your letters *there*, and, as they will be of importance, beg they may be taken care of, particularly those written in *a female hand*, of which description, many may be expected.

"Having thus introduced you to, and fixed you, recruit-like, in *good quarters*, I consider it almost unnecessary to say, however *bad* you may *imagine* the wine, I doubt not your own *prudence* will point out the characteristic necessity for drinking enough, not only to afford you the credit of reeling to bed by the aid of the banister, but the collateral comfort of calling yourself 'damned queer' in the morning, owing entirely to the villainous adulteration of the wine, for, when *mild* and *genuine*, you can take off *three* bottles 'without winking or blinking.' When rousing from your last somniferous reverie in the morning, ring the bell with no small degree of energy, which will serve to convince the whole family you are awake; upon the entrance of either *chamberlain* or *chambermaid*, vociferate half a dozen questions in succession, without waiting for a single reply. As, What morning is it? does it hail, rain, or shine? Is it a frost? Is my breakfast ready? Has anybody enquired for me? Is my groom here? &c., &c. And here it becomes directly in point to observe, that a *groom* is become so evidently necessary to the *ton* of the present day (particularly in the neighbourhood of Bond Street) that a great number of *Gentlemen* keep a *groom*, who cannot (except upon *credit*) keep a *horse;* but then, they are always upon 'the look out for horses;' and, till they are obtained, the employment of *the groom* is the embellishment of *both ends* of his master, by first dressing his head, and then polishing his boots and shoes.

"The trifling ceremonies of the morning gone through, you will sally forth in search of adventures, taking that great Mart of *every* virtue, 'BOND STREET,' in your way.

Here it will be impossible for you (between the hours of *twelve* and *four*) to remain, even a few minutes, without falling in with various 'feathers of your wing,' so true it is, in the language of Rowe, 'you herd together,' that you cannot fear being long alone. So soon as three of you are met, adopt a Knight of the Bath's motto, and become literally 'Tria juncta in uno,' or, in other words, link your arms so as to engross the whole breadth of the pavement ; the *fun* of driving fine women, and old dons, into the *gutter*, is exquisite, and, of course, constitutes *a laugh* of the most *humane* sensibility. Never make these excursions without *spurs*, it will afford not only *presumptive* proof of your *really* keeping a horse, but the lucky opportunity of *hooking* a fine girl by the gown, apron, or petticoat ; and, while she is under the distressing mortification of disentangling her-self, you and your companions can add to her dilemma by some indelicate *innuendo,* and, in the moment of extrication, walk off with an exulting exclamation of having 'cracked the muslin.' Let it be a fixed rule never to be seen in the LOUNGE without a *stick,* or *cane ;* this, dangling in a string, may accidentally get between the feet of any female in passing ; if she falls, in consequence, that can be no fault of *yours,* but the effect of her indiscretion.

"By way of relief to the sameness of the scene, throw yourself loungingly into a chair at Owen's,[1] cut up a *pine* with the greatest *sang froid,* amuse yourself with a jelly or two, and, after viewing with a happy *indifference* whatever may present itself, throw down a *guinea* (without con-descending to ask a question) and walk off ; this will not only be politically inculcating an idea of your *seeming* liberality upon the present ; but paving the way to *credit* upon a *future* occasion. I had hitherto omitted to mention the necessity for previously providing yourself with *a glass* suspended from your button-hole by a string) the want of

---

[1] This probably was the shop of *Owen and Bradley* whose names first appear in the *London Directory* of 1812, as fruiterers, 77, New Bond Street.—J.A.

which will inevitably brand you with *vulgarity*, if not with indigence; for the true (and, formerly, 'unsophisticated') breed of *Old John Bull* is so very much altered by *bad crosses*, and a deficiency in constitutional stamina, equally affecting the *optic nerves*, that there are very few men of fashion can see *clear* beyond the *tip* of the *nose*.

"At the breaking up of the parade, stroll, as it were, accidentally into the Prince of Wales's Coffee house, in Conduit Street, walk up with the greatest ease, and consummate confidence to every box, in rotation; look at everybody with an inexplicable *hauteur*, bordering upon contempt; for, although it is most likely you will know *little* or *nothing* of *them*, the great object is, that they should have a *perfect knowledge* of *you*. Having repeatedly, and vociferously, called the waiter when he is most *engaged*, and, at each time asked him various questions equally frivolous and insignificant, seem to skim the surface of the *Morning Post* (if disengaged), humming the *March* in *Blue Beard*,[1] to show the *versatility* of your genius; when, finding you have made yourself sufficiently *conspicuous*, and an object of general attention (or rather attraction), suddenly leave the room, but not without such an *emphatical* mode of *shutting* the *door*, as may afford to the various companies, and individuals, a most striking proof of your departure."

[1] "The grand Dramatic Romance of Blue Beard; or, Female Curiosity." The Words by George Colman the younger—the Music composed and selected by M. K. (Michael Kelly). London, 1798.

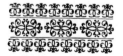

CHAPTER XXXI.

"THE Three Mr. Wiggins's" are *real* "Bond Street Loungers," and are portraits of Lord Llandaff and his brothers, the Hon. Montagu, and George, Matthews. They were dandies of the purest water, with their white waistcoats and white satin knee-ribbons. The title is taken from a farce by Allingham, called "Mrs. Wiggins," played at the Haymarket, May 27, 1803. It is very laughable, and turns upon the adventures of an old man named Wiggins, and three Mrs. Wiggins's. It was very popular, and gave the title to another caricature of Gillray's.

As will be seen, they wore powder, but this curious fashion was on its last legs—the *Crops*, or advanced Whigs, having given it its death blow; still, it struggled on for some years yet. There is a little story told in the *Morning Herald* of the 20th of June, 1804, which will bear reproduction: "The following conversation occurred on Monday last, in the Gallery of the House of Commons. A gentleman, very much powdered, happened to sit before another who did not wear any. During the course of the debate, the son of *powder* in front, frequently annoyed, by his nodding, or rather his *noddle*, his neighbour in the rear, for which he apologized, as often as any notice was taken of it. At last, the influence of Morpheus became so powerful, that the rear rank man found his arm perfectly painted with

THE THREE MR. WIGGINS'S.

powder, in such a manner as to produce some *ignition* in his temper, and repel his annoyer with a little more *spunk*[1] than he showed on any of the former occasions. This

---

[1] This word has two meanings, which are here played upon. One is *spirit* or *pluck;* the other is the name indifferently for match splints, or dry, rotten wood.

being resented, the other presented his arm, and said, ' Sir, you should not be angry; for, if I wished for such an ornament as this, I should, this morning, have left that office to my hair-dresser. I am a man of such independence that I would not, willingly, be indebted to you for a single *meal,* and here you have forced on me a bushel. If I had been your greatest enemy, you could do nothing more severe, than to *pulverize* me; and, as I have given you no intentional offence, I must beg of you, in future, not to *dust my jacket.*' This sally had all the effect for which it was intended, and, instead of exchanging cards, the affair ended, like some senatorial speeches, in a *laugh.*"

As all the members of the family, including the domestics had to be powdered, most houses of any pretension had a small room set apart for the performance, called "the powdering room," or closet, where the person to be operated upon went behind two curtains, and, by putting the head between the two, the body was screened from the powder, and the head received its due quantity, without injury to the clothes.

Still, all the world was not rich, and, therefore, with some, economy in clothing was a necessity. As is usual, when a want appears, it is met; and in this case it certainly was, in a (to us) novel manner — *Morning Post,* January 12, 1805: "INTERESTING to the PUBLIC. W Welsford, Tailor, No. 142, Bishopsgate Street, respectfully informs the Public, that he continues to pursue the plan, originally adopted by him, six years since, of SUPPLYING CLOTHES, on the following terms:—

Four Suits of Superfine Clothes, the old Suits to be returned, in one year ...	£16	0	0
Five Suits	18	18	0
Six Suits	21	10	0

"Those Gentlemen who should not prefer the above

Contract, may be supplied at the undermentioned reduced price:

A Coat of the best Superfine Cloth, complete £2 12 0
A Fine Fancy Waistcoat 0 14 0
Superfine double-milled Cassimere Breeches 1 4 0
Superfine Pantaloons ... ... 1 0 0."

Nor was this the only practical economy in dress in that age. Hats, which were then, as a rule, made of Beaver, were somewhat expensive articles; and, in looking diligently over the newspapers of the times, I found that here, again, a want arose, and was met. These Beaver hats got shabby, and could be repaired; a firm advertising that "after several years' practice they have brought the Art of Rebeavering Old Hats to greater perfection than it is possible to conceive; indeed, they are the only persons that have brought it to perfection; for, by their method, they can make a gentleman's old hat (apparently not worth a shilling) as good as it was when new. . . . Gentlemen who prefer Silk hats, may have them silked, and made waterproof."

Hats were rendered dearer than they would, otherwise, have been, by their having to pay a tax—the only portion of personal clothing which did so. This tax, of course, was evaded; so we find, in the *Morning Post*, May 20, 1810, the following "CAUTION TO HATTERS. A Custom prevailing among hatters, of pasting the stamp upon the lining, by which the same stamp may frequently be sold with different hats successively, they are required by the Commissioners of the Stamp Duties, to conform, in selling hats, to the provisions of the Act of the 36th of George III., cap. 125, secs. 3, 4, 7, 9, which directs that the lining, or inside covering of every hat shall, itself, be stamped; and it is the intention of the Commissioners to prosecute for the penalties of that Act, inflicted on all persons guilty of violating its regulations. Persons purchasing hats are requested to be careful in seeing that they are duly stamped upon the lining itself, and not by a separate piece of linen affixed to it; and reminded that the Act above-mentioned (sec. 10) inflicts a penalty of £10 upon persons buying, or wearing, hats not legally stamped."

ORIGINALS. A HINT TO THE BON TON.

We have seen it recommended to the Bond Street Lounger that it was absolutely necessary for him to have an eye-glass suspended from his button-hole; and the same fashion is mentioned in the *Morning Post*, August 28, 1806: "The town has been long amused with the *quizzing glasses* of our modern fops, happily ridiculed by a door-key in O'Keefe's whimsical farce of *The Farmer*. A Buck has lately made his appearance in Bond Street, daily, between two and four o'clock, with *a Telescope*, which he occasionally applies to his eye, as he has a glimpse of some object passing on the other side of the street, worth *peeping* at. At the present season, we cannot but recommend this practice to our fashionable readers, who remain in the Metropolis. It indicates friendship, as it shows a disposition to *regard* those who are at a *distance*."

There have been, in all ages of fashion, some who outvied the common herd in eccentricity of costume; and the early nineteenth century was no exception to the rule. It is true that it had not, in the time of which I write, arisen to the dignity of a "pea-green Haines ;" but still, it could show its "Green Man." "BRIGHTON, September 25, 1806. Among the personages attracting, here, public notice, is an original, or *would-be* ori-

ORIGINALS. A HINT TO THE BON TON.

ginal, generally known by the appellation of ' the Green Man.' He is dressed in green pantaloons, green waistcoat, green frock, green cravat ; and his ears, whiskers, eyebrows, and chin, are better powdered than his head, which is, however, covered with flour. He eats nothing but green fruits and vegetables ; has his rooms painted green, and furnished with a green sofa, green chairs, green tables, green bed, and green curtains. His gig, his livery, his portmanteau, his gloves, and his whip, are all green. With a green silk handkerchief in his hand and a large watch chain, with green seals fastened to the green buttons of his green waistcoat, he parades every day on the Steyne, and in the libraries, erect like a statue, walking, or, rather, moving to music, smiling and singing, as well contented with his own dear self, as well as all those round him, who are not few." That he had money was evident, for his green food, including, as it did, choice fruit, would sometimes cost him a guinea a day; besides which, he was seen at every place of amusement, and spent his money lavishly. Eventually, he turned out to be a lunatic, and, after throwing himself out of windows, and off a cliff, he was taken care of.

The two preceding illustrations are manifest exaggerations of costume; but the germ of truth which supplies the satire is there; and, with them, the men's dress of this period is closed.

CHAPTER XXXII.

Ladies' dress — French costume — Madame Recamier — The classical style — " Progress of the toilet "—False hair—Hair-dresser's advertisement—The Royal Family and dress—Curiosities of costume.

IN ladies' dress more allowance must be made for the caprices of fashion ; it always has been their prescriptive right to exercise their ingenuity, and fancy, in adorning their persons ; and, save that the head-dress is somewhat caricatured, the next illustration gives a very good idea of the style of dress adopted by ladies at the commencement of 1800, some phases of which we are familiar with, owing to their recent reproduction—such as the *décolletée* dress, and clinging, and diaphonous skirt, as well as the long gloves.

However, the eccentricities of English costume, at this period, were as nothing compared with their French sisters. The Countess of Brownlow,[1] speaking, as an eye-witness, says: "The Peace of 1802 brought, I suppose, many French to England ; but I only remember one, the celebrated Madame Recamier, who created a sensation, partly by her beauty, but still more by her dress, which was vastly unlike the unsophisticated style, and *poke* bonnets, of the English women. She appeared in Kensington Gardens, *à l'antique*,

[1] "Slight Reminiscences of a Septuagenarian," by Emma Sophia, Countess of Brownlow, p. 2. London, 1867.

PARIS FASHIONS FOR WINTER DRESS—1800.

a muslin dress clinging to her form like the folds of the
drapery on a statue ; her hair in a plait at the back, and
falling in small ringlets round her face, and greasy with
huile antique ; a large veil thrown over the head, completed
her attire, that not unnaturally caused her to be followed
and stared at."

The French Revolution and early Consulate were emi-

FASHIONS, EARLY 1800.

nently classical, as regards ladies' dress; and, as a matter
of course, the mode was followed in England, but never
to the extent that it was in France. No one can doubt
the beauty of this style of dress ; but it was one totally
unfitted for out-door use, and even for evening dress. It
was very slight, and then only fitted for the young and
graceful, certainly not for the middle-aged and rotund.

There was a ladies' magazine, which began in 1806,
called *La belle Assemblée ;* and à very good magazine it

FASHIONABLE FURBELOES; OR, THE BACK FRONT OF A LADY OF
FASHION, IN THE YEAR 1801.

LIGHT HEAD-DRESSES AND LONG PETTICOATS FOR THE YEAR 1802.

is.   In it, of course, are numerous fashion plates ; but I
take it that they were then, much as now, intended to be
looked at as indications of the fashion, more than the fashion
itself.   Certainly, in the contemporaneous prints, I have
never met with any costume like them, and I much prefer
for accuracy of detail, to go to the pictorial satirist, who,
if he did somewhat exaggerate, did so on a given basis,
an actual costume ; and, moreover, threw some life and
expression into his groups, which render them better worth

PREPARING FOR A BALL—1803.

looking at, than the
meaningless lay-
figures, which serve
as pegs, on which
to hang the clothes
of the fashion-
monger.

The next three
illustrations, which,
although designed
by an amateur, are
etched by Gillray,
give us a glimpse
of the mysteries of
the toilet such as
might be sought
for in vain else-
where ; they are
particularly valuable, as they are in no way exaggerated,
and supply details otherwise unprocurable.

After these revelations, no one will be surprised to find
that ladies wore false hair.   It has been done in all ages ;
when done, it is no secret, even from casual observers.   It
was thoroughly understood that it was worn, for was there
not always standing witness in the windows of Ross in
Bishopsgate Street, and especially in the two bow windows
of Cryer, 68, Cornhill—one of which had twenty blocks of

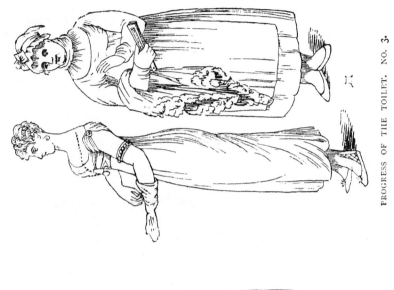

PROGRESS OF THE TOILET. NO. I.

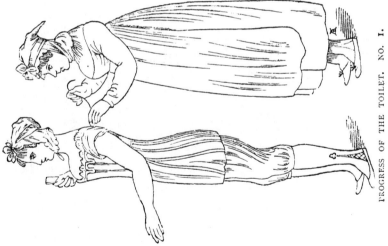

PROGRESS OF THE TOILET. NO. 3.

gentleman's, and the other twenty-one of lady's perukes.
One West-end *coiffeur* thus advertises—*Morning Post*,
March 18, 1800:

"Correct Imitations of Nature.
"To Ladies of Rank and Fashion.
"T. Bowman's House and Shop being now repaired, is

PROGRESS OF THE TOILET. NO. 2.

re-opened with every conveniency and accommodation. His
new Stock consists of:

"I. Full Dress Head-dresses, made of long hair,
judiciously matched, and made to correspond with Nature
in every part; the colours genuine; they will dress in any
style the best head of hair is capable of; and, in beauty,
are far superior. Price 4, 5, 6½, 8, 10, 12, 15, and 20 guineas.

"II. REAL NATURAL CURL HEAD-DRESSES. These cannot be described ; they must be seen. Price 5 guineas.

"III. FORCED NATURAL CURL HEAD-DRESSES are made of such of the Natural Curled Hairs, as have not a sufficient curl ; therefore it is assisted by Art : with fine points, of a soft and silky texture, very beautiful. Price 4 guineas.

"IV. PLAIN CURLED HEAD-DRESSES are made of Hair, originally straight, but curled by baking, boiled, &c. Price 3 guineas.

"V. The TRESSE À LA GRECQUE, when put over the short head-dress, is a complete full dress. Price half-a-guinea, 1, 1½, 2, 3, 4, and 5 guineas.

" In order to account for the apparent high prices of the above, it is necessary to observe, that there are as many qualities of Hair as of Silk, Fur, or Wool (the guinea, and the guinea and a half Wigs, as they are called, can only be made of the refuse, or of Hair procured in this Country) ; all that Bowman uses is collected at Fairs, from the French Peasants, on the Continent, which (from the present[1] convulsed state) is now very dear ; as, notwithstanding the artful and false insinuations of interested persons, the importation of last year is not more than one-fifth of former years, and no part of it Men's Hair.

" ☞ One thing T. B. intreats Ladies to observe, that he does not expose, or dress his best articles on Heads, Poupées, or Dolls, for Show, the common trick at the Cheap Shops, to hide Defects, as many Ladies know to their cost. His Head-dresses are, until they are sold, the same as a Head of Hair that wants cutting ; they are then cut and trimmed to suit the Countenance, or fancy, of the wearer. No article is sold that is not in every respect perfect in fitting ; and the most disinterested advice given as to what is fashionable, proper, and becoming. Ladies'

[1] *Sic in orig.*

Hair dressed at 3s. 6d., 5s., and 7s. 6d.—No. 102, New Bond Street."

A few days later on, the same paper (March 21, 1800) relates a fearful story. "Yesterday a bald-pated lady lost her wig on Westminster Bridge; and, to complete her mortification, a near-sighted gentleman, who was passing at the time, addressed the back of her head, in mistake for her face, with a speech of condolence."

In June of the same year, the same paper takes the ladies to task for their *décolletée* dresses. "The ladies continue to uncover their necks *behind*, and well they may; for, since they are covering them *before*, they cannot be so much afraid of *back-biting.*"

The Queen and the Princesses set practical lessons in social economy to the ladies of England. The latter were not ashamed to embroider their own dresses for a drawing-room, and the Queen, in order to encourage home manufactures, used Spitalfields silk, or stuffs made in this country; and "stuff balls," like our "calico" ditto, were not uncommon.

At the end of the first decade of the century costumes became even more bizarre; although, of course, *Les Invisibles* is an exaggeration. The ordinary out-door dress of ladies of this year is shown in the two following illustrations.

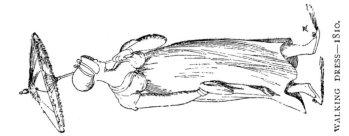

WALKING DRESS—1810.

GRACE, FASHION, AND MANNERS. FROM THE
LIFE—1810.

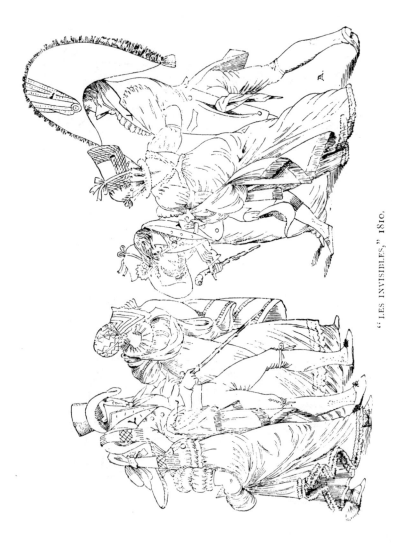

"LES INVISIBLES," 1810.

CHAPTER XXXIII.

Diversions of people of fashion—Daily life of the King—Children—Education—
Girls' education—Matrimonial advertisements—Gretna Green marriages—
Story of a wedding ring—Wife selling—" A woman to let."

THE Essayists of Anne's time did good work, and left precious material for Social History behind them, when they good-humouredly made fun of the little follies of the day; and two satirical prints of Rowlandson's follow so well in their footprints that I must needs transcribe them. "May 1, 1802. *A Man of Fashion's Journal.* 'Queer dreams, owing to Sir Richard's claret, always drink too much of it—rose at one—dressed by half-past three—took an hour's ride—a good horse, my last purchase, remember to sell him again—nothing like variety—dined at six with Sir Richard—said several good things—forgot 'em all—in high spirits—quizzed a parson—drank three bottles, and loung'd to the theatre—not quite clear about the play—comedy or tragedy—forget which—saw the last act—Kemble toll loll—not quite certain whether it was Kemble or not—Mrs. Siddons monstrous fine—got into a hack—set down in St. James's Street—dipp'd a little with the boys at hazards—confounded bad luck—lost all my money.'"

"May 1, 1802. *A Woman of Fashion's Journal.* 'Dreamt of the Captain—certainly a fine man—counted my card money — lost considerably — never play again with the Dowager—breakfasted at *two*, . . . dined at seven at Lady Rackett's—the Captain there—more than usually agreeable—went to the Opera—the Captain in the party—house prodigiously crowded—my *ci devant* husband in the opposite box—rather *mal à propos*—but no matter—*telles choses sont*—looked into Lady Squander's *roût*—positively a mob —sat down to cards—in great luck—won a cool hundred of my Lord Lackwit, and fifty of the Baron—returned home at five in the morning—indulged in half an hour's reflection —resolved on reformation, and erased my name from the Picnic Society.'"

This style of life was taken more from the Prince of Wales than the King, whose way of living was very simple; and, although this book is intended more to show the daily life of the middle classes, than that of Royalty, still a sketch of the third George's private daily life cannot be otherwise than interesting. It was this quiet, unassuming daily life of the King, together with his affliction, which won him the hearts of his people.

Morning Post, November 7, 1806: "When the King rises, which is generally about half-past seven o'clock, he proceeds immediately to the Queen's saloon, where His Majesty is met by one of the Princesses; generally either Augusta, Sophia, or Amelia; for each, in turn, attend their revered Parents. From thence the Sovereign and his Daughter, attended by the Lady in Waiting, proceed to the Chapel, in the Castle, wherein Divine Service is performed by the Dean, or Sub-Dean : the ceremony occupies about an hour. Thus the time passes until nine o'clock, when the King, instead of proceeding to his own apartment, and breakfasting alone, now takes that meal with the Queen, and the five Princesses. The table is always set out in the Queen's noble breakfasting-room, which has been recently decorated with very excellent modern hangings, and, since the late improvements by Mr. Wyatt, com-

mands a most delightful and extensive prospect of the
Little Park. The breakfast does not occupy more than
half an hour. The King and Queen sit at the head of the
table, according to seniority. Etiquette, in every other
respect is strictly adhered to. On entering the room the
usual forms are observed, according to rank. After breakfast, the King generally rides out on horseback, attended
by his Equerries ; three of the Princesses, namely, Augusta,
Sophia, and Amelia, are usually of the party. Instead of
only walking his horse, His Majesty now proceeds at a good
round trot. When the weather is unfavourable, the King
retires to his favourite sitting-room, and sends for Generals
Fitzroy, or Manners, to play at chess with him. His
Majesty, who knows the game well, is highly pleased when
he beats the former—that gentleman being an excellent
player. The King dines regularly at two o'clock ; the
Queen and Princesses at four. His Majesty visits, and
takes a glass of wine with them, at five. After this period,
public business is frequently transacted by the King in
his own study, wherein he is attended by his Private
Secretary, Colonel Taylor. The evening is, as usual,
passed at cards, in the Queen's Drawing-room, where
three tables are set out. To these parties many of the
principal nobility, &c., residing in the neighbourhood, are
invited. When the Castle clock strikes ten, the visitors
retire. The supper is then set out, but that is merely a
matter of form, and of which none of the Family partake.
These illustrious personages retire at eleven o'clock to rest
for the night, and sleep in undisturbed repose until they
rise in the morning. The journal of one day is the history
of the whole year."

Children were, in those days, "seen and not heard ;" and
were very different to the precocious little prigs of the
present time. The nursery was their place, and not the
unlimited society of, and association with, their elders, as
now. When the time for school came, the boys were

taught a principally classical education, which was considered, as now, an absolute necessity for a gentleman.
Modern languages, with the exception of French and
Italian, were not taught. German and the Northern
languages were unknown, and Spanish only came to be
known during, and after, the Peninsular War. There was
no necessity for learning them. As a rule, people did not
travel, and, if they did, their *courier* did all the conversation for them ; and there was no foreign literature to speak
of which would induce a man to take the trouble to learn
languages. The physical sciences were in their infancy,
and chemistry,
with its wonder-
ful outcome of
electricity, was
in its veriest
babyhood : so
that boys were
not cumbered
with too much
learning.

GROUP OF CHILDREN, 1808.

As to young
ladies' educa-
tion, they had,
as they must devoutly have blessed, had they the gift of
prescience, no Girton, nor Newnham, nor St. Margaret's, nor
Somerville Halls. Their brains were not addled by exams,
or Oxford degrees. Here is their curriculum of study, with
its value, in the year 1800. " Terms :—The Young Ladies
are boarded, and taught the English and French languages,
with grammatical purity and correctness, history and
needle-works, for twenty-five guineas per annum, washing
included ; parlour boarders, forty guineas a year; day
boarders, three guineas per quarter ; day scholars, a
guinea and a half. No entrance money expected, either
from boarders or day scholars. Writing, arithmetic, music,

FILIAL AFFECTION; OR, A TRIP TO GRETNA GREEN.

dancing, Italian, geography, the use of the globes, and astronomy, taught by professors of eminence and established merit.—Wanted a young lady of a docile disposition, and genteel address, as an apprentice, or half-boarder; she will enjoy many advantages which are not to be met with in the generality of schools. Terms thirty guineas for two years."

A few years of school, and then, how to get a husband—the same then, as it is now, and ever will be. Matrimonial advertisements were very common, and bear the stamp of authenticity; but the following beats all I have yet seen: "MATRIMONY—To Noblemen, Ladies, or Gentlemen. Any Nobleman, Lady, or Gentleman, having a female friend who has been unfortunate, whom they would like to see comfortably settled, and treated with delicacy and kindness, and that might, notwithstanding errors, have an opportunity of moving in superior life, by an Union with a Gentleman holding rank in His Majesty's service, who has been long in possession of a regular and handsome establishment, and whose age, manners, and person, are such (as well as Connections) as, it is to be presumed, will not be objected to, may, by addressing a few lines, post paid, to B. Price, Esqre., to be left at the Bar of the Cambridge Coffee House, Newman Street, form a most desirable Matrimonial union for their friend. The Advertiser is serious, and therefore hopes no one will answer this from idle motives, as much care has been taken to prevent persons from gaining any information, to gratify idle curiosity. The most inviolable honour and secrecy may be relied on, and is expected to be observed throughout the treaty. If the Lady is not naturally vicious, and candour is resorted to, the Gentleman will study, by every means in his power, to promote domestic felicity."

Marriage at *Gretna Green* was then in full force, and many were the Couples who went post on that Northern road, and were married by the blacksmith—as we see in

Rowlandson's picture. These Marriages, which were, according to the law of Scotland, perfectly legal and binding, provided the contracting parties avowed themselves to be man and wife before witnesses, were only made illegal by Act of Parliament in 1856, and now it is necessary for one of the parties married, to have resided in Scotland for twenty-one days.

A curious story about a wedding ring is told in the *Morning Post* of the 3rd of December, 1800, under the heading "Clerkenwell Sessions":

A TRIP TO GRETNA GREEN (ROWLANDSON).

"The Prosecutor, a young man, lately out of his apprenticeship, and in very confined circumstances, applied, about a month ago, to the Parish of Shoreditch, and stated, that, it having been his wish to marry a young woman in the same street where he worked, but not having money sufficient to buy the wedding ring, and, his intended spouse being as poor as himself, he hoped their Worships would advance him a small sum to accomplish the purchase; and then added, that they had already been three times asked in Church, and the morrow (Sunday) was the day appointed for the ceremony.

"The Vestry taking into consideration the good character

of the applicant, ordered five shillings to be paid him, and the defendant, who is overseer of that parish, was requested to furnish him with a ring, which he did, the same night about ten o'clock, and charged for it 7s. 6d. Before leaving the shop the purchaser said he hoped it was worth the money, when the overseer replied it was good gold, and added, you may pledge it at any pawnbroker's in the town for 7s. The witness was then satisfied and departed.'

"On the Monday following, the affairs of the newly married couple not having assumed the most flourishing aspect, the bridegroom was necessitated to resort to a neighbouring pawnbroker's shop, when, to the surprise of the party, the ring was declared to be worth nothing, it being a metal composition gilt. Upon this discovery he made application to a Magistrate; the affair went before the Grand Jury, who found a true bill against the jeweller, and the matter was yesterday brought into Court, but in consequence of the absence of material witnesses, the further investigation of this business stands over to a future day." I regret to say there is no further record of this case.

On this class, the marriage tie lay lightly, and a rough, and summary, method was sometimes used to dissolve it. In a book of mine [1] I have already mentioned the practice of wife-selling, as being in vogue at this time. What I then said, can be further confirmed by examples which come within the range of this book.

Morning Herald, March 11, 1802: "On the 11th of last month, a person sold, at the market cross, in Chapel en le Frith, a wife, a child, and as much furniture as would set up a beggar, for eleven shillings!"

Morning Herald, April 16, 1802: "A Butcher sold his wife by auction the last market day at Hereford. The lot brought £1 4s. and a bowl of punch."

Annual Register, February 14, 1806: "A man named

[1] "Old Times." London: Nimmo, 1885.

John Gorsthorpe exposed his wife for sale in the market, at Hull, about one o'clock ; but, owing to the crowd which such an extraordinary occurrence had gathered together, he was obliged to defer the sale, and take her away. About four o'clock, however, he again brought her out, and she was sold for 20 guineas, and delivered, in a halter, to a person named Houseman, who had lodged with them four or five years."

Morning Post, October 10, 1807 : " One of those disgraceful scenes, which have, of late, become too common, took place on Friday se'nnight at Knaresborough. Owing to some jealousy, or other family difference, a man brought his wife, equipped in *the usual style*, and sold her at the market cross for 6d. and a quid of tobacco ! "

In the *Doncaster Gazette* of March 25, 1803, a sale is thus described : " A fellow sold his wife, as a cow, in Sheffield market-place a few days ago. The lady was put into the hands of a butcher, who held her by a halter fastened round her waist. ' What do you ask for your cow ?' said a bystander. 'A guinea,' replied the husband. ' Done !' cried the other, and immediately led away his bargain. We understand that the purchaser and his ' cow ' live very happily together."

Enough examples have been given to show that the French idea of wives being sold in Smithfield, and elsewhere, is founded on fact ; indeed, there is no reason to disbelieve the writer of " Six mois à Londres in 1816," when he describes a wife sale he saw at Smithfield—at which the lady was offered at the price of 15s., and, at that price, was eventually purchased, after due examination, " Comme il avait examiné quelques instans auparavant, une jument que je l'avais vu marchander."

We must not throw stones at our grandfathers because this custom was in their midst. I could quote numerous instances of it, from time to time, down to our own days. *Vide* the *South Wales Daily News*, May 2, 1882, where, at

Alfreton, a woman was sold by her husband, in a public-house for a glass of ale; and, again, in the *Pall Mall Gazette*, October 20, 1882, where it is recorded, that, at Belfast, a certain George Drennan sold his wife to one O'Neill, for one penny and a dinner.

But, before dismissing the social status of women of this class, at that time, I cannot help chronicling a singular custom, which, however, appears to be peculiarly local.

Annual Register, March 22, 1806: " A WOMAN TO LET! There is a custom, which, most likely, is peculiar to a small district in the western part of Cumberland. A few days ago, a gentleman from the neighbourhood of Whitehaven, calling upon a person, at his house in Ulpha, was informed that he was not at home; he was gone to church; there was '*a woman to let!*' On enquiry as to the meaning of this singular expression, it was thus explained :—When any single woman, belonging to the parish, had the misfortune to prove with child, a meeting of the parishioners is called, for the purpose of providing her a maintenance in some family, at so much a week, from that time to a limited time after delivery; and, this meeting (to give it the greater sanction), is uniformly holden in the church, where the *lowest* bidder has the *bargain!* And on such occasions, previous notice is given, that on such a day, there will be a ' woman to let.' "

CHAPTER XXXIV.

ONE vice the women of that age had, in common with the men, and that was Gambling—which, perhaps, was not so bad among the former, as during the last years of the preceding century, when Ladies Archer, and Buckinghamshire, and Mrs. Concannon were pilloried, and scourged metaphorically by the Satirists, as they were promised to be treated, physically, by Lord Kenyon. Their race was run—as expressed in the *Morning Post*, January 15, 1800: " Society has reason to rejoice in the complete downfall of the Faro Dames, who were so long the disgrace of human nature. Their *die* is cast, and their *odd tricks* avail no longer. The *game* is up, and very few of them have *cut* with *honours*."

Mrs. Concannon still kept on, but not in London, as is seen by the following paragraph. *Morning Herald*, December 18, 1802: " The visitors to Mrs. Concannon's *petits soupers*, at *Paris*, are not attracted by *billets* previously circulated, but by *cards*, afterwards *dealt out*, in an elegant and scientific manner; not to mince the matter.

they are the rendezvous of *deep play :* and the only questionable point about the matter is, whether the *Irish*, or the *French*, will prove victors at the close of so desperate a winter's campaign."

Still, we find even in the Royal circle, where the utmost gravity of demeanour, and purity of manner, were to be found, the card table was *the* evening's amusement. " The evening is, as usual, passed at cards, in the Queen's Drawing Room, where three tables are set out." And cards were still the staple entertainment both for men and women, at night. Naturally, the latter did not play for such high stakes as the men did ; but they contrived to make, or lose, a sufficient sum, either to elate, or to depress them, and experience, as far as in them lay, all the fierce feelings of the gambler. Nay, some made a pitiful profit out of their friends—in the shape of " card money "—which meant that the players put so much, every game, into a pool (generally the snuffer tray) to pay for the cards, and something for the servants.

It was a practice in its death throes, having been mortally wounded, by public opinion, at the end of the last century ; but the little meanness still obtained—*vide* the *Morning Herald*, December 15, 1802 : " In a pleasant village near the Metropolis, noted for its constant 'tea and turn out parties,' the extortion of *Card Money* had, lately, risen to such a pitch, that it was no unusual thing for the *Lady* of the House, upon the breaking up of a table, to immediately examine the sub-cargo of the candlestick, and, previous to the departure of her guests, proclaim aloud the lamentable defalcation of a pitiful shilling, which they might, perchance, have forgot to *contribute*. We are happy to find that some of the most respectable people in the place have resolved to discountenance and abolish this *shabby genteel* custom, which has too long prevailed ; a shameful degradation of everything like English hospitality."

But they sometimes played as high as did the opposite

sex—the climax, perhaps, coming in the following, from
the *Morning Post*, April 5, 1805 : " The sum lately lost at
play by a Lady of high rank is variously stated. Some
say it does not amount to more than £200,000, while others
assert that it is little short of £700,000. Her Lord is very un-
happy on the occasion, and is still undecided with respect to
the best mode to be adopted in the unfortunate predicament."

The men lost and gained large sums of a night ; and, for
that age, gaming had reached its climax. Little birds
whisper [1] that it is not much better now ; but, at all events,
it is not so open. From the highest to the lowest—from
the Heir Apparent, and the two great leaders of party, Fox
and Pitt, down to the man who could only afford to punt
his shilling, or half-crown, at a " silver hell "—all were

---

[1] From the *Globe*, January 26, 1885 :

" WEST END GAMBLING HOUSES.

" TO THE EDITOR OF THE GLOBE.

" Sir,—Can it be true—as rumour has it—that in an old-established gambling
club, not 100 miles from St. James's Street, enormous sums are nightly staked,
and that fortunes rapidly change hands ?   I hear that three men sat down a few
nights ago to play écarté in this said club, and that one of their number was at
a certain period of the evening a loser of the enormous sum of £100,000.   That
when this very impossible figure was reduced to limits within which the winners
considered the loser could pay, play ceased and the party broke up.   The next
day—so runs the story—one of the winners called with bills to the amount of
£26,000, drawn on stamped paper, for the loser to accept.   This gentleman,
however, though he freely admits having played, states that, having dined not
wisely but too well, he has no sort of recollection of losing any specific sum,
but merely a hazy idea that fabulously large amounts were recklessly staked all
round, and no accounts kept.   In other words, he repudiates, and finally, after
a lengthened discussion, has consented to place himself in the hands of a friend
to decide what he is to pay.   If this is true, and I have no reason to doubt it,
I can only stigmatize the whole affair as a public scandal, and the police should
promptly interfere and shut up a club where such disgraceful things occur.
When Jenks's baccarat 'hell' was closed, and Mr. J. Campbell Wilkinson
and his six associates were each fined £500 (hence the very excellent *bon mot*
which appeared in the *Sporting Times* that 'Jenks' babies' had become
'Jenks' monkeys'), the public were justified in believing that, at last, there
was not to be one law for the rich and another for the poor, and that in future
men who broke the law by gambling for thousands, would have the same justice
meted out to them as those who did so by tossing for coppers.   However, it
appears such hopes were premature, and before this happy state of things is
arrived at, further attention must be drawn to the matter, hence this letter, for
which I sincerely trust you will be able to find space.—I am, Sir, yours, &c.,
" A Hater of Professional Gamblers.

"January 24th."

bitten, more or less, by this mania of gaming. The magistrates lashed the petty rogues when they were caught, but winked discreetly at the West-end Clubs, and ordered no raids upon them. There they might win or lose their thousands, secure that the law would not stretch out its arm to molest them. There the nobility, legislators, country gentlemen, and officers of the army, met together on a common footing, to worship the Demon of Play.

There were three principal Clubs—White's, Brookes', and Boodles'. White's was originally a "Chocolate House" in William the Third's time, but became a private club early in the eighteenth century, and was used by the Tories. It was a club always noted for high play and betting, and very curious some of their bets were, the old wager book being still preserved. Brookes' was the Whig Club, and was then conducted by that

> "liberal Brookes, whose speculative skill
> Is hasty credit and a distant bill;
> Who, nurs'd in Clubs, disdains a vulgar trade,
> Exults to trust, and blushes to be paid."

Among the members of this club were the Prince of Wales, and, of course, his *fidus Achates*, Sheridan, besides the great Charles James Fox, who here played deeply, and whose name is oft recorded in the wager book, which, however, is of older date, and was kept when the club was held at Almack's.

"Lord Northington bets Mr. C. Fox, June 4, 1774, that he (Mr. C. F.) is not called to the bar before this day four years."

"March 11, 1775. Lord Bolinbroke gives a guinea to Mr. Charles Fox and is to receive a thousand from him whenever the debt of this country amounts to 171 millions. Mr. Fox is not to pay the £1,000 till he is one of His Majesty's Cabinet."

"April 7, 1792. Mr. Sheridan bets Lord Lauderdale

and Lord Thanet, twenty-five guineas each, that Parliament will not consent to any more lotteries after the present one voted to be drawn in February next."

At all the clubs, gaming was practised more or less. *Morning Herald*, June 16, 1804 : " A noble Lord, lately high in office, and who manifests a strong inclination to be rein-

GREAT SUBSCRIPTION ROOM AT BROOKES'S.

stated in his political power, lost at the UNION, a night or two back 4,000 guineas before twelve o'clock ; but, continuing to play, his luck took a turn, and he rose a winner of a thousand before five the next morning."

Again, to show the large sums then won and lost at gambling, take the following newspaper cuttings.

Morning Post, June 30, 1806: "The Marquis of H——d is said to have been so successful at play this season, as to have cleared £60,000. The Earl of B——e has won upwards of £50,000, clear of all deductions. A Right Reverend is stated to be amongst those who are *minus* on this occasion."

Morning Post, July 8, 1806: "A certain noble Marquis, who has been so very fortunate this season in his gaming speculations, had a run of ill luck last week. At one sitting, his lordship was *minus* no less a sum than *thirteen thousand pounds !*"

Morning Post, July 15, 1806: "The noble Marquis, who has been so great a gainer, this season, at *hazard*, never plays with any one, from a PRINCE, to a *Commoner*, without having the stakes *first* laid on the table. His lordship was always considered as a *sure card*, but now his fame is established, from the circumstance of his having cleared £35,000, after deducting all his losses for the last six months."

But, although the magistrates shut their eyes to the sins of the great, and punished the small, when brought before them, the Government systematically demoralized the people by means of lotteries. True, it was a great temptation, for it yielded a revenue to the State of about £350,000, besides the licenses of the brokers, £50 each. Very jealous was the Government to protect its children from the pernicious effects of private lotteries; they were *anathema*, and, besides, they would absorb some of the profit, which otherwise would have gone into the pockets of a paternal rule. In this decade, there were but two private lotteries, and, for both of them, a special act of Parliament was required, viz., that of the Pigot diamond in 1800, and Boydell's pictures in 1805.

This illustration is by Pyne, and, like all his drawing, is

extremely graphic. It represents the Life Guards, who then had to perform many of the duties of our police, conveying the Lottery wheels, from Somerset House (or Somerset Place, as it was then called) to Cooper's Hall, in Basinghall Street, where the Lottery was then drawn. There were four sledges employed for the purpose, two carrying the wheels containing the tickets, with their blanks, or prizes, and the other two bore the cases for the wheels. They were drawn by three horses each.

For many years the Lottery had been drawn at Guildhall, but it was afterwards removed to Cooper's Hall.

LIFE GUARDS ESCORTING A LOTTERY WHEEL.

At both places the tickets were drawn out of the wheels by two scholars of Christ's Hospital, or Bluecoat boys—who were thus selected for this office because their youth, and supposed integrity,[1] rendered them less liable than

[1] In May, 1775, a Bluecoat boy confessed that he had been tampered with, and had concealed a ticket, which was afterwards drawn. A man was arrested as the accomplice, but was discharged ; but the Lottery Committee, in order to prevent a similar fraud, moved the following resolution (December 12, 1775), which was afterwards always adhered to : "That it be requested of the *Treasurer of Christ's Hospital*, not to make known who are the twelve boys nominated for drawing the lottery till the morning the drawing begins ; which said boys are all to attend every day, and the two who are to go on duty at the wheels, are to be taken promiscuously from amongst the whole number, by either of the Secretaries, without observing any regular course, or order ; so that no boy shall know when it will be his turn to go to either wheel."

other boys, to be tampered with.   The accompanying illustration gives a very life-like presentment of the scene.

The last public Lottery, in England, was drawn in
October, 1826.

Needless to say that Gambling, either in the form of
card playing, dicing, or lotteries, was not the only way that
fools and rogues could throw away their money.   Still
there were two resources left—the Turf, and Cock-fighting.
The Turf was undoubtedly purer then than now, when it
has reached such a pitch of refinement in blackguardism,

DRAWING THE LOTTERY AT COOPER'S HALL.

and scoundrelism, that it must soon either be swept away,
or violently reformed.   Racing then was more for encouraging a breed of horses, swift, yet of such staying powers as
to be able to run a four-mile heat without breaking down :
not like our "exaggerated greyhounds," who can barely
stagger over a course of six furlongs, or three quarters of a
mile.

The stakes were not so high, and although there was
much betting on a race, yet it was among the upper class,
or men who could afford to lose to each other, and in the
society of their equals ; and not as at present, when a lord

is on familiar terms with a ruffian, so long as he will give the odds required, and may possibly be able to pay if he loses; nor, then, did shop boys make books on races, or talk learnedly of double events, &c., and such scenes as can now be witnessed any race day in Fleet Street, were utterly unknown, and undreamt of. A King's plate of £100 was then considered worth running for, and noblemen, and gentlemen, matched their horses one against the other, in a proper spirit of emulation.

There was a fair amount of racing literature—"Baily's Racing Register," "Pick's Racing Calendar," "The Turf Register," "The Racing Calendar," and "The Sporting Magazine," and I know, and care not, whether this is an exhaustive list. From some of them we get some curious names of race horses, for their owners then, seem to have run riot in the nomenclature of their animals. What should we say nowadays to such names as "Kiss in a Corner," "Jack, come tickle me," "Jenny, come tye me," "I am little, pity my condition," "Jack's my favourite," "Britons, strike home," "Why do you slight me?" "Turn about, Tommy," "Sweeter when clothed," "Watch them and Catch them," "First time of Asking," "Fear not, Victorious," "Hop, step, and jump," &c., &c.

As a curious incident of manners in the early century, I may mention that two ladies, Lady Lade and Mrs. Thornton (wife of Col. Thornton), both rode matches in public. Mrs. Thornton's brother-in-law, Mr. Flint, was stopping at the Colonel's seat of Thornville, and riding with the lady in its grounds. They had a gallop, and Mrs. Thornton's old horse, aided by her good riding, beat her antagonist, which so nettled him, that he challenged her to a further trial, which took place publicly, on the last day of the York August Meeting, 1804. Mrs. Thornton's horse broke down, and she lost; but she did not omit to wail publicly over the matter, asserting that otherwise she would have won, and that her opponent took unfair advantage of her.

This exhibition of herself seems to have fired her ambition, for we read in the *Morning Post*, August 20, 1805 :

"Mrs. Thornton is to ride 9 st. against Mr. Bromford, who is to ride 13 st., over the York Course, four miles ; to run the last race on Saturday in the next August meeting, for four hogsheads of Coti Roti p.p. and 2,000 guineas h. ft. ; and Mrs. T. bets Mr. B. 700 gs. to 600 gs. p.p.; the 2,000 gs. h. ft. provided it is declared to the Stewards four days before starting. Mrs. T. to have her choice of four horses.

" Mr. B. to ride Allegro, sister to Allegranti.

" N.B. Colonel T., or any gentleman he may name, to be permitted to follow the lady over the course, to assist her in case of any accident."

When it came to the pinch, Mr. Bromford declined the race, paid his forfeit, and the lady walked over. Later in the day, however, she raced Buckle, a jockey, mounted on Allegro—carrying 13 st. 6 lb., whilst Mrs. Thornton scaled 9 st. 6 lb.—and she beat the professional by half a neck. This match does not seem to have been for any money, but merely for the honour of the thing.

Before quitting the subject of horses, I cannot help mentioning that both Tattersall, and Aldridge, were in existence, as equine auctioneers, a position which, their thorough integrity has consolidated, and preserved to the present day.

CHAPTER XXXV.

Cock-fighting—Its illegality—Public recognition of it—Description of company at a cock-fight—High stakes—Bull-baiting—Debate thereon in the House of Commons—Prize-fighting—Famous pugilists—George IV. as a patron of the Ring—Attempts to put down prize-fighting—Female physical education—Cudgel-playing, and other sports.

COCK-FIGHTING was another way of gambling—a barbarous pastime, yet of great antiquity, and, changing the name of the combatants to quails, or partridges, extending all over the world, especially in the East. The Greeks had their Cock-fights, the Romans fought both cocks and quails. Of its introduction into England there is no certain date, but Fitz-Stephen, who died in 1191, mentions schoolboys as fighting their cocks on Shrove Tuesday. Edward III., Henry VIII., Elizabeth, and Cromwell, all prohibited Cock-fighting ; yet, so popular was it, that no prohibition was of any avail, and the Royal fulminations passed unheeded, and fell into desuetude almost as soon as uttered.

In the time of which I write, Cocking was a recognized sport, publicly advertised. *Morning Post*, January 5, 1805 : " Cocking, to be Fought on Monday, January 7, 1805, and continue all the week, at the Cock Pit Royal, South side of St. James's Park, the Gentlemen of Suffolk, and the Gentlemen of Hampshire's MAIN OF COCKS, for Five

Guineas the battle, and One Hundred Guineas the odd. To begin fighting each day precisely at Half-past Five o'clock." Indeed, " Cock-fighting, Shooting, and Military Carriages " were advertised.

The Cock Pit Royal was in Bird Cage Walk, St. James's Park, and was a great institution, until the expiration of its lease in 1816, when the landlord refused to renew. Of a sketch of its interior (by Rowlandson, and Pugin, in their " Microcosm of London ") the following description is given, which will better help to illustrate the *sport* than any words of mine, as the account is contemporary :

" This print may, without undue partiality, be acknowledged to excel that of Hogarth, upon the same subject. It is different in one particular : here the satire is general, not personal ; a collection of peers and pickpockets, grooms and gentlemen, *bons-vivants* and bullies ; in short, a scene which produces a medley of characters, from the highest to the lowest, has seldom been painted with an adherence to nature so strict and so interesting. The principal figure in the front row seems to anticipate the loss of the battle ; his neighbour to the right appears to have some *eggs in the same basket ;* whilst a stupid sort of despair in the countenance of the next figure proclaims that all hope is lost ; the smiling gentleman on his left seems to be the winner. The clenched fists and earnest features of the personage in the same row, between two sedate contemplaters of the fight, make one feel that sort of interest which arises from a belief that victory depends upon only a little assistance being given at that particular moment to the bird upon whose side he has betted. In the centre, and on the highest row behind, are two figures, apparently intended as hurling defiance to the whole company ; they are certainly offering odds, which no one is disposed to take. A little to the left, and just above the smart officer with a cocked hat, is a group inimitably portrayed. A parcel of *knowing ones,* who have betted pretty high, finding themselves in the *wrong box*, appear very desirous of *edging off*, and are attacking all together a personage who has been too much for them ; his attitude is expressive, and, with his fingers thrust into his ears, seems to indicate that he will take no more bets ; whilst the two figures (one in a cocked hat) to the left appear to enjoy the humorous expedient. . . . On the right we discover a pugilistic exhibition, and at a little distance horsewhips and sticks brandished in the air ; all these are the natural accompaniments of the scene. Upon the whole, this picture has great merit, and conveys a more perfect idea of the confusion and bustle of a Cockpit than any description." This was written in 1808-9.

Sometimes very large sums depended upon these combats—*vide Morning Post*, April 28, 1800 : "A *main of cocks* is to be fought this week at Newmarket, as interesting to the sporting world as that, last summer, at York. The match is *ostensibly* made between Mr. Cussans, and Mr. Germain ; but Sir Harry Vane Tempest, and others we could name, are supposed to be the real principals. It is for 1,000 guineas a side, and forty guineas each battle. Great sums are depending, and much money will be sported."

The last Act against Cock-fighting was 12 and 13 Vic., cap. 92 (August 1, 1849) ; but if any one imagines that, therefore, this *amusement* is extinct, he is very much mistaken.

Another cruel, yet intensely national sport, was Bull-baiting. Hardly a country town of note but had its "Bull-ring" ; and, although the bull had but a circumscribed range, being tied by a rope to a stake, yet the dogs did not always get the best of the combat, and many a tyke met his death, or went a limping cripple for the remainder of his days. I have already noted one bull-baiting in the account of the *Jubilee* rejoicings at Windsor in October, 1709, and that must suffice.

A few years previously it had been made the subject of a debate in the House of Commons, where much special pleading in its favour was exhibited. On May 24, 1802,[1] Mr. John Dent, M.P. for Lancaster, moved that the Bill to prevent Bull-baiting and Bull-running be read a second time. Sir Richard Hill pleaded the cause of the poor bulls, not very eloquently, but as earnestly as he could. He pointed out that an Act had been passed for the abolition of Bull-baiting in Ireland, and he called upon the Irish members to support this Bill.

Then up rose the Right Hon. W. Windham, M.P. for Norwich, and he contended that the cruelty was no greater than that comprised in the sports of hunting, shooting, and fishing. "If the effects of one were to be viewed through the medium of a microscope, why were not the consequences of the other to be scrutinized with equal severity?" In the course of a long speech he warmed to his view of the subject, until, at last, in the fervour of his eloquence, he burst into the following : "He believed that the bull felt a satisfaction in the contest, not less so than the hound did when he heard the sound of the horn which summoned him to the chase. True it was, that young bulls, or those that were never baited before, showed reluctance to be tied to the stake ; but those bulls, which, according to the language of the sport, were called *game* bulls, who were used to baiting, approached the stake and stood there, while preparing for the contest, with the utmost composure. If the bull felt no pleasure, and was cruelly dealt with, surely the dogs had also some claim to compassion ; but the fact was, that both seemed equally arduous in the conflict ; and the bull, like every other animal, while it had the better side, did not appear to feel unpleasantly ; it would be ridiculous to say he felt no pain ; yet, when on such occasions he exhibited no sign of terror, it was a demonstrable proof that he felt some pleasure."

[1] "Parliamentary History," vol. xxxvi.

Mr. Courtenay rose to a much greater height. Said he: "What a glorious sight to see a dog attack a bull! It animates a British heart—

'To see him growl, and snap, and snarl, and bite,
Pin the bull's nose, and prove instinctive might.'

Besides, if bull-baiting was given up, the characteristic of our British dogs, so classically celebrated in the Augustan age of literature, would be totally lost. Claudian says: 'Magnaque taurorum fracturæ colla Britannæ.' Symmachus mentions seven Irish bull-dogs: 'Septem Scottici canes,' as then first produced in the circus at Rome, to the great admiration of the people.'"

General Gascoyne considered it an amusement which the lower orders were entitled to ; and it was "with regret he observed a disposition in many of the members to deprive the poor of their recreations, and force them to pass their time in chaunting at conventicles."

Then the gentle William Wilberforce rose, and rebuked the former speakers, telling them that he thought the subject had been treated with too much levity. "The evidence against the practice was derived from respectable magistrates. From such evidence he had derived a variety of facts, which were too horrid to detail to the House. A bull—that honest, harmless, useful animal—was forcibly tied to a stake, and a number of bull-dogs set upon him. If he was not sufficiently roused by the pain of their attacks, the most barbarous expedients were hit upon to awake in him that fury which was necessary to the amusement of the inhuman spectators. One instance of the latter kind he would state. A bull had been bought for the sole purpose of being baited ; but, upon being fixed to the stake, he was found of so mild a nature that all the attacks of the dogs were insufficient to excite him to the requisite degree of fury ; upon which those who bought him refused to pay the price to the original owner, unless he could be

made to serve their purposes: the owner, after number-
less expedients, at last sawed off his horns, and poured into
them a poignant sort of liquid, that quickly excited the
animal to the wished-for degree of fury. When bulls were
bought merely for the purpose of being baited, the people
who bought them wished to have as much diversion (if
diversion, such cruelty could be called) as possible, for their
money. The consequence was that every art, even fire,
had been employed to rouse the exhausted animal to fresh
exertions, and there were instances where he had expired
in protracted agonies amidst the flames. It had been said,
that it would be wrong to deprive the lower orders of their
amusements, of the only cordial drop of life which supported them under their complicated burthens. Wretched,
indeed, must be the condition of the common people of
England, if their whole happiness consisted in the practice
of such barbarity!"

Sheridan joined Wilberforce; but the Bill was thrown
out by 64 to 51; and the practice of Bull-baiting was only
declared illegal in 1835, when it was included in the Act
against Cruelty to Animals, 5th and 6th William IV., cap.
59.

There was yet another brutal sport, not wholly unconnected with money and betting, which was then at its
apogee, and that was Prize-fighting. This decade was at
its Augustan period, when the ruffians, who mauled each
other for lucre's sake, were petted and fêted as much as
ever were the gladiators in the time of Rome's decline—
the names of the pugilists then living being those of the
greatest renown in the history of the prize ring. Even
people who are not tainted with a love of the "Noble Art
of Self-defence" must have heard of Jem Belcher, John
Gully, page to George IV., and M.P. for Pontefract;
Dutch Sam, Tom Crib, and his black adversary Thomas
Molineaux; these names are as familiar to every school-
boy as those of the Homeric heroes. It was an age of

muscle, not of brains; and the use of the fists was encouraged as the arbiter in disputes which nothing but a little blood-letting could appease, in preference to the duels, or to that utter abhorrence of all Englishmen—the knife.

Doubtless, boxing is commendable in many ways, and should form part of every man's physical education, not only to the great advantage of his muscular system, and consequent good health, but, should occasion ever require the use of his fists, he is armed at once with weapons in whose use he is well trained; but that is very different from two men, possibly very good friends, spending long months in getting themselves in the best possible physical condition for pounding each other into a mass of bruised jelly, in order to put some money in their pockets, and afford sport and amusement to a parcel of debased brutes, whatever their social position might be.

The Prince of Wales in his younger days was, to a small extent, a " Patron of the Ring," *i.e.*, he once went to a meeting which took place at Smitham Bottom, near Croydon, on June 9, 1788, where he saw three fights, one between the celebrated John Jackson—whose beautiful tomb is in Brompton Cemetery—and Fewterel, of Birmingham ; and, on Jackson's winning, he sent him, by the hand of his friend, Colonel Hanger, a bank-note. The next fight was between Stephen Oliver, nicknamed " Death," with a Jew, named Elisha Crabbe, which ended in " Death's " defeat ; and the third encounter was between two outsiders.

Again he was present at three fights which took place on the Brighton race-course, on August 6, 1788. In the third—which was between Tom Tyne, "the Tailor," and Earl—Tyne hit his opponent a sharp, left-handed blow on the side of the head, which drove him against the rail of the stage. He fell insensible, and expired very shortly afterwards. The Prince of Wales openly expressed his determination to never again witness a prize-fight—and this he kept—also to settle an annuity on Earl's widow and children ; but history is silent as to whether this was ever carried out.

Of course, then as now, the better-thinking portion of the nation discountenanced these blackguard exhibitions, which were mainly supported by the " fast " set of that day —the JERRY HAWTHORNS and CORINTHIAN TOMS of the next decade. It is refreshing to read such paragraphs as the following :

Morning Post, January 11, 1808 : " PRIZE FIGHTING. We are happy to hear that there is some prospect of this most disgraceful and mischievous practice being put an end to by the interference of the Legislature. The consequences resulting from it become every day more and more serious, and, without a vigorous effort to terminate the evil, we may shortly expect to find numerous families reduced to the extremes of poverty and wretchedness, in consequence of those who have hitherto supported them by their industry having given themselves up to idleness and blackguardism, by entering the foul ranks, and becoming the constant associates of prize-fighting vagabonds."

Ibid.: " The magistrates are *beginning* to do their duty ; they, last week, dissolved a meeting of Boxers who were sparring for money. His Majesty's Navy wants able-bodied men, and those lovers of fighting could hardly complain, if they were compelled to box with *French* instead of *English* men."

Morning Post, February 3, 1808 : " PRIZE FIGHTING. We are rejoiced to find that we have not in vain called attention to the growing evil of this disgraceful, mischievous, and baleful practice. Mr. Justice GROSE, in his Charge to the Grand Jury, yesterday, particularly noticed its pernicious effects, and forcibly urged the necessity of a speedy remedy ; and we may, therefore, hope, ere long, to see the progress of this species of blackguardism and vice effec-

tually arrested. We shall take an early opportunity of
offering some further reflections upon the subject."

But nothing came of it. It is now illegal, but we know
well enough, that fights frequently take place. The police
are half-hearted over it, knowing it to be a thankless task
even to effect a capture; for no magistrate ever inflicts
more than a very nominal punishment, either on principals
or accessories.

That the physical education of the fair sex was attended

CUDGEL PLAYING—1800.

to, 'ong before these days of female gymnastic exercises, is
evidenced by the following advertisement in the *Morning
Post*, February 20, 1810: "PATENT GRAND EXERCISE
FRAMES particularly intended for Young Ladies, the use of
which will not only remove deformities, but will infallibly
produce health, strength, symmetry, beauty, and superior
elegance of deportment," &c.

The lower classes in the Metropolis were naturally
debarred from manly sports, by want of room; so that

almost their sole muscular exercise was Skittles. But, in
the country, a wholesome rivalry was engendered among
the rustic youth, by means of foot-racing, wrestling, and
Cudgel-playing. The latter still survives in Berkshire,
where many a crown has been cracked at the Scouring of
the White Horse (of late years fallen into desuetude), and
many an old "gamester" still lingers, who can tell long
yarns of the hats he has won. At fairs, too, and holidays,
the young lasses used to race for smocks, and many sports
were in vogue that are now never practised, save when
resuscitated at some Harvest Home, or some country school
feast.

CHAPTER XXXVI.

Hunting then, and now—Hunting near the Metropolis—The Epping Hunt—Fishing—Shooting then, and now—Guns—Methods of proving gun barrels—Big charges—Introduction of the Percussion Cap—Size of bags—Colonel Thornton's bet.

OF course there was Hunting, both Fox and Stag, but it was not carried out on the same principles then as now. A man, then, kept a pack of hounds for his own amusement, that of his friends, and the neighbourhood generally. A meet, then, was a great social gathering of neighbours, at which, for the time, all were on a courteous equality, engendered by similarity of taste, and cemented by means of the Master, who, at some great expense, kept the pack for others' use. Now, " the old order changes, yielding place to new ; " the probability is that it is a subscription pack—with the subscriptions not too well paid, and the Master frequently changing, owing to his quarrels with his masters, the subscribers, who carp at his doings, and try to dictate their own views. The railway brings down the " London Contingent "—sporting stockbrokers, solicitors, tailors, and publicans—in fact, all who can scrape together the necessary money to hire the " hunter," and pay its fare to the nearest station to the meet. These people have no sympathy with the farmers, no relations with the county, spend no money, because

21

they return to London at night, care nought for the damage they do, which, probably, is done in ignorance; and it is no wonder that, now-a-days, hunting is not so popular among tenant farmers as it might be—and it is pretty safe to prophesy, that in many districts, before many more years, it will be reckoned as a thing of the past.

Then, however, there was never heard a whisper of the

FOX-HUNTING BREAKFAST.

scarcity of foxes. A fox found poisoned, or shot, would have been considered as an indelible disgrace to the district. The word *vulpecide* was not coined, because the crime had not been committed. No farmer ever sent in a claim to the Hunt, and only old women, cottagers, ever wanted compensation for the gander, or the two or three hens that they had lost; as to warning off land, it had never been dreamt of, much less practised.

In other ways, too, hunting was different—both horses, and hounds were heavier, and slower then; it was not the pace of the run that was discussed at night, but its length, and the behaviour of both hounds, and horses. Fox hunting began much earlier in the morning than it does now; and a good solid meal of cold meat, washed down with a tankard of home brewed, was vastly superior to a modern "lawn meet" breakfast, with its wines and liqueurs, to "steady the nerves," to say nothing of the flask of "jumping powder." Sport, too, was found much nearer the Metropolis then than now. *Morning Post*, August 14, 1805: "To SPORTSMEN and others.—A Deputation to be granted of the very extensive Manors of HORNSEY and FINCHLEY, in the County of Middlesex, with the liberty of Hunting and Shooting over, and upon, the said Manors, abounding with game," &c.

The Epping Hunt, too, where the citizens [1] annually met

PERCH-FISHING—1804.

on Easter Monday, to vindicate their right to hunt in the Forest, was not the farce it afterwards became. Most men, then, were accustomed to horseback, and could manage to stick on somehow.

Fishing and shooting were, of course, as popular as now. Of the former we have had little to learn since Isaac Walton's time, and the illustration shows us that the

---

[1] There is a story told of a Lord Mayor in times long past, who went a-hunting in Epping Forest. Some one riding past him saluted him with, "My Lord! the Hare comes this way." His lordship bravely drew his trusty sword, and, flourishing it, exclaimed, "Let him come! let him come! I thank my God, I fear him not."

"Contemplative Man," in the early part of this century, knew how to combine his "Recreation" with the charms of female society.

Shooting, like hunting, was a totally different thing, in the first ten years of the century, to what it is now. There were no battues, no hot, and elaborate, luncheons, no being posted in "warm corners," no army of beaters, no breech-loaders, and two attendants to load for you, and, at the end of a days sport, no waggon-loads of slain to be sent off to market to help pay, in some part, the expenses of breeding, and keeping, such a head of game. Then, a man went out,

AFTER A DAY'S SHOOTING—1809.

preferably with a friend or two, soon after an early break-fast, accompanied by Don and Ponto, who were his con-stant companions in his walks, and whose education he had personally superintended ; to watch their intelligent move-ments was in itself one of the pleasures of the day. When a covey rose, not a shot was wasted, if possible, for, by the time the gun was reloaded, the birds would be far off. A bit of bread and cheese, as luncheon, at the nearest farm-house, or the village pub.; if the former, a brace of birds, or a hare left, with a kindly message. Enough game to carry home, without being tired, plenty for the larder, and some for friends ; then dinner, some punch—and Betty would come with the chamber candle and warming-pan, to find the party asleep and quite ready for bed.

The Guns, with which our grandfathers shot, were vastly inferior to our modern breechloader; the workmanship was good, but the flint-lock, with its tardy firing, and the very weak powder then in use, did not render the "birding gun" a very efficient weapon.

Thornhill, who wrote the *Shooting Directory* in 1804, is as great an authority on the subject of guns as any of his contemporaries; and he had quite sense enough to see that

COCK SHOOTING WITH SPANIELS—1804.

the old-fashioned long barrel of four feet, or more, carried no further than one of three feet, and he counselled the musket length of two feet ten inches, as the standard length for fowling-piece barrels, and preferred one that carried its shot close, to one that scattered. The method of proving "that a barrel will not burst, was to get a ball to fit the exact bore, and put the exact weight of the ball in powder, with which load, and fire it off by a train; if it does not burst, you need be under no apprehension. This is called

Tower-proof; or put in double the quantity of powder and shot."

He recommends as a proper charge for a fowling-piece of ordinary calibre, a drachm and a quarter, or a drachm and a half, of good powder, and an ounce, or an ounce and a quarter, of shot ; and, when treating on the subject of recoil, he gives one or two anecdotes of overloading. "The overloading of the piece is the reason of the recoil ; respecting sportsmen who are in the habit of overloading with shot, such are properly ridiculed in a treatise published some time since, entitled, 'Cautions to Young Sportsmen,' in which we find an advertisement levelled at some persons who were going to a Pigeon Shooting Match at *Ballingbear-Warren House.* It was as follows : 'Take notice, that no person will be allowed to load with more than four ounces of shot.' A gamekeeper to whom this author mentioned the story, told him he thought it a pretty fair allowance, and, on being told what charge and weight of shot he generally used, replied, he divided a pound into five charges. . . . A friend of the gentleman who relates this story, seeing his keeper equipped for a pigeon match, had the curiosity to examine his charge, and, after trying it with his rammer, expressed his surprise at finding it rather less than usual. 'Oh, sir,' replied the keeper, 'I have only put in the powder yet ;' and, on putting in the shot, the charge, altogether, was *eleven* fingers. The reason he assigned was ' that he always liked to give his piece a belly full.'"

The Percussion Cap, which was destined to make such a revolution in small arms, was patented April 11, 1807, by the inventor, the Rev. A. J. Forsyth, of Belhelvie, Aberdeenshire. It soon came into use, for we find an advertisement in the *Morning Post*, December 23, 1808: "To SPORTSMEN. The PATENT GUN-LOCK invented by Mr. Forsyth is to be had at No. 10, Piccadilly, near the Haymarket. Those who may be unacquainted with the excellence of this Invention are informed that the inflammation is produced without the assistance of flint, and is much more rapid than in the common way. The Lock is so constructed as to render it completely impervious to water, or damp of any kind, and may, in fact, be fired under water."

Grouse, partridge, and other shooting, commenced on the same dates as now, and game certificates were as necessary then, as at the present time. Heavy bags were not the rule. Thornhill supplies us with his ideal of a luxurious sportsman of his time, with every appliance for slaughter, and game *ad libitum.* Compare his butcher's bill with that of a modern *battue.* " A man of fortune, surrounded with gamekeepers (let us suppose the scene for the present in Norfolk), pointers, setters, &c., without number, *Manton* [1] Guns, and all in compleat retinue, going out at, perhaps, twelve o'clock (the hour of indolent, and *feather bed* gunners), into the highest preserved covers in that County, where the game is so very tame, that twenty birds may be killed in a few hours ; their servants with clean guns ready, and, if necessary, loaded by them ; and probably, if the dog of one of these *elegant* sportsmen is admired, or gains credit, if his master is asked his name, he makes for answer ' he really cannot tell you, but will ask his game-keeper.' "

A large bag is spoken of by Daniel, in his *Field Sports,* where he says that in 1796, on Mr. Colquhoun's manor at Wretham, in Norfolk, the Duke of Bedford, and six other gentlemen, killed eighty cock pheasants, and forty hares, besides some partridges, in one day.

Mr. Coke, of Holkham, kept up a wonderful head of game, so that his performances ought not to be looked upon in the light of phenomenal sportsmanship, because his victims were so plentifully to hand. As an instance, on October 7, 1797, upon his manor at Warham, and within a mile's circumference, he bagged forty brace of partridges,

[1] Joseph Manton was at that time *the* great gun maker.

in eight hours, at ninety-three shots ; and, on the previous day, over the same ground, he killed twenty-two brace and a half, in three hours.   In 1801, he killed, in five days, *seven hundred and twenty-six partridges.*

In January, 1803, Mr. Coke, Sir John Shelley, and Tom Sheridan went to Lord Cholmondeley's place at Houghton, in Norfolk, and killed there, in one day, to their three guns only, fourteen and a half brace of hares, sixteen couples of rabbits, twenty-four brace of pheasants, thirteen brace of partridges, and sixteen couples of woodcock.

In the *Morning Post* of the 21st of January, 1801, we find : " Col. Thornton some time ago made a bet that he would kill 400 head of game at 400 shots, the result was, that, in the year 1800, he bagged 417 head of game (consisting of part-ridges, pheasants, hares, snipe, and woodcock) at 411 shots. Enumerated amongst these are a black wild duck, and a white pheasant cock, and at the last point he killed a brace of cock pheasants, one with each barrel ; on the leg of the one last killed (an amazing fine bird) was found a ring, proving that he had been taken by Colonel Thornton when hawking, and turned out again in the year 1792."

CHAPTER XXXVII.

A Cockney's account of the First of September—Pigeon shooting—Out-door games —Cricket—High stakes—Lord's cricket ground—Trap and ball—Billiards— Life of Andrews the billiard player.

PASSING from recounting the feats of legitimate sportsmen, let us unbend, and indulge in a contemporary account of his cockney congener—*Times*, September 2, 1803 :

"A COCKNEY'S ACCOUNT OF YESTERDAY,
BEING
THE FIRST OF SEPTEMBER.

" Having sat up all night to be ready and fresh in the morning, four of us met at the Obelisk, in St. George's Fields, from whence we proceeded with our dogs, arms, and ammunition, to Lambeth Marsh, where we expected to have great sport, but found nothing except a cat, which we all fired at ; but being only four in number, and a cat having nine lives, we missed killing her, though, as we believe, she was severely wounded. In this discharge we broke a bell glass in a gardener's ground, so, fearing that we might, on that account, be taken up for poachers, we made the best of our way to Tothill Fields ; here we reloaded our pieces, and gave our dogs a piece of bread each, but the fox dog would not eat his. We then proceeded to look about for sport, when two Westminster boys claimed the place as their manor, and drove us out of it. We now beat all about Jenny's Whim, and seeing something swimming across the water, which a waterman's boy told us was a dab-chick, we all fired, but without success, but the terrier caught it, as it ran up the bank and it proved to be the largest rat we had ever seen.

" As we passed through the five Fields, Chelsea, we saw several pigeons, but they flew so fast that none of us could take aim.

" On the other side of Battersea Bridge, met two men driving *geese.* Offered them eighteenpence, which they accepted, for a shot at the flock, at twenty yards. Drew lots who should fire first ; it fell to *Billy Candlewick's* chance, who, from his father belonging many years ago to one of the regiments of City Militia, knew something of taking aim.

" The goose driver stepped the ground, and Billy took aim for above ten minutes, when, shutting both his eyes lest the pan might flash in his sight, he snapped, and missed fire. He took aim a second time, snapped and missed again. Borrowed *Bob Tape's* scissars, and hammered the flint—snapped, and missed fire a third time—thought the Devil had got hold of the gun, examined her, found she was neither loaded nor primed. The goose driver refused to let Billy try again, so we gave him another sixpence, and he sold us a lame gander, which we placed at about six yards, and, taking a shot apiece at him, killed him, and put him in *Ned Thimble's* cabbage net.

" Passed over Clapham Common, where we saw several parties, but would not interfere with their sport.

" In our way to Stockwell, *Ned Simple* fired at a pigeon, which was perched on the top of a tree, and shot a man's hat and wig off, who stood underneath it. As we thought he might be killed, we set off as hard as we could run, but were pursued and overtaken by two gardeners, who insisted upon being paid two shillings for destroying a scarecrow. We paid the money very readily, and kept our counsel.

"When we came in sight of the Swan, at Stockwell, we all ran as hard as we could to see who should get in first as we had settled to breakfast there. Unfortunately, our gun being cock'd, I made a stumble, and the trigger being touched by something, off went the piece, and lodged the contents in the body of a *sucking pig* that was crossing the road. The squeaking of the poor little animal roused the maternal affections of the sow, and set the fox dog, the terrier, the Newfoundland bitch, and the mastiff, a barking. The noise of the sow, the pig, and the dog, with the report of the gun, brought the people of the house, and, indeed, of the neighbourhood ; and, being threatened by one, and laughed at by another, we thought it best to buy the pig at four shillings, which we did, and put it into *Bob Tape's* game bag, which, by the bye, was nothing but half a bolster tick.

"We now beat every bush with the muzzle of our guns, set the dogs on the pigs, and found but one chaffinch, which was rather wild, not letting us come within eight yards, so that we could not make sure of our bird. We hunted him from spray to spray for above an hour, without being able to get in a parallel line, so as to take sure aim when, at last, he was killed by a little boy, who knocked him down with a stone. Bought him, and put him into the net with the goose.

"Hunted a weazle for above an hour, and lost him. The terrier was remarkably staunch.

"Crossing a field near Camberwell, we thought we saw a covey of partridges at the side of a ditch ; so we all made up to them with our guns cock'd, tying the dogs to our legs, that they might not run in, and spring the game.

"What we thought to be a covey of partridges, proved to be a gang of gypsies, who were squatted under the hedge, peeling turnips and paring potatoes for dinner. It was the mercy of God we did not fire on them, as all our pieces were up to our shoulders, and we had but one eye open, apiece, when that, which we took to be the *old cock*, rose up, and said in a loud voice, 'What the devil are ye about?'

" After much difficulties, and but little sport, got, by the direction of the gypsies, into the Greenwich road, where, being rather fatigued, we stopped at the Halfway house, until a coach came by, when, mounting the roof, and the box, we were conveyed near Blackheath, to our unspeakable joy.

" Never saw the Heath before—amazed at the number of furze bushes, and the wide extent there is for game. Had an excellent chase after a jackass, when the mastiff tore his leg. Kept close together for fear of losing each other.

" Got down near a large round house, shot at a flock of sparrows, and killed one, which we think is a cock, his head being rather black.

" Saw several brother sportsmen out, who had killed nothing but a hedge hog and a tame jack daw, which belonged to the public house at New Cross Turnpike.

" Got up to the main road, fired at a yellow hammer, and frightened the horses in the Dover stage. The guard threatened to shoot us, and we took to our heels.

" Saw some black game flying very high. They looked for all the world like crows.

" The terrier came to a point at a thick bunch of fern. We were now sure this must be a covey of partridges, and we prepared accordingly. The mastiff ran in, and brought out one of the young ones. It proved to be a nest of grass mice : took every one, and put them into the bolster. Grass mice were better than nothing.

" Much fatigued, and agreed to shoot all the way home, fired off our guns at the foot of Greenwich Hill, and were laughed at by the inhabitants—loaded them again, and fired at a sheet of paper for half an hour without putting a grain in it.

"We went into a cow-house, near Bermondsey Spa, to get some milk for the dogs, and, laying down upon a heap of straw, we all fell fast asleep. We were awakened by the entrance of a cow and her calf, when we found we had been robbed of our dogs and our guns.

"We went into a public house to console ourselves for our loss, where we stayed till it was dark, that we might not be seen returning in such an unsportsmanlike manner.

"Agreed on the way what stories we should tell about the day's amusement and success : parted at the Monument, and went to our respective homes."

There was evidently the same tender-hearted sentiment then, as now, with regard to the "tournament of doves"— see the *Morning Post*, November 19, 1810 : "The expert marksmen in *pidgeon killing matches* are very properly denominated *slaughtermen ;* four of these *humane* gentlemen shot no less than *thirty-six*, for mere amusement, the other day on Finchley Common."

Perhaps the principal out-door game (for football, as a game, was not yet organized, and hockey and golf had but local fame and habitations) was Cricket ; and even this friendly sport, and generous rivalry, as we know it, was then contaminated by being played for money. Two or three examples, in one year, will be sufficient to show the motive of the game.

Morning Herald, July 1, 1802 : "CRICKET. Tuesday was played a grand match of Cricket on Hampstead Heath, between eleven Gentlemen of the Mary le bone Club, and nine Gentlemen of Hampstead and Highgate, with two men given, for 500 guineas, which was won by the latter, by 112 runs."

Ibid., July 15, 1802: "CRICKET. Tuesday was played a grand match of Cricket, at Chigwell, Essex, between eleven Gentlemen of Chigwell and eleven Gentlemen of the Mile End Club, for 500 guineas, which was won by the latter by 23 runs. Even betting at starting.

"Yesterday a grand match of Cricket was played at Camberwell, between eleven Gentlemen of Camberwell and Peckham, and eleven Gentlemen of Clapham, for 500 guineas, which was won by the former by three wickets."

Ibid., September 3, 1802: "CRICKET. Monday last, and two following days, was played a grand match of Cricket, on Ripley Green, Surrey, between eleven Gentlemen of All England, and twenty-two Gentlemen of Surrey, for 1,000 guineas, which was won by the former in one in (? innings), and twenty-five runs."

Lord, whose Cricket-ground was afterwards bought by the M.C.C., and which still goes by his name, then had the ground now covered by Harewood and Dorset Squares: the date of removal thence to the present ground is noted in an advertisement in the *Morning Post*, April 21, 1809: "CRICKET GROUND. LORD begs to inform the Noblemen and Gentlemen, lovers of Cricket, that he has enclosed and levelled a large piece of Ground, at the top of Lisson Grove, a short distance from his old Ground, which, for size and beauty of situation cannot be excelled, which will be ready for playing on by the beginning of May, to be known by the name of Lord's Saint John's Wood Cricket Ground."

Then also was played a game, now practically defunct in this country, but vigorous enough in America, where it is known as Base-ball. *Morning Herald*, September 22, 1802: "On Monday last was finished, at Haverstock Hill, near Hampstead, a grand Match of *Trap* and *Ball*, between twenty-five Gentlemen of the *Law*, and five of the *Gospel*, which was won by the former."

Billiards was an old indoor game, which had somewhat fallen into abeyance, but was reviving, for we read, in the *Morning Post*, September 28, 1809: "Billiards are becoming very fashionable; it is an amusement of a gentlemanly cast—giving at once activity to the limbs, and grace to the person. A match was played yesterday at Kidman's."

From this illustration, which is taken from a little book entitled, " New Instructions for Playing in all its Varieties, the Game of Billiards," &c., 1801, there seems to have been but little difference either in the play, or in the furniture of the room, between the past and the present times. They must have played a somewhat heavy, and dead game, though, for neither india-rubber cushions, nor slate tables, were known. The rules for the game are similar to our own.

This little book gives a curious biography, which I am tempted, as it is short, to copy.

BILLIARDS—1801.

" *Account of* MR. ANDREWS, *the celebrated Billiard Player.*

" Mr. Andrews was born to an easy independent fortune, but, commencing life at a time that he was incapable of judging of the world, or of himself, was led away by a single passion ; for he was not actuated by any other. He devoted himself entirely to the blind goddess, and worshipped her incessantly, under the form of two ivory balls. He was remarkably thin, not very tall, though above the middle size : his face was a perfect vacuum with respect to every possible idea except Billiards. So infatuated was he in pursuing this game, to attain the summit of excellence at it, that he sacrificed days, nights, weeks, months, and years to it.

"At length he arrived at such a degree of perfection, as well in the theoretical, as in the practical part of the game, that there was no player in Europe could equal him, except one, who was the celebrated Abraham Carter, who kept the tables at the corner of the Piazzas, Russel Street, Covent Garden. Mr. Andrews was the most devoted adept of this game that ever nature produced; he seemed but to vegetate in a Billiard Room, and, indeed, he did little more in any other place. He was a perfect Billiard Valetudinarian, in the most rigid significance of the expression. He ate, drank, slept, walked, nay, talked but to promote the system of the balls. His regimen was tea, and toast and butter, for breakfast, for dinner, and for supper.

"It might reasonably be imagined, that so regular a professor would obtain all the advantages that could result from the science. He won considerable sums, but knew not the value of money; and when playing for only five or ten pounds, he took no pains, but seemed perfectly indifferent about winning or losing. There was a latent finesse in this, but it did not operate to his advantage: he was laying by for bets, but as they were seldom offered, the strength of his play being very well known, he often lost by repeated small sums, very considerable ones.

"It is generally believed, however, that he has played for more money at billiards than any other person ever did. The following is a remarkable circumstance: he, one night, won of Col. W——e upwards of £1,000, and the Colonel appointed to meet him the next day to go with him to the City, to transfer Stock to him for the amount of the sum lost. Being in a hackney coach, they tossed up who should pay for it. Andrews lost, and upon this small beginning he was excited to continue, till he had lost the whole sum he had won the night before at billiards. When the coachman stopped to get down, he was ordered to get up again, and drive them back, as they had no occasion to get out.

"By these pursuits he lost very large sums which he had won at billiards; and, in a few years, hazard, and other games of chance, stripped him of every shilling he could command. He had still left a small annuity which he endeavoured to dispose of, but it was so securely settled upon himself that he could not sell it; otherwise it is probable that it would soon have been transferred at the gaming table. He very lately lived in a retired manner in Kent, where he declared to an intimate old acquaintance that he never knew contentment when he was rolling in money; but, since he was obliged to live upon a scanty pittance, he thought himself one of the happiest men in the universe."

CHAPTER XXXVIII.

IN the Dawn of the Nineteenth Century, the theatre was
a favourite amusement for the good folks, probably
because there were no other public forms of amusement, if we except an occasional concert or masquerade.
The stage supplied this want, and the people took due
advantage of it. The audience, through much frequenting,
were critically educated, and demanded good acting. This,
as a rule, they obtained, partially, as I think, because there
were fewer actors, and, consequently, not so many mediocre
performers as now, and partly owing to the constant change
of performance—there being no "long runs," as we know
them, where an actor mechanically goes through the same
part for hundreds of nights, until, like Sothern, he absolutely, and unconsciously, adopts his own mannerisms, and
spoils himself for a fresh part.

The richer, and titled classes, were not content with
witnessing professional skill, but strove to emulate and
surpass the performers at their own amateur entertain-
ments, and the most notable of these private societies was
the Pic Nic Society.

There were eight Theatres in London, *i.e.*, when one or other was not burnt down—namely, The King's, Haymarket; Covent Garden; Drury Lane; Theatre Royal, Haymarket; The Royalty, in Goodman's Fields; Sadlers Wells; Astley's; and the Royal Circus, now the Surrey, on the other side the river.

Of course, as would be only natural, the best actors were at the West-end Theatres, and to show their calibre, one has only to mention such names as John Philip Kemble, Munden, Bannister, Dowton, Elliston, Liston, Mrs. Siddons, Fawcett, Mrs. Jordan, Kelly, Johnstone, Young, Cooke, &c. No wonder, that with such actors, the stage was popular. Their names are still a tradition of excellence to the profession, and the performances, with one notable exception, in the O. P. Riots, were listened to with great decorum, and there was a vast improvement upon the rougher manners of the previous century.

I can only find the mention of one *fracas* in the whole ten years, and the report of that, in the *Annual Register*, December 26, 1801, shows how very far the audience were from sympathizing with the offender. "At Covent Garden Theatre the holiday folks were inclined to be mischievous. As soon as the curtain drew up to commence the play of 'Richard the Third,' a wine glass was thrown on the stage by way of prologue, but without exciting much observation; a few minutes after, determined to attract notice, a quart bottle was thrown from the two-shilling gallery on the stage; it grazed the hat of Mr. Betterton, who was playing Tressel to Murray's Henry VI., knocked out some of the jewels, and, falling on the stage, rolled down to the lamps unbroken. The audience were thunderstruck, the play stood still, and, for a few seconds, every one gazed with amazement. Satisfied of what had been done, a general burst of indignation broke out over the house, and 'throw him over!' 'turn him out!' were vociferated from all quarters. The villain was pointed out by his neighbours, sitting in the front row of the two-shilling gallery. He was seized, the people in the pit, and the boxes, rising up, and considerable agitation prevailed. The fellow, who was drunk, held by the iron railing, and refused to retire. This provoked the resentment against him still more, and the cries of vengeance were loud and general. Three or four laid hold of him, and seemed as if they would drag rail and all away ; at last, they succeeded in taking him out of the theatre."

In this decade appeared a theatrical phenomenon—the like of which has never been seen since ; in the shape of a boy, who was endowed with a truly marvellous gift of acting—one Master William Henry West Betty, surnamed " The Infant Roscius," who was born at Shrewsbury, September 13, 1791. His parents were extremely respectable, and in easy circumstances—so that it was not from need, but from pure inclination, that he adopted the stage as a profession. Whilst yet a child, he was fond of declamation with action, and, before he was twelve, he acted the part of Osman in Voltaire's tragedy of Zara, at the Theatre, Belfast. He was, at that time, residing in Ireland, and the theatres, having been closed for some time previously, owing to the disturbed state of the country, were glad of any attraction when they did open—so Betty took an engagement at the above theatre, for four nights, on the understanding that he was to share the house, after deducting twelve pounds, for the expenses of the house. His first performance was on the 19th of August, 1803, when he was not yet twelve years old. Next day he was the talk of Belfast, and on the other three nights he played Norval, Rolla, and Romeo.

Then he went to Dublin, Cork, Glasgow, Edinburgh, and Birmingham, at which latter place he was heard by Mr. Justice Graham, one of the Board of Management of Drury Lane Theatre. He reported about the infant genius, and proposals were made, which were too low to be acceptable.

He was afterwards engaged to play at Covent Garden, and, owing to an informality in the agreement, Drury Lane got hold of him on the intervening nights, at the same salary.

Whoever was his *entrepreneur*, he did his work well, and the puff preliminary was very delicately administered. The first notice of this kind that I can find, is in the *Morning Herald*, August 6, 1804. " A very extraordinary phenomenon has lately burst upon the *theatrical* world. A boy of the name of Beatie, not exceeding twelve years of age, reads and enacts all the principal of Shakespeare's characters, in a stile of superiority that astonishes the most experienced Actors. He has performed in Ireland, and is now exciting general astonishment at Edinburgh Off the stage his manners are puerile, as he is often seen playing at marbles in a morning, and Richard the Third in the evening. He is rather short of his age, slight made, but has great expression of countenance.

The moment he begins to converse upon stage business, he appears an inspired being. He has a pleasant turn for repartee, which makes his company much sought for. The Edinburgh Manager expressed his fears, at first rehearsal, that his voice would not fill the house. 'My dear Sir,' replied the little hero of the buskin, 'I beg you will be under no apprehensions upon that score, for, if my voice does not fill your house, probably my playing will!'"

THE YOUNG ROSCIUS, AS FREDERICK, IN " LOVERS' VOWS."

Here is an anecdote of him, probably got up to suit the public. *Morning Herald*, November 16, 1804 : "The *Young Roscius*, who is in all respects *play ful*, lately hesitated in going on the stage when he was to perform *Richard.* Young, the chief Liverpool actor, told him the stage was waiting, and urged him to appear. The boy declared, that, unless Young would bend his back, that he might have *one jump at leap-frog*, he would not appear. After some demur at this whimsical request, and some useless remonstrance, Young was obliged to submit ; and the little fellow then went upon the stage, and performed his part with admirable spirit."

Kept always before the public, in this manner, no wonder curiosity was stimulated to the highest pitch, and that when he did appear, he received an ovation. The mildest contemporary account of his *début* in London, is in the *Morning Herald*, of the 3rd of December, 1804, and I extract a portion. "On Saturday evening (December 1st) this prodigy of early excellence, whose merits have been as much extolled in the provinces, as they have been sceptically regarded in the Metropolis, met the *fiery ordeal* of a London audience. There has not been, within our recollection, any manifestation of public anxiety which can be quoted, as equalling that displayed on this occasion. At one o'clock the doors of the Pit and Gallery were besieged with expectants. At five, the outer doors of the box passages were forced open, and the boxes were occupied by an immense crowd, who forcibly ejected the persons stationed to keep places. The numbers still poured in with such rapidity, and pressure, that some hundreds leaped from the Boxes into the Pit, which was so crowded by this accession, that numbers must have perished, but for the humane attentions of some Ladies in the Boxes, who assisted in raising them, and passing them to the lobbies. The number outside the House and in the passages still continued to increase, though every effort

was made to assure them that their exertions must be
unavailing. We have not heard of any fatal accident, but
the faintings, bruises, and minor contingencies are beyond
all enumeration."

The play was "Barbarossa" (by Dr. Browne), and Master
Betty took the part of *Selim*. In the second scene—"Where
he sounds the feelings of *Othman*, he showed exquisite
judgment and sensibility. In the close of the scene when
he says:

> ' Oh! thou hast rous'd a thought on which revenge
> Mounts with redoubled fire!'

his fine blue eyes lighted up a countenance full of expression—his attitudes were graceful and appropriate, and the
strong emotion seemed to pervade every fibre of his frame.
The applauses which greeted his entrée were redoubled,
and loud *huzzas* and *bravos* resounded through the Theatre.
In the third act, with his mother, his *pathos* and his
judgment were both transcendent. When to the caution
of *Othman* he replies, . . . the energy of his delivery was
such as to leave all description at a distance: but the
closing soliloquy was the very climax of excellence. . . .

" In passing from particulars to generals, we feel ourselves at a loss how to proceed. We cannot try him as a
boy, who comes forward with such superior pretensions.
We cannot rate him as a *man*, when so many means of
future excellence are as yet unripened and undisclosed.
When we mention that his step is firm and manly—his
gesticulation free and unembarrassed—and his delivery and
emphasis in general most correct, we speak of things which
might, possibly, through tuition be acquired. But the
intelligence of manner—the eloquence of the eye when
speech was denied—the rapid yet judicious transitions
from prostrate affliction to dignified resentment—are
qualities which a GARRICK might display, but which he
never could transfuse. We do not mean to hold forth this

youth as a model of perfection, but that, at his age, and with so few opportunities, he should approach so nearly to perfection, is the wonder which it is our province to record."

THEATRICAL LEAP-FROG.

The great JOHN KEMBLE was said to have been much put out at the amount of attention this child received, and Rowlandson caricatured the young Roscius leaping over "Black Jack's" head.

The crowding to see him still continued, and there is

an amusing caricature by Ansell of the difficulties to be
encountered, in order to obtain a glimpse of the precocious boy.   The scene is vividly depicted.   " Has
any lady lost a flannel dickey?"   "Who owns a shoe?"
" That Dickey belongs to me, young man," exclaims a
lady whose dress bears palpable tokens of the fray.   A

VAIN ATTEMPT TO SEE YOUNG ROSCIUS.

plaintive voice is heard bewailing, "I'm a bran new hat out
of pocket;" whilst a cripple inquires, "Has any of the good
people found a Crutch?"

All sorts of *ruses* were attempted, in order to see
Master Betty without inconvenience.   Here is one of
them—*Morning Herald*, December 14, 1804: "A curious

trick was last night discovered at Drury Lane Theatre. Some of the Performers in the Orchestra had been induced to yield their places to as many *sprigs* of fashion, who entered with their violins under their arms, and with *greased bows*, that they might not interrupt the harmony to which they could not contribute. The fraud was discovered in time, and the *falsetto* fashionables were civilly ushered back to the *outer door!*"

He was presented to the Prince of Wales at Carlton House; and, on the 5th of December, 1804, when he was acting at Covent Garden, the King and the Royal Family went to Drury Lane to see the " School for Scandal," and the King having expressed a wish to see the marvellous boy, Sheridan had him fetched, and hence the illustration of " The Introduction," by J. B. Sheridan introduces him to the King as " The Wonder of the Theatrical World—A Diamond amongst Pebbles—A Snowdrop in a Mud-pool—The Golden Fleece of the *Morning Chronicle!* The Idol of the *Sun!* The Mirror of the *Times!* The Glory of the *Morning Post!* The Pride of the *Herald!* and the finest Cordial of the Publican's *Advertiser.*" The young Roscius thus presented, makes his bow to the Royal Couple, saying, " Never till this hour stood I in such a presence, yet there is something in my breast which makes me bold to say that Norval ne'er will shame thy favour."

He also visited the Duke of Clarence, and Charles James Fox; and, when he had an illness, probably induced by over excitement, and petting, so numerous were the inquiries after his precious health, that bulletins had to be issued.

At Drury Lane his first appearance was as enthusiastically received, as at Covent Garden; and, if possible, more riotously, for the mob broke all the windows within their reach, on the Vinegar Yard side of the Theatre, and, when the passages were thrown open, the balustrades, on

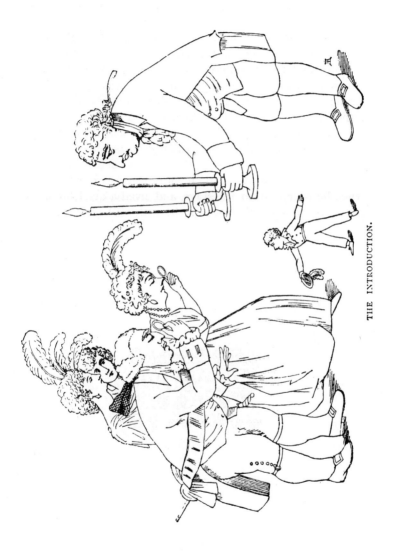

THE INTRODUCTION.

both sides of the staircase which led to the boxes, were entirely demolished.

From 1805 to 1808, he principally played at the provincial theatres, and in the latter year, being seventeen years of age, he was entered as a gentleman Commoner of Christ's College, Cambridge, and also was gazetted as Cornet in the North Shropshire Yeomanry Cavalry. His father died in 1811, and he then left Cambridge, residing on an estate his father had purchased, near Shrewsbury. Here he stayed till he was twenty years old, when his passion for the stage revived; and he acted, with occasional intermissions, until he was thirty-two years old, when he retired from the stage, and lived a quiet life until his death, which took place on the 24th of August, 1874.

CHAPTER XXXIX.

Betty's imitators—Miss Mudie, "The Young Roscia"—Her first appearance in London—Reception by the audience—Her fate—Ireland's forgery of "Vortigern and Rowena"—Fires among the theatres—Destruction of Covent Garden and Drury Lane.

BETTY'S success raised up, of necessity, some imitators—there were other Roscii, who soon disappeared; and, as ladies deny the sterner sex the sole enjoyment of all the good things of this world, a Roscia sprang into existence—a Miss Mudie, who entered on her theatrical career, even earlier than Master Betty. *Morning Post*, July 29, 1805 : "The Young Roscia of the Dublin Stage (only seven years old), who is called the *Phenomenon*, closed her engagement there on Monday last, in the part of *Peggy*, in the *Country Girl*, which she is stated to have pourtrayed with 'wonderful archness, vivacity, and discrimination.'"

Children, such as this, however precocious, are, of course simply ridiculous, and we are not astonished to find fun being made of them. Says the *Morning Post*, October 21, 1805 : "A young Lady was the other day presented by her nurse and mamma to one of our managers for an engagement. She came recommended by the testimony of an *amateur*, that she was a capital representative of the *Widow Belmour*. The manager, after looking at her from head to foot, exclaimed, ' But how old is Miss ? ' ' Seven years old, sir, next Lammas,' answered the nurse, ' bless her pretty face.' ' Oh ! Mrs. Nurse,' replies the manager, gravely, ' *too old, too old ;* nothing above *five years* will now do for *Widow Belmour.*' "

Old playgoers had not quite lost all their wits, although they had been somewhat crazy on the subject of young Roscius ; but he was then fourteen, whilst this baby was only seven. However, the *Phenomenon* appeared, and duly collapsed, the story of which I should spoil did I not give it in the original. Here it is, as a warning to ambitious *débutantes—Morning Post*, November 25, 1805 :

" COVENT GARDEN. The play of the *Country Girl* was announced at this house, on Saturday evening, for the purpose of introducing to a London audience, a very young lady, a Miss MUDIE, in the character of Miss *Peggy.* Miss Mudie has played, as it has been reported, but we doubt the truth of the report, with great success at Dublin, Liverpool, Birmingham, &c., where she has been applauded and followed nearly as much as Master BETTY. The people of London seem to have been aware that these reports were unfounded, for no great degree of curiosity prevailed to see her on Saturday.

" The audience received this child very favourably on her entrance. She is said to be ten years of age, but in size she does not look to be more than five. She is extremely diminutive, and has not the plump, comely, countenance of an infant : her nose is very short ; her eyes not well placed ; she either wants several teeth, or is, perhaps, shedding them ; and she speaks very inarticulately. It was difficult to understand what she said. When she attempts expression of countenance, her features contract about the nose, and eyes, in a way that gives reason to suppose she is older than her person denotes. She seems to have a young body with an old head.

" In the first passages of her part, she appeared to give

some satisfaction, and was loudly applauded ; an in-
dulgent audience wishing, no doubt, to encourage her to
display her full powers ; but when she was talked of as a
wife, as a mistress, and an object of love, the scene became
so ridiculous that hissing and horse laughing ensued. She
made her *début* before Miss BRUNTON, a tall, elegant,
beautiful woman, and looked in size just as if Miss
BRUNTON'S fan had been walking in before her ; Miss
MUDIE the married woman, and Miss BRUNTON the
maiden ! When she was with her husband, Mr. MURRAY,
no very tall man, she did not reach higher than his knee,
and he was obliged to stoop even to lay his hand upon her
head, and bend himself down double to kiss her ; when she
had to lay hold of his neckcloth to coax him, and pat his
check, he was obliged to stoop down all fours that she
might reach him ! The whole effect was so out of nature,
so ludicrous, that the audience very soon decided against
Miss Mudie. At first they did not hiss when she was on
the stage, from delicacy ; but, in her absence, hissed the
performance, to stop the play, if possible. But as she
persevered confidently they hissed her, and at last called
vehemently, *Off ! off !* Miss Mudie was not, however,
without a strong party to support her ; but the noise increased to that degree in the latter scenes that not a word
could be heard, on which Miss Mudie walked to the front
of the stage with great confidence and composure, not
without some signs of indignation, and said :

"'LADIES AND GENTLEMEN,

"'I know nothing I have done to offend you, and
has set (*sic*) those who are sent here to hiss me ; I will be
very much obliged to you to turn them out.'

"This speech, which, no doubt had been very imprudently
put into the infant's mouth, astonished the audience ;
some roared out with laughter, some hissed, others called
Off ! off ! and many applauded. Miss Mudie did not
appear to be in the slightest degree chagrined or em-

barrassed, and she went through the scene with as much glee as if she had been completely successful. At the end of it the uproar was considerable, and a loud cry arising of *Manager! Manager!* Mr. KEMBLE came forward. In substance he said :

"'LADIES AND GENTLEMEN,

"' Miss Mudie having performed at various provincial theatres with great success, her friends thought themselves authorised in presenting her before you. It is the duty, and the wish, of the proprietors of this House to please you ; and to fulfil both, was their aim in bringing forward Miss Mudie. 'The Drama's laws, the Drama's patrons give'—Miss Mudie intends to withdraw herself from the stage ; but I entreat you to hear her through the remainder of her part.'"

She came on the stage again, but the audience would not listen to her, and Miss Searle had to finish her part. What became of this self-possessed child I know not; according to the *Morning Post*, April 5, 1806, she joined a children's troupe in Leicester Place, where, "though deservedly discountenanced at a great threatre, she will, no doubt, prove an acquisition to the infant establishment."

Late in the last century, the literary and theatrical world had been thrown into a state of high excitement, by the announcement of the discovery of an original play by Shakespeare, called "Vortigern and Rowena," which was acted at Drury Lane, and condemned, as spurious, the first night ; but belief in it lasted for some time, and the question was of such importance, that the *Morning Post*, in 1802, took the suffrages of the fashionable world, as to its authenticity. The question was set at rest in 1805 by the forger himself, one William Henry Ireland, who had the audacity to publish a book[1] in which he unblushingly details all his forgeries, and his method of doing them. It

---

[1] "The Confessions of William Henry Ireland, containing the Particulars of his Fabrication of the Shakespeare Manuscripts." London, 1805.

is an amusing volume, and has recently been utilized by a novelist.[1] The absolute forgeries are still in existence, including the pseudo-lock of Shakespeare's hair; and they changed owners some few years since, when they were sold by auction at very low prices.

There was a great fatality among theatres; there were but few of them, and they were continually being burnt down. The Opera House in 1789 ; The Pantheon 1792 ; Astley's Amphitheatre, September 17, 1794. This theatre was unlucky. It again fell a victim to the flames, September 1, 1803 ; and Astley, on this occasion, seems to have met with an accident—*Times*, September 7, 1803 : "Fortunately for Mr. Astley, almost the whole of his plate was at Lower Esher, from which place he reached the Amphitheatre in one hour and a quarter. It was not till he came to Vauxhall that his horse fell ; the same presentiment which foreran the former conflagration of his property, the moment he heard the gate bell ring, he exclaimed to Mrs. Astley, 'They come to tell me that the Theatre is on fire.'"

The Surrey Theatre, or, as it was then called, the Royal Circus, was destroyed by fire August 12, 1805 ; and Covent Garden was burnt down September 20, 1808—the fire being supposed to have been caused by a piece of wadding from a gun fired during the performance of Pizarro. It was, of course, a tremendous conflagration, and unfortunately resulted in loss of life, besides the loss of many original scores of Handel, Arne, and other eminent composers, together with Handel's organ.

Plans for a new theatre were soon got out, and Mr. Smirke (afterwards Sir Robert, to whom we owe the beautiful British Museum, and the General Post Office) was the architect. The first stone was laid, with much Masonic pomp, on the 31st of December, 1808, by the Prince of Wales, the Duke of Sussex, and a distinguished circle of guests, being present. The weather was unpropitious, but immense

[1] " Talk of the Town," by James Payn.

crowds of people were present ; and it is curious to learn, as showing the defective police of the time, that " The Horse Guards patrolled the streets, and several of the Volunteer Corps did duty on the occasion."

Within two months from the above date, Drury Lane Theatre was totally destroyed by fire. On the 24th of February, about 11 p.m., it was discovered, and it did not take long before the whole was in a blaze ; not for want of precautions, for it seems they had adopted the best accepted preventitives of a great theatrical conflagration known to modern architects, viz., an iron curtain, and a huge reservoir of water on the top of the building—the latter being described as " a mere bucket full to the volume of fire on which it fell, and had no visible effect in damping it," which may be comforting for modern playgoers to remember. Nor was it long in burning ; by 5 a.m. " the flames were completely subdued "—that is, there was nothing left to burn. Very little was saved, only a bureau and some looking-glasses, from Mrs. Jordan's dressing-room, and the " Treasury " books and some papers. Sheridan took his loss, outwardly, with great *sang froid,* one anecdote affirming that, on a remark being made to him that it was a wonder he could bear to witness the destruction of his property, he replied, " Why ! where can a man warm himself better than at his own fire-side ? " However, by his energy, he soon found temporary premises for his company, and, having obtained a special license from the Lord Chamberlain, he took the Lyceum and opened it on the 25th of September, or, within a week of the fire.

CHAPTER XL.

The O. P. Riots—Causes of—Madame Catalani—Kemble's refutation of charges—
Opening of the theatre, and commencement of the riots—O. P. medals, &c.—
" The house that Jack built "—A committee of examination—Their report—
A reconciliation dinner—Acceptation of a compromise—" We are satisfied "—
Theatre re-opens—Re-commencement of riots—The proprietors yield, and the
riots end.

WE now come to the celebrated O. P. Riots, which find no parallel in our theatrical history, and which would require at least two thick volumes to exhaust. Never was there anything so senseless ; never could people have been more persistently foolish ; they would listen to no reason ; they denied, or pooh-poohed, every fact.

O. P. represents " Old Prices," and, as the management of the new theatre had raised the price of their entertainment, as they had a perfect right to do, these people demanded that only the old prices should be charged for admission. It was in vain that it was pointed out that very early notice was given of the intended rise, as indeed it was, directly after the destruction of the fire—*vide Morning Post*, September 24, 1808 : " The Managers, we understand, intend to raise the price of admission, when they open at the Opera to 7s. for the boxes, and to 4s. for the pit. The admission for the galleries to remain as before. Much clamour has already been excited against this innovation, but we think unjustly."

Had this been the only grumble, probably no more would have been heard of it, but all sorts of rumours got about—That the proprietors, of whom Kemble was one (and, except on the stage, he was not popular), would make a handsome profit out of the insurance, and sale of old materials; that the increased number of private boxes, with their ante-rooms, were built for the special purpose of serving as places of assignation for a debauched aristo-

MADAME CATALANI.

cracy; and, therefore, a virtuous public ought to rise in its wrath against them. And last, but not least, they tried to enlist patriotic feelings into the question, and appealed to the passions of the mob—(remember we were at war with the French, and the ignorant public could not discriminate much between the nationality of foreigners) as to whether it was fair to pay such enormous nightly sums to a foreigner—which sums were partly the cause of the rise in price—when native talent was going unappreciated.

This foreigner was Madame Angelica Catalani, a lady who was born at Sinigaglia, in 1779. At the early age of twelve, when at the convent of St. Lucia, at Gubbio, her beautiful voice was remarkable, and when she left the convent, at the age of fifteen, she was compelled to get a living on the stage, owing to her father's ruin.

At sixteen, she made her *début* at Venice, in an opera by Nasolini; and she afterwards sang at Florence, at La Scala in Milan, at Trieste, Rome, and Naples. Her fame got her an engagement at Lisbon, where she married M.

Valabrègue, a French officer attached to the Portuguese Embassy ; but she still kept to her name of Catalani— at all events, on the stage. From Lisbon she went to Madrid, thence to Paris, where she only sang at concerts ; and, finally, in October, 1806, she came to London, where she speedily became the rage. According to one biographer (Fétis), she gained immense sums here ; but I much doubt his accuracy. He says : "In a single theatrical season which did not last more than four months, she gained about 180,000

CATALANI.

francs (£7,200), which included her benefit. Besides that, she gained, in the same time, about 60,000 francs (£2,400) by *soirées* and private concerts. They gave her as much as 200 guineas for singing at Drury Lane, or Covent Garden—'God save the King,' and ' Rule, Britannia,' and £2,000 sterling were paid her for a single musical fête."

This, according to the scale paid her at Covent Garden, said by her opponents to be £75 per night, must be excessive; but the mob had neither sense, nor reason, in the matter; she was a foreigner, and native talent was neglected. Her name suggested a subject to the caricaturist, of which he speedily availed himself.

These were the principal indictments against Kemble (for he, as manager, had to bear the brunt of the riot) and the proprietors replied to them categorically—*vide Morning Post*, September 18, 1809:

"It is stated that the old materials of the Theatre were estimated at £25,000.

For £25,000, read £1,000. The bricks were of so little value, that not one old brick was used in the building, and the greater part now lie buried near Hart Street.

It is stated that instead of twelve private boxes, they have now thirty-four, being an addition of twenty-two private boxes.

For 22 read 12 additional private boxes. In fact, the Proprietors contend that they have no private boxes, as all of them are let annually to the Public. They are taken by the higher classes of society, and, by that means, the first and second circles of boxes are left free for the public at large. What the Proprietors gain by them annually, they lose nightly.

It is stated that £50,000 was received from the Insurance of the Theatre.

For £50,000, read £42,000. 'Tis true that £3 or 4,000 was received from the insurance of houses, now included in the Theatre; but it was forgotten that the Proprietors paid near £28,000

It is asserted that Madame Catalani is the cause of the advance on the prices.

for those houses, to insulate the Theatre, and render the avenues safe and commodious. The increased ground rent of which will be a heavy and lasting incumbrance on the Theatre.

The Proprietors have already given their reasons to the Public, which existed long before Madame Catalani's engagement. As well might it be said that the increased prices were caused by Mrs. Siddons, whose engagement is fifty guineas a night and a clear benefit ; or by the other eminent English Performers of the Theatre, whose salaries amount to £32,000."

There was good sound sense in this refutation, yet something is wanting to explain more fully the riot which was to come, and which, at all events, was popularly supposed to relate to the structure of the building, and to the rise in prices. The following is much condensed from a contemporary account of the theatre :

" The Pit of this Theatre is very spacious. . . . The two Galleries are comparatively small, there *not being accommodation in the upper, for more than* 150 *or* 200 *persons !* The Upper Gallery is divided into five compartments, and may thus be considered a tier of five boxes, with a separate door at the back of each. These doors open into a spacious lobby, one side of which is the back of the gallery, and the other the exterior wall of the Theatre, with the windows into the street. The lobby to the middle gallery beneath is similarly situated. Under the gallery is a row of *private boxes*, constituting the whole third tier! They consist of 26 in number, with a private room behind each. The Carpeting was laid down in these boxes on Saturday last ; but the furniture of each, and also of the adjoining room, will be according to the taste of the several occupants, among whom are some of the Royal Dukes."

And now I have to chronicle one of the most senseless phases of public opinion that ever made a page, or a paragraph, of history. The Theatre opened on September 18, 1809, with " Macbeth " and " The Quaker," but not one word that was delivered on the stage could be heard by the audience.

When the curtain drew up, Kemble delivered an address, which was extremely classical—all about Æschylus, Thespis, and Sophocles, of which the people present knew nothing, until they saw the next morning's papers. Instead of listening, they sang " God save the King " with all the power of their lungs, and in good order ; but that once over, then, with one consent, they began to yell " No KEMBLES—no theatrical tyrants—no domineering Napoleons !—What! will you fight, will you faint, will you die, for a Shilling ?—No imposition !—no extortion !—English charity.—Charity begins at home.—No foreigners—No CATALANIS."

Somebody in the boxes addressed the frantic mob, but nothing was heard of his speech, and a magistrate named Read, attended by several Bow Street officers, came on the stage, and produced the Riot Act ; it was no good—he could not be heard, and yet, among the audience, were many men of position, and even some of the Royal Dukes.

The second night the row was as bad, and it now was becoming organized. People brought placards, which began mildly with " The Old Prices," and afterwards deve-

loped into all sorts of curious things. One was displayed
in the first circle of the boxes, and " TOWNSEND,[1] heading
a posse of constables, rushed into the pit to seize this
standard of sedition, together with the standard bearers.
A contest ensued of the hottest kind, staffs and sticks were
brandished in all directions ; and, after repeated onsets
and retreats, Townsend bore away a few of the standards,
but failed in capturing the standard bearers. He retired
with these imperfect trophies. But, as the oppositionists
kept the field of battle, they claimed the victory, which
they announced to the boxes and galleries with three
cheers. The standard bearers in the boxes were not
equally successful. They were but few in number, and
not formed into a compact body, and had, besides, their
rear and flanks open to the attack of the enemy. Some of
them we saw seized from behind, and dragged most rudely
out of the boxes, and treated, in every respect, with a rigour
certainly *beyond* the *law.* One of them, who had all the
appearance of a gentleman, was accompanied by a lady,
who screamed at seeing the rudeness he suffered, and then
flew out of the box to follow him. This vigorous activity
on the part of the constables made the placards disappear
for a time ; but they were soon after hoisted again in the
pit, and hailed with acclamations every time they were
observed."

On the third night the uproar was as great, many of the
lights had been blown out, and the place was a perfect
pandemonium ; when Kemble, in dress suit of black, and
chapeau bras, appeared, and obtained a momentary hearing.
" Ladies and gentlemen," said he, " permit me to assure
you that the proprietors are most desirous to consult your
wishes (loud and continued applause). I stand here, to
know what you want." If the noise and uproar could
have been greater than before, it was after this brusque,

[1] A famous *Bow Street Runner*, and one in great favour with, and attendance on, Royalty.

and unfortunate, speech. "*You know what we want—the question is insulting—Off! off! off!*" For five minutes did the great man face his foes, and then he retired. Then some one in the boxes addressed the audience in a speech calculated to inflame, and augment, the riot; and Kemble once more came forward with a most sensible exposition as to the sum spent on the theatre, its appointments, and company. He might as well have spoken to the wind.

Night after night this scene of riot continued, varied only by the different noises—of bugle and tin horns, rattles, clubs, yelling, &c.—and the manifold placards, which differed each night, and were now not disturbed. There were O. P. medals struck—how many I know not—but there are three of them in the British Museum. One, which is struck both in white metal and bronze, has *obv.* John Bull riding an Ass (Kemble), and flogging him with two whips—Old and New Prices. *Leg.* FROM *N* TO *O* JACK YOU MUST GO ; *in exergue—*

> JOHN BULL'S ADVICE TO YOU, IS GO.
> 'TIS BUT A STEP FROM N TO O.

Rev. a P within an O, surrounded by laurel, and musical emblems. *Leg.* GOD SAVE THE KING ; *in exergue,* MAY OUR RIGHTS AND PRIVILEGES REMAIN UNCHANGED. Another has *obv.* Kemble's head with asses' ears ; and the third, which was struck when Mr. Clifford was being prosecuted for riot, has *obv.* Kemble's head with a fool's cap on ; *leg.* OH ! MY HEAD AITCHES ; *in exergue,* OBSTINACY.

Then, too, the Caricaturists took up the tale and worked their wicked will upon the theme. I only reproduce one —by Isaac Cruikshank (father to George) which was published 28th September, 1809.

On the 22nd of September Kemble came forward and said, *inter alia,* that the proprietors, anxious that their conduct

This is the house that *Jack* [1] built.

These are the BOXES painted so neat, with snug room and sofa all complete,
Where assignations are made by the *Great* that visit the House that Jack built.

[1] *John* Kemble.

These are the Pigeon Holes over the Boxes, painted so neat, &c.

This is the CAT engaged to squall, to the poor in the Pigeon
Holes, &c.

This is John Bull with his *Bugle Horn*
Who hissed the CAT engaged to
squall, &c.

This is the Thieftaker[1] shaven and shorn
That took up John Bull with his *Bugle
Horn*, &c.

This is the Manager, full of scorn, who *Raised the Price* to the People forlorn,
And directed the Thieftaker shaven and shorn to take up John Bull, &c.

[1] Townsend—a very good likeness.

should be fully looked into, were desirous of submitting their books, and their accounts, to a committee of gentlemen of unimpeachable integrity and honour, by whose decision they would abide. Meanwhile the theatre would be closed, and Madame Catalani, cancelling her engagement, went to Ireland.

"THE DEPARTURE FOR IRELAND.

"WHEN *Grimalkin* [1] the Spy, took a peep at the house,
  And saw such confusion and strife,
He stole to the Green-room as soft as a Mouse,
  And thus he address'd his dear wife :
'MON DIEU ! don't sit purring, as if all was right,
  Our measure of meanness is full,
We cannot stay here to be bark'd at all night,
  I'd rather be toss'd by a *Bull.*' "

The committee of gentlemen (of whom the well-known John Julius Angerstein was one), published their report, and balance sheet, which was publicly advertised on the 4th of October, and they agreed that the profit to the shareholders on the capital, employed during the six years, was 6⅜ per cent. per annum, and that during that time they had paid £307,912. This, of course, would not satisfy the mob, and on the re-opening of the theatre on the 4th of October there was the same riot with its concomitant din of cat calls, rattles, horns, trumpets, bells, &c. For a few days the riot was not so bad, although it still continued ; but, on the 9th of October, it broke out again, and the proprietors were compelled to take proceedings at Bow Street against some of the worst offenders. This had the effect, for a time, of stopping the horns, rattles, bells, bugles, &c., but the rioters only exchanged one noise for another, for now they imitated all the savage howlings of wild beasts, and it seemed as if Pidcock's Menagerie had been turned into the theatre.

This soon got too tame, and on the 20th of October they

[1] Supposed to be Madame Catalani's husband. She died at Paris, of cholera, 12th of June, 1849.

began fighting among themselves, and stripping the baize
off the seats. On the 24th, the proprietors issued a very
proper address to the people, showing that they were not
getting exorbitant profits, and, consequently, the prices
were not too high ; but it had no effect until the Grand
Jury found true bills against some of the rioters, when
there was a lull for a time, which might have been permanent, had not Brandon, the boxkeeper, charged a Mr.
Clifford with having created a commotion in the pit. After
examination, however, at Bow Street, he was released—
and then the mob had another grievance. Brandon must
be dismissed ; nor only so—on the 5th of November a mob
went to Bloomsbury Square, and broke the windows in
Kemble's house, after which, there was another lull ; then
on the 25th the turbulent spirits broke out again, because
it was the fiftieth night, or *jubilee*, of the riots. A few of
them were charged at Bow Street, but that did not stop
the riot till nearly the middle of December, when there
was another lull in the storm.

Both sides were getting weary of the strife ; and, on the
14th of December, a dinner was held at the Crown and
Anchor Tavern, Covent Garden, at which Kemble met
the Opposition, and a compromise was entered into, and
agreed upon, that the boxes were to remain the same price
—7s.—the pit was to revert to the old price of 3s. 6d.; and
the galleries to remain as they were ; the private boxes,
at the end of the season, were to be again restored, and
appropriated to the accommodation of the public. The
rioters wanted Brandon to be discharged, and at night,
when he had to appear before his sweet masters, they
saluted him with volleys of oranges, and walking-sticks ;
and, the next night, it was announced that Brandon had
been sacrificed to public opinion, and had been dismissed.[1]
One or two more apologies for small *lâches*, and King Mob
produced a placard, " WE ARE SATISFIED."

[1] He was afterwards reinstated.

But they were not ; they wanted the boxes reduced to 6s. ; and, having so long had license, the ferment was not subdued at once. Take the 19th of December, for instance ; Kemble was hissed, on his appearance on the stage, and when he spoke the lines—

> " The times are out of joint—Oh, cursed spite !
> That ever I was born to *set them right ! "*—

there was an universal shout of derision.

For the remainder of that season there was peace ; but, when the new season opened, on September 10, 1810, with " The Beggar's Opera," and " Raising the Wind," it was found that part of the treaty had not been carried out; as, although the centre portion of the first tier, had been converted into public boxes ; yet, on either side, were still the objectionable private boxes, which, last year, had so excited the prudishly virtuous indignation of a howling mob. " No foreign sofas ! No Italian private boxes." In vain did Kemble point out that, since the conclusion of the treaty, an Act of Parliament had been passed for the rebuilding of Drury Lane Theatre, which allowed the proprietors to have as many private boxes as they might find convenient ; and, consequently, would place Covent Garden at a decided disadvantage; therefore, his proprietary had hoped the public would condone the fact of their still retaining a few private boxes. Oh, no ! The O. P. dance, and the O. P. song, were immediately revived in all their glory, and the remainder of the evening was spent in the old manner, minus the accompaniment of horns, rattles, or placards ; but a quart bottle was thrown from the gallery into the pit, and the management offered a reward of fifty guineas for the conviction of the offender.

Next night there were two placards exposed: " O. P. We have been imposed on ! " " O. P. The Treaty is broken ; open War ! " The night after, the row got worse. On the 14th of September it was as bad as last year—

watchmen's rattles were freely used, and mewing, barking, groaning, braying, and whistling, made a hideous chorus. The O. P. dance was changed to the "Contract" dance, but still was danced to the tune of the O. P. hornpipe.

The proprietors, after their bitter experience of the previous year, felt that, however right they might be, they could not contend against the *force majeure* of the mob ; and, on the 16th of September, they pledged themselves "that next season (when they will again have returned into their possession) the eight annual boxes shall be given up, and let to the public, at large, as nightly boxes." It was no use ; that night the row was as bad as ever ; and, after that performance, the theatre was closed to make the alterations in the boxes, which were thrown open to the public. The theatre was re-opened on the 24th of September, and the performances passed off without interruption. And so ended the eventful O. P. Riots.

CHAPTER XLI.

"The Pic-nic Club"—Its supporters—Its entertainment—Its short life—Automata and wool pictures—Almack's—Pidcock's Menagerie—"The Invisible Girl"—Vauxhall—Sir Roger de Coverley — Price of admission, &c. — Ranelagh Gardens.

THE theatre, although the main source of amusement, was not the only one. There were masquerades at the Pantheon, and a private theatrical club, called the "Pic-nic Club," of which a Captain Caulfield was the manager. Lady Buckinghamshire—foremost in this, as in gaming—was one of its chief supporters; and it took its name from every one drawing lots, as to what should be his, or her, share of the entertainment. This club consisted of the leaders of fashion—the Prince of Wales, Lords Cholmondeley, Valletort, Carlisle, Spooner, Kirkcudbright, and Derby; and, of course, "old Q," the Duke of Queensberry. Sir Lumley Skeffington, also, was an ornament to the society; whilst the lady members besides Lady Albina Buckinghamshire, numbered in their ranks, Lady Salisbury, Lady Jersey, and Mrs. Fitzherbert. It was *crème de la crème*, and I find them chronicled in the *Morning Herald* of March 16, 1802, thus: "The *Pic-nic* Club met last night for the first time, in the Tottenham Street Rooms.[1] The Entertainment commenced with a

[1] Used also for the concerts of Ancient Music.

Prologue by Colonel Greville, which was followed by a French Proverb. An Act of the *Bedlamites*, a piece translated from the French, for the occasion, was then performed. A French Proverb, and an Epilogue, succeeded; and the whole succeeded with a *Pic-nic* Supper, provided from a tavern.[1] The company was not numerous, though 300 cards of invitation were issued. Madame Parisot,[2] disapproving of the *dilettanti* project, refused to take any part in the performance. It being apprehended that the public peace might be disturbed by this irregular assemblage, the Bow Street officers held themselves in readiness to act, during the whole of the evening, but happily there was no occasion for their services."

The society afterwards moved to the Argyle Rooms, then most highly proper, and fashionable. There were several caricatures of this society from Gillray's pencil, one of which (the next illustration) I reproduce.

Here Gillray has given, as a contrast, Lord Valletort "the neatest of little beaux," and the smallest man in the Club, and Lord Cholmondeley, who was very tall and stout. Lady Buckinghamshire, whose *embonpoint* Gillray never spared, plays the piano, and Lady Salisbury, who from her love of hunting, was frequently satirized under the name of Diana, performs on a hunting horn. The fashionable papers of the day were, during the season, seldom without a paragraph of this society, but it did not last long, and its death is recorded in the *Times*, February 28, 1803: "The Pic-nic Society is at an end. Many of its members, at a late meeting, wished to continue the Theatrical amusements, but no person would undertake the management of them."

In 1801, there were to be seen in Spring Gardens, Maillardet's Automata, where a wooden lady performed on

---

[1] This marks, as much as anything, the manners of the times. Fancy the *upper ten*, now-a-days, ordering their supper from a tavern!

[2] The famous ballet-dancer of that time.

THE PIC-NIC ORCHESTRA.

the piano ; also Miss Linwood's Exhibition of Needlework,
first at the Hanover Square Rooms, and afterwards at
Saville House, Leicester Square, where were exhibited
marvels of crewel work. There are one or two of her
pictures in the South Kensington Museum ; but her
" Salvator Mundi," after Carlo Dolci, for which she refused
3,000 guineas, she bequeathed to the Queen. She had a
rival, whose name, however, has not been so well perpetuated—*vide* the *Morning Post*, June 4, 1800 : " The
wool pictures, so much talked of among the connoisseurs,
are certainly executed with very great taste. Miss Thomp-
son has brought her art to very great perfection," &c.
These were shown in Old Bond Street.

Then, for the extremely select, during the season, was
Almack's [1] which, then, was not quite so exclusive as afterwards. *Morning Herald*, April 27, 1802 : " Almack's, King
Street, St. James' Square. James and William Willis most
respectfully inform the Nobility and Gentry, the first
SUBSCRIPTION BALL will be on Thursday, the 29th instant,
under the patronage of her Grace the Duchess of Devonshire, the Marchioness of Townshend, and the Countess of
Westmoreland. Tickets One Guinea each." The same
newspaper has also an advertisement of a new Panorama
of Paris. This was by a M. de Maria ; and there was
also another, " Barker's Panorama," in Leicester Square.

Those who liked such exhibitions could see the Phantas-
magoria, at the Lyceum Theatre, where the Magic Lantern
was exhibited with novel effects, such as moving eyes and
limbs, but they had not yet attained the height of " dis-
solving views." Pidcock's Menagerie [2] was the only sub-

---

[1] Otherwise Willis's Rooms.
[2] This Collection was sold in March, 1810—*vide Morning Post*, March 22,
1810 : " The sale at Pidcock's, Exeter 'Change, has been well attended. The
skeleton of the famous elephant was put up at 20 guineas, and knocked down
at 55. The skeleton of the spermaceti whale, sixty-six feet long, which formerly
appeared in Rackstraw's Museum, sold for nine guineas. Many scarce and
beautiful birds sold at low prices, and the whole collection, consisting of 205
lots, produced about £140."

stitute they then had for our " Zoo," and was situate
in Exeter 'Change. It is thus described in a guide to
London, 1802 : "A collection of divers beasts and birds,
only exceeded in rarity by those of the Royal Menagerie,
in the Tower."

The " Invisible Girl " was exhibited in Leicester Square,
and was "a globe of glass suspended by a ribbon, under
which four tubes are adapted, but they do not communicate
therewith, and are likewise insulated ; by these, conversation is carried on with an invisible lady, who answers every
question, breathes on you, and tells every visitor whatever
they hold in their hands, in an instant. This exhibition is
open from ten o'clock until six. Price of admittance, *two
shillings and sixpence.*"

There were two famous out-door places of amusement,
now no more, namely, Vauxhall, and Ranelagh. Vauxhall,
was formerly called Foxhall, or Spring Garden, and is thus
described in No. 383 of the *Spectator :* "We were now
arrived at Spring Garden, which is excellently pleasant at
this time of the year. When I considered the fragrancy of
the walks and bowers, with the choir of birds that sung
upon the trees, and the loose tribe of people that walked
under their shades, I could not but look upon the place
as a kind of Mahometan paradise. Sir Roger told me it
put him in mind of a little coppice by his house in the
country, which his chaplain used to call an aviary of
nightingales. ' You must understand,' says the knight,
' that there is nothing in the world that pleases a man in
love, so much as your nightingale. Ah, Mr. Spectator, the
many moonlight nights that I have walked by myself, and
thought on the widow by the music of the nightingale !'
He, here, fetched a deep sigh, and was falling into a fit of
musing, when a mask, who came behind him, gave him a
gentle tap upon the shoulder, and asked him if he would
drink a bottle of mead with her ? But the knight being
startled at so unexpected a familiarity, and displeased to

be interrupted in his thoughts of the widow, told her, ' she was a wanton baggage ; ' and bid her go about her business."

These gardens opened about the middle of May, and closed about the end of August ; they were only open three days a week—Monday, Wednesday, and Friday ; and

VAUXHALL GARDENS—1808-9.

the price of admission was 3s. 6d., the concert commencing at eight, the attendance averaging from 5,000 to 15,000. At the end of the first part of the concert, about 10 p.m., a curtain was drawn up, and disclosed " a view of a bridge, a water mill, and a cascade ; while coaches, waggons, soldiers, and other figures were exhibited as crossing that bridge." The orchestra, which I reproduce, was a blaze of light, and, altogether, in the gardens, at that time, were 37,000 lamps. Occasionally, a display of fireworks took place ; whilst, to add to the attractions of the gardens, there were recesses, and alcoves, provided, where suppers, and refreshment, could be procured. .

Ranelagh Gardens were in Chelsea, about where the Barracks now stand. The amusements provided were almost identical with Vauxhall, but, although considered a place of summer resort, its season commenced in February, and closed at the end of May, or the middle of June. The general price of admission was half a crown ; but, on a masquerade night, it rose to 10s. 6d. or £1 1s., but that included supper and wine. There were particular fête nights, notably of the Pic-nic Society, when the price of admission varied from 5s. to 7s. 6d.

CHAPTER XLII.

THESE open-air concerts showed that there was a
natural taste for music in the English character,
and when we look at the composers who then
flourished, and at the singers who expounded their works,
we must own that the dawn of the century could fairly hold
its own with its latter days. Dr. Arnold, Dr. Callcott
(whose glees are still sung in many a home), Shield, Stevens,
and Clementi, were among the composers ; and, for singers
—was there not Mrs. Billington, with her extraordinarily
sweet voice, her forcible expression, and flexible execution ?

Gillray here has kept an excellent likeness of our *prima
donna*, and, probably, did not much exaggerate her proportions. She was paid remarkably well, as most *divas*
are, and, if the satirical prints, and newspaper reports of
the time, do not belie her, she was as voracious after
" Refreshers " as a modern Queen's Counsel, or she could
not appear.

Here we see Mrs. Billington utterly prostrate, until revived by golden pills, of which Sheridan is bringing a good
supply. We can see what she earned from a newspaper
cutting, or two.

MRS. BILLINGTON, AS CLARA, SINGING A BRAVURA (1802).

Morning Post, June 12, 1800 : " Mrs. Billington is engaged for the King's Theatre next season, and she is to have two thousand guineas."

Morning Post, July 15, 1801 : " Mrs. Billington after *humming* all the Theatres, has, at last, fixed on the *hive* in Covent Garden, where she will, no doubt, make much *buzz* and *honey* next season. Articles were signed between her and Mr. Harris yesterday. This we can state as a *positive*

THEATRICAL DOCTORS RECOVERING CLARA'S NOTES.

fact. It is with much pleasure we find she has resolved to return to the English stage ; she will revive our Operas, of late fallen into disrepute, and bring music again into fashion. The terms are very liberal, but not more so than we expected so extraordinary, so charming a singer, to obtain. She is to have three thousand guineas, and a free benefit, besides fifty guineas per night at the oratorios ; this altogether will amount to upwards of four thousand pounds for the season, and this season is not to extend beyond half a year."

PLAYING IN PARTS.

[*Gillray*, 15*th May*, 1801.

Morning Herald, April 2, 1802 : " Mrs. Billington will net this single season, by her professional abilities, no less than *eleven thousand pounds !* "

Mdlle. Mara, too, whose rich, sweet voice was so often heard in oratorio, got her fifty guineas a night at Drury Lane, in the year 1800, so that we see that in those old days " singing women " were well paid. Mrs. Crouch, that sweet songstress, and rival of the Billington, although she had quitted the stage through an unfortunate accident, which injured her voice, died in this decade, on the 2nd of October, 1805. There were many more of respectable calibre, but none with the exception of Storace, to compare with the three named.

Among male voices Incledon, and Braham, were preeminent. Incledon had a beautifully rich voice, the successful cultivation of which was doubtless owing to his early training, under the celebrated William Jackson, at Exeter Cathedral.

Many of us now living can remember having heard John Braham sing, although, of course, only in his decadence. His was a wonderfully successful musical career, not only here, but on the Continent ; but then he had a most rare voice, and one of such extensive range, that he could sing airs written for Mdlle. Mara.

No other male singers of this period are worthy of note, nor do we find many good, or lasting, names among the instrumentalists. Wesley on the organ, Clementi and Cramer on the pianoforte, F. Cramer on the violin, about exhaust the list. But the people were musical at heart and there is no greater fallacy than to think the English were ever otherwise. Small and select parties would meet of an evening, and perform concerted chamber music. The illustration by Gillray is slightly caricatured, but it gives a very fair view of such a domestic scene.

Or, we might take another drawing-room scene, in

which only two are actors, and are executing a duet to a harp accompaniment.

That good, and what we term severe, music was then appreciated, we have evidence in the existence of the "Academy of Ancient Music," which was held at the Crown and Anchor Tavern, Covent Garden—an institution which began in Queen Anne's reign, under the conduct of the celebrated musician, Dr. John Christopher Pepsuch; and, till 1737, no ladies were admitted in the audience. In

HARMONY BEFORE MATRIMONY—1805.

another twenty years it assumed more of the form of a public concert; and, in 1786, the society migrated to Free-mason's Hall, where, in 1788, it was resolved to admit ladies as subscribers. The subscription, which, at its com-mencement, was only half a guinea, rose, by degrees, to five guineas, and then settled down to four, which covered a season of six, or eight, concerts.

There was a split in the musical camp, and a branch of the parent society seceded, and established themselves at the Opera House, in the Haymarket, under the title of "The Concert of Ancient Music," or "King's Concerts." They afterwards moved to the Hanover Square Rooms. The concerts commenced in February, and continued till the end of May. Six directors, chosen from the nobility, selected, in turn, the pieces for each concert—at which all modern music was utterly excluded, and nothing could be played unless twenty-five years old. So strictly was this carried out, that if the director for the night introduced anything more modern, he was (and it was done more than once) fined in a very considerable sum. There were also popular concerts held at the Hanover Square rooms, during the season, to which the admission was generally half a guinea.

And yet, with all this reverence for old music, it was found impossible to make a success of a "Commemoration of Dr. Arne," which took place at Ranelagh on June 10, 1802; the expenses being £100, and the actual receipts for the night only £26! Well may the newspaper editor end the paragraph with "Poor Thomas Arne!"

In contradistinction to this, a Competition of Pipers, which was annual, seems to have been a great success. The Highland Society of London gave the prizes, three in number: 1st, a handsome set of pipes with a silver plate, and forty merks Scots; 2nd and 3rd, thirty merks, and it was decided at the Theatre Royal, Edinburgh, before an enthusiastic audience.

The principal dance of this period was the country dance; but the valse had already been introduced, and rapidly came into favour, although it was held to be fast, and rather indecent, and was danced in a somewhat different style to what it is nowadays.

LA VALSE—1819.

WALTZER AU MOUCHOIR—1800.

CHAPTER XLIII.

PAINTING was not at its highest at this time, and yet there were many buyers, even for the pictures then painted. The Royal Academy of Art (founded in 1765, when it received its Charter, on the 26th of January, as the Incorporated Society of British Artists, a name afterwards changed in 1768) was then located at Somerset House, where life classes were held, and instruction given, as shown in the illustration on the next page.

But, as yet, there was no National Gallery of Paintings, that was reserved till a latter period, when Government bought the collection of John Julius Angerstein, Esq., in 1824. This formed the nucleus of our magnificent collection. His gallery, at his house in Pall Mall, had long held high rank among the private picture collectors, he having two Murillos, for which he paid 3,500 guineas. The Duke of Bridgewater's, the Marquis of Lansdowne's, the two, or rather three, Hopes', Lord Radstock's, the Duke of Northumberland's, the Duke of Devonshire's, and the

25

Miniatures at Strawberry Hill, were all magnificent collections; whilst Mr. Charles Townley, at his residence in
Park Lane, had the finest collection of antique statues
and busts, &c., in the world. These are now in the British
Museum.

The principal painters of this decade, although numerous,
do not represent a school likely to be perpetuated, although, as we read them, they are well known; many are
respectable, two or three are famous. First must come
Benjamin West, President of the Royal Academy, who

DRAWING FROM LIFE AT THE ROYAL ACADEMY—1808.

then lived in Newman Street: and, indeed, if we look at
the addresses of these old painters, we find them very
humble compared with the palatial habitations of some of
our modern painters. As a *Master*, West will never live,
he was a respectable painter, but even in his own time, was
not over belauded.

There was James Barry, who was once professor of
painting to the Academy, but was deposed, *en plein cour*,
because he could, or would, not confine his lectures to their
proper subjects, besides being coarse and libellous. This

made him hypochondriac, and he, besides, became poor—
a position somewhat alleviated by an annuity which was
subscribed for him. He died in 1806. His dwelling was
in Castle Street, Oxford Street.

Henry Fuseli lived in Queen Anne Street, East. His
pictures were noted for the extravagance of their conception, and their anatomy; he delighted in painting the
horrible, and supernatural, and was, perhaps, seen at his
best in his Milton Gallery, which was opened in 1798, and
closed July 19, 1800.

John Opie made a name, which still lives among collectors, but he never will rank as an Art Master. He
owed much of his celebrity to Dr. Wolcott (Peter Pindar),
who, an artist himself, tried to bring his *protégé* into
notoriety. He lived in Berner's Street, Oxford Street, and
died in 1807.

De Loutherbourg and his imitator, Sir Francis Bourgeois,
are hardly worthy of a notice. The latter, certainly, left a
collection of pictures to Dulwich Gallery, with £10,000 to
keep them in preservation; £2,000 for the repair of the
gallery, and a complimentary bequest of £1,000 to the
Masters and Fellows of Dulwich College.

The genius of the age was, undoubtedly, Joseph Mallord
William Turner, who ranks as one of our greatest land-
scape painters. Like all other artists, he had his periods
of excellence; but, when at his best, he was unapproach-
able. Thoroughly appreciated in this decade, he died not
so long ago, December 19, 1851.

From Turner to James Northcote is a long step, but
they were on the same footing as Royal Academicians.
He tried to be, as some of our modern R.A.'s do, an
universal genius; but the verdict of posterity has not
endorsed his pretensions. He lived then in Argyll Street,
and did not die until July 13, 1831.

Another Academician, Thomas Stothard, deserves
notice, and will be most remembered for his " Canterbury

Pilgrims;" but his style was mannered, and did he paint now, he, probably, would not get a living.

Sir Thomas Lawrence did not then occupy the position he afterwards filled, of President of the Royal Academy; but he had the rare honour of being made a "Supplemental Associate;" a rank conferred, because his youth would not entitle him to ask for the ordinary Associateship. He was then living modestly in Greek Street, Soho, and did not charge much for his pictures. In 1802 he only got thirty guineas for a three-quarter size, and sixty guineas for a half-length portrait. In 1806, he obtained fifty guineas for three-quarter, and whole length, two hundred guineas. 1808 saw his prices still go higher, similar sizes eighty and three hundred guineas; and in 1810, he charged one hundred guineas for a head, and four hundred guineas for a full length. Handsome prices, yet poor pay compared to what our pet artists now get.

Robert Smirke, R.A., then living in Charlotte Street, was a painter of English *genre* pictures, and was very fond of painting scenes from Don Quixote. Sir David Wilkie, however, painted *genre* subjects inimitably, and stood pre-eminent in this branch of art, at the period of which I write.

Sir William Beechey was a respectable portrait painter, and filled that office to Her Majesty Queen Charlotte, but he was not a Sir Joshua. He then lived at Great George Street, Hanover Square; but he died at Hampstead, in 1839, at a good old age of over eighty. John Hoppner, R.A., was another portrait painter of the time, as was also Sir Martin Archer Shee, President R.A., then living in Cavendish Square.

Westall, as being an Academician, deserves a passing notice, and Reinagle, too; but neither have made a name that will live. One minor painter deserves to be mentioned, Henry Bone, the enamel painter, whose collection of his own works (valued at £10,000) was offered to the nation for £4,000, refused, and sold under the hammer for £2,000. John Singleton Copley was still alive, as was also Angelica Kauffman, nor must the name of Sir George Howland Beaumont be omitted ; but he was more of an amateur than professional artist.

That erratic genius, George Morland, died in 1806, at the early age of forty-two. Fecund in producing pictures as he was, he never could have painted a tithe

CONNOISSEURS EXAMINING A COLLECTION OF GEORGE MORLAND.

part of the genuine Morlands that have been before the public, and ·the secret of these forgeries probably lies in the fact, that his pictures, painted from such familiar models, as sheep and pigs, were so easily imitated. After his death a collection of his pictures was exhibited, and Gillray gave a very graphic sketch of it. The connoisseurs were well known. The old gentleman in the foreground looking through his reversed spectacles is Captain Baillie.

Behind him, and using a spy glass, is Caleb Whiteford, a friend of Garrick. The tall stout man, nearest the wall, is said to be a Mr. Mitchell, a banker ; but although I have carefully examined the ten years' lists of bankers, I cannot find his name mentioned as a partner in any firm. And, I believe, the figure without a hat, is generally considered to be Christie the Auctioneer.

The foregoing is a tolerably correct list of the most eminent artists of the commencement of the century, many names of minor note, being of necessity, left out.

In sculptors, this decade was rich. The veteran Nollekens still worked, and continued to work, till his eighty-second year, and was then living in Mortimer Street. In Newman Street lived Thomas Banks, R.A., whose colossal statue of Achilles bewailing the loss of Briseis, is now in the hall of the British Institution. Sir Francis Chantrey, R.A., was then a young, and rising, sculptor, as yet but little known. John Flaxman, R.A., was then in his zenith, being made professor of sculpture to the Royal Academy in 1810. His successor, Sir Richard Westmacott, was made A.R.A., in 1805 ; and these names alone form an era of glyptic art unparalleled in English history.

Engravers, too, furnish a list of well-known names, among whom, for delicacy of work, Francis Bartolozzi probably stands pre-eminent, his engravings challenging competition at the present day. There were also Thomas Holloway, and William Sharp ; but, perhaps, the most popular names—none of whom will ever rank as first-class engravers—are Gillray, Rowlandson, and Isaac and George Cruikshank. Their names were on every lip, and their works the theme of every tongue. Nor must we forget John Boydell, who was Alderman and Lord Mayor of the City of London. Not only an engraver by profession, he encouraged art, by commissioning the first artists of the day to paint pictures, which he afterwards had engraved, notably his magnificent Shakespeare, than which there is no more sumptuous English edition. On this he spent no less than £350,000, and by this expenditure of capital, and bad trade, owing to the war with France, and the stoppage of commercial relations with the Continent, he fell into debt, and was obliged to get an Act of Parliament passed to enable him to get rid of the original pictures and plates, of his Shakespeare Gallery, by a lottery, which was drawn in 1804.

Besides the Shakespeare Gallery in Pall Mall, and Alderman Boydell's Gallery in Cheapside, there were several dealers' collections—the chief of which was "The European Museum," Charles Street, St. James's Square. Here pictures, some of them good, were on sale on commission, and, to prevent its being merely a lounge, a shilling was charged for admission.

Not to be forgotten are the two Water Colour Societies —"The Exhibition of Paintings in Water Colours," established in 1804, and located in 1808 in Bond Street. Reinagle was treasurer, and its members were Messrs. G. Barrett, J. J. Chalon, J. Christall, W. S. Gilpin, W. Havell, T. Heaphy, J. Holworthy, F. Nicholson, N. Pocock, W. H. Pyne, S. Rigaud, S. Shelley, J. Smith, J. Varley, C. Varley, and W. F. Wells. The associate members were Miss Byrne, and Messrs. J. A. Atkinson, W. Delamotte, P. S. Munn, A. Pugin, F. Stevens, and W. Turner.

The other society was started in 1808 or 1809, under the title of "The Associated Artists in Water Colours," and their first exhibition was held at 20, Lower Brook Street, Grosvenor Square, where a picture gallery already existed.

It is a thankless task to attempt to give a list of names of literary note, of this epoch, because, as in the case of foregoing lists, it is impossible to avoid giving some critic occasion to slay—an omitted name, being a heinous sin, outweighing all the patient hard work of research and reading, necessary for the writing of a book like this. Still an attempt thereat is bound to be made :

Austen, Jane.
Baillie, Joanna.
Barbauld, Mrs.
Beckford, Peter.
Beckford, William.
Bentham, Jeremy.
Bloomfield, Robert.
Brougham, Henry.
Byron, Lord.
Campbell, Thomas.
Canning, George.
Chapone, Mrs.
Coleridge, S. T.
Crabbe, George.
Cobbett, William.
Cumberland, Richard.
Cunningham, Allan.
D'Israeli, Isaac.
De Quincey, Thomas.
Dibdin, T. F., D.D.
Edgeworth, Miss.
Godwin, William.
Hazlitt, William.
Heber, Bishop.
Hemans, Mrs.
Hogg, James.
Hook, Theodore.
Holcroft, Thomas.
Inchbald, Mrs.

Keats, John.
Lewis, M. G. (Monk).
Lingard, John.
Lamb, Charles.
Landor, W. S.
London, John.
Lysons, Daniel.
Maturin, Charles Robert.
Montgomery, James.
Malthus, Rev. T. R.
Mill, James.
Moore, Thomas.
More, Hannah.
Morgan, Lady.
Opie, Mrs.
Porter Miss A. M.
Porter, Miss Jane.
Rogers, Samuel.
Roscoe, W.
Shelley, P. B.
Scott, Sir W.
Southey, Robert.
Smith, Sydney.
Tooke, John Horne.
Trimmer, Mrs.
Turner, Sharon.
Wilberforce, W.
Wollstonecroft, Mary.
Wordsworth, W.

This was an age of dear books, and not of literature for the million. We are apt to think that three volumes for a novel is rather too much—when it can be, and is, afterwards, published comfortably in one; but, in those days, novels ran to four or five volumes, as may be seen by only taking one advertisement. *Morning Post*, July 18, 1805 : "Family Annals; a Domestic Tale, in 5 Vols. 25s. by Mrs. Hunter of Norwich. The Demon of Sicily;

a Romance. 4 Vols., 20s. Friar Hildargo ; a Romance. 5 Vols., 25s."

Mudie's Library was not, but Hookham's, and Colburn's were in existence, and Ebers' started in 1809.

It was a great age for the collection of first editions, unique copies, and large paper books ; and, thanks to the industry, and good taste of this era, priceless treasures have been preserved to us, which might otherwise have been lost. It was a peculiarly classical age, the excavations at Pompeii, and Herculaneum, and the systematic spoliation of Etruscan tombs then going on, whetted men's appetites, and even the Prince of Wales helped to contribute towards the stock of classical lore : " The business of unrolling the Herculaneum MSS. at Portici, under the direction of M. Hayter, and at the expense of His Royal Highness the Prince of Wales, proceeds with success and rapidity. One hundred and thirty MSS. have already been opened, or are unfolding, and M. Hayter hopes to be able to decypher the six hundred, which still remains in the museum. Eleven young persons are constantly employed in un-rolling the MSS., and two more, in copying or drawing them. M. Hayter expects to find a Menander entire, an Ennius, and a Polybius," &c. I give this extract merely to show the classical taste of the time.

Attention was also being aroused to Oriental literature, and the two Ouseley's gave a great impetus to its study. Major Ouseley brought over from Bengal, in 1805, 15,000 volumes of Arabic, Persian, and Sanskrit MSS., besides a vast museum of Oriental curiosities. The Major had peculiar facilities, and opportunities, for forming his collection, as he was for some time *aide de camp* to the Nawab of Oude. His brother, Sir William, also possessed a choice library of some 800 Arabic, Persian, and Turkish MSS.

Not only here, but on the Continent, philology was looking up, for we find that the Pope, whilst in Paris, at the Coronation of Napoleon, visited the National Printing

Office, and, as he passed along the galleries, 150 presses furnished him with a sheet each, upon which was printed the Lord's Prayer in a different language or dialect.　Asia furnished 46 ; Europe, 75 ; Africa, 12 ; America, 17.

In fact, literature was beginning to be aggressive, and, actually, to ask for a club of its own ; and in 1808 the *Alfred Club* took premises in Albemarle Street, and continued its existence till 1855, when it was merged in the Oriental.　It was extremely dull, and was christened by the wicked wits, the *Half read ;* and Lord Alvanley was a member until the seventeenth Bishop saw proposed, and then he gave up.

CHAPTER XLIV.

OF the London Daily papers that were then existing, but two are now alive—the *Morning Post* (the *Doyen* of the daily press) and the *Times*. They were heavily taxed, in 1800, with a 3d. stamp per copy. In July, 1804, this was made 3½d.; pamphlets, half-sheet, ½d.; whole sheet, 1d.; an Almanac had to have a shilling stamp; and a perpetual Calendar, one of 10s. And this oppressive stamp, with a comparatively limited circulation, meant death to a newspaper. In 1809, the *Morning Post*, and other papers, boldly went in for a halfpenny rise, and gave its reasons—May 20: " Since the settlement with Government took place, which fixed the price at sixpence, every article necessary for the composition of a Newspaper, has increased in price to an unprecedented extent. Paper has risen upwards of fifty per cent.; Types upwards of eighty per cent.; Printing Ink thirty-five per cent.; Journeymen's wages ten per cent., and everything else in the same proportion. It is therefore unnecessary for us to observe, that the advance of One Halfpenny per Paper will go but a short way towards placing the Proprietors in the same situation, in respect to profits allowed, in which they were left by the settlement of 1797 ; and, under all these considerations, the Public, we trust, will not deem us unreasonable in availing ourselves of the parliamentary provision that has just been made in favour of all Newspapers.   The Bill will receive the Royal Assent this day, and on Monday, the Price of the *MORNING POST, in common with that of other Newspapers,* will be Sixpence Halfpenny."

Then, as now, the backbone of a Newspaper was its advertisements, and then also, did each Newspaper laud itself as being the best advertising medium, owing to its superior circulation.   We, who are accustomed to see huge posters setting forth sworn affidavits that the daily circulation of some London newspapers amounts to some quarter of a million if not more, will feel some surprise when we learn that the *Morning Post*, of June 10, 1800, the then leading paper, published a sworn return (and exulted over their number and success) of 10,807 newspapers printed in the week June 2–7, or a daily average of 1,800 copies.

The *World*, at one time a rival, had published its circulation when it reached 1,500 daily, and thus laid claim to be considered a good advertising medium ; and this was when newspapers were selling at 3d. each.   In 1800 they were 6d. each, and the extra tax had diminished the circulation of the *Morning Post* during the previous summer by one-third, which fall they claim to have recovered, and to have raised their circulation in five years from 400 to 1,800 daily.   In June, 1796, the *Times* published its number ; and again in 1798, when it confessed to a fall of 1,400 in its daily sale.

In 1806 there was a very pretty little war as to the circulation of rival newspapers.

The *Times* opened the ball on the 15th of November by inserting a paragraph, "Under the Clock" : " ☞ *We are under the necessity of requesting our Correspondents and*

Advertisers not to be late in their communications, if intended for the next day's publication; as the extraordinary Sale of THE TIMES, *which is decidedly superior to that of every other Morning Paper, compels us to go to press at a very early hour."*

The *Morning Post*, November 17th (which number is unfortunately missing in the British Museum file), challenged the statement—to which the *Times* replied on the 18th : "*This declaration of our Sale, a Morning Paper of yesterday has thought proper to contradict, and boldly claims the superiority. We have only to say on the subject, that, if the Paper will give an attested account of its daily Sale for the last two Months, we will willingly publish it."*

And now the strife was waxing hot, for the *Morning Post* on the 21st of November wrote : "We admit the sale of his Paper may, *for the present*, be many hundreds beyond any other, except the MORNING POST, the decided superiority of which, we trust, he will no longer affect to dispute. . . . We pledge ourselves to PROVE that the regular sale of the MORNING POST is little short of a thousand per day superior to that of his paper."

Of course the *Times*, of the 22nd of November, calls this a preposterous boast, and wishes statistics for the last two months.

Thus goaded, the *Morning Post*, of the 24th of November, issued affidavits from its printers and publisher, that its circulation, even at that dead season, was upwards of 4,000 daily, and that during the sitting of Parliament it reached, and exceeded 5,000, the editor remarking : "What is meant by regular Sale, is the Number which is daily served to SUBSCRIBERS. . . . If those who, by the Low Expedient of selling their Papers by the noisy nuisance of Horn Boys, take into their accounts the extra Papers so sold, it is not for us to follow so unworthy an example ; to such means the MORNING POST never has recourse."

The *Times*, November 25th, has the last of this wordy warfare, declaring that its circulation sometimes reached 7,000 or 8,000 a day: and I should not have introduced this episode, had it not have given such a perfect insight into the working of the press of that date, which would have been unobtainable but for this quarrel.

The British Museum then stood where now it does, only Montague House, in which its treasures were then enshrined, was totally unfitted for their reception—for instance, a collection of Egyptian antiquities were kept in two sheds in the courtyard. The whole of the antiquities, and rarities, were in sad want of arrangement, and classification, and as many impediments, as possible, were placed in the way of visitors.

Take what it was like in 1802 : " Persons who are desirous of seeing the Museum, must enter their name and address, and the time at which they wish to see it, in a book kept by the porter, and, upon calling again on a future day, they will be supplied with printed tickets, free of expense, as all fees are positively prohibited. The tickets only serve for the particular day and hour specified ; and, if not called for the day before, are forfeited.

" The Museum is kept open every day in the week, except Saturday, and the weeks which follow Christmas day, Easter, and Whitsunday. The hours are from nine till three, except on Monday and Friday, during the months of May, June, July, and August, when the hours are only from four till eight in the afternoon.

" The spectators are allowed three hours for viewing the whole—that is, an hour for each of the three departments. One hour for the Manuscripts and Medals ; one for the natural and artificial productions, and one for the printed books. Catalogues are deposited in each room, but no book must be taken down except by the officer attending, who will also restore it to its place. Children are not admitted.

" Literary characters, or any person who wishes to make

use of the Museum for purposes of study and reference, may obtain permission, by applying to the trustees, or the standing committee. A room is appointed for their accommodation, in which, during the regular hours, they may have the use of any manuscript or printed book, subject to certain regulations."

On the 8th of June, 1804, the Trustees somewhat modified the arrangements, and instead of visitors having to call twice about their tickets, before their visit, they might be admitted the day of application (Monday, Wednesday, or Friday only) subject to the following rule :

"Five Companies, of not more than 15 persons each, may be admitted in the course of the day ; namely, one at each of the hours of 10, 11, 12, 1, and 2. At each of these hours the directing officer in waiting shall examine the entries in the book ; and if none of the persons inscribed be exceptionable, he shall consign them to the attendant, whose turn it will be to conduct the companies through the House.

" Should more than fifteen persons inscribe their names, for a given hour, the supernumeraries will be desired to wait, or return at the next hour, when they will be admitted preferably to other applicants."

The Museum Gardens were a great attraction, and were much visited. So much, indeed, were they thought of, that, in an advertisement of a house to let, it is stated, as a great recommendation that it commands "a view of the Museum Gardens, and a part of Hampstead Heath."

There were other museums, notably the Leverian Museum, the collection of Sir Ashton Lever, of Alkington, near Manchester, a *virtuoso* of the first water. He spent very large sums on this collection, which consisted mainly of specimens of natural history (over 5,000 stuffed birds), fossils, shells, corals, a few antiquities, and the usual country museums' quota of South Sea Island weapons, and dresses. There was much rubbish, as we should term it—

according to the *Gentleman's Magazine* of May, 1773 (p. 200), like a double-headed calf, a pig with eight legs, two tails, one backbone, and one head. Some pictures of birds in straw very natural, a basket of paper flowers, a head of his present Majesty, cut in Cannel Coal ; a drawing of Indian ink of a head of a late Duke of Bridgwater, &c., &c.

The collection had, of course, much increased, when in 1785, Sir Ashton Lever, shortly before his death, disposed of it by lottery. The winner, Mr. Parkinson, built " a very elegant and well-disposed structure for its reception, about a hundred yards from the foot of Blackfriars Bridge, on the Surrey side." [1] The admission was one shilling. Presumably it did not pay, for it was sold by auction in 1806. The sale lasted sixty-five days. The number of lots being 7,879, and the catalogue occupying 410 octavo pages. Then there were the museums of the two Hunters— that of Dr. William Hunter, F.S.A., &c. In the period of which I treat, his anatomical specimens, coins, &c., were exhibited at the Theatre of Anatomy, in Great Windmill Street, whence, according to his will, they were after a certain time transferred to the University of Glasgow, where they now are. His brother John, who was also a F.R.S., had a grand collection of anatomical preparations, which was purchased by the Government for £15,000, and deposited, *pro bono publico*, in the College of Surgeons.

[1] Afterwards known as " The Rotunda."

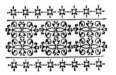

CHAPTER XLV.

Medical—The Doctor of the old School—The rising lights—Dr. Jenner—His
discovery of vaccination for smallpox—Opposition thereto—Perkins's Metallic
Tractors—The "Perkinean Institution"—His cures—Electricity and Galvanism
—Galvanizing a dead criminal—Lunatic Asylums—Treatment of the insane—
The Hospitals.

APROPOS of Doctors—the medical and surgical
branches of the profession were emerging from
empiricism, and science was beginning to assert
herself, and laying the foundation of the English School of
Medicine, the finest the world has yet seen. The doctor of
the old school (as given in the next page) was still extant,
with his look of portentous sagacity, his Burghley-like shake
of the head, his bag with instruments and medicaments,
and the cane—always the gold-headed cane—which came
in so useful, and gave such a look of sapience when applied
to the side of the nose, affording time for consideration
before giving an opinion on a doubtful case—a relic of
the time when, in its gold top, was carried a febrifuge, such
as aromatic vinegar, or the such like. Similar types are
also given in a political caricature by Isaac Cruikshank.

But these old quacks were disappearing, and the pro-
genitors of the present hardworking, energetic, and scientific men, our medical advisers, were arising, and I append
a list, imperfect as it may be, which contains names
of world-wide reputation, and thoroughly well known to

26

every fairly educated Englishman. They are taken in
no sequence, chronological or otherwise. Sir Anthony
Carlisle, F.R.S., President of the Royal College of Surgeons ; Sir Charles Mansfield Clarke, so famous for his
treatment of the Diseases of Women and Children ;
Sir Astley Paston Cooper ; Sir Henry Halford ; that
rough old bear John Abernethy ; Dr. Matthews Baillie

A DOCTOR OF THE OLD SCHOOL—1803.

the brother of Joanna Baillie ; Sir Benjamin Collins
Brodie—then a young man ; Dr. Edward Jenner, of
whom more anon ; Wm. Lawrence, F.R.S., Surgeon
Extraordinary to the Queen ; Sir Charles Bell, another
famous Surgeon, whose " System of Anatomy," is still
a text book ; Geo. James Guthrie, and many others ;
but a sufficient number of well-known names have been

given to warrant the assertion that it was an exceptionally brilliant time of English medicine and surgery.

Perhaps the medical man of this era, to whom the whole world is most indebted, is Dr. Jenner, who thoroughly investigated the wonderfully prophylactic powers of the cow pock. He had noticed that milkers of cows could not, as a rule, be inoculated with the small-pox virus—a means of prevention then believed in, as the patient generally suffered but slightly from the inoculation, and it was then a creed, long since exploded, that small-pox could not be taken twice. This fact of their resistance to variolous inoculation set him thinking, and he came to the conclusion that they had absorbed into their systems, a counter poison in the shape of some infection taken from the cows. He made many experiments, and found that this came from a disease called the cow pock, and that the vaccine lymph could not only be taken direct from the cow, but also by transmission from the patients who had been inoculated with that lymph, and whence the present system of so-called vaccination—the greatest blessing of modern times.

Jenner, of course, was opposed ; fools do not even believe in vaccination now, and great was the battle for, and against, in the medical profession, and many were the books written *pro* and *con.* " Vaccination Vindicated," Ed. Jones ; " A Reply to the Anti-Vaccinists," Jas. Moore ; "The Vaccine Contest," Wm. Blair ; "Cow Pock Vaccination," Rowland Hill ; " Birch against Vaccination," " Willan on Vaccination," &c., &c.

Gillray could not, of course, leave such a promising subject alone, and he perpetrated the accompanying illustration. Here Dr. Jenner (a very good likeness) is attending to his patients—vaccinating, rather too vigorously, one lady—the lymph, in unlimited quantity, being borne by a workhouse boy, and receiving his patients who are exhibiting the different phases of their vaccination. As a rule, they seem to have " taken " too well.

THE COW POCK; OR, THE WONDERFUL EFFECTS OF THE NEW INOCULATION!

(*Vide the publications of yᵉ Anti-Vaccine Society.*)

A quack, who flourished early in the century, far better
deserved the caricaturists' pencil than Jenner, and he
got it. The illustration on this page represents an
American quack, named Perkins, who pretended to
cure various diseases by means of his metallic tractors
—operating on John Bull. The paper on the table
is the *True Briton*, and it reads thus: "Theatre—dead
alive—Grand Exhibition in Leicester Square. Just arrived
from America the Rod of Æsculapius. Perkinism in all

METALLIC TRACTORS—1802.

its glory, being a certain cure for all Disorders, Red Noses,
Gouty Toes, Windy Bowels, Broken Legs, Hump backs.
Just discovered, Grand secret of the Philosopher's Stone,
with the true way of turning all metals into Gold."

The truth is, that, at the end of the eighteenth century,
Galvani and Volta, Sir Joseph Banks, in connection with
the Royal Society, and all the scientific men of the day,
were deeply interested in solving the mysteries of electricity; and, as nobody, as yet, knew much about it, the
public were liable to be gulled by any empiric, and Benja-

min Douglas Perkins was the very man to do it. He,
and others, wrote several pamphlets on " The Influence of
Metallic Tractors on the Human Body, in removing various
Inflammatory Diseases," and such like, and opened a *Perkinean Institution* in London.   He must have been fairly
successful, for his advertisements lasted some years.   His
published cures were miraculous : " A Lady was afflicted
with an Erysipelas in her face. . . . In a few minutes she
cheerfully acknowledged that she was quite well."   " A
man aged 37 had, for several years, been subject to the
Gout.   I found him in bed, and very much distressed with
the disease in one of his feet.   After I had operated upon
it with the Tractors he said the pain was entirely gone."
" A Lady burned her hand.   I, happily, called at the house
immediately after the accident, and applied the Tractors.
In about ten minutes, the inflammation disappeared, the
vesication was prevented, and she said the pain was gone."
The price of these " blessings to men " was five guineas a
set ; and he explains them in the specification of the
patent granted him on the 10th March, 1798, where, speaking of Galvanism, he says, " Among the metals that may
be thus characterised, I have found none more eminently
efficacious in removing diseases than the combinations of
copper, zinc, and a small proportion of gold : a precise
quantity of each is not necessary : also iron united to a
very small proportion of silver and platina ; an exact proportion of these also not necessary.   These are constructed
with points, and of such dimensions as convenience shall
dictate.   They may be formed with one point, or pointed
at each end, or with two or more points.   The point of the
instrument thus formed I apply to those parts of the body
which are affected with diseases, and draw them off on the
skin, to a distance from the complaint, and usually towards
the extremities."

Electricity was then a new toy, of which no one, as yet,
knew the use, and they amused themselves with it in

various ways, one of which must serve as an example. *Times*, January 22, 1803 : "The body of *Forster*, who was executed on Monday last for murder, was conveyed to a house not far distant, where it was subjected to the *Galvanic process* by Professor ALDINI, under the inspection of Mr. KEATE, Mr. CARPUE, and several other professional gentlemen. M. ALDINI, who is the nephew of the discoverer of this most interesting science, showed the eminent and superior powers of *Galvanism* to be far beyond any other stimulant in nature. On the first application of the process to the face, the jaw of the deceased criminal began to quiver, and the adjoining muscles were horribly contorted, and one eye was actually opened. In the subsequent part of the process, the right hand was raised and clenched, and the legs and thighs set in motion. It appeared to the uninformed part of the bystanders as if the wretched man was on the eve of being restored to life. This, however, was impossible, as several of his friends who were under the scaffold had violently pulled his legs, in order to put a more speedy termination to his sufferings. The experiment, in fact, was of a better use, and tendency. Its object was to show the excitability of the human frame, when this animal electricity is duly applied. In cases of drowning or suffocation, it promises to be of the utmost use, by reviving the action of the lungs, and, thereby, rekindling the expiring spark of vitality. In cases of apoplexy, or disorders of the head, it offers, also, most encouraging prospects for the benefit of mankind. The professor, we understand, has made use of *Galvanism*, also, in several cases of insanity, and with complete success."

This latter part—the cure of the insane by means of electricity—has not been verified by practice. Their treatment was very inefficient, although, even then, whips and chains were disappearing—especially in the public madhouses, which were at that time Bethlehem, and St. Luke's Hospitals. Bethlehem Hospital was then situated in

Moorfields, and the major part of it had been built in 1675. Over the entrance gates were two sculptured representations of Raving and Melancholy madness, by Cibber; these are now in the hall of the present hospital. Patients remained until they were cured, or for twelve months if not cured. In the latter case if it was thought that a further sojourn might be of use, they were re-admitted, and they also were permanently kept, were they hopelessly incurable, and dangerous to society. There were then about 260

WOMEN'S WARD, ST. LUKE'S—1808.

patients who might be visited by their friends every Monday and Wednesday, from 10 to 12 a.m. Visitors were only admitted by an order from a governor—a vast improvement on the old plan, when a visitor could always obtain admission by payment of a small fee. In fact, in Queen Anne's reign, and later, it formed, with the lions at the Tower, and the wax figures at Westminster Abbey, one of the chief sights in London, thus causing a scandal to the institution, and, without doubt, injuring the patients.

St. Luke's Hospital for the insane was in Old Street,

City Road, and was built because Bethlehem was inadequate to the relief of *all indigent lunatics ;* and their treatment was fairly rational, even those who were obliged to wear straight jackets having their meals together, so as to afford some little break in the monotony of their miserable lives. Each patient had a separate sleeping apartment, and there were two large gardens, one for men, the other for women, where pleasant recreation could be taken in fine weather.

The other medical hospitals were—Bartholomew's, St. Thomas's, Guy's, St. George's, the London, Middlesex, the Westminster Infirmary, and the Lock Hospital, in Grosvenor Place. The majority of these had regular medical schools, as now, but there were, also, many private lecturers and demonstrators of anatomy, as also professors of natural and experimental philosophy, and chemistry.

CHAPTER XLVI.

THE Royal Institution had just been founded (incorporated 13th January, 1800), and the Gresham lectures were held. The Royal Institution was patronized by its big elder brother, the Royal Society, for in the minutes of the proceedings of the latter, on the 15th of April, 1802, is the following :

"Resolved, that . . . the Royal Society be requested to direct their Secretaries to communicate from time to time to the Editor of the Journals of the Royal Institution, such information respecting the Papers read at the Meetings of the Society, as it may be thought proper to allow to be published in these Journals."

In the first ten years of this century, no great scientific discoveries were made ; the most prominent being the researches of that marvellous scientist and Egyptologist, Dr. Thomas Young,[1] in connection with physical optics, which led to his theory of undulatory light.[2] Yet there were good men coming forward, the pioneers of this present

---

[1] He was elected a Fellow of the Royal Society—the "guinea stamp" of a scientific man, *at the age of* 21.

[2] See "A Course of Lectures on Natural Philosophy and the Mechanic Arts" by Dr. Thomas Young. 2 vols. 1807.

age, to whose labours we are much indebted ; and any decade might be proud of such names as Faraday, Banks, Rennie, Dr. Wollaston, Count Rumford, Humphrey Davy, and Henry Cavendish, whose discovery of the gaseous composition of water laid the foundation of the modern school of chemistry.

The Society of Arts, too, was doing good work, and the Society of Antiquaries, and the Linnæan Society, were also in existence; but the Horticultural, and Geological Societies, alone, were born during this ten years.

Ballooning was in the same position as now, *i.e.*, bags of gas could, as is only natural, rise in the air, and be carried whither the wind listed ; and, especially in the year 1802, ærostatics formed one of the chief topics of conversation, as Garnerin and Barrett were causing excitement by their ærial flights.

Man had enslaved steam, but had hardly begun to utilize it, and knew but very little of the capabilities of its energetic servant. Then it was but a poor hard-working drudge, who could but turn a wheel, or pump water. Certainly a steamboat had been tried on the Thames, and Fulton's steamboat *Clermont* was tried on the Seine in 1803, at New York in 1806, and ran on the Hudson in 1807 ; but the locomotive was being hatched. The use of iron rails to ease the draft was well known, and several patents were granted for different patterns of rail, but they were mainly used in mines, to save horse power. Under the date of 24th March, 1802, is a " Specification of the Patents granted to Richard Trevithick and Andrew Vivian, of the Parish of Camborne, in the County of Cornwall. Engineers and Miners, for Methods for improving the construction of Steam Engines, and the Application thereof for driving Carriages, and for other purposes." Here, then, we have the germ of the locomotive, which has been one of the most powerful agents of civilization the world ever saw. But it was not till 1811 that the locomotive was used, and then only on a railway connected with a colliery.

It was not a mechanical age, or rather, applied mechanics was as a young child, and babbled sillily. The only thing I regret, in writing this book, is the time I have wasted in looking over Patent Specifications, to find something worthy to illustrate the mechanical genius of the time. The most useful invention I have found, is the paper-making machine. This was originally the conception of a Frenchman, Louis Robert, who sold his invention to Didot, the great printer, who, bringing it to England, got Fourdrinier to join with him in perfecting it. It did not, Minerva-like, spring ready armed from its parent's brain; but was the subject of several patents; but the one which approaches nearest to, and is identical in all essential points with, the present paper-making machine, is his "Specification, enrolled pursuant to Act of Parliament of the 47th of George the Third, of the Invention of Henry Fourdrinier and Sealy Fourdrinier, of Sherborne Lane, London, and John Gamble, of Saint Neots, in the County of Huntingdon, Paper Manufacturers; for making Paper by means of Machines, for which several Letters Patent have been obtained at different periods. Term extended to 15 years from 14th August, 1807." This extension had been obtained by means of an Act of Parliament passed the previous session, and the machine was capable of making the endless web of paper now in vogue.

The primitive state of our manufactures at this date may be, perhaps, best understood by a typical illustration or two, taken by Pyne, a most conscientious draughtsman, who drew all his studies from nature. The first, on the next page, is an Iron Foundry, casting shot.

Coals were very dear, and that was owing to two things. First, that only the Sunderland district coals were used in London, because they only could, in any quantity, be shipped to London; the vast Staffordshire, and other

inland basins, being out of the question, owing to lack of
carriage, except where a canal was handy; and the other
reason for their high price was that there being no steam
vessels, a contrary wind would keep the coal-ships out of
port, and, consequently, denude the market.

The inland coals were cheap enough in their own
localities—*vide* the *Morning Post*, August 6, 1800: "At
Oldham, in Lancashire, the best coals are only 6s. 9d.
equal to a London chaldron.[1]   At Barnsley, in Yorkshire,
the best coals are sold at the pit's mouth for only 1½d.

AN IRON FOUNDRY—1802.

per cwt.   Surely, permission ought to be granted for coals
to be brought to London, if they can be conveyed by
water.   This might be done, as the canals from Lancashire
are now cut so as a barge with twenty-five tons of coals
would arrive in London in fourteen days.   They cost at
the pit only 8s. 4d. per ton."

But not only were they unattainable, but many of the
coal-fields from which we now draw our supplies were
absolutely unknown.   Here is an instance—*Morning Post*,

[1] Thirty-six bushels, similar to the sealed measure kept at the Guildhall,
heaped up; average weight, 28½ cwt.   The Newcastle chaldron weighed
53 cwt.

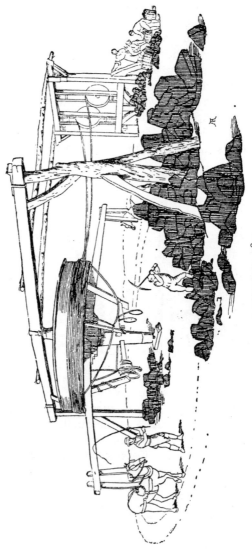

A COLLIERY—1302.

July 25, 1805 : " A very fine *stratum* of coal, 15 feet deep, has been lately discovered on the Earl of Moira's estate at Donnington, and by which the Leicestershire Canal Shares have been doubled in their value."

In looking at the following list of prices of coals, it must be borne in mind that these are the market prices for coals *ex ship;* and it was reckoned that 12s. per ton was a fair price to allow for metage, carriage, and profit. Add this, and remember that a sovereign at the commencement of the century had the purchasing power of, and, consequently, worth about 30s.; it will then be seen that coals were excessively dear—such as would now practically extinguish every manufacture.

Even in 1800, when coals were only about 48s. or 48s. 6d., the price was considered so excessive, that a Committee of the House of Commons sat upon the subject, and issued a report, imputing it to the following causes :

" 1. The agreement among the Coal Owners in the North, called ' The Limitation of Vends,' by which each colliery on the Tyne is limited, so as not to exceed a certain quantity in each year. Those Coal Owners who are found to have shipped more than their stipulated quantities, being bound to make a certain allowance at the end of each year, to those who have shipped less, and to conform to certain other regulations adopted by the Coal Owners on the river Wear.

" 2. The detention of the ships at Newcastle, waiting for the best coals, sometimes a month or six weeks.

" 3. The want of a market in London which would admit of a competition, perfectly free, in the purchase of coals.

" 4. The circumstance of the coal-buyer being, in many instances, owners both of ship and cargo ; which (as appears by the evidence) leads to considerable abuse.

" 5. The want of a sufficient number of Meters, and of

craft, for unloading the ships on their arrival in the river, and the occasional delays in procuring ballast on their return voyage.

"6. The practice of mixing the best coals with those of an inferior quality, and selling the whole so mixed as of the best kind ; and

"7. To frauds in the measurement, carriage, and delivery of coals."

That there were great profits made by coals, there can be no doubt. Mr. Walter, the proprietor of the *Times*, had been a coal-factor, and had failed in business, before he started his newspaper—in which, in its early days, he keenly scanned the state of the Coal Market for the benefit of the public.

Here is a paragraph advertisement from the *Morning Herald*, June 2, 1802, which shows that our grandfathers could advertise in as catching a style as the present generation : " On Saturday, the following conversation occurred between two sailors opposite Somerset House : 'Ah ! Sam, how are you ?' 'Why, Jack, when I saw you, a few days ago, I *was near a Gentleman ;* but now, through my folly, am a *complete beggar !* ' 'Cheer up, Sam, for you are *near* a Gentleman now. I have just received all my prize money and wages ; we have been partners in many a hard battle; we will be partners now. I am going to the London Sea Coal Company, in Southampton Street, Holborn, to buy a score of coals; and, by retailing of which, I'll prove to you, there's a devilish deal more satisfaction and pleasure than in throwing the gold dust away on bad women or public-houses." This company were in September, 1804, selling their coals at 58s. per chaldron.

October 8, 1804 : " Pool [1] price of coals : Wallsend, 54s. 6d.; Hebburn and Percy, 52s. 6d.; Wellington, 52s. 3d.;

[1] That part of the Thames from the east side of London Bridge is called "The Pool."

Temples, 51s. 8d.; Eighton, 48s. 3d. Eight ships at market, and all sold. The addition of 12s. to the above will give the price at which the coals should be delivered in town."

That was in face of approaching winter. In summer time the price was naturally lower—July 1, 1805: "Coals. Monday, 24 June, 20 cargoes sold from 39s. 3d. to 49s. 6d. per chaldron. Wednesday, 26 do.; 10 ditto 42s. 9d. to 49s. Friday, 28: 15 ditto 43s. 9d. to 49s. 6d. in the Pool."

In February, 1808, the retail price of coals was 64s.; and this did not include metage and shooting. In October, 1809, they rose to 74s., and in November of the same year they reached 84s

CHAPTER XLVII.

The Navy—Sailor's carelessness—"The Sailor's Journal"—The sailor and "a dilly"—Dress of the sailors—Rough life both for officers and men –Number of ships in Commission—Pressing—A man killed by a press-gang—Mutinies— That of the *Danäe*—Mutiny on board the *Hermione*, and cold-blooded slaughter of the officers—Mutiny in Bantry Bay—Pay of the officers—French prisoners of war.

IT was the fashion then, as it is now, to portray a sailor, as a harum-scarum, jovial, rollicking, care-for-nought ; and doubtless, in the main, he was, at that time, as unlike as possible to the blue-riband, savings-bank Jack that he very frequently is now. Prize money was pretty plentiful; such things as a temperance captain and ship, were unknown ; and the constant active service in which they were engaged, with its concomitant insecurity to life and limb, must have made them somewhat reckless, and inclined to enjoy life, after their fashion, whilst they still possessed that life. Rowlandson—May 30, 1802— drew two of them in a caricature, called "The Sailor's Journal." They are dividing a bowl of punch, one is smoking, the other gives his mate some extracts from his Journal : " Entered the port of London. Steered to Nan's lodgings, and unshipped my Cargo ; Nan admired the shiners—so did the landlord—gave 'em a handful a-piece ; emptied a bottle of the right sort with the landlord to the

health of his honour Lord Nelson. All three set sail for
the play ; got a berth in a cabin on the larboard side—
wanted to smoke a pipe, but the boatswain wouldn't let
me ; remember to rig out Nan like the fine folks in the
cabin right ahead. Saw Tom Junk aloft in the corner of
the upper deck—hailed him ; the signal returned. Some
of the land-lubbers in the cockpit began to laugh—tipped
them a little foremast lingo till they sheered off. Emptied
the grog bottle ; fell fast asleep—dreamt of the battle of
Camperdown. My landlord told me the play was over—
glad of it. Crowded sail for a hackney coach. Squally
weather—rather inclined to be sea-sick. Gave the pilot a
two pound-note, and told him not to mind the change. In
the morning, looked over my Rhino—a great deal of it, to
be sure; but I hope, with the help of a few friends, to spend
every shilling in a little time, to the honour and glory of
old England."

This was the ideal, and typical, sailor ; the reality was
sometimes as foolish. *Morning Herald*, June 12, 1805 :
" One day last week a sailor belonging to a man-of-war at
Plymouth had leave to go on shore ; but, having staid
much longer than the allowed time, he received a sharp
reprimand on his return. Jack's reply was that he was
very sorry, but that he had taken a *dilly* (a kind of chaise
used about Plymouth) for the purpose of making the
utmost haste, but the coachman could not give him change
for half a guinea, and he, therefore, was obliged to keep
him driving *fore* and *aft* between Plymouth and the Dock,
till he had *drove* the half-guinea out ! Unfortunately for
poor Jack, it so happened, that when the half-guinea
was *drove out*, he was set down at the spot whence he
started, and had just as far to walk, as though he had not
been drove at all."

When in full uniform, a sailor in the Royal Navy was
a sight to see—with his pigtail properly clubbed and
tied with black silk. We have already seen them in the

picture of Nelson's funeral car, and the accompanying illustration is of the same epoch, and shows a British sailor weeping over Lord Nelson's death.

It was a rough school, both for officers and men. We may judge somewhat of what the life of the former was like by Captain Marryat's novels; but, lest they should be highly coloured, let us take a few lines from the first page of the "Memoir of Admiral Sir Edward Codrington":[1]

BRITISH SAILOR—1805.

"He spent nine years at sea as a midshipman; and I have repeatedly heard him say, that during those nine years (so important for the formation of character) he never was invited to open a book, nor received a word of advice or instruction, except professional, from any one. More than that, he was thrown among a set in the gun-room mess, older than himself, whose amusement it was—a too customary amusement in those days—to teach the lad to drink, and to lead him into their own habitual practice in that respect."

If this was the case with the officers, how did the men fare? Volunteer recruits did not come from the pick of the labouring class, and the pressed men soon fell into the ways of those surrounding them. No doubt they were better off in the Royal Navy than in the Mercantile Marine; but the ship's stores of that day consisted but of salt pork, and beef, the latter being indifferently called *junk* or *old horse*. The biscuits, too, were nothing like those now supplied on board Her Majesty's ships. Wheat was

---

[1] Edited by his daughter, Lady Bourchier. London, 1873.

very dear, and these sailors did not get the best of that. Inferior corn, bad package, and old age soon generated weevils, and the biscuit, when these were knocked out, was often but an empty shell. Bullied by their officers, and brutally flogged and punished for trifling faults, Jack's life could not have been a pleasant one; and we can hardly wonder that he often deserted, and sometimes mutinied. Yet, whenever a fight was imminent, or did actually occur, all bad treatment was banished from his mind, and he fought like a Briton.

And there were many ships to man. Not only were all our dockyards hard at work building and repairing, but prizes were continually coming in ; and the French men-of-war were better designed than ours—in fact, it may be said that we learned, at that time, our Naval Architecture from the prizes we took. In October, 1804, there were in commission 103 ships of the line, 24 fifty-gun vessels, 135 frigates, and 398 sloops—total 660. In March, 1806, there were 721 ships in commission, of which 128 were of the line. On January 1, 1808, there were 795 in commission, 144 being ships of the line. Many of these were taken from the French, as the following exultant paragraph from the *Annual Register*, August 19, 1808, will show :

" It must be proudly gratifying to the minds of Britons, as it must be degradingly mortifying to the spirit of Bonaparte, to know that we have, at this moment, in the British Navy, 68 sail of the line, prizes taken from the enemies of this country at different periods, besides 21 ships carrying from 40 to 50 guns each, 62 ships from 30 to 40 guns each, 15 carrying from 20 to 30 guns each, and 66 from 10 to 20 guns each ; making a total of 232 ships."

To man these ships, &c., some 100,000 men were needful, and as they would not come of their own will, they must be taken *vi et armis*. Impressing men for the King's Naval Service had always been in use since the fourteenth century, so that it was no novelty ; but it must have been hard indeed for a sailor coming from a long voyage (and they had long voyages in those days—no rushing three times round the world in a twelvemonth, and time to spare), full of hope to find his wife and children well, to be bodily seized, without even so much as landing, and sent on board a King's ship, to serve for an indefinite period. A few extracts from the newspapers will show what a press was like.

Morning Post, January 21, 1801 : " The press for seamen on the river and on shore is warmer than was ever known in any former war."

Times, March 11, 1803 : " The impress service, particularly in the Metropolis, has proved uncommonly productive in the number of excellent seamen. The returns at the Admiralty of the seamen impressed on Tuesday night amounted to 1,080, of whom no less than two-thirds are considered prime hands. At Portsmouth, Portsea, Gosport, and Cowes, a general press took place the same night. Every merchant ship in the harbours and at Spithead, was stripped of its hands, and all the watermen deemed fit for His Majesty's service were carried off. Upwards of six hundred seamen were collected in consequence of the promptitude of the measures adopted. . . . Government, we understand, relies upon increasing our naval force with ten thousand seamen, either volunteers, or impressed men, in less than a fortnight, in consequence of the exertions which are making in all the principal ports. Those collected on the river, and in London, will be instantly conveyed to Chatham, Sheerness, and Portsmouth. Several frigates and gun brigs have sailed for the islands of Jersey and Guernsey with impress warrants."

Times, May 9, 1803 : " On Sunday afternoon two gallies, each having an officer and press-gang in it, in endeavouring to impress some persons at Hungerford Stairs, were resisted by a party of coal-heavers belonging to a wharf adjoining, who assailed them with coals and glass-bottles ;

several of the gang were cut in a most shocking manner, on their heads and legs, and a woman who happened to be in a wherry, was wounded in so dreadful a manner, that it is feared she will not survive. . . . The impress on Saturday, both above and below Bridge, was the hottest that has been for some time ; the boats belonging to the ships at Deptford were particularly active, and it is supposed they obtained upwards of two hundred men, who were regulated (*sic*) on board the *Enterprize* till late at night, and sent in the different tenders to the Nore, to be put on board such ships whose crews are not completed. . . . The impressed men, for whom there was not room on board the *Enterprize*, on Saturday were put into the Tower, and the gates shut, to prevent any of them effecting their escape."

Morning Herald, December 11, 1804 : "A very smart press took place yesterday morning upon the river, and the west part of the town. A great many useful hands were picked up."

Morning Post, May 8, 1805 : "The embargo to which we alluded in our Paper of Monday has taken place. At two o'clock yesterday afternoon, orders for that purpose were issued at the Custom House, and upwards of a thousand able seamen are said to have been already procured for the Navy, from on board the ships in the river."

Morning Post, April 11, 1808 : "On Saturday the hottest press ever known took place on the Thames, when an unprecedented number of able seamen were procured for His Majesty's service. A flotilla of small smacks was surrounded by one of the gangs, and the whole of the hands, amounting to upwards of a hundred, were carried off."

These raids on seamen were not always conducted on "rose-water" principles, and the slightest resistance met with a cracked crown, or worse. Witness a case tried at the Kingston Assizes, March 22, 1800, where John Salmon, a midshipman in His Majesty's navy, was indicted for the wilful murder of William Jones. The facts of the case were as follow. The prisoner was an officer on board His Majesty's ship *Dromedary*, lying in the Thames off Deptford. He and his lieutenant, William Wright (who was charged with being present, and assisting), went on shore on the night of the 19th of February, with nine of the crew, on the impress service ; Wright had a pistol, Salmon a dirk, one of the sailors a hanger, and the rest were unarmed. After waiting some time in search of prey, the deceased, and one Brown, accompanied by two women, passed by ; they were instantly seized upon, and carried to a public-house, from whence they endeavoured to effect their escape ; a scuffle ensued, in the course of which the deceased called out he had been pricked. At this time three men had hold of him—a sufficient proof that he was overpowered—and whoever wounded him, most probably did so with *malice prepense*. The poor fellow was taken, in this state, to a boat, and thence on board a ship, where, for a considerable time, he received no medical assistance. The women, who were with him, accompanied him to the boat, and he told them that the midshipman had wounded him, and that he was bleeding to death ; that every time he fetched his breath, he felt the air rushing in at the wound. He was afterwards taken to the hospital, and there, in the face of death, declared he had been murdered by the midshipman. The case was thoroughly proved as to the facts, but the prisoner was acquitted of the capital charge of murder, and I do not know whether he was ever prosecuted for manslaughter.

Men thus obtained, could scarcely be expected to be contented with their lot, and, therefore, we are not surprised to hear of more than one mutiny—the marvel is there were so few. Of course, they are not pleasant episodes in history, but they have to be written about.

The first in this decade (for the famous mutiny at the Nore occurred in the previous century), was that on board the *Danäe*, 20 guns, Captain Lord Proby. It is difficult to accurately ascertain the date, for it is variously given in different accounts, as March 16th, 17th, and 27th, 1800; but, at all events, in that month the *Danäe* was cruising off the coast of France, with some thirty of her crew, and officers, absent in prizes, and having on board some French-men who had been captured on board the privateer *Borde-lais*, and had subsequently entered the English service. On board was one Jackson (who had been secretary to Parker, the ringleader of the Nore Mutiny in 1798), who had been tried for participation in that mutiny and ac-quitted, since when, he had borne a good character, refusing the rank of petty officer which had been offered to him, giving as a reason, that being an impressed man, he held himself at liberty to make his escape whenever he had a chance, whereas, if he took rank, he should consider himself a volunteer.

With him as a ringleader, and a crew probably contain-ing some fellow sufferers, and the Frenchmen, who would certainly join, on board, things were ripe for what followed. The ship was suddenly seized, and the officers overpowered, Lord Proby and the master being seriously wounded. The mutineers then set all sail, and steered for Brest Harbour, and on reaching Camaret Bay, they were boarded by a lieutenant of *La Colombe*, who asked Lord Proby to whom he surrendered. He replied, to the French nation, but not to the mutineers. *La Colombe* and the *Danäe* then sailed for Brest, being chased by the *Anson* and *Boadicæa*, and would, in all probability, have been captured, had not false signals been made by the *Danäe* that she was in chase. Lord Proby had previously thrown the private code of signals out of his cabin window. They were all confined in Dinan prison.

The *Hermione*, also, was carried over to the enemy by a mutinous crew; but in October, 1800, was cut out of Porto Cavello, after a gallant resistance, by the boat's crew of the

Surprise, Captain Hamilton, and brought in triumph to Port Royal, Jamaica. On this occasion justice overtook two of the mutineers, who were hanged on the 14th of August—one in Portsmouth Harbour, the other at Spithead. Another of the mutineers, one David Forester, was afterwards caught and executed, and, before he died, he confessed (*Annual Register*, April 19, 1802), " That he went into the cabin, and forced Captain Pigot overboard, through the port, while he was alive. He then got on the quarter deck, and found the first lieutenant begging for his life, saying he had a wife and three children depending on him for support ; he took hold of him, and assisted in heaving him overboard alive, and declared he did not think he would have taken his life had he not first took hold of him. A cry was then heard through the ship that Lieutenant Douglas could not be found : he took a lantern and candle, and went into the gun-room, and found the Lieutenant under the marine officer's cabin. He called in the rest of the people, when they dragged him on deck, and threw him overboard. He next caught hold of Mr. Smith, a midshipman ; a scuffle ensued, and, finding him likely to get away, he struck him with his tomahawk, and threw him overboard. The next cry was for putting all the officers to death, that they might not appear as evidence against them, and he seized on the Captain's Clerk, who was immediately put to death."

I have to chronicle yet one more mutiny, happily not so tragical as the last, but ending in fearful punishment to the mutineers. It occurred principally on board the *Temeraire* then in Bantry Bay, but pervaded the squadron ; and the culprits were tried early in January, 1802, by a court martial at Portsmouth, for " using mutinous and seditious words, and taking an active part in mutinous and seditious assemblies." Nineteen were found guilty, twelve sentenced to death, and ten, certainly, hanged.

There seems to have been no grumble about their pay,

or food, or accommodation—a sea life was looked upon as a hard one, and accepted as such. The officers, at all events, did not get paid too well, for we read in the *Morning Post*, October 19, 1801 : "We understand the Post Captains in the Navy are to have eight shillings a day instead of six. And it is supposed that Lieutenants will be advanced to four shillings instead of three." They occasionally got a haul in prize money—like the *Lively*, which in August, 1805, was awarded the sum of £200,000 for the capture of some Spanish frigates.[1]

Spite of everything, the naval power of England reached the highest point it has ever attained, and no matter whatever grievances they may have been suffering from, the sailors, from the admiral to the powder monkey, behaved nobly in action, and, between the Navy and Army, we had rather more prisoners of war to take care of than was agreeable. Speaking of an exchange of prisoners, the *Morning Post*, October 15, 1810, says: "There are in France, of all kinds of prisoners and detained persons, about 12,000; in England there are about 50,000 prisoners," and the disproportion was so great that terms could not be come to.

[1] Lord St. Vincent had a lawsuit which was decided in March, 1801, for an eighth share of two Spanish ships captured in 1799. Its value was £9,674, and he won his case.

CHAPTER XLVIII.

The Army—Number of men—Dress—Hair-powder—Militia—Commissions easily obtained—Price of substitutes—The Volunteers—Dress of the Honourable and Ancient Artillery Company—Bloomsbury Volunteers, and Rifle Volunteers —Review at Hatfield—Grand rising of Volunteers in 1803.

IN the year 1800, our Army consisted of between 80,000 and 90,000 men, besides the foreign legions, such as the Bavarians, in our pay. In 1810, there were 105,000, foreigners not included.

The British soldier of that day was, outwardly, largely compounded of a tight coat and gaiters, many buttons and straps, finished off with hog's lard and flour; and an excellent representation of him, in the midst of the decade, is taken from a memorial picture of the death of Nelson, and also from his funeral; but these latter may have been volunteers, as they were much utilized on that occasion. Be they what they may, both had one thing in common— the pig-tail—which was duly soaped, or larded and floured, until flour became so scarce that its use was first modified, and then discontinued, about 1808. Otherwise the variety of uniforms was infinite, as now.

Of the threatened Invasion I have already treated. Of the glorious campaigns abroad I have nothing to say, except that all did their duty, or more, with very few blunders, if we except the Expedition to the Scheldt.

From the highest to the lowest, there was a wish to be with the colours. Fain would the Prince of Wales have joined any regiment of which he was colonel, on active service, and, in fact, he made application to be allowed to do so, but met with a refusal, at which he chafed greatly. Should any one be curious to read the " Correspondence between His Majesty, The Prince of Wales, the Duke of York, and Mr. Addington, respecting the Offer of Military Service made by His Royal Highness the Prince of Wales," it can be found in the appendix to the chronicle of the *Annual Register* for 1803, pp. 564, &c.

The Army was fighting our battles *abroad*, so that for the purposes of this book, we are left only to deal with the Militia and Volunteers. The Militia were in a state of almost permanent embodiment, except during the lull about 1802. March, 1803, saw them once more under arms; the Yeomanry had not been disembodied. Commissions in the Militia seem to have been easily procurable. *Morning Post*, December 3, 1800 : " MILITIA ENSIGNCY. A young Gentleman of respectability can be introduced to an Ensigncy in the Militia, direct," &c. *Times*, July 2, 1803 : " An Adjutancy of English Militia to be sold," &c. Substitutes could be bought, but at fluctuating prices, according to the chance of active service being required. When first called out in 1803, one could be got for £10 ; but the *Times*, September 15, 1803, in its Brighton news, says : " The price of substitutes now is as high as forty guineas, and this tempting boon, added to the stimulus of patriotism, has changed the occupation of many a Sussex swain." The *Annual Register*, October 15, 1803, says : " Sixty pounds was last week paid at Plymouth for a substitute for the Militia. One man went, on condition of receiving 1s. per day during the war, and another sold himself for 7s. 3d. per lb."

The Volunteer movement has been glanced at when treating of the threatened Invasion of 1803. There had,

BRITISH SOLDIER—1805.

SOLDIERS—1806.

DRESSING PIG-TAILS IN THE OPEN AIR—1801.

HON. ARTILLERY COM-
PANY—1803.

VOLUNTEER RIFLE CORPS—1803.

BLOOMSBURY AND INNS OF COURT VOLUNTEER—1803.

in the previous century, been a grand Volunteer force called into existence, but nothing like the magnificent general uprising that took place in 1803. Their uniforms, and accoutrements, nearly approached the regulars, as ours do now ; but there was much more scope for individual fancy. The Honourable and Ancient Artillery Company wore a blue uniform, with scarlet and gold facings, pipe-clayed belts, and black gaiters. The Bloomsbury, and Inns of Court Volunteers dressed in scarlet, with yellow facings, white waistcoat and breeches, and black gaiters, whilst the Rifles were wholly clad in dark green.

The whole of the old Volunteers of 1798 did not disband ; some old corps still kept on. On June 18, 1800, the King, accompanied by his family, the Ministers, &c., went to Hatfield, the seat of the Marquis of Salisbury, and there reviewed the Volunteers and Militia, to the number of 1,500, all of whom the Marquis most hospitably dined. Of this dinner I give a contemporary account, as it gives us a good insight into the fare of a public entertainment, especially one given by a nobleman, in honour of his sovereign and country : "80 hams, and as many rounds of beef ; 100 joints of veal ; 100 legs of lamb ; 100 tongues ; 100 meat pies ; 25 rumps of beef roasted ; 100 joints of mutton ; 25 briskets ; 25 edge bones of beef ; 71 dishes of other roast beef ; 100 gooseberry pies : besides very sumptuous covers at the tables of the King, the Cabinet Ministers, &c. For the country people, there were killed at the Salisbury Arms, 3 bullocks, 16 sheep, and 25 lambs. The expense is estimated at £3,000."

There was a grand Volunteer Review on July 22, 1801, of nearly 5,000 men, by the Prince of Wales, supported by his two brothers, the Dukes of York and Kent, some 30,000 people being present.

But the moment invasion was threatened, there sprang, from the ground, armed men. A new levy of 50,000 regulars was raised, and the Volunteers responded to the call for men in larger numbers than they did in 1859-60. In 1804, the " List of such Yeomanry and Volunteer Corps as have been accepted and placed on the Establishment in Great Britain," gives a total of 379,943 officers and men (effective rank and file 341,687), whilst Ireland furnished, besides 82,241 officers and men, a grand total of 462,184, against which we can but show some 214,000, less about 5,000 non-efficients, with a much larger population.

CHAPTER XLIX.

THE Volunteers were a useful body. They served as police, and were duly drummed to church on the National Fast and Thanksgiving days, to represent the national party; and, as I do not know whether the terms under which they were called into being, are generally known, I venture to transcribe them, even though they be at some length. *Times*, September 30, 1803:

"REGULATIONS
for the
ESTABLISHMENTS, ALLOWANCES, &c.
of
CORPS and COMPANIES of VOLUNTEER INFANTRY,
accepted subsequently to August 3, 1803.

War Office, September 3, 1803.

" A Regiment to consist of not more than 12 Companies, nor less than 8 Companies.

" A Battallion to consist of not more than 7 Companies, nor less than 4 Companies.

" A Corps to consist of not less than 3 Companies.

"Companies to consist of not less than 60, nor more than 120 Privates.

"To each Company 1 Captain, 1 Lieutenant, 1 Second Lieutenant or Ensign.

"*It is, however, to be understood that where the establishment of any Companies has already been fixed at a lower number by Government, it is to remain unaltered by the Regulation.*

"Companies of 90 Privates and upwards to have 2 Lieutenants and 1 Second Lieutenant or Ensign ; or 3 Lieutenants, if a Grenadier or Light Infantry Company.

"Regiments consisting of 1,000 Privates to have 1 Lieut.-Col. Commandant, 2 Lieut.-Colonels, and 2 Majors.

"No higher rank than that of Lieut.-Col. Commandant to be given, unless where persons have, already, borne high rank in His Majesty's forces.

"Regiments of not less than 800 Privates, to have 1 Lieut.-Col. Commandant, 1 Lieut.-Colonel, and 2 Majors.

"Regiments of not more than 480 Privates to have 1 Lieut.-Col. Commandant, 1 Lieut.-Colonel, and 1 Major.

"Battalions of less than 480 Privates to have 1 Lieut.-Colonel, and 1 Major.

"Corps consisting of 3 Companies, to have 1 Major Commandant, and no other Field Officer.

"Every Regiment of 8 Companies, or more, may have 1 Company of Grenadiers, and 1 Company of Light Infantry, each of which to have 2 Lieutenants instead of 1 Lieutenant, and 1 Second Lieutenant or Ensign.

"Every Battalion of 7 Companies, and not less than 4, may have 1 Company of Grenadiers, or 1 Company of Light Infantry, which Company may have 2 Lieutenants instead of 1, and 1 Second Lieutenant or Ensign.

"One Serjeant and 1 Corporal to every 20 Privates.

"One Drummer to every Company, when not called out into actual service.

"Two Drummers when called out.

" Staff.

" An Adjutant, Surgeon, Quarter-Master, and Serjeant-Major, may be allowed on the establishment of Corps of sufficient strength, as directed by the Militia Laws ; but neither the said Staff Officers, nor any other Commissioned Off. er, will have any pay or allowance whatever, except in the following cases, viz. :

" If a Corps, or any part thereof, shall be called upon to act in cases of riot or disturbance, the charge of constant pay may be made for such services, for all the effective Officers and Men employed on such duty, at the following rates, the same being supported by a Certificate from His Majesty's Lieutenant, or the Sheriff of the County ; but, if called out in case of actual invasion, the corps is to be paid and disciplined in all respects, as the regular Infantry ; the Artillery Companies excepted, which are then to be paid as the Royal Artillery.

Per diem.	*s.*	*d.*
Field Officer or Captain of a Company	9	5
Lieutenant	5	8
Second Lieutenant or Ensign	4	8
Adjutant	8	0
Quarter-Master	5	8
Surgeon	10	0
Serjeant-Major, and 2s. 6d. per week in addition	1	6
Serjeant	1	6
Corporal	1	2
Drummer	1	0
Private	1	0

" The only instances in which pay will be allowed, by Government, for any individual of the Corps when not so called out, are those of an Adjutant and Serjeant-Major, for whom pay will be granted at the rates following : Adjutant 6s. a day, Serjeant-Major 1s. 6d. per diem, and 2s. 6d. per week—in addition, if authorized by His Majesty's Secretary of State, in consequence of a particular application from the Lord Lieutenant of the County, founded upon the necessity of the case ; but this indulgence cannot be allowed under any circumstances unless the Corps to which the Adjutant may belong, shall consist of not less than 500 effective rank and file, and he shall have served at least five years as a Commissioned Officer in the Regulars, embodied Militia, Fencibles, or East India Company's Service ; and, unless the Corps to which the Serjeant-Major may belong, shall consist of not less than 200 effective rank and file, and he shall have served at least three years in some of His Majesty's forces.

" Drill Serjeants of Companies are to be paid by the Parishes to which their respective Companies belong, as is provided in the 43rd Geo. III. cap. 120. sec. 11, and no charge to be made for them in the accounts to be transmitted to the War Office.

" Pay at the rate of one shilling per man per day for twenty days' exercise within the year to the effective Non-commissioned Officers—(not being Drill Serjeants paid by the Parish) Drummers and Privates of the Corps, agreeably to their terms of service. No pay can be allowed for any man who shall not have attended for the complete period of twenty days.

" When a charge of constant pay is made for an Adjutant, or Serjeant-Major, his former services must be particularly stated in the pay list wherein the first charge is made.

" The allowance for clothing is twenty shillings per man, once in three years, to the effective non-commissioned officers, drummers, and privates of the Corps.

" The necessary pay lists will be sent from the War Office, addressed to the several Commandants, who will take care that the Certificates be regularly signed whenever the twenty days' exercise shall have been completed, and the clothing actually furnished to the man. The allowance for the twenty days' exercise may be drawn for immediately, and that for clothing, in one month from the receipt of such pay lists at the War Office, by bills, signed by the several Commandants, at thirty days' sight, upon the general agent : unless any objection to the latter charges shall be signified officially to the said Commandant in the meantime.

" The whole to be clothed in red, with the exception of the Corps of Artillery, which may have blue clothing, and Rifle Corps, which may have green, with black belts.

" Serjeant-Major receiving constant pay and Drill Serjeants paid by the parish, to be attested, and to be subject to military law, as under 43 Geo. III. cap. 121.

" All applications for arms and accoutrements should be made through the Lord Lieutenant of the County, directly to the Board of Ordnance, and all applications for ammunition, for exercise, or practice, should be made through the inspecting Field Officers of Yeomanry and Volunteers to the Board of Ordnance annually. Ammunition for service should be drawn through the medium of the inspecting Field Officer, from the depôt under the orders of the General Officer of the District.

" The arms furnished by the Board of Ordnance to Corps of Volunteer Infantry are as follows : Musquets, complete with accoutrements ; drummer's swords ; drums with sticks ; spears for serjeants.

" The articles furnished to Volunteer Artillery by the Board of Ordnance, are pikes, drummer's swords, and drums with sticks.

" Spears are allowed for Serjeants, and pikes to any extent for accepted men not otherwise armed.

" The following allowances, in lieu of accoutrements, &c., when required, may be obtained on application by the Commandant of the Corps to the Board of Ordnance : 10s. 6d. per set in lieu of accoutrements ; 3s. each drummer's sword belt ; 2s. each drum carriage.

" Such Corps as have offered to serve free of expense, and have been accepted on those terms, can claim no allowance under these heads of service.

" Every Officer, Non-commissioned Officer, Corporal, Drummer, and Private Man, to take the oath of allegiance and fidelity to His Majesty, his heirs and successors.

" If the Commandant of a Corps should at any time desire an augmentation in the establishment thereof, or alteration in the title of the Corps, or the names, or dates of commissions of the officers, the same must be transmitted through the Lord Lieutenant of the County, in order to the amendment being submitted to His Majesty.

" All effective Members of Volunteer Corps and Companies accepted by His Majesty, are entitled to the exemptions from ballot allowed by 42 Geo. III. cap. 66, and Geo. III. cap. 121, provided that such persons are regularly returned in the muster rolls to be sent in to the Lord Lieutenant, or Clerk of the General Meetings of his County, *at the times, in the manner,* and certified upon honour by the Commandant, *in the form* prescribed by those Acts, and schedules thereto annexed.

" The Monthly Returns should be transmitted to the Inspecting Field Officer appointed to superintend the District in which the Corps is situated, and to the Secretary of State for the Home Department."

Thus, we see that the regulations for the Volunteers were very similar to what they are now.

Of course the arms served out to them were, to our modern ideas, beneath contempt. There were a few Rifle Corps, who were armed with what was then called the Brunswick Rifle. It was short, because the barrel was very thick and heavy. The rifling was poly-grooved, the bullet spherical, and somewhat larger than the bore, so that when wrapped in a greased linen patch (carried in a box, or trap, in the butt of the gun) it required a mallet applied to the ramrod—to drive the bullet home—and fill up the grooves of the rifling. Of course it was a far

superior weapon to the musket, or " Brown Bess " [1]—which
was not calculated even to "hit a haystack" at thirty
yards. The *Morning Post*, July 24, 1810, thus speaks of
the shooting of a Corps: "The Hampstead Volunteers
fired at a target yesterday on the Heath. Many excellent
shots were fired, and some nearly entered ' the Bull's eye.' "

They were always holding Volunteer reviews, and having
Volunteer dinners, and Volunteers, generally, were raised
to the rank, at least, of demigods—they were the saviours
of their country. Never was there such bravery as that
of these fire-eaters : and, if *Boney* dared show his nose on
English soil—why—every British Volunteer would, in-
dividually, capture him ! Volunteering even made them
moral, and religious—*teste* the *Times*, September 3, 1803 :
" Since the formation of Volunteer Corps, the very
manners of many have taken a more moral turn : public-
houses are deserted for the drill, our churches are better
frequented, profane swearing is banished, every man looks
to his character, respects the Corps in which he is enrolled,
and is cautious in all he says or does, lest he should
disgrace the name of a *British Volunteer*."

There was a large Patriotic Fund got up, which on
December 31, 1803, amounted in *Consols* to £21,000, and
in *Money*, to £153,982 5s. 7d., and it must be remembered
that the taxes were very heavy. But there is an individual
case of patriotism I cannot help chronicling, it is so typical

[1] So called from the brown barrel. At one time all gun barrels were not
only bright, but burnished—the date of the abolition of which, is fixed by the
following—*Morning Post*, October 3, 1808 : " The system of cropping the
hair of the soldiers is on the point of being followed up by the adoption of a
plan which will, no doubt, give equal satisfaction to the whole army : we
mean the abolition of that absurd practice of polishing the arms, which, in
some regiments, has been carried to such an excess as materially to injure the
piece, and render it totally unfit for use in half the time estimated for fair wear
in usual service. Fire-locks upon a new principle, with brown locks and
barrels, have been already issued to the light companies of several regiments,
and the Board of Ordnance have received orders to complete the issue to the
remainder of the army, with all the expedition possible ; in consequence of
which, a requisition has been made of the gunsmiths in the several regiments
to repair, without loss of time, to the Royal Manufactory of Arms at Lewisham."

of the predominant feeling of that time, that a man, and his goods, belonged to his country, and should be at his country's disposal. *Times*, September 6, 1803 : " A Mr. Miller,[1] of Dalswinton, in Scotland, has written a letter to the Deputy Lieutenants of the County wherein he resides, in which he says : ' I wish to insure my property, my share in the British Constitution, my family, myself, and my religion, against the French Invasion. As a premium, I offer to clothe and arm with pikes one hundred Volunteers, to be raised in this, or any of the neighbouring parishes, and to furnish them with three light field pieces ready for service. This way of arming, I consider superior with infantry, whether for attack or defence, to that now in use ; but as to this, Government must determine. I am too old and infirm to march with these men, but I desire my eldest son to do so. He was ten years a soldier in the Foot and Horse service. In case of an invasion, I will be ready to furnish, when requested, 20 horses, 16 carts, and 16 drivers ; and Government may command all my crops of hay, straw, and grain, which I estimate at 16,700 stones of hay, 14 lbs. to the stone, 14,000 bushels of pease, 5,000 bushels of oats, 3,080 bushels of barley.' "

[1] Dalswinton is in county Dumfries, and the estate was about 5,000 acres, formerly belonging to the Comyns, but it came into the possession of Patrick Miller, Esq., who built a fine mansion on the site of the old castle. He was a man well up to his time, for here, in 1788, he launched, on a lake, the first steamboat ever attempted.

CHAPTER L.

IT would be utterly impossible, whilst writing of things military, of this part of the century, to ignore the Clarke Scandal—it is a portion of the history of the times.

Mrs. Mary Ann Clarke was of humble parentage, of a lively and sprightly temperament, and of decidedly lax morality. She had married a stonemason named Clarke, who became bankrupt; she, however, cleaved to him and his altered fortunes, until his scandalous mode of living induced her to separate from him, and seek a livelihood as best she might. Her personal attractions, and lively disposition, soon attracted men's notice, and after some time she went upon the stage, where she essayed the *rôle* of Portia. There must have been some fascination about her, for each of her various lovers rose higher in the social scale, until, at last, she became the mistress of the Duke of York, and was installed in a mansion in Gloucester Place. Here the establishment consisted of upwards of twenty servants. The furniture is described as having been most magnificent The pier glasses cost from 400 to 500 pounds each, and her wine glasses, which cost upwards of two guineas apiece, sold afterwards, by public auction, for a guinea each.

She kept two carriages, and from eight to ten horses, and had an elegant mansion at Weybridge, the dimensions of which may be guessed, by the fact that the oil cloth

MRS. CLARKE.

for the hall cost fifty pounds. The furniture of the kitchen at Gloucester Place cost upwards of two thousand pounds.

These things swallowed up a great deal of money, and, although the Duke had a fine income, yet he had the capacity for spending it ; nor only so—could contract debts

with great facility, so that the money which he nominally
allowed Mrs. Clarke (for it was not always paid), was insufficient to provide for such extravagance, and other means
had to be found. This was done by her using the influence
she possessed over the Duke, and getting him to grant
commissions in the army, for which the recipients paid Mrs.
Clarke a lower price than the regulation scale. The satirical
prints relating to her are most numerous. I only reproduce two. Her levée was supposed not only to be attended

MRS. CLARKE'S LEVÉE.[1]

by military men, but by the clergy ; and it was alleged that
applications had been made through her both for a bishopric,
and a deanery, and that she had procured for Dr. O'Meara,
the privilege of preaching before Royalty. But it was
chiefly in the sale of army commissions that she dealt, thus
causing young officers to be promoted " over the heads "

---

[1] Mrs. Clarke is saying :

 " Ye Captains and ye Colonels, ye parsons wanting place,
  Advice I'll give you gratis, and think upon your case,
  If there's any possibility, for you I'll raise the dust,
  But then you must excuse me, if I serve myself the first.

of veterans. Certainly her scale of prices, compared with those of the regulation, were very tempting, resulting in a great saving to the recipient of the commission.

	MRS. CLARKE'S PRICE.	REGULATION PRICE.
A Majority	£900	£2,600
A Captaincy	700	1,500
A Lieutenancy	400	550
An Ensigncy	200	400

I have no wish to go into the minute details of this

MILITARY LEAP FROG; OR, HINTS TO YOUNG GENTLEMEN.

scandal, but on January 27, 1809, G. Lloyd Wardell,[1] Esq., M.P. for Oakhampton, began his indictment of the Duke of York, in this matter, before the House of Commons; and he showed that every sale effected through Mrs. Clarke's means, was a robbery of the Half Pay Fund, and he asked for a Parliamentary Committee to investigate the affair; this was granted, and Mrs. Clarke, and very numerous

[1] Commonly known as Colonel Wardell, or Wardle. His real military rank was Major, in which capacity he served in Sir W. W. Wynne's regiment during the rebellion in Ireland.

witnesses were examined. The lady was perfectly self-
possessed, and able to take care of herself; and the evidence,
all through, was most damaging to the Duke. Mrs. Clarke
is thus described in the *Morning Post* of Friday, February
3, 1809: "Mrs. Clarke, when she appeared before the House
of Commons, on Wednesday, was dressed as if she had
been going to an evening party, in a light blue silk gown
and coat, edged with white fur, and a white muff. On her
head she wore a white cap, or veil, which at no time was let
down over her face. In size she is rather small, and does

THE PRODIGAL SON'S RESIGNATION.

not seem to be particularly well made. She has a fair,
smooth skin, and lively blue eyes, but her features are not
handsome. Her nose is rather short and turning up, and
her teeth are very indifferent; yet she has the appearance
of great vivacity of manners, but is said not to be a well-
bred or accomplished woman. She appears to be about
thirty-five years of age."

The Duke took the extraordinary course of writing a
letter to the Speaker of the House of Commons, whilst the
matter was *sub judice*, in which he asserted his innocence;

and, foreseeing what was to follow, gave out that for the future he meant to be a very good boy, and that he would retrench in his expenditure, in order to attempt to liquidate his debts.

The House eventually found that there was nothing in the evidence to prove personal corruption, or criminal connivance on the part of His Royal Highness ; but, although thus partially whitewashed, the public opinion against him was too strong, and he placed his resignation, as Commander in Chief, in the King's hands.

Places were openly bought and sold, although it was known to be illegal, such advertisements as the following being common—*Morning Post*, June 14, 1800 :

" PUBLIC OFFICES.

" A YOUNG MAN of good Connections, well educated in writing and accounts, and can find security, wishes for a Clerkship in any of the Public Offices. Any Lady or Gentleman having interest to procure such a situation, will be presented with the full value of the place. The greatest secrecy and honour will be observed."

So common were they, that it was found necessary to issue notices on the subject. Here is one :

" *Custom House, London, December* 7, 1802.

" WHEREAS Advertisements have, at different times, appeared in the Newspapers, offering Sums of Money for the procuring of Places, or Situations, in the Customs, inserted either by persons not aware of the serious consequences which attach upon transactions of this nature, or by persons of a different description, with a view to delude the ignorant, and unwary : The Commissioners of His Majesty's Customs think it necessary to have it generally made known that, in addition to the punishment which the Common Law would inflict upon the offence of bribing, or

attempting to bribe, any person entrusted with the disposal
of any Office, the Statute passed in the fifth and sixth year
of the reign of King Edward the Sixth, inflicts the penalty
of incapacity to hold such office in the person purchasing, and the forfeiture of office in the person selling ; and
that in case any such place or situation, either shall have
been, or shall hereafter be procured, or obtained, by such
Corrupt means, they are determined to enforce the penalties of the Law, and to prosecute the offenders with the
utmost severity. And they do hereby promise a Reward
of One Hundred Pounds, to any person or persons who
will give information and satisfactory proof, of any place
or situation in the Customs being so obtained, so that the
parties concerned therein may be proceeded against
accordingly."

Duels were most frequent, so much so, as not to excite
any interest in the student of history of that time, for it is
difficult to pick up a newspaper and not find one recorded.
The reasons are not always given, but it did not take much
to get up a duel ; any excuse would serve. As an example,
let us take the duel between Colonel Montgomery, and
Captain Macnamara, at Chalk Farm (April, 1803) in which
the former was killed, and the latter wounded. Lord
Burghersh, in giving evidence before the coroner's jury,
said : "On coming out of St. James's Park on Wednesday
afternoon, he saw a number of horsemen, and Colonel
Montgomery among them ; he rode up to him ; at that
time, he was about twenty yards from the railing next to
Hyde Park Gate. On one side of Colonel Montgomery
was a gentleman on horseback, whom he believed was
Captain Macnamara. The first words he heard were uttered
by Colonel Montgomery, who said : ' Well, Sir, and I will
repeat what I said, if your dog attacks mine, I will knock
him down.' To this, Captain Macnamara replied, ' Well,
Sir, but I conceive the language you hold is arrogant, and

29

not to be pardoned.'   Colonel Montgomery said : ' This is not a proper place to argue the matter ; if you feel yourself injured, and wish for satisfaction, you know where to find me.' "   And so these two poor fools met, and one was killed—all because two dogs fought, and their masters could not keep their temper !

CHAPTER LI.

Police—Dr. Colquhoun's book—The old Watchmen—Their inadequacy admitted
—Description of them—Constables—" First new mode of robbing in 1800 "—
Robbery in the House of Lords—Whipping—Severe sentence—The Stocks—
The Pillory—Severe punishment—Another instance.

THE police authorities very seldom attempted to interfere with these duels ; indeed, practically there was no police. There were some men attached to the different police courts, and there were the parochial constables with their watchmen ; but, according to our ideas, they were the merest apology for a police. Indeed, our grandfathers thought so themselves, and Dr. Colquhoun wrote a book upon the inefficiency of the police, which made a great stir. It was felt that some better protection was needed, as may be seen from two contemporary accounts : "Two things in London that fill the mind of the intelligent observer with the most delight, are the slight restraints of the police, and the general good order. A few old men armed with a staff, a rattle, and a lantern, called watchmen, are the only guard throughout the night against depredation ; and a few magistrates and police officers the only persons whose employment it is to detect and punish depredators ; yet we venture to assert that no city, in proportion to its trade, luxury, and population, is so free from danger, or from depredations, open or concealed, on property."

"The streets of London are better paved, and better lighted than those of any metropolis in Europe; we have fewer street robberies, and scarcely ever a midnight assassination. Yet it is singular, where the police is so ably regulated, that the watchmen, our guardians of the night, are, generally, old decrepit men, who have scarcely strength

WATCHMEN GOING ON DUTY—1808.

to use the alarum which is their signal of distress in cases of emergency."

Thus we see that even contemporaries were not enthusiastic over their protectors; and a glance at the two accompanying illustrations fully justify their opinion. "The Microcosm of London," from which they are taken, says: "The watch is a parochial establishment supported by a parochial rate, and subject to the jurisdiction of the magistrates: it is necessary to the peace and security of the Metropolis, and is of considerable utility: but that it might be rendered much more useful, cannot be denied. That the watch should consist of able-bodied men, is, we presume, essential to the complete design of its institution, as it forms a part of its legal description: but that the watchmen are persons of this character, experience will not vouch; and why they are so frequently chosen from

WATCH-HOUSE. MARYLEBONE—1808.

among the aged, and incapable, must be answered by those who make the choice. In the early part of the last century, an halbert was their weapon; it was then changed into a long staff; but the great coat and the lantern are now accompanied with more advantageous implements of duty—a bludgeon, and a rattle. It is almost superfluous to add, that the watch-house is a place where the appointed watchmen assemble to be accoutred for their nocturnal rounds, under the direction of a Constable, whose duty, being taken by rotation, enjoys the title of Constable of the night. It is also the receptacle for such unfortunate persons as are apprehended by the watch, and where they remain in custody till they can be conducted to the tribunal of a police office, for the examination of the magistrate.

The following little anecdote further illustrates the inefficiency of these guardians of the peace—*Morning Herald*, October 30, 1802: "It is said that a man who presented himself for the office of watchman to a parish at the West-end of the town, very much infested by depredators, was lately turned away from the vestry with this reprimand: 'I am astonished at the impudence of such a great, *sturdy, strong* fellow as you, being so *idle* as to apply for a *Watchman's* situation, when you are capable of labour!'"

CONSTABLES—1805.

Part of their duty was to go their rounds once every hour, calling out the time, and the state of the weather, and this was done to insure their watchfulness, but it must also have given warning to thieves. This duty done, they retired to a somewhat roomy sentry box, where, should they fall asleep, it was a favourite trick of the mad wags of the town to overturn them face downwards. Being old and infirm, they naturally became the butts and prey of the bucks, and bloods, in their nocturnal rambles; but such injuries as they received, either to their dignity, or persons, were generally compounded for by a pecuniary recompense.

The Constable, was a superior being, he was the *Dogberry*, and was armed with a long staff.

Crime then was very much what it is now ; there is very little new under the sun in wickedness—still, the *Morning Post* of February 3, 1800, has the

" FIRST NEW MODE OF ROBBING

in 1800.

" A few days past, a man entered a little public-house, near Kingston, called for a pint of ale, drank it, and, whilst his host was away, put the pot in his pocket, and, without even paying for the beer, withdrew. The landlord, re-turning, two other men, who were in the room, asked him whether he knew the person who had just left the house ? ' No,' he replied. ' Did he pay for the ale ? ' said they. ' No,' answered the other. ' Why, d—n him,' cried one of the guests, ' he put the pot in his pocket.' ' The devil, he did ! ' exclaimed the host, ' I will soon be after him.'

" Saying this, he ran to the door, and the two men with him. ' There, there, he's going round the corner now!' said one, pointing. Upon which the landlord immediately set off, and, cutting across a field, quickly came up to him. 'Holloa! my friend,' said he, ' you forgot to pay for your beer.' ' Yes,' replied the other, ' I know that ! ' ' And, perhaps you know, too,' added the host, ' that you took away the pot ? Come, come, I must have that back again, at any rate.' ' Well, well,' said the man, and put his hand into his pocket, as if about to return the pot ; but, instead of that, he produced a pistol, and robbed the ale-house keeper of his watch and money.

" This might seem calamity enough for the poor man ; but, to fill up his cup of misfortune to the brim, he found, on reaching his home, that the two he had left behind, had, during his absence, plundered his till, stolen his silver spoons, and decamped."

One of the most audacious robberies of those ten years, was one which took place on September 21, 1801, when the House of Lords was robbed of all the gold lace, and the ornaments of the throne, the King's arms excepted, were stripped, and carried away.   Nor was the thief ever found.

For minor offences the punishments were, Whipping, the Stocks, and the Pillory ; for graver ones, Imprisonment, Transportation, and DEATH.

As a specimen of the offence for which Whipping was prescribed, and the whipping itself, take the following— *Morning Post*, November 4, 1800 : " This day, being hay-market day at Whitechapel, John Butler, pursuant to his sentence at the last General Quarter Sessions, held at Clerkenwell, is to be publicly whipped from White-chapel Bars, to the further end of Mile End, Town, the distance of two miles, for having received several trusses of hay, knowing them to have been stolen, and for which he gave an inferior price."

The Stocks were only for pitiful rogues and vagabonds, and for very minor offences ; but the Pillory, when the criminals were well known, and the crime an heinous one, must have been a very severe punishment; for, setting aside the acute sense of shame which such publicity must have awoke in any heart not absolutely callous, the physical pain, if the mob was ill-tempered, must have been great. As a proof, I will give two instances.

The first is from the *Morning Herald*, January 28, 1804 : " The enormity of Thomas Scott's offence, in endeavouring to accuse Capt. Kennah, a respectable officer, together with his servant, of robbery, having attracted much public notice, his conviction, that followed the attempt, could not but be gratifying to all lovers of justice.   Yesterday, the culprit underwent a part of his punishment ; he was placed in the pillory, at Charing Cross, for one hour.   On his first appearance, he was greeted by a large mob, with a discharge of *small shot*, such as *rotten eggs, filth*, and *dirt* from the streets, which was followed up by dead cats, rats, &c., which had been collected in the vicinity of the Metropolis by the boys in the morning. When he was taken away to Cold Bath Fields, to which place he is sentenced for twelve months, the mob broke the windows of the coach, *and would have proceeded to violence* [1] had the Police Officers not been at hand."

The other is taken from the *Annual Register*, September

PILLORY. CHARING CROSS.

27, 1810: "Cooke, the publican of the Swan, in Vere Street, Clare Market, and five others of the eleven miscreants convicted of detestable practices, stood in the pillory in the Haymarket, opposite to Panton Street. Such was the degree of popular indignation excited against these wretches, and such the general eagerness to witness their punishment that by ten in the morning all the windows and even the roofs of the houses were

[1] The italics are mine.—J. A.

crowded with persons of both sexes; and every coach, waggon, hay-cart, dray, and other vehicle which blocked up great part of the streets, were crowded with spectators.

"The Sheriffs, attended by the two City marshals, with an immense number of constables, accompanied the procession

THE PILLORY.

of the prisoners from Newgate, whence they set out in the transport caravan, and proceeded through Fleet Street and the Strand; and the prisoners were hooted and pelted the whole way by the populace. At one o'clock, four of the culprits were fixed in the pillory, erected for, and accommodated to, the occasion, with two additional wings, one being allotted to each criminal. Immediately a new torrent of popular vengeance poured upon them from all sides ; blood, garbage, and ordure from the slaughter houses, diversified with dead cats, turnips, potatoes, addled eggs, and other missiles to the last moment.

"Two wings of the pillory were then taken off to place Cooke and Amos in, who, although they came in only for the second course, had no reason to complain of short allowance. The vengeance of the crowd pursued them back to Newgate, and the caravan was filled with mud and ordure.

"No interference from the Sheriffs and police officers could restrain the popular rage ; but, notwithstanding the immensity of the multitude, no accident of any note occurred."

CHAPTER LII.

Smuggling—An exciting smuggling adventure—The Brighton fishermen and the Excise—"Body-snatching"—"Benefit of Clergy"—Tyburn tickets—Death the penalty for many crimes—"Last dying Speech"—The "condemned pew" at Newgate—Horrible execution at Jersey—The new drop—An impenitent criminal.

THE offence of Smuggling, now all but died out, was common enough, and people in very good positions in life thought it no harm to, at least, indirectly participate in it. The feats of smugglers were of such every-day occurrence, that they were seldom recorded in the papers, unless there were some peculiar circumstances about them, such as shooting an excise man, or the like. In one paper, however, the *Morning Post*, September 3, 1801, there are two cases, one only of which I shall transcribe. "A singular circumstance occurred on Tuesday last, at King Harry Passage, Cornwall. A smuggler, with two ankers of brandy on the horse under him, was discovered by an exciseman, also on horseback, on the road leading to the Passage. The smuggler immediately rode off at full speed, pursued by the officer, who pressed so close upon him, that, after rushing down the steep hill to the Passage, with the greatest rapidity, he plunged his horse into the water, and attempted to gain the opposite shore. The horse had not swam half way over, before, exhausted with fatigue, and the load on his back, he was on the

point of sinking, when the intrepid rider slid from his
back, and, with his knife, cut the slings of the ankers,
and swam alongside his horse, exerting himself to keep his
head above water, but all to no purpose ; the horse was
drowned, and the man, with difficulty, reached the shore.
The less mettlesome exciseman had halted on the shore,
where he surveyed the ineffectual struggle, and, afterwards,
with the help of the ferryman, got possession of the
ankers."

Sometimes it was done wholesale, see the *Morning
Herald*, February 17, 1802 : " Last Thursday morning, the
Brighton fishermen picked up at sea, and brought to shore,
at that place, upwards of five hundred casks of Contraband
spirits, of which the Revenue officers soon got scent,
and proceeded, very actively, to unburden the fishermen.
This landing and seizing continued, with little intermission,
from six to ten, to the great amusement of upwards of two
thousand people, who had became spectators of the scene.
When the officers had loaded themselves with as many
tubs as they could carry, the fishermen, in spite of their
assiduity, found means to convey away as many more, and
by that means seemed to make a pretty equal division.
The above spirits, it appeared, had been thrown overboard
by the crew of a smuggling vessel, when closely chased by
a Revenue Cutter."

We may claim that one detestable offence, then rife, is
now extinct. I allude to " Body-snatching." It is true
that anatomists had, legally, no way of procuring subjects
to practise on, other than those criminals who had been
executed, and their bodies not claimed by their friends ;
but, although the instances on record are, unfortunately
numerous, I have already written of them in another
book, and once is quite sufficient.

Of one or two legal curiosities now extinct, I may
mention " Benefit of Clergy," an institution established in
our early history, in order to screen a clerk, or learned man,

from the consequences of his crime.   In case of felony, one had but to plead ability to read, and prove it, and the sentence was commuted to branding the hand with a hot iron.   It was a privilege much abused, but it lingered on until 1827, when it was abolished by the Act, 7 and 8 Geo. IV. cap. 28.

Another curious custom, now also done away with, we meet with, in an advertisement in the *Morning Herald*, March 17, 1802 : "WANTED, one or two Tyburn Tickets, for the Parish of St. George's, Hanover Square.   Any person or persons having the same to dispose of, may hear of a purchaser," &c.   These tickets were granted to a prosecutor who succeeded in getting a felon convicted, and they carried with them the privilege of immunity from serving all parochial offices.   They were transferable by sale (but only once), and the purchaser enjoyed its privileges.   They were abolished in 1818.   They had a considerable pecuniary value, and in the year of their abolition, one was sold for £280 !

"Tyburn" reminds us of the fearful numbers sentenced to death at that time.   The law sadly wanted reformation in this respect ; besides murder, coining, forgery, &c., many minor offences were punishable with death, although all convicted and sentenced were not executed ; some being reprieved, and punished with transportation.   George III. had a great dislike to capital punishment, and remitted the sentence to as many as he could.   Take as an example of the awful severity of the law, only one sessions at the Old Bailey, ending September 24, 1801 : "Sentence of death was then passed upon *Thomas Fitzroy*, alias *Peter Fitzwater*, for breaking and entering the dwelling-house of James Harris, in the daytime, and stealing a cotton counterpane. *Wm. Cooper* for stealing a linen cloth, the property of George Singleton, in his dwelling-house.   *J. Davies* for a burglary.   *Richard Emms* for breaking into the dwelling-house of Mary Humphreys, in the daytime, and stealing a pair of stockings. *Richard Forster* for a burglary. *Magnus Kerner* for a burglary, and stealing six silver spoons. *Robert Pearce* for returning from transportation. *Richard Alcorn* for stealing a horse. *John Nowland* and *Rd. Freke* for burglary and stealing four tea spoons, a gold snuff-box, &c. *John Goldfried* for stealing a blue coat. *Joseph Huff,* for stealing a lamb, and *John Pass* for stealing two lambs."

In fact, the "Tyburn tree" was kept well employed, and yet, apparently, the punishment of death hardly acted as a deterrent. A sad, very sad street cry, yet one I have often

THE CONDEMNED SERMON. NEWGATE.

heard, was of these poor wretches ; true, it had been made specially to order, in Catnach's factory for these articles, in Monmouth Court, Seven Dials ; but still it was the announcement of another fellow-creature having been done to death.

The executions which would arise from the batch of sentences I have just recorded, would take place at Newgate. The last person hanged at Tyburn, having suffered, November 7, 1783, and the above illustration shows in a peculiarly graphic manner, the *condemned sermon,* which was preached to those about to die on the morrow. To make the service thoroughly intelligible to them, and to

THE LAST DYING SPEECH AND CONFESSION.

impress them with the reality of their impending fate, a coffin was set in the midst of the " condemned pew."

Crowds witnessed the 'executions, which took place in the front of Newgate, and on one occasion, on the 23rd of February, 1807, an accident occurred, by the breaking of the axle of a cart, whereon many people were standing; they were not only hurt, but the crowd surged over them, and it ended in the death of twenty-eight people, besides injuries to many more.

We have seen, in February, 1885, a murderer reprieved, because the drop would not act; but in the following instance, the criminal did suffer, at all events, actual pain. It happened at Jersey, on the 11th of May, 1807, and is thus chronicled in the *Annual Register* for that year: " After hanging for about a minute and a half, the executioner suspended himself to his body; by whose additional weight the rope extended in such a manner that the feet of the criminal touched the ground. The executioner then pulled him sideways, in order to strangle him; and being unable to effect this, got upon his shoulders; when, to the no small surprise of the spectators, the criminal rose straight upon his feet, with the hangman upon his shoulders, and loosened the rope from his throat with his fingers. The Sheriff ordered another rope to be prepared; but the spectators interfered, and, at length, it was agreed to defer the execution till the will of the magistrates should be known. It was subsequently determined that the whole case should be transmitted to His Majesty, and the execution of the sentence was deferred till His Majesty's pleasure should be known."

A platform which suddenly disappeared from under the criminal seems to have been invented in 1807, for we read under 27th of July of that year, that John Robinson was executed at York " on the new drop," but something of the same kind had certainly been used in 1805.

As a rule, the poor creatures died creditably; but there

30

is one case to the contrary, which is mentioned in the *European Magazine*, vol. xlvii. pp. 232–40. A man named Hayward was to be hanged for cutting and maiming another. The scene at the execution is thus described : "When the time for quitting the courtyard arrived, Hayward was called to a friend to deliver him a bundle, out of which he took an old jacket, and a pair of old shoes, and put them on. ' Thus,' said he, ' will I defeat the prophecies of my enemies ; they have often said I should die in my *coat* and *shoes*, and I am determined to die in neither.' Being told it was time to be conducted to the scaffold, he cheerfully attended the summons, having first ate some bread and cheese, and drank a quantity of coffee. Before he departed, however, he called out, in a loud voice, to the prisoners who were looking through the upper windows at him, ' Farewell, my lads, I am just a going off ; God bless you ! ' ' We are sorry for you,' replied the prisoners. ' I want no more of your pity,' rejoined Hayward ; ' keep your snivelling till it be your own turn.' Immediately on his arrival upon the scaffold, he gave the mob three cheers, introducing each with a ' Hip, ho ! ' While the cord was preparing he continued hallooing to the mob.

"It was found necessary, before the usual time, to put the cap over his eyes, besides a silk handkerchief, by way of bandage, that his attention might be entirely abstracted from the spectators. . . . He then gave another halloa, and kicked off his shoes among the spectators, many of whom were deeply affected at the obduracy of his conduct."

CHAPTER LIII.

BUT of all brutal sentences, that for the crime of high treason, was the worst. When Colonel Despard was sentenced to death for conspiracy, on the 9th of February, 1802, the words used by the Judge, were as follow :—

" The only thing now remaining for me, is the painful task of pronouncing against you, and each of you, the awful sentence which the law denounces against your crime, which is, that you, and each of you (here his lordship named the prisoners severally), be taken to the place from whence you came, and from thence you are to be drawn on hurdles to the place of Execution, where you are to be hanged by the neck, but not until you are dead ; for while you are still living, your bodies are to be taken down, your bowels torn out, and burnt before your faces ! your heads are to be then cut off, and your bodies divided each into four quarters, and your heads and quarters to be then at the King's disposal ; and may the Almighty God have mercy on your Souls."

In this case the disembowelling and dismemberment were remitted, but they were dragged to the place of execution on a *hurdle*, which, in this instance, was the body of a small cart, on which two trusses of clean straw were laid. They were hanged, and after hanging for about twenty-five minutes, "*till they were quite dead*," they were cut down. "Colonel [1] Despard was first cut down, his body placed upon saw dust, and his head on a block. After his coat had been taken off, his head was severed from his body. The executioner then took the head by the hair, and carrying it to the edge of the parapet on the right hand, held it up to the view of the populace, and exclaimed, "This is the head of a traitor — EDWARD MARCUS DESPARD ! . . . The bodies were then put into their different shells, and are to be delivered to their friends for interment."

Another relic of barbarism was the driving a stake through the body of a suicide, and burying him at the junction of a cross road—*Morning Post*, April 27, 1810: "The Officers appointed to execute the ceremony of driving a stake through the dead body of *James Cowling*, a deserter from the London Militia, who deprived himself of existence, by cutting his throat, at a public-house in Gilbert Street, Clare Market, in consequence of which, the Coroner's Jury found a verdict of Self-murder, very properly delayed the business until twelve o'clock on Wednesday night, when the deceased was buried in the cross roads at the end of Blackmoor Street, Clare Market."

The motive for this practice was, that by fastening the body to the ground, by means of a stake, it rendered it "of the earth, earthy," and thus prevented its perturbed spirit from wandering about. It is believed that the last burial of a suicide in London, at a cross road, was in June, 1823, when a man, named Griffiths, was buried about half-past one a.m., at the junction of Eaton Street, Grosvenor Place,

[1] The *Times*, February 22, 1805.

and the King's Road, but no stake was driven through the body.

The Prisons in London were fairly numerous, but several of them were for debtors, whose case was very evil. There they languished, many in the most abject poverty, for years, trusting to the charity of individuals, or to funds either bequeathed, or set aside, for bettering their condition. In 1804, an Act was passed (44 Geo. III. cap. 108, afterwards repealed by the Stat. Law. Rev. Act, 1872) for the Relief of Insolvent Debtors, and they were not slow in taking advantage of it. Not only had they poverty, and loss of liberty, to contend with, but gaol fever, which carried them off at times, and cleared the prisons. So contagious was it, that in February, 1805, almost all the cadets at Woolwich suffered from it, and several died. It was imported into the school, by one of the cadets, who had been to visit some prison.

The prisons were as follow, in 1805 :—

1. King's Bench Prison, for debtors on process or execution, and for persons under sentence for misdemeanour, &c. This was in St. George's Fields, Southwark, and was considered more wholesome than the London prisons. There were districts surrounding the prison both here, and at the Fleet, where prisoners could dwell, without going inside, by payment of fees. The prisoners inside the King's Bench, could but obtain leave to go out once every term, or four times a year. There were 300 rooms in the prison, but it was always full, and decent accommodation was even more expensive to obtain, than at the Fleet.

2. The Fleet Prison was one belonging to the Courts of Common Pleas, and Chancery, to which debtors might remove themselves from any other prison, at the expense of six or seven pounds. A contemporary account says :

" It contains 125 rooms, besides a common kitchen, coffee and tap rooms, but the number of prisoners is generally so great, that two, or even three, persons are obliged to submit to the shocking inconvenience of living in one small room!! Those who can afford it, pay their companion to *chum* off, and thus have a room to themselves. Each person so paid off, receives four shillings a week. The prisoner pays one shilling and threepence a week for his room without furniture, and an additional sevenpence

INTERIOR OF FLEET PRISON.

for furniture. Matters are sometimes so managed, that a room costs the needy and distressed prisoner from ten to thirteen shillings a week.

"Those who have trades that can be carried on in a room, generally work, and some gain more than they would out of doors, after they become acquainted with the ways of the place. During the quarterly terms,[1] when the court sits, prisoners, on paying five shillings a day, and on giving security, are allowed to go out when they please, and there is a certain space round the prison, called the *rules*, in which prisoners may live, on furnishing two good securities to the warden for their debt, and on paying about 3 per cent. on the amount of their debts to the warden. The rules extend only from Fleet Market to the London Coffee House, and from Ludgate Hill to Fleet Lane, so that lodgings are bad, and very dear. Within the walls there is a yard for walking in, and a good racquet ground."

3. Ludgate Prison, or Giltspur Street Compter, for debtors who were freemen of the City of London.

4. Poultry Compter—a dark, small, ill-aired dungeon—used as a House of Detention.

5. Newgate—which was the gaol both for Criminals, and Debtors, for the County of Middlesex. On the debtors' side, the overcrowding was something terrible. The felons', or State side, as it was called, was far more comfortable, and the criminals better accommodated. The prison might, then, be visited on payment of two or three shillings to the turnkeys, and giving away a few more to the most distressed debtors.

6. The New Prison, Clerkenwell, was also a gaol for the County of Middlesex, and was built in 1775. The fare here was very meagre—only a pound of bread a day.

7. Prison for the liberty of the Tower of London, Wellclose Square.

8. Whitechapel Prison, for debtors in actions in the Five Pounds Courts, or the Court of the Manor of Stepney.

9. The Savoy Prison, used as a Military prison, principally for deserters.

---

[1] These days amounted to 80 or 90 in the year.

10. Horsemonger Lane Gaol, the County prison for Surrey.

11. The Clink, a small debtors prison in Southwark.

12. The Marshalsea Gaol, in Southwark, for pirates.

13. The House of Correction, Cold Bath Fields, which was built according to a plan of Howard, the philanthropist, on the basis of solitary confinement. At this time it was dreaded as a place of punishment, and went

HOUSE OF CORRECTION. COLD BATH FIELDS.

by the name of the Bastille. (Its slang name now is *the Steel*.)

The prisoners were not too well fed. A pound of bread, and twopenny worth of meat a day, and a very fair amount of work to do—was not calculated to make it popular among the criminal classes.

It was the only prison in which the inmates wore uniform. That of the men was blue jacket and trousers, with yellow stockings, whilst the women had a blue jacket and blue petticoat. They had clean linen every week; so that, probably, it was a healthy prison. One good thing about it was, that a portion of the prisoners' earnings was reserved, and given to them when they quitted prison.

14. City Bridewell, Blackfriars, was a house of Correction for the City.

15. Tothill Fields, Bridewell, was a similar institution for Westminster.

16. New Bridewell, Southwark, for Surrey.

Besides these public prisons, were several private establishments used as provisional prisons—kept by the Sheriff's Officers, called *lock-up*, or, *sponging houses*, where for twelve, or fourteen shillings a day, a debtor might remain, either until he found the means to repay the debt, or it was necessary to go to a public prison, when the writ against him became returnable. They were nests of extortion and robbery.

The Police Offices in London were :

The Mansion House.	Lambeth Street, Whitechapel.
Guildhall.	High Street, Shadwell.
Bow Street.	Union Street, Southwark.
Hatton Garden.	Queen's Square, Westminster.
Worship Street.	Great Marlborough Street.

Wapping New Stairs, for offences committed on the Thames. Of those *extra* the City, Bow Street was the chief, and the head magistrate there, was called the Chief Magistrate, and received a stipend of £1,000 per annum ; a large sum in those days. He was assisted by two others, at a salary of £500 each.

Dr. Patrick Colquhoun called so much attention to the inefficiency of the police, that a Committee of the House of Commons, in the session of 1798, sifted the matter, and from the report of this Committee, only, can we gather the criminal statistics of the kingdom (at least with regard to its expense).

BOW STREET POLICE OFFICE—1808.

The amount of the general expense of the criminal police of the kingdom, is stated by the Committee as follows :

1st. The annual average of the total expense of the seven public offices in the Metropolis from their institution in 1792, to the end of the year 1797 ... ... £18,281 13 6

2nd. Total expenses of the office in Bow Street in the year 1797, including remuneration to the magistrates in lieu of fees, perquisites, &c., and the expense of a patrol of sixty-eight persons 7,901 7 7

Total for the Metropolis £26,183 6 1

The other expenses for the prosecution and conviction of felons, the maintenance, clothing, employment, and transportation of convicts, to which may be added the farther sums annually charged on the county rates, amounted in 1797 to £215,869 13 10½

In 1804, it was estimated that there were 2,044 beadles and watchmen, and 38 patrols, on nightly duty in, and around the Metropolis. Of these, the City proper, with its 25 wards, contributed 765 watchmen, and 38 patrols.

The poor were pretty well taken care of. Besides the parochial workhouses, there were 107 endowed almshouses, and many other like institutions ; the City Companies, it was computed, giving upwards of £75,000, yearly, away in charity. There were very many institutions for charitable, and humane purposes—mostly founded during the previous century—for the relief of widows and orphans, deaf and dumb persons, lunatics, relief of small debtors, the blind, the industrious poor, &c. And there were 1,600 Friendly Societies in the Metropolis, and its vicinity, enrolled under the Act, 33 George III. cap. 54. These had 80,000 members, and their average payments were £1 each per annum.

For education in London, there were :

16 Inns of Court and Chancery, for education in the law.

5 Colleges, viz., Zion College, Gresham, Physicians, Doctors Commons, and Herald's College.

62 Schools or public Seminaries, such as Westminster, the Blue Coat, St. Paul's, Merchant Taylors, Charterhouse, &c., educating some 5,000 children.

237 Schools, belonging to the different parishes, educating some 9000.

3,730 Private Schools.

4,050 Total Seminaries of Education.

This does not include nearly twenty educational establishments such as the Orphan Working School, the Marine Society, Freemasons School, &c.

And there were about the same number of Religious and Moral Societies, such as the Society for Promoting Christian Knowledge, the Society for the Propagation of the Gospel in Foreign Parts, Religious Tract Society, Missionary Societies, &c.; besides a number of Sunday Schools—so that we see education, and philanthropy, were hard at work in the DAWN OF THE NINETEENTH CENTURY.

THE END.

INDEX.